High Performance Computing for
Big Data
METHODOLOGIES AND APPLICATIONS

T0330909

Chapman & Hall/CRC
Big Data Series

SERIES EDITOR
Sanjay Ranka

AIMS AND SCOPE

This series aims to present new research and applications in Big Data, along with the computational tools and techniques currently in development. The inclusion of concrete examples and applications is highly encouraged. The scope of the series includes, but is not limited to, titles in the areas of social networks, sensor networks, data-centric computing, astronomy, genomics, medical data analytics, large-scale e-commerce, and other relevant topics that may be proposed by potential contributors.

High Performance Computing for
Big Data
METHODOLOGIES AND APPLICATIONS

EDITED BY **CHAO WANG**

CRC Press
Taylor & Francis Group

CRC Press is an imprint of the
Taylor & Francis Group, an **informa** business

A CHAPMAN & HALL BOOK

CRC Press
Taylor & Francis Group
6000 Broken Sound Parkway NW, Suite 300
Boca Raton, FL 33487-2742

First issued in paperback 2020

© 2018 by Taylor & Francis Group, LLC
CRC Press is an imprint of Taylor & Francis Group, an Informa business

No claim to original U.S. Government works

ISBN 13: 978-0-367-57289-1 (pbk)
ISBN 13: 978-1-4987-8399-6 (hbk)

Visit the Taylor & Francis Web site at
http://www.taylorandfrancis.com

and the CRC Press Web site at
http://www.crcpress.com

Contents

Preface

$\mathbf{A}$S SCIENTIFIC APPLICATIONS HAVE become more data intensive, the management of data resources and dataflow between the storage and computing resources is becoming a bottleneck. Analyzing, visualizing, and managing these large data sets is posing significant challenges to the research community. The conventional parallel architecture, systems, and software will exceed the performance capacity with this expansive data scale. At present, researchers are increasingly seeking a high level of parallelism at the data level and task level using novel methodologies for emerging applications. A significant amount of state-of-the-art research work on big data has been executed in the past few years.

This book presents the contributions of leading experts in their respective fields. It covers fundamental issues about Big Data, including emerging high-performance architectures for data-intensive applications, novel efficient analytical strategies to boost data processing, and cutting-edge applications in diverse fields, such as machine learning, life science, neural networks, and neuromorphic engineering. The book is organized into two main sections:

1. "Big Data Architectures" considers the research issues related to the state-of-the-art architectures of big data, including cloud computing systems and heterogeneous accelerators. It also covers emerging 3D integrated circuit design principles for memory architectures and devices.

2. "Emerging Big Data Applications" illustrates practical applications of big data across several domains, including bioinformatics, deep learning, and neuromorphic engineering.

Overall, the book reports on state-of-the-art studies and achievements in methodologies and applications of high-performance computing for big data applications.

The first part includes four interesting works on big data architectures. The contribution of each of these chapters is introduced in the following.

In the first chapter, entitled "Dataflow Model for Cloud Computing Frameworks in Big Data," the authors present an overview survey of various cloud computing frameworks. This chapter proposes a new "controllable dataflow" model to uniformly describe and compare them. The fundamental idea of utilizing a controllable dataflow model is that it can effectively isolate the application logic from execution. In this way, different computing frameworks can be considered as the same algorithm with different control statements to support the various needs of applications. This simple model can help developers better understand a broad range of computing models including batch, incremental, streaming, etc., and is promising for being a uniform programming model for future cloud computing frameworks.

In the second chapter, entitled "Design of a Processor Core Customized for Stencil Computation," the authors propose a systematic approach to customizing a simple core with conventional architecture features, including array padding, loop tiling, data prefetch, on-chip memory for temporary storage, online adjusting of the cache strategy to reduce memory traffic, Memory In-and-Out and Direct Memory Access for the overlap of computation (instruction-level parallelism). For stencil computations, the authors employed all customization strategies and evaluated each of them from the aspects of core performance, energy consumption, chip area, and so on, to construct a comprehensive assessment.

In the third chapter, entitled "Electromigration Alleviation Techniques for 3D Integrated Circuits," the authors propose a novel method called TSV-SAFE to mitigate electromigration (EM) effect of defective through-silicon vias (TSVs). At first, they analyze various possible TSV defects and demonstrate that they can aggravate EM dramatically. Based on the observation that the EM effect can be alleviated significantly by balancing the direction of current flow within TSV, the authors design an online self-healing circuit to protect defective TSVs, which can be detected during the test procedure, from EM without degrading performance. To make sure that all defective TSVs are protected with low hardware overhead, the authors also propose a switch network-based sharing structure such that the EM protection modules can be shared among TSV groups in the neighborhood. Experimental results show that the proposed method can achieve over 10 times improvement on mean time to failure compared to the design without using such a method, with negligible hardware overhead and power consumption.

In the fourth chapter, entitled "A 3D Hybrid Cache Design for CMP Architecture for Data-Intensive Applications," the authors propose a 3D stacked hybrid cache architecture that contains three types of cache bank: SRAM bank, STT-RAM bank, and STT-RAM/SRAM hybrid bank for chip multiprocessor architecture to reduce power consumption and wire delay. Based on the proposed 3D hybrid cache with hybrid local banks, the authors propose an access-aware technique and a dynamic partitioning algorithm to mitigate the average access latency and reduce energy consumption. The experimental results show that the proposed 3D hybrid cache with hybrid local banks can reduce energy by 60.4% and 18.9% compared to 3D pure SRAM cache and 3D hybrid cache with SRAM local banks, respectively. With the proposed dynamic partitioning algorithm and access-aware technique, our proposed 3D hybrid cache reduces the miss rate by 7.7%, access latency by 18.2%, and energy delay product by 18.9% on average.

The second part includes eight chapters on big data applications. The contribution of each of these chapters is introduced in the following.

In the fifth chapter, entitled "Matrix Factorization for Drug–Target Interaction Prediction," the authors first review existing methods developed for drug–target interaction prediction. Then, they introduce neighborhood regularized logistic matrix factorization, which integrates logistic matrix factorization with neighborhood regularization for accurate drug–target interaction prediction.

In the sixth chapter, entitled "Overview of Neural Network Accelerators," the authors introduce the different accelerating methods of neural networks, including ASICs, GPUs, FPGAs, and modern storage, as well as the open-source framework for neural networks. With the emerging applications of artificial intelligence, computer vision, speech recognition, and machine learning, neural networks have been the most useful solution. Due to the low efficiency of neural networks implementation on general processors, variable specific heterogeneous neural network accelerators were proposed.

In the seventh chapter, entitled "Acceleration for Recommendation Algorithms in Data Mining," the authors propose a dedicated hardware structure to implement the training accelerator and prediction accelerator. The training accelerator supports five kinds of similarity metrics, which can be used in the user-based collaborative filtering (CF) and item-based CF training stages and the difference calculation of SlopeOne's training stage. A prediction accelerator that supports these three algorithms involves an accumulation operation and weighted average operation during their prediction stage. In addition, this chapter also designs the bus and interconnection between the host CPU, memory, hardware accelerator, and some peripherals such as DMA. For the convenience of users, we create and encapsulate the user layer function call interfaces of these hardware accelerators and DMA under the Linux operating system environment. Additionally, we utilize the FPGA platform to implement a prototype for this hardware acceleration system, which is based on the ZedBoard Zynq development board. Experimental results show this prototype gains a good acceleration effect with low power and less energy consumption at run time.

In the eighth chapter, entitled "Deep Learning Accelerators," the authors introduce the basic theory of deep learning and FPGA-based acceleration methods. They start from the inference process of fully connected networks and propose FPGA-based accelerating systems to study how to improve the computing performance of fully connected neural networks on hardware accelerators.

In the ninth chapter, entitled "Recent Advances for Neural Networks Accelerators and Optimizations," the authors introduce the recent highlights for neural network accelerators that have played an important role in computer vision, artificial intelligence, and computer architecture. Recently, this role has been extended to the field of electronic design automation (EDA). In this chapter, the authors integrate and summarize the recent highlights and novelty of neural network papers from the 2016 EDA Conference (DAC, ICCAD, and DATE), then classify and analyze the key technology in each paper. Finally, they give some new hot spots and research trends for neural networks.

In the tenth chapter, entitled "Accelerators for Clustering Applications in Machine Learning," the authors propose a hardware accelerator platform based on FPGA by the combination of hardware and software. The hardware accelerator accommodates four clustering algorithms, namely the k-means algorithm, PAM algorithm, SLINK algorithm, and DBSCAN algorithm. Each algorithm can support two kinds of similarity metrics, Manhattan and Euclidean. Through locality analysis, the hardware accelerator presented a solution to address the off-chip memory access and then balanced the relationship between flexibility and performance by finding the same operations. To evaluate the performance of the accelerator, the accelerator is compared with the CPU and GPU, respectively, and then it gives the corresponding speedup and energy efficiency. Last but not least, the authors present the relationship between data sets and speedup.

In the eleventh chapter, entitled "Accelerators for Classification Algorithms in Machine Learning," the authors propose a general classification accelerator based on the FPGA platform that can support three different classification algorithms of five different similarities. In addition, the authors implement the design of the upper device driver and the programming of the user interface, which significantly improved the applicability of the accelerator. The experimental results show that the proposed accelerator can achieve up to 1.7× speedup compared with the Intel Core i7 CPU with much lower power consumption.

In the twelfth chapter, entitled "Accelerators for Big Data Genome Sequencing," the authors propose an accelerator for the KMP and BWA algorithms to accelerate gene sequencing. The accelerator should have a broad range of application and lower power cost. The results show that the proposed accelerator can reach a speedup rate at 5× speedup compared with CPU and the power is only 0.10 w. Compared with another platform the authors strike a balance between speedup rate and power cost. In general, the implementation of this study is necessary to improve the acceleration effect and reduce energy consumption.

The editor of this book is very grateful to the authors, as well as to the reviewers for their tremendous service in critically reviewing the submitted works. The editor would also like to thank the editorial team that helped to format this task into an excellent book. Finally, we sincerely hope that the reader will share our excitement about this book on high-performance computing and will find it useful.

Acknowledgments

CONTRIBUTIONS TO THIS BOOK were partially supported by the National Science Foundation of China (No. 61379040), Anhui Provincial Natural Science Foundation (No. 1608085QF12), CCF-Venustech Hongyan Research Initiative (No. CCF-VenustechRP1026002), Suzhou Research Foundation (No. SYG201625), Youth Innovation Promotion Association CAS (No. 2017497), and Fundamental Research Funds for the Central Universities (WK2150110003).

Editor

Chao Wang received his BS and PhD degrees from the School of Computer Science, University of Science and Technology of China, Hefei, in 2006 and 2011, respectively. He was a postdoctoral researcher from 2011 to 2013 at the same university, where he is now an associate professor at the School of Computer Science. He has worked with Infineon Technologies, Munich, Germany, from 2007 to 2008. He was a visiting scholar at the Scalable Energy-Efficient Architecture Lab in the University of California, Santa Barbara, from 2015 to 2016. He is an associate editor of several international journals, including *Applied Soft Computing, Microprocessors and Microsystems, IET Computers & Digital Techniques, International Journal of High Performance System Architecture*, and *International Journal of Business Process Integration and Management*. He has (co-)guest edited special issues for *IEEE/ACM Transactions on Computational Biology and Bioinformatics, Applied Soft Computing, International Journal of Parallel Programming*, and *Neurocomputing*. He plays a significant role in several well-established international conferences; for example, he serves as the publicity cochair of the High Performance and Embedded Architectures and Compilers conference (HiPEAC 2015), International Symposium on Applied Reconfigurable Computing (ARC 2017), and IEEE International Symposium on Parallel and Distributed Processing with Applications (ISPA 2014) and he acts as the technical program member for DATE, FPL, ICWS, SCC, and FPT. He has (co-)authored or presented more than 90 papers in international journals and conferences, including seven ACM/IEEE Transactions and conferences such as DATE, SPAA, and FPGA. He is now on the CCF Technical Committee of Computer Architecture, CCF Task Force on Formal Methods. He is an IEEE senior member, ACM member, and CCF senior member. His homepage may be accessed at http://staff.ustc.edu.cn/~cswang

Contributors

Marc Belleville
CEA-LETI
Grenoble, France

Alberto Bosio
LIRMM, CNRS
Montpellier, France

Yong Chen
Computer Science Department
Texas Tech University
Lubbock, TX

Yuanqing Cheng
Beihang University
Beijing, China

Jeng-Nian Chiou
Department of Computer Science &
    Information Engineering
National Cheng Kung University
Tainan, Taiwan

Dong Dai
Computer Science Department
Texas Tech University
Lubbock, TX

Luigi Dilillo
LIRMM, CNRS
Montpellier, France

Haijie Fang
School of Software Engineering
University of Science and Technology
    of China
Hefei, China

Patrick Girard
LIRMM, CNRS
Montpellier, France

Lei Gong
Department of Computer Science
University of Science and Technology
    of China
Hefei, China

Gangyong Jia
Department of Computer Science
    and Technology
Hangzhou Dianzi University
Hangzhou, China

Yun-Kae Law
Department of Computer Science &
    Information Engineering
National Cheng Kung University
Tainan, Taiwan

Shiming Lei
Department of Computer Science
and
School of Software Engineering
University of Science and Technology
    of China
Hefei, China

Xi Li
Department of Computer Science
University of Science and Technology
    of China
Hefei, China

Xiao-Li Li
Institute of Infocomm Research(I2R)
A*STAR
Singapore

Yanhua Li
Department of Computer Science
Tsinghua University
Beijing, China

Ing-Chao Lin
Department of Computer Science &
    Information Engineering
National Cheng Kung University
Tainan, Taiwan

Yong Liu
Institute of Infocomm Research(I2R)
A*STAR
Singapore

Yuntao Lu
Department of Computer Science
University of Science and Technology
    of China
Hefei, China

Fan Sun
Department of Computer Science
University of Science and Technology
    of China
Hefei, China

Aida Todri-Sanial
LIRMM, CNRS
Montpellier, France

Arnaud Virazel
LIRMM, CNRS
Montpellier, France

Pascal Vivet
CEA-LETI
Grenoble, France

Aili Wang
Department of Computer Science
and
School of Software Engineering
University of Science and Technology
    of China
Hefei, China

Chao Wang
Department of Computer Science
University of Science and Technology
    of China
Hefei, China

Min Wu
Institute of Infocomm Research(I2R)
A*STAR
Singapore

Chongchong Xu
Department of Computer Science
University of Science and Technology
  of China
Hefei, China

Yiwei Zhang
Department of Computer Science
University of Science and Technology of
  China
Hefei, China

Youyang Zhang
Department of Computer Science
Tsinghua University
Beijing, China

Youhui Zhang
Department of Computer Science
Tsinghua University
Beijing, China

Peilin Zhao
Ant Financial
Hangzhou, China

Yangyang Zhao
Department of Computer Science
University of Science and Technology
  of China
Hefei, China

Xuehai Zhou
Department of Computer Science,
University of Science and Technology
  of China
Hefei, China

I

Big Data Architectures

CHAPTER 1

Dataflow Model for Cloud Computing Frameworks in Big Data

Dong Dai and Yong Chen

Texas Tech University

Lubbock, TX

Gangyong Jia

Hangzhou Dianzi University

Hangzhou, China

CONTENTS

1.1 INTRODUCTION

In recent years, the Big Data challenge has attracted increasing attention [1–4]. Compared with traditional data-intensive applications [5–10], these "Big Data" applications tend to be more diverse: they not only need to process the potential large data sets but also need to react to real-time updates of data sets and provide low-latency interactive access to the latest analytic results. A recent study [11] exemplifies a typical formation of these applications: computation/processing will be performed on both newly arrived data and historical data simultaneously and support queries on recent results. Such applications are becoming more and more common; for example, real-time tweets published on Twitter [12] need to be analyzed in real time for finding users' community structure [13], which is needed for recommendation services and target promotions/advertisements. The transactions, ratings, and click streams collected in real time from users of online retailers like Amazon [14] or eBay [15] also need to be analyzed in a timely manner to improve the back-end recommendation system for better predictive analysis constantly.

The availability of cloud computing services like Amazon EC2 and Windows Azure provide on-demand access to affordable large-scale computing resources without substantial up-front investments. However, designing and implementing different kinds of scalable applications to fully utilize the cloud to perform the complex data processing can be prohibitively challenging, which requires domain experts to address race conditions, deadlocks, and distributed state while simultaneously concentrating on the problem itself. To help shield application programmers from the complexity of distribution, many distributed computation frameworks [16–30] have been proposed in a cloud environment for writing such applications. Although there are many existing solutions, no single one of them can completely meet the diverse requirements of Big Data applications, which might need batch processing on historical data sets, iterative processing of updating data streams, and real-time continuous queries on results together. Some, like MapReduce [16], Dryad [17], and many of their extensions [18,19,31–33], support synchronous batch processing on the entire static datasets at the expense of latency. Some others, like Percolator [21], Incoop [22], Nectar [23], and MapReduce Online [34], namely incremental systems, offer developers an opportunity to process only the changing data between iterations to improve performance. However, they are not designed to support processing of changing data sets. Some, like Spark Streaming [35], Storm [24], S4 [25], MillWheel [26], and Oolong [27], work on streams for asynchronous processing. However, they typically cannot efficiently support multiple iterations on streams. Some specifically designed frameworks, like GraphLab [28] and PowerGraph [29], however, require applications to be expressed in a certain manner, for example, vertex-centric, which is not expressive for many Big Data applications.

Currently, to support various applications, developers need to deploy different computation frameworks, develop isolated components (e.g., the batch part and streaming part) of the applications based on those separate frameworks, execute them separately, and manually merge them together to generate final results. This method is typically referred to as *lambda architecture* [36]. This clearly requires a deep understanding of various computing frameworks, their limitations, and advantages. In practice, however, the computing frameworks may utilize totally different programming models, leading to diverse semantics and execution flows and making it hard for developers to understand and compare them fully. This is controversial to what cloud computation frameworks target: hiding the complexity from developers and unleashing the computation power. In this chapter, we first give a brief survey of various cloud computing frameworks, focusing on their basic concepts, typical usage scenarios, and limitations. Then, we propose a new *controllable dataflow execution* model to unify these different computing frameworks. The model is to provide developers a better understanding of various programming models and their semantics. The fundamental idea of controllable dataflow is to isolate the application logic from how they will be executed; only changing the control statements can change the behavior of the applications. Through this model, we believe developers can better understand the differences among various computing frameworks in the cloud. The model is also promising for uniformly supporting a wide range of execution modes including batch, incremental, streaming, etc., accordingly, based on application requirements.

1.2 CLOUD COMPUTING FRAMEWORKS

Numerous studies have been conducted on distributed computation frameworks for the cloud environment in recent years. Based on the major design focus of existing frameworks, we categorize them as batch processing, iterative processing, incremental processing, streaming processing, or general dataflow systems. In the following subsections, we give a brief survey of existing cloud processing frameworks, discussing both their usage scenarios and disadvantages.

1.2.1 Batch Processing Frameworks

Batch processing frameworks, like MapReduce [16], Dryad [17], Hyracks [37], and Stratosphere [38], aim at offering a simple programming abstraction for applications that run on static data sets. Data models in batch processing frameworks share the same static, persistent, distributed abstractions, like HDFS [39] or Amazon S3 [40]. The overall execution flow is shown in Figure 1.1: developers provide both *maps* and *reduce* functions, and the frameworks will automatically parallelize and schedule them accordingly in the cloud cluster. As shown in Figure 1.1, the programming models offered by these batch processing systems are simple and easy to use, but they do not consider multiple iterations or complex data dependencies, which might be necessary for many applications. In addition, they do not trace the intermediate results, unless users explicitly save them manually. This might also lead to a problem if the intermediate results generated from *map* functions are needed for other computations.

1.2.2 Iterative Processing Frameworks

Iterative applications run in multiple rounds. In each round, they read the outputs of previous runs. A number of frameworks have been proposed for these applications recently. HaLoop [18] is an extended version of MapReduce that can execute queries written in a variant of recursive SQL [41] by repeatedly executing a chain of MapReduce jobs. Similar systems include Twister [19], SciHadoop [31], CGLMapReduce [32], and iMapReduce [33]. Spark [20] supports

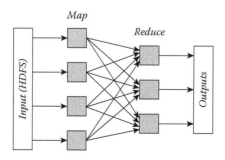

FIGURE 1.1   Batch processing model (MapReduce).

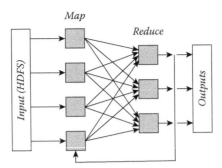

FIGURE 1.2   Iterative processing model. (From Ekanayake, J., et al., *Proceedings of the 19th ACM International Symposium on High Performance Distributed Computing*, ACM, pp. 810–818, 2010, Publisher location is Chicago, IL.)

a programming model similar to DryadLINQ [42], with the addition of explicit in-memory caching for frequently reused inputs. The data model for those iterative processing frameworks extends batch processing with the ability to cache or buffer intermediate results from previous iterations, as shown in Figure 1.2. The programming model and runtime system are consequently extended for reading and writing these intermediate results. However, they are not able to explicitly describe the sparse computational dependencies among parallel tasks between different iterations, which is necessary to achieve the desired performance for many machine learning and graph algorithms. Developers need to manually manage the intermediate results, for example, by caching, buffering, or persisting accordingly.

1.2.3 Incremental Processing Frameworks

For iterative applications, an optimization called *incremental processing*, which only processes the changed data sets, can be applied to improve performance. Incremental computation frameworks take the sparse computational dependencies between tasks into account and hence offer developers the possibility to propagate the unchanged values into the next iteration. There are extensions based on MapReduce and Dryad with support for such incremental processing, following the basic programming model showing in Figure 1.3. MapReduce Online [34] maintains states in memory for a chain of MapReduce jobs and reacts efficiently to additional input records. Nectar [23] caches the intermediate results of DryadLINQ [42] programs and uses the semantics of LINQ [43] operators to generate incremental programs that exploit the cache. Incoop [22] provides similar benefits for arbitrary MapReduce programs by caching the input to reduce stages and by carefully ensuring that a minimal set of reducers is re-executed upon a change in the input. There are also incremental processing frameworks that leverage asynchronously updating distributed shared data structures. Percolator [21] structures a web indexing computation as triggers that are fired when new values are written. Similar systems include Kineograph [44] and Oolong [27]. Our previous work, Domino [45], unifies both synchronous and asynchronous execution into a single trigger-based framework to support incremental processing (shown in Figure 1.4). However, none of these incremental optimizations can be applied to continuous streams that are often used in a cloud environment.

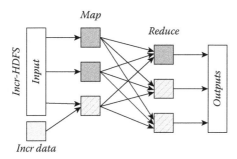

FIGURE 1.3   Incremental computing framework (Incr-MapReduce example).

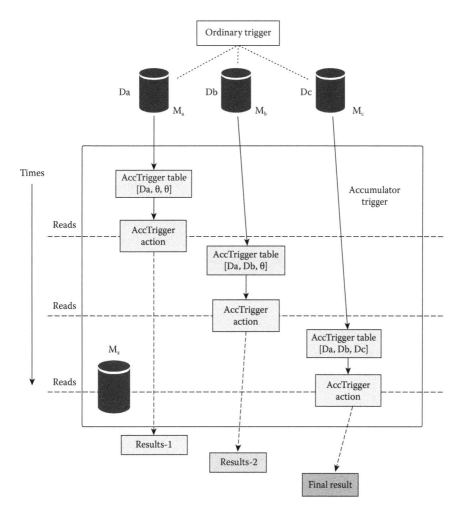

FIGURE 1.4   Domino programming model example. (From Dai, D., et al., *Proceedings of the 23rd International Symposium on High-Performance Parallel and Distributed Computing*, ACM, Vancouver, Canada, pp. 291–294, 2014.)

1.2.4 Streaming Processing Frameworks

Streaming processing frameworks provide low-latency and stateless computation over external changing data sets. Spark Streaming [35] extends Spark [46] to handle streaming input by executing a series of small batch computations. MillWheel [26] is a streaming system with punctuations and sophisticated fault tolerance that adopts a vertex API, which fails at providing iterative processing on those streams. Yahoo! S4 [25], Storm [24], and Sonora [47] are also streaming frameworks targeting fast stream processing in a cloud environment. Most of the existing streaming processors can be traced back to the pioneering work done on streaming database systems, such as TelegraphCQ [48], Aurora [49], and STREAM [50]. The key issue of existing streaming processing frameworks is that they do not support iterations and possible incremental optimizations well. In this proposed project, we aim at supporting iterative processing on streams with fault-tolerance mechanisms and scalability (Figure 1.5).

1.2.5 General Dataflow Frameworks

Numerous research studies have been conducted on general dataflow frameworks recently. CIEL [51] is one such study and supports fine-grained task dependencies and runtime task scheduling. However, it does not offer a direct dataflow abstraction of iterations or recursions nor can it share states across iterations. Spinning [52] supports "bulk" and "incremental" iterations through a dataflow model. The monotonic iterative algorithms can be executed using a sequence of incremental updates to the current state in an asynchronous or synchronous way. REX [53] further supports record deletion in incremental iterations. Bloom^L [54] supports fixed-point iterations using compositions of monotone functions on a variety of lattices. A differential dataflow model from Frank et al. [55] emphasizes the differences between dataflows and abstracts the incremental applications as a series of computation on those differences. Naiad [11] extends the differential dataflow model by introducing time constraints in all programming primitives, which can be used to build other programming models. However, these existing dataflow systems share similar limitations that motivate this proposed research. First, they are limited to streaming processing and are not easy to use on static data sets. Second, they do not support different execution semantics for the same application, which needs fine-grained controls over the data

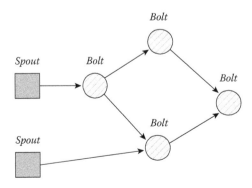

FIGURE 1.5 Streaming processing framework (Storm).

flows. The time constraint introduced by Naiad is a good start but needs significant extensions to be easily used. Third, the results generated from iterative algorithms on mutation streams are not clear enough: information to describe how the results were generated, such as whether they are just intermediate results or the complete, accurate results, is missing.

1.3 APPLICATION EXAMPLES

Big Data applications include recommendation systems, many machine learning algorithms, neural networks training, log analysis, etc. They typically process huge data sets that may be static or dynamic (like streaming), contain complex execution patterns like iterative and incremental processing, and require continuous results to direct further operations. We take the problem of determining the connected component structure [56] of a graph as an example. This is a basic core task used in social networks like Twitter [12] or Facebook [57] to detect the social structure for further data analysis [58]. The connected component problem can be formulated as follows: given an undirected graph $G = (V, E)$, partition the V into maximal subsets $V_i \subset V$, so that all vertices in the same subset are mutually reachable through E. The label propagation algorithm is most widely used for solving such a problem. Specifically, each vertex will be first assigned an integer label (initially the unique vertex ID) and then iteratively updated to be the minimum among its neighborhood. After i steps, each vertex will have the smallest label in its i-hop neighborhood. When it converges, each label will represent one connected component, as shown in Figure 1.6.

Assuming developers need to implement such a distributed label propagation algorithm for a huge social network, which may contain billions of vertices and edges, they will need the help from distributed computation frameworks. We discuss four scenarios below, showing the programming models and semantics of existing computation frameworks. We will further discuss how these scenarios can be uniformly modeled by the controllable dataflow model in next section.

Scenario 1: Finding Connected Components of a Static Graph. This scenario is the simplest case, which basically applies the label propagation algorithm to a static graph. Since the algorithm is iterative, previous results (i.e., label assignment) will be loaded and updated in each iteration. Batch processing frameworks including MapReduce [16] and Dryad [17] run such an application by submitting each iteration as a single job.

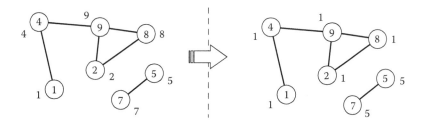

FIGURE 1.6   Run label propagation algorithm to get the connected components. The minimal ID will be spread to all vertices in each component (i.e., 1 and 5).

The iterative processing frameworks [18,19,31–33,35] can be used to cache the intermediate results in memory to improve the performance. These implementations are fine in terms of building a proof-of-concept prototype, but they cannot provide the best performance. In fact, it is obvious that there is no need to load the entire outputs of previous iterations and overwrite them with newly calculated ones in each iteration. It is expected that as more iterations of the algorithm are executed, fewer changes happen on vertex labels. This pattern is referred to as *sparse computational dependencies* [28], which can be utilized by incrementally processing only changed labels to improve the performance.

Scenario 2: Incremental Optimization of Connected Components on Static Graph. To incrementally process changed data each time, the incremental processing frameworks provide an active working set (*w*), which gathers all the vertices that change their labels in the previous iteration to users in each iteration. Initially, *w* consists of all vertices. Each time, vertices are taken from *w* to propagate their labels to all neighbors. Any neighbor affected by these changed labels will be put into *w* for the next iteration. Whenever *w* is empty, the algorithm stops. Frameworks like GraphLab [28], Pregel [59], and Percolator [21] support such incremental processing. The incremental processing can be further improved with priority [60], where the active working set (*w*) is organized as a priority queue. For example, we can simply sort all vertices in *w* based on their labels to improve the performance, as the smaller labels are more likely to prevail in the main computation.

Scenario 3: Asynchronous Incremental Optimization of Connected Components on Static Graph. The performance can be further improved by allowing asynchronous incremental processing in the framework. The incremental processing framework used in the previous scenario requires global synchronizations between iterations, which causes performance degradation when there are stragglers (nodes that are notably slower than others). An asynchronous framework can avoid this problem and improve the performance in many cases. However, from the algorithm's perspective, not all iterative algorithms converge in an asynchronous manner. Even for those that converge, the synchronous version may lead to faster convergence, even as it suffers from stragglers. It is necessary for the computation framework to provide different execution semantics including asynchronous, synchronous, or even a mix of them [61] for developers to choose and switch to achieve the best performance.

Scenario 4: Connected Components of Streaming Graph. The straightforward strategy of applying the connected component algorithm on a mutating graph is to run it on the snapshot of the entire graph multiple times. Systems like Streaming Spark [35] belong to this category. A significant drawback of such an approach is that previous results will be largely discarded and next computations need to start from the scratch again. In contrast, the majority of stream processing frameworks like S4 [25], Storm [24], and MillWheel [26] are designed to only process streaming data sets. When used for iterative algorithms, the results from different iterations running on different data sets of streams may overwrite each other, leading to inconsistent states. In addition to this limitation, all these existing frameworks lack the capability of providing a way to manage continuous results, which may be generated as intermediate results or complete, accurate results.

1.4 CONTROLLABLE DATAFLOW EXECUTION MODEL

In this research, we propose a new general programming and execution model to model various cloud computing frameworks uniformly and flexibly. Specifically, we propose a *controllable dataflow execution model* that abstracts computations as imperative functions with multiple dataflows.

The proposed controllable dataflow execution model uses graphs to represent applications, as Figure 1.7 shows. In dataflow graphs, vertices are execution functions/cores defined by users. The directed edges between those vertices are data flows, which represent the data dependency between those executions. The runtime system will schedule parallel tasks into different servers according to such dataflow graphs and hence benefit developers by transparent scaling and automatic fault handling. Most existing distributed computation frameworks, including the best-known representatives like MapReduce [16], Spark [46], Dryad [17], Storms [24], and many of their extensions, can be abstracted as a special case of such general dataflow model. The key differences among different computation frameworks can be indicated by the term *controllable*, which means the dataflows are characterized and managed by control primitives provided by the model. By changing control primitives, even with the same set of execution functions, developers will be able to run applications in a completely different way. This uninformed model is critical for developers to understand development, performance tuning, and on-demand execution of Big Data applications. In the following subsections, we describe how to utilize the proposed model for the same label propagation algorithm discussed in the Section 1.3 under different scenarios.

ALGORITHM 1.1:   INIT(INPUT_DS, OUTPUT_DS)

1.   **if** *input_ds* **is** init-data-stream {
2.   **for** node **in** *input_ds*{
3.   node_label = node_id
4.   **for** neighbor **in** node's neighbors{
5.   output_ds.add(neighbor, node_label)
6.   }
7.   }
8.   }
9.   **else**{
10.   **for a** node **in** *input_ds*{
11.   **for a** neighbor in node's neighbors{
12.   output_ds.add(neighbor, node_label)
13.   }
14.   }
15. }

ALGORITHM 1.2:   MIN(INPUT_DS, OUTPUT_DS)

1. **for** node in input_ds{
2.   output_ds(node, min(node, node_label))
3. }

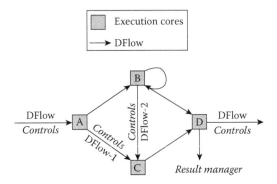

FIGURE 1.7   A sample dataflow model.

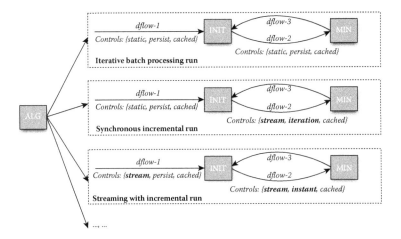

FIGURE 1.8   Three different implementations of the same algorithm using different control primitives.

Figure 1.8 shows how to use control primitives to control the same label propagation algorithm in three different scenarios, which correspond to Scenarios 1, 2, and 4 described in Section 1.2 (we omit Scenario 3 as it is similar to Scenario 2). In this example, although there are three different execution scenarios, the algorithm contains the same two execution cores: INIT and MIN (as shown in Algorithms 1.1 and 1.2). INIT takes *dflow-1* as input, initializes the label for each node to be its own ID, and broadcasts this label to its all neighbors as *dflow-2*. MIN accepts *dflow-2*, calculates the minimal label for each node, and outputs it as *dflow-3* back to INIT, which will again broadcast this new label to all neighbors as *dflow-2*. The algorithm is iterative and will repeat until no new label is created. The key difference among these three scenarios is the control primitive shown in Figure 1.8. Before describing how they can change the application execution, we first describe the meanings of control primitives as follows:

- *Static* means the dataflow is generated from a static data set. Also, for any static dataflows, unless they are fully generated and prepared, their following execution cores will not start.

- *Stream* indicates the dataflow is generated from a changing data set. The dependent execution cores can run on a small changing set each time without waiting.

- *Persist* means the dataflow will be persistent. It can be visited like accessing normal files later. For those dataflows that do not persist, the execution core cannot read the data again unless the previous executions are rerun.

- *Cached* means the dataflow can be cached in memory if possible, which can significantly improve the performance for future use (up to the system resource limit).

- *Iteration* works with stream dataflows only. It means that this streaming dataflow will not start its dependent execution core unless the entire current iteration has finished.

- *Instant* also works with streaming dataflows only. It indicates that the dataflow will start its dependent dataflow immediately once new data arrives.

Using these control primitives, as shown in Figure 1.8 and explained below, we can uniformly describe different cloud computing frameworks using the same algorithm. These executions are for different usage scenarios and present completely different execution patterns, which cover the multiple computation frameworks, as Section 1.2 describes.

1. *Scenario 1*: Iterative batch processing runs in a MapReduce fashion, where all intermediate results are stored and reloaded for the next iteration. We can define all three dataflows as *{static, persist, cached}*, which means the dataflows are static, can be persisted for future access, and can be cached if possible to improve the performance. Execution cores will not start unless all data are loaded.

2. *Scenario 2*: Synchronous incremental runs with incremental optimizations. We change the control mechanisms on *dflow-2* and *dflow-3* to *{stream, iteration, cached}*. Through streaming, the execution cores can process the broadcasted node labels without fully loading them. Control primitive iteration is critical in this example. It holds the start of MIN and INIT until the previous iteration finishes. For example, MIN will not output a new label for node i unless it has compared all possible labels generated from other nodes in this iteration.

3. *Scenario 3*: Streaming with incremental runs on a changing graph. We can change the control primitives on *dflow-1* to *{stream, persist, cached}* to denote it is a stream. In addition, we use "persist" to indicate that the whole graph will be persisted for future use, which is necessary as they will be needed for later processing. Furthermore, we also change *dflow-2* and *dflow-3* to instant. This means that both MIN and INIT will start as soon as there are new data shown in the dataflows, which might lead to inconsistent results for some algorithms. For the label propagation algorithm, they should be able to produce correct results with better performance.

Through this example, we show that, through the controllable dataflow model, we can use the same or similar algorithms to program applications that are designed for different usage scenarios with different performance requirements. This will help developers to better understand the programming models and semantics of various cloud computing frameworks and also points to a promising future for a unified programming model for Big Data applications.

1.5 CONCLUSIONS

In recent years, the Big Data challenge has attracted increasing attention. To help shield application programmers from the complexity of distribution, many distributed computation frameworks have been proposed in a cloud environment. Although there are many frameworks, no single one can completely meet the diverse requirements of Big Data applications. To support various applications, developers need to deploy different computation frameworks, develop isolated components of the applications based on those separate frameworks, execute them separately, and manually merge them together to generate the final results. This clearly requires an in-depth understanding of various computing frameworks and their limitations and advantages. In this chapter, we first give a brief survey of various cloud computing frameworks, focusing on their basic concepts, typical usage scenarios, and limitations. Then, we propose a new *controllable dataflow execution* model to unify these different computing frameworks. We believe the proposed model will provide developers a better understanding of various programming models and their semantics. The model is also promising to uniformly support a wide range of execution modes including batch, incremental, streaming, etc., according to application requirements.

REFERENCES

1. *Big Data*, http://en.wikipedia.org/wiki/Big data.
2. *Core Techniques and Technologies for Advancing Big Data Science and Engineering (BIGDATA)*, 2009, http://www.nsf.gov/funding/pgm summ.jsp?pims id=504767&org=CISE.
3. *DARPA Calls for Advances in Big Data to Help the Warfighter*, 2009, http://www.darpa.mil/NewsEvents/Releases/2012/03/29.aspx.
4. *Obama Administration Unveils BIG DATA Initiative*, 2009, http://www.whitehouse.gov/sites/default/files/microsites/ostp/big data press release final 2.pdf.
5. M. Bancroft, J. Bent, E. Felix, G. Grider, J. Nunez, S. Poole, R. Ross, E. Salmon, and L. Ward, 2009, HEC FSIO 2008 workshop report, in High End Computing Interagency Working Group (HECIWG), Sponsored File Systems and I/O Workshop HEC FSIO, 2009.
6. A. Choudhary, W.-K. Liao, K. Gao, A. Nisar, R. Ross, R. Thakur, and R. Latham, 2009, Scalable I/O and analytics, *Journal of Physics: Conference Series*, vol. 180, no. 1, p. 012048.
7. J. Dongarra, P. Beckman, T. Moore, P. Aerts, G. Aloisio, J.-C. Andre, D. Barkai, et al., 2011, The international exascale software project roadmap, *International Journal of High Performance Computing Applications*, vol. 25, no. 1, pp. 3–60.
8. G. Grider, J. Nunez, J. Bent, S. Poole, R. Ross, and E. Felix, 2009, Coordinating government funding of file system and I/O research through the high end computing university research activity, *ACM SIGOPS Operating Systems Review*, vol. 43, no. 1, pp. 2–7.
9. C. Wang, J. Zhang, X. Li, A. Wang, and X. Zhou, 2016, Hardware implementation on FPGA for task-level parallel dataflow execution engine, *IEEE Transactions on Parallel and Distributed Systems*, vol. 27, no. 8, pp. 2303–2315.

10. C. Wang, X. Li, P. Chen, A. Wang, X. Zhou, and H. Yu, 2015, Heterogeneous cloud framework for big data genome sequencing, *IEEE/ACM Transactions on Computational Biology and Bioinformatics (TCBB)*, vol. 12, no. 1, pp. 166–178.

11. D. G. Murray, F. McSherry, R. Isaacs, M. Isard, P. Barham, and M. Abadi, 2013, Naiad: A timely dataflow system, in *Proceedings of the Twenty-Fourth ACM Symposium on Operating Systems Principles*, ACM, Farmington, PA, pp. 439–455.

12. *Twitter*, http://www.twitter.com/.

13. M. Girvan and M. E. Newman, 2002, Community structure in social and biological networks, *Proceedings of the National Academy of Sciences*, vol. 99, no. 12, pp. 7821–7826.

14. *Amazon*, http://www.amazon.com/.

15. *Ebay*, http://www.ebay.com/.

16. J. Dean and S. Ghemawat, 2008, MapReduce: Simplified data processing on large clusters, *Communications of the ACM*, vol. 51, no. 1, pp. 107–113.

17. M. Isard, M. Budiu, Y. Yu, A. Birrell, and D. Fetterly, 2007, Dryad: Distributed data-parallel programs from sequential building blocks, in *Proceedings of the 2nd ACM SIGOPS/EuroSys European Conference on Computer Systems 2007*, ser. EuroSys '07, New York: ACM, pp. 59–72.

18. Y. Bu, B. Howe, M. Balazinska, and M. D. Ernst, 2010, HaLoop: Efficient iterative data processing on large clusters, *Proceedings of the VLDB Endowment*, vol. 3, no. 1–2, pp. 285–296.

19. J. Ekanayake, H. Li, B. Zhang, T. Gunarathne, S.-H. Bae, J. Qiu, and G. Fox, 2010, Twister: A runtime for iterative MapReduce, in *Proceedings of the 19th ACM International Symposium on High Performance Distributed Computing*, ACM, Chicago, IL, pp. 810–818.

20. M. Zaharia, M. Chowdhury, T. Das, A. Dave, J. Ma, M. McCauley, M. Franklin, S. Shenker, and I. Stoica, 2012, Resilient distributed datasets: A fault-tolerant abstraction for in-memory cluster computing, in *Proceedings of the 9th USENIX Conference on Networked Systems Design and Implementation*, Berkeley, CA: USENIX Association, p. 2.

21. D. Peng and F. Dabek, 2010, Large-scale incremental processing using distributed transactions and notifications, *OSDI*, vol. 10, pp. 1–15.

22. P. Bhatotia, A. Wieder, R. Rodrigues, U. A. Acar, and R. Pasquin, 2011, Incoop: MapReduce for incremental computations, in *Proceedings of the 2nd ACM Symposium on Cloud Computing*, ACM, Cascais, Portugal, p. 7.

23. P. K. Gunda, L. Ravindranath, C. A. Thekkath, Y. Yu, and L. Zhuang, 2010, Nectar: Automatic management of data and computation in datacenters, *OSDI*, vol. 10, pp. 1–8.

24. *Storm*, https://storm.apache.org//.

25. L. Neumeyer, B. Robbins, A. Nair, and A. Kesari, 2010, S4: Distributed stream computing platform, in IEEE International Conference on Data Mining Workshops (ICDMW), 2010, IEEE, Sydney, Australia, pp. 170–177.

26. T. Akidau, A. Balikov, K. Bekiroglu, S. Chernyak, J. Haberman, R. Lax, S. McVeety, D. Mills, P. Nordstrom, and S. Whittle, 2013, Millwheel: Fault-tolerant stream processing at internet scale, *Proceedings of the VLDB Endowment*, vol. 6, no. 11, pp. 1033–1044.

27. C. Mitchell, R. Power, and J. Li, 2011, Oolong: Programming asynchronous distributed applications with triggers, in *Proceedings of the SOSP*, ACM, Cascais, Portugal.

28. Y. Low, J. Gonzalez, A. Kyrola, D. Bickson, C. Guestrin, and J. M. Hellerstein, 2010, Graphlab: A new framework for parallel machine learning, arXiv preprint arXiv:1006.4990.

29. J. E. Gonzalez, Y. Low, H. Gu, D. Bickson, and C. Guestrin, 2012, PowerGraph: Distributed graph-parallel computation on natural graphs, *OSDI*, vol. 12, no. 1, p. 2.

30. W. Gropp, E. Lusk, and A. Skjellum, 1999, *Using MPI: Portable parallel programming with the message-passing interface,* vol. 1, MIT Press, Cambridge, MA.

31. J. B. Buck, N. Watkins, J. LeFevre, K. Ioannidou, C. Maltzahn, N. Polyzotis, and S. Brandt, 2011, Scihadoop: Array-based query processing in hadoop, in *Proceedings of 2011 International Conference for High Performance Computing, Networking, Storage and Analysis*, ACM, Seattle, WA, p. 66.

32. J. Ekanayake, S. Pallickara, and G. Fox, MapReduce for data intensive scientific analyses, in IEEE Fourth International Conference on eScience, 2008, eScience'08, IEEE, Indianapolis, IN, pp. 277–284.
33. Y. Zhang, Q. Gao, L. Gao, and C. Wang, 2012, iMapReduce: A distributed computing framework for iterative computation, *Journal of Grid Computing*, vol. 10, no. 1, pp. 47–68.
34. T. Condie, N. Conway, P. Alvaro, J. M. Hellerstein, K. Elmeleegy, and R. Sears, 2010, Mapreduce online, *NSDI*, vol. 10, no. 4, p. 20.
35. M. Zaharia, T. Das, H. Li, S. Shenker, and I. Stoica, 2012, Discretized streams: An efficient and fault-tolerant model for stream processing on large clusters, in *Proceedings of the 4th USENIX Conference on Hot Topics in Cloud Computing*, Berkeley, CA: USENIX Association, p. 10.
36. *Lambda Architecture*, http://lambda-architecture.net/.
37. V. Borkar, M. Carey, R. Grover, N. Onose, and R. Vernica, 2011, Hyracks: A flexible and extensible foundation for data-intensive computing, in IEEE 27th International Conference on Data Engineering (ICDE), 2011, IEEE, Hannover, Germany, pp. 1151–1162.
38. D. Wu, D. Agrawal, and A. El Abbadi, 1998, Stratosphere: Mobile processing of distributed objects in java, in *Proceedings of the 4th Annual ACM/IEEE International Conference on Mobile Computing and Networking*, ACM, Dallas, TX, pp. 121–132.
39. D. Borthakur, 2007, The hadoop distributed file system: Architecture and design, *Hadoop Project Website*, vol. 11, p. 21.
40. *Amazon S3*, http://www.amazon.com/s3.
41. C. J. Date and H. Darwen, 1987, *A guide to the SQL standard*, vol. 3, New York: Addison-Wesley.
42. Y. Yu, M. Isard, D. Fetterly, M. Budiu, U. Erlingsson, P.K. Gunda, and J. Currey, 2008, DryadLINQ: A system for general-purpose distributed data-parallel computing using a high-level language, *OSDI*, vol. 8, pp. 1–14.
43. E. Meijer, B. Beckman, and G. Bierman, 2006, LINQ: Reconciling object, relations and xml in the. net framework, in *Proceedings of the 2006 ACM SIGMOD International Conference on Management of Data*, ACM, Chicago, IL, pp. 706–706.
44. R. Cheng, J. Hong, A. Kyrola, Y. Miao, X. Weng, M. Wu, F. Yang, L. Zhou, F. Zhao, and E. Chen, 2012, Kineograph: Taking the pulse of a fast-changing and connected world, in *Proceedings of the 7th ACM European Conference on Computer Systems*, ACM, Bern, Switzerland, pp. 85–98.
45. D. Dai, Y. Chen, D. Kimpe, R. Ross, and X. Zhou, 2014, Domino: An incremental computing framework in cloud with eventual synchronization, in *Proceedings of the 23rd International Symposium on High-Performance Parallel and Distributed Computing*, ACM, Vancouver, BC, pp. 291–294.
46. M. Zaharia, M. Chowdhury, M. J. Franklin, S. Shenker, and I. Stoica, 2010, Spark: Cluster computing with working sets, in *Proceedings of the 2nd USENIX Conference on Hot Topics in Cloud Computing*, USENIX, Berkeley, CA, p. 10.
47. F. Yang, Z. Qian, X. Chen, I. Beschastnikh, L. Zhuang, L. Zhou, and J. Shen, 2012, *Sonora: A platform for continuous mobile-cloud computing*, Technical Report, Citeseer.
48. S. Chandrasekaran, O. Cooper, A. Deshpande, M. J. Franklin, J. M. Hellerstein, W. Hong, S. Krishnamurthy, S. R. Madden, F. Reiss, and M. A. Shah, 2003, TelegraphCQ: Continuous dataflow processing, in *Proceedings of the 2003 ACM SIGMOD International Conference on Management of Data*, ACM, San Diego, CA, pp. 668–668.
49. D. J. Abadi, D. Carney, U. Çetintemel, M. Cherniack, C. Convey, S. Lee, M. Stonebraker, N. Tatbul, and S. Zdonik, 2003, Aurora: A new model and architecture for data stream management, *The International Journal on Very Large Data Bases*, vol. 12, no. 2, pp. 120–139.
50. A. Arasu, B. Babcock, S. Babu, M. Datar, K. Ito, I. Nishizawa, J. Rosenstein, and J. Widom, 2003, Stream: The Stanford stream data manager (demonstration description), in *Proceedings of the 2003 ACM SIGMOD International Conference on Management of Data*, ACM, San Diego, CA, pp. 665–665.

51. D. G. Murray, M. Schwarzkopf, C. Smowton, S. Smith, A. Madhavapeddy, and S. Hand, 2011, CIEL: A universal execution engine for distributed data-flow computing, *NSDI*, vol. 11, p. 9.

52. S. Ewen, K. Tzoumas, M. Kaufmann, and V. Markl, 2012, Spinning fast iterative data flows, *Proceedings of the VLDB Endowment*, vol. 5, no. 11, pp. 1268–1279.

53. S. R. Mihaylov, Z. G. Ives, and S. Guha, 2012, REX: Recursive, delta-based data-centric computation, *Proceedings of the VLDB Endowment*, vol. 5, no. 11, pp. 1280–1291.

54. N. Conway, W. R. Marczak, P. Alvaro, J. M. Hellerstein, and D. Maier, 2012, Logic and lattices for distributed programming, in *Proceedings of the Third ACM Symposium on Cloud Computing*, ACM, San Jose, CA, p. 1.

55. F. D. McSherry, R. Isaacs, M. A. Isard, and D. G. Murray, Differential dataflow, May 10 2012, US Patent App. 13/468,726.

56. J. E. Hopcroft and R. E. Tarjan, *Efficient algorithms for graph manipulation*, Communications of the ACM, New York, 1971.

57. *Facebook*, http://www.facebook.com/.

58. A. Broder, R. Kumar, F. Maghoul, P. Raghavan, S. Rajagopalan, R. Stata, A. Tomkins, and J. Wiener, 2000, Graph structure in the web, *Computer Networks*, vol. 33, no. 1, pp. 309–320.

59. G. Malewicz, M.H. Austern, A.J. Bik, J.C. Dehnert, I. Horn, N. Leiser, and G. Czajkowski, 2010, Pregel: A system for large-scale graph processing, in *Proceedings of the 2010 ACM SIGMOD International Conference on Management of Data*, ACM, Indianapolis, IN, pp. 135–146.

60. Y. Zhang, Q. Gao, L. Gao, and C. Wang, 2011, Priter: A distributed framework for prioritized iterative computations, in *Proceedings of the 2nd ACM Symposium on Cloud Computing*, ACM, p. 13.

61. C. Xie, R. Chen, H. Guan, B. Zang, and H. Chen, 2014, *SYNC or ASYNC: Time to fuse for distributed graph-parallel computation, Technical report*, Shanghai Jiao Tong University, http://ipads.se.sjtu.edu.cn/projects/powerswitch/PowerSwitch-IPADSTR-2013-003.pdf.2.2.2.

CHAPTER 2

Design of a Processor Core Customized for Stencil Computation

Youyang Zhang, Yanhua Li, and Youhui Zhang

Tsinghua University

Beijing, China

CONTENTS

2.1 INTRODUCTION

Energy efficiency is the key issue for high-performance computing [1]. The root of this problem lies in that the free ride of clock frequency and chip power efficiency improvements is over. Thus, power has been the main constraint for future system designs.

Much research has proved that efficient designs must be specific to the application and/or algorithm classes. They usually employ alternative approaches (instead of general-purpose processors) to construct high-performance computing systems, including FPGA, embedded processors, and accelerators.

For example, Customizable Domain-Specific Computing of UCLA [2] is carrying out the development of a general methodology for creating novel customizable architecture platforms and the associated software tools to achieve orders of magnitude computing efficiency improvement for applications in a specific domain. The Custom Computing Research Group of ICST [3] also conducts research in various areas of specialized computing platforms, including research on models, architectures, development methods, and some applications of custom-designed systems. More concrete examples are as follows: (1) the BlueGene and SiCortex (http://www.purdue.edu/uns/x/2008a/080610McCartneySICortex.html) supercomputers, which are based on embedded processor cores that are more typically seen in automobiles, cell phones, and so on; (2) FPGA, which has been used as an application accelerator in computing systems more and more [4–6]; and (3) Xeon Phi coprocessors manufactured by Intel (based on the MIC architecture) [7], which are specially designed for HPC segments and only support a subset of the X86-64 ISA.

The design philosophy of customizable processors is opposite to that of general-purpose processors: the latter focuses a great deal on backward compatibility and the wide range of application adaptability. Thus for a concrete class of applications of algorithms, the general-purpose processor usually cannot achieve a fairly high power efficiency. For instance, an NERSC/CRD study on the dual-core AMD processor of the Cray XT3 and XT4 systems showed that a number of applications that were supposed to be memory-bound are in fact constrained by other microarchitectural bottlenecks in the existing processors and that different applications have different balance requirements. In contrast, the chip area of general-purpose processors is usually more than 100 times of the embedded chips. Therefore, how to utilize the chip resources efficiently and accordingly is the key point.

From the aspect of microarchitecture, customization usually means to adapt some application-specific features to improve the running efficiency [8–15]; this strategy will limit the applicability more or less.

Our work is different: it presents a systematic approach to enhance a preliminary customizable processor core with some common architecture features. Specifically, we enhance a single and very simple core with those needed hardware features combined with software optimizations, including data prefetch, DMA, on-chip memory, and SIMD methods.

In summary, we present the following contributions:

1. We present a systematic approach to customize a simple core with common architecture features: a wide variety of software/hardware codesigns have been examined, including array padding, loop tiling, data prefetch, on-chip memory for temporary storage, online adjusting the cache strategy to reduce memory traffic, memory-IO, and DMA for the overlap of computation (instruction-level parallelism).

2. For stencil computations, we have employed all customization strategies and evaluated each of them from the aspects of core performance, energy consumption, chip area, and so on to construct a comprehensive assessment.

3. Other computations, such as the vector and matrix arithmetic, have been evaluated, too, which proves the applicability of this technique.

2.2 RELATED WORK

2.2.1 Customizable Design and Processors

The customizable processor is one of the key components. Such a fully featured processor usually consists of a base processor design and a design tool environment that permits significant adaptation of that base processor by allowing system designers to change major processor functions. In particular, the instruction set can be extended by the application developer.

Tensilica's Xtensa is a typical instance, which provides a base design that the designer can extend with custom instructions and datapath units (http://tensilica.com/). Manually creating ISA extensions gives larger gains: Tensilica reports speedups of 40×–300× for kernels such as FFT, AES, and DES encryption.

We use the Xtensa Xplorer IDE as the evaluation tool and use the LX4 core as the starting point of enhancement. The Xtensa Xplorer contains a cycle-accurate core simulator with power estimator, which can be recreated according to the latest core configuration. Thus, we can get the running energy consumption and the chip area under a given CMOS process.

2.2.2 Application-Specific Microarchitecture

CPUs tailored to meet the requirements of HPC applications have been widely used. The K computer (http://www.fujitsu.com/global/about/tech/k/) customized its SPARC64 VIIIfx cores for high-performance applications, including the SIMD extension, a larger floating point register file, etc. Green Flash [8,9] proposed a new approach to scientific computing that chooses the science target first and designs systems for applications. The special design of the tailored Xtensa processor cores for parallel models is focused on how to build the CMP and higher level structures. Instead, we focus on the single core design.

Anton [10] was designed and built specially for molecular dynamics simulations of proteins and other biological macromolecules. Besides 32 pipelined ASIC modules, each Anton processing node contains four Tensilica cores and eight specialized but programmable SIMD cores (called *geometry cores*).

Customized CPUs can also match an ASIC solution's performance within 3× of its energy and within the comparable area for H.264 encoding [11]. Customized Xtensa cores have three broad strategies: (1) merging frequently used sequential operations into a single instruction; (2) very long instruction word (VLIW) and SIMD techniques; (3) the creation of application-specific data storage with fused functional units.

Fidjeland et al. [16] designed a customizable multiprocessor for application-optimized inductive logic programming, a form of symbolic machine learning. It can yield speedups of up to 15× over software running on a Pentium 4 machine.

Some research has developed ways to generate customization automatically: Atasu et al. [17] presented Fast Instruction SyntHesis (FISH), a system that supports automatic generation of custom instruction processors. Grad and Plessl [18] studied the feasibility of instruction set specialization for reconfigurable ASICs at run time; they proposed effective ways of pruning the design space to reduce the run time of instruction set extension algorithms by two orders of magnitude.

2.2.3 Stencil Computation

Applications often perform nearest-neighbor computations, called *stencils*. In a stencil operation, each point in a grid is updated with weighted contributions from a subset of its neighbors. These operations are then used to build solvers that range from simple Jacobi iterations to complex multigrid and adaptive mesh refinement methods [19]. As described by Colella [20], stencil computation is usually the kernel of structured grid applications, and the latter has been regarded as one of the seven important numerical methods for science and engineering.

As described by Zhang and Mueller [21], the stencil computation can be presented by the following equation over a 3D rectangular domain:

$$C(i,j,k) = \sum_m A_m * B(i \pm I_m, j \pm J_m, k \pm K_m)$$

$$+ \sum_l A_l(i,j,k) * B(i \pm I_l, j \pm J_l, k \pm K_l) \tag{2.1}$$

The center point and some neighboring points in the input grid (Array B) are weighted by either scalar constants (Am) or elements in grid variables (Al (i, j, k)) at the same location as the output.

The offsets (Im/Jm/Km and Il/Jl/Kl) that constrain how the input data is accessed are all constant. We call their maxima the *halo margins of three dimensions*.

Then, a stencil calculation is called an *N-point stencil*, where N is the total number of input points used to calculate one output point.

The data structures of stencil calculations are typically much larger than the capacity of data caches. In addition, the amount of data reuse depends on the number of points in a stencil. So these computations generally achieve a low fraction of theoretical peak performance; the speed of main memory data transfer is not high enough to avoid stalling the computational units on microprocessors. Reorganizing these stencil calculations to take full advantage of memory hierarchies has been the subject of much investigation. A study of stencil optimization [22] on (single-core) cache-based platforms found that tiling optimizations were primarily effective when the problem size exceeded the on-chip cache's capacity.

Another related work is Ref. [23]. Datta et al. [23] developed some effective software optimization strategies for stencil computation for a broad set of multicore architectures in the current HPC literature, including X86/UltraSparc CPUs, graphics processing units (GPUs), and CELL. However, none of the customizable processors were mentioned. Ref. [24] presents a domain-specific approach to automatically generate code tailored to different processor types, instead of writing hand-tuned code for GPU accelerators.

The stencil computation was also optimized to exploit the parallelism of GPUs [23,25,26] and reconfigurable architectures of FPGAs [27,28].

Unlike previous work customizing software for hardware, our work customizes the hardware and carries out the codesign.

2.3 CUSTOMIZATION DESIGN

2.3.1 Customization Flow

We examine a wide variety of optimizations, including the following:

1. Software optimizations (array padding and loop tiling) combined with cache adoption

2. Bandwidth optimizations: prefetch and fine-tuning of the cache attribute dynamically

3. DMA with the memory on-chip

4. SIMD

Rather than application-specific hardware, these are common architecture features: some are used for the ILP exploration, some for bandwidth optimizations, and others for the overlap of memory-IO and computation. And according to what we know, there is no real architecture that has applied them together.

2.3.2 Array Padding and Loop Tiling

Array padding and loop tiling are common software optimizations. The novelty of our work is that, owing to the features of the customizable processor, the cache's configuration can also be customized. Therefore, we can codesign hardware/software together to adjust the power consumption and the chip area.

The array padding transformation sets a dimension to a new size in order to reduce cache-set conflicts; tiling for locality requires grouping points in an iteration space into smaller blocks, allowing reuse in multiple directions when the block fits in a faster memory (L1 cache in this work). Both are directly dependent on the d-cache's configurations.

Specific to stencil computations, as mentioned in Refs. [29,30], to carefully select tile dimensions is important to avoid cache conflicts. Because there are quite a few, researchers have explored the tiling optimizations for the stencil.

2.3.3 Bandwidth Optimizations

Processors may also support software prefetching instructions, which is available on all cached data addresses. Then software can control the prefetch operations directly, and no miss history table is needed. However, it can only express a cache line's worth of memory level parallelism once.

For stencil, some existing researchers [31,32] have claimed that prefetching does not provide significant speedup because the innermost loop in the stencil kernel is predominantly memory bandwidth-bound and the tiling technique (if employed, as we did) also contributes to less effective prefetching. However, it is a general-purpose feature anyway, and we still consider it for customization.

For the second, we try to avoid unnecessary memory accesses. For example, on write-allocate architectures, a write miss will cause the allocation of a cache line. However, for a data region that will be totally overwritten, this transfer is useless. Then, a good solution is to adjust the cache attribute of a given address range during the run time while the remaining is unchanged.

The final method here is about the on-chip memory, which is an alternative to cache. Its access latency is usually the same as that of cache, while it is not transparent to software. We use it with the DMA mechanism together; details are presented in Section 2.3.5.

2.3.4 SIMD and DMA

Here, we introduce new SIMD instructions to enhance the floating-point processing capability of the simple core, and the DMA mechanism is also employed, as the stencil kernel is predominately bound by memory bandwidth.

As we know, modern general-purpose processors are usually equipped with SIMD instructions for floating-point data, which is highly valuable for scientific computing and multimedia processing. However, the ability of floating point processing is the shortcoming of normally customizable cores: they usually own a single floating point processing unit, and no SIMD is supported. Therefore, we have to enhance the corresponding capability to adapt to high-performance computing.

Generally speaking, DMA allows certain hardware modules to access system memory independently of the CPU. Owing to DMA, the core can do other operations as the data transfer is in progress, which is especially meaningful if the data amount is large and/or the transfer is relatively slow.

We intend to use the DMA engine to transfer data from the external memory into the memory on-chip directly to overlap the communication with computation. It works

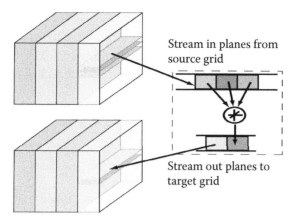

Stream in planes from
source grid

Stream out planes to
target grid

FIGURE 2.1   Visualization of circular queue.

like the CELL processor, which transfers data to and from the main memory and local memories. However, most modern processors lack this feature.

For stencil computation, one optimization, known as *circular queue* [23], is promising. This approach allocates a shadow copy (called a *queue*) of the planes of a tile in the local memory; data on planes are streamed (by load instructions or DMAs) into the queue, processed, and streamed back. It is often beneficial to double buffer operations as well. Figure 2.1 illustrates the circular queue.

2.3.5   Stencil Computation and Others

This 19-point stencil performs an out-of-place iteration; the halo value is 1 for all three dimensions. Values are weighted by elements in grid variables, A, which apparently increases the data-transmission pressure and lacks the temporal locality. For each grid point, this stencil will execute 37 floating point operations and 39 memory references.

Because the stencil is computation- and memory-access-intensive, we intend to enhance the preliminary core with the following techniques:

1. Floating-point SIMD instruction(s), combined with the DMA and memory on-chip solutions

2. Bandwidth optimizations, including data prefetching and adjusting the cache attribute to prevent filling the overwritten regions

3. Hardware/software hybrid optimizations to improve cache efficiency.

In the next section, we customize the core accordingly.

2.3.5.1 Seven-Point Stencil Computation

This seven-point stencil reads and writes in two distinct arrays. For each grid point, this stencil will execute 13 floating point operations over 7 values. The customization techniques used by the 19-point stencil are employed here, too.

2.3.5.2 Dense-Matrix Multiplication

Mainly we use the new floating-point SIMD instruction to enhance the computation capability and implement a circular-queue-like mechanism to DMA the data into on-chip memory. In addition, the common timing and data padding techniques are also employed.

2.3.5.3 Vector Inner Products and Vector Scaling

These can be regarded the basic operations of dense matrix multiplication. Therefore the similar SIMD and DMA techniques are used, too.

2.4 IMPLEMENTATION

We use the Xtensa LX4 core as the starting point of customization (its configurations were introduced in Section 2.2.1).

1. For software optimization, with the help of Pluto [33], an automatic locality-optimization tool can achieve the source-to-source transformation; we have tried some different strategies of data padding and loop tiling on the core simulator. Then we found the best strategy and the corresponding cache configurations: one 16-KB, two-way set-associative write-back d-cache with 256-B cache-line.

   Of course, greater capacities or higher set-association degrees will lead to better performance. However, we found that the performance improvement is limited while the additional chip area is relatively larger. Therefore, we select this compromise configuration, which is called the *tiling case* in the following subsections.

   Moreover, owing to the DMA method presented in Subsection 2.3.5, the cache configuration can be reduced more, which will be introduced in detail later.

2. For hardware prefetch, the Xtensa processor offers such an option. Internally, the prefetch logic has a miss history table, which keeps track of the cache misses that have occurred; and the prefetch buffers that keep track of the cache line addresses will be prefetched. There is a configurable number of prefetch buffers (8 or 16). It also supplies prefetch instructions, DPFR, DPFW, DPFRO, and DPFWO; all prefetch a single cache line into the prefetch buffer.

   Array C of the target computation will be overwritten; thus the attribute of allocate-on-write-miss is a burden for it. So we are faced with a trade-off because the usual attribute of write-back-and-allocate-on-write-miss has been proved better. Fortunately, LX4 processors support data region control operations so it can set cache attributes of a given region of memory; we can set the cache attributes of Array C as write-back-but-no-allocate-on-write-miss while keeping the remaining part as the normal. Specifically, the processor could modify the corresponding attributes in the memory management unit (MMU).

3. We employ the ISA extension technique of customizable CPUs to enhance the floating-point processing capability. We implement the add and multiply operations of floating points using the integer operations. Because the SIMD technique of integer operations is supported inherently by LX4, we implement the SIMD version of add and multiply operations of floating points.

The detailed design flow is as follows:

Step 1: According to the ANSI/IEEE Std 754-1985 specification, we implement the add and multiply operations (referred to as *floatadd* and *floatmul* in the following contents) of two single precision floating point values using the Tensilica Instruction Extension (TIE) language.

Step 2: We introduce one 288-bit register and three 96-bit registers (referred to as *vec* and *mat1~3* in the following contents) that are used to occupy up to nine consecutive values of Array A and three groups of three consecutive values of Array B, respectively.

Step 3: Based on the instruction fusion and SIMD mechanisms of TIE, we design the final instruction and operation unit, which can complete up to nine add and multiply operations in one instruction.

Now, the new scalar MADD instruction is able to support the computation of up to nine pairs of floating point objects in parallel. Tests show that the new instruction can complete the computation of the innermost loop in 30 cycles (if the cache is perfect), while the original FPU spends about 80 cycles (the cache is perfect, too).

4. The Xtensa processor can contain up to 128 KB local SRAM, and its access latency is just one cycle. We allocated a double buffer in the local memory for the DMA transfer.

It supports the inbound DMA option, which means that other cores or DMA engines can transfer data into the local memories directly in parallel with the processor pipeline. The software can deal with the completion of DMA operations through polling mode or interrupt mode.

We focus on Array A, whose transmission pressure is the largest; other data is still accessed through the d-cache. The whole computation procedure can be described as follows:

a. Initialize the engine.

b. DMA the first data segment of Array A to Buffer 1.

c. Wait for the completion (in polling mode).

d. DMA the follow-up data into Buffer 2.

e. Execute the floating-point computations on Buffer 1 (other data accesses are handled as normal).

f. DMA the follow-up data into Buffer 1.

g. Execute the computations on Buffer 2.

h. Goto Step d till the end.

Thus DMA operations are decoupled from execution.

In our implementation, a simple seven-stage Xtensa LX processor is used as the DMA engine, and the system sketch map is presented. These two cores are connected with two TIE ports: one is used to export the core's DMA request to the controller; the other feeds back the operation results.

Moreover, the introduction of DMA (and local memories) can decrease the pressure on the d-cache, remarkable because only the data of Arrays B and C will be cached. Then, we have gotten another best cache configuration: one 8-KB, two-way set-associative d-cache with the 64-B cache line. For this configuration, the performance is almost the same as the larger cache, while the area cache and energy consumption both decrease.

2.5 TEST RESULTS AND ANALYSIS

Based on the IDE provided by Tensilica, we have carried out evaluations for each above-mentioned optimization step from the aspects of core performance, power consumption, and chip area. The array scale is set as $512 \times 512 \times 3$. We also compare the design with other architectures; at last, we illustrate that the scalability of our customization is good.

2.5.1 Tiling and Padding

We tested the naïve version of the preliminary core at first. We then optimized the source code as described in Section 2.3.1 and adjusted the configurations of the d-cache at the same time to find out the best combination. Finally, we found that one 16-KB, two-way set-associative d-cache with the 256-B cache line (which is called the *tiling case* and is used as the reference in the following comparisons) is the most optimized: its performance is almost 2.4 times higher than the naïve version, while the power consumption is only about 55% (the typical case), which is presented in Table 2.1 (the worst and typical cases of the 45-ns CMOS technology are both given).

2.5.2 Prefetch

Our test shows that the hardware prefetch itself hardly brings any improvement; its software counterpart can get very limited performance promotion, even less than 0.5%.

We think the reason is that the cache line is fairly long (256 B). Therefore the data to be used in the near future has been loaded implicitly; moreover, the tiling technology has utilized the locality fully. Test results have also confirmed it: prefetch increases the memory read throughput by about 12% while it decreases the miss rate of d-cache by only 0.1 percentage points.

TABLE 2.1   Naïve versus Tiling

	Frequency (GHz)	Cycles	Energy (pJ)
Naïve case	1.399	158727991	25850857119
	(1.102)	(158728187)	(26813094601)
Tiling case	1.398	64933263	14276508076
	(1.102)	(64872830)	(14693772179)

Note: Values of the worst case are in brackets.

2.5.3 No-Allocate

This is a simple but very efficient method because it causes little increase of the chip area: compared with the tiling case, to set the cache attributes of Array C as write-back-but-no-allocate-on-store improves performance by about 1.6% and decreases energy consumption by 2% (the typical case in Table 2.2).

Specifically, test results show that this optimization can reduce the memory throughput by about 3.7%.

2.5.4 SIMD

ILP optimization has improved the real application performance by about 15% while increasing power consumption by 8% (the typical case in Table 2.3). Because this application is mainly memory-bound, the computation speedup cannot improve the application performance as much as in the ideal situation (Section 2.4).

Moreover, the number of data load operations is only 76.5% of the reference case. We believe that the registers have increased the effective storage capacity on-chip; some memory reads have been avoided.

2.5.5 DMA

As described in Section 2.4, we load the data into the local RAM in parallel. Specifically, two banks of 16-KB on-chip RAM are allocated; each one is equipped with an independent port to avoid access conflicts. The data size of one DMA transfer operation is 6 KB.

Moreover, the Tensilica environment provides software modules to support the simulation of a system including more than one core. Then a simple seven-stage Xtensa LX processor is used here as the DMA engine to simplify the performance, energy consumption, and chip area evaluation.

TABLE 2.2   Tiling versus No-Allocate

	Frequency (GHz)	Cycles	Energy (pJ)
No-allocate case	1.398	63898275	13993398996
	(1.102)	(63705119)	(14403185813)
Tiling case	1.398	64933263	14276508076
	(1.102)	(64872830)	(14693772179)

Note: Values of the worst case are in brackets.

TABLE 2.3   Tiling versus SIMD

	Frequency (GHz)	Cycles	Energy (pJ)
SIMD case	1.395	55575543	15495768744
	(1.098)	(55583405)	(16826161157)
Tiling case	1.398	64933263	14276508076
	(1.102)	(64872830)	(14693772179)

Note: Values of the worst case are in brackets.

Because DMA transfers bypass the d-cache, it is reasonable to shrink the cache now: typical-case tests show that DMA can improve performance by 14% and increase the energy by 21% when the d-cache size is set as 8 KB and the miss rate has been reduced to 0.5%.

Specifically, the time overhead of DMA has occupied about 29% of the computation part (including the data load/store operations), which is hidden to an extent degree. On the other hand, the DMA transfer interferes issued from the d-cache, which partially offsets the overlap.

If the cache strategy customization and SIMD are implemented at the same time, the performance increase is 29%, while the energy consumption is increased by 17%. This is the best result we have gotten. All results are given in Table 2.4.

Finally, we give chip areas of all the above-mentioned configurations (the typical case) in Table 2.5, including areas of each component.

2.5.6 Preliminary Comparison with X86 and Others

We roughly compared our design with a general-purpose processor, the Intel® Xeon® Processor X5560, which is also produced by the 45-nm CMOS process. The corresponding parameters are listed in Table 2.6.

X5560 is a four-core processor. Here, we simply take one-fourth of its nominal power consumption, as well as the chip area. The drawback of this simplification lies in that 1/4 of the shared on-chip 8-MB L3-cache of X86 has been regarded as one part of the core. The whole L3-cache has been used in reality, although only one single core is employed from the aspect of computation. Therefore, we believe this simplification is acceptable.

TABLE 2.4 Tiling versus DMA and the Best Case

	Frequency (GHz)	Cycles	Energy (pJ)
Best case	1.395	46561339	16708308961
	(1.098)	(46564309)	(17461403831)
DMA case	1.395	56160632	17332648838
	(1.098)	(56060762)	(15527598614)
Tiling case	1.398	64933263	14276508076
	(1.102)	(64872830)	(14693772179)

Note: Values of the worst case are in brackets.

TABLE 2.5 All Cases

	Tiling Case	No-Allocate Case	SIMD Case	DMA Case	Best Case
Overall area (mm²)	0.388	0.388	0.713	0.624	0.914
Core	0.233	0.233	0.268	0.268	0.268
Cache and local memory	0.155	0.155	0.155	0.312	0.312
SIMD	N/A	N/A	0.290	N/A	0.290
DMA	N/A	N/A	N/A	0.044	0.044

TABLE 2.6 Customized Core versus X86

	Power (W)	Chip Area (mm²)	Frequency (Ghz)	Application Performance(s)
Our design	0.5	0.914	1.395	33
	(0.41)	(1.14)	(1.098)	(42)
X5560	24	66	2.8	18

Note: Values of the worst case are in brackets.

TABLE 2.7 Customized Core versus GPU and FPGA (Typical Case)

	Best Case		GPU			FPGA	
		[23]	[25]	[26]	[27]	[28]
Throughput (GFlop/s)	0.82	36	51.2	64.5	35.7	102.8
Efficiency (MFlop/s/W)	1660	76.5	n/a	n/a	n/a	785.0

We can see that it can achieve an order of magnitude higher performance per watt; its application performance is about 50% of that of X86, while the chip area is 0.91 mm² (typical case) to about 1.14 mm² (worst case), 1/58 to 1/72 of the X86 core area. Of course, we have made a simplification here; this comparison is for reference only.

In addition, we compare it with reference designs [23,25–28] based on GPU or FPGA; the best numbers from them are compared with our performance of the typical case, to provide a fair comparison. Detailed data are listed in Table 2.7.

From the aspect of performance (throughput), our design is much slower because of its simple structure and resource consumption. However, for performance per watt, it is a little more than an order of magnitude higher than GPUs and is comparable to FPGA; its programming flexibility is apparently much higher, too.

2.5.7 Scalability

We test the performance of different scales of the target application, from $256 \times 256 \times 3$ to $2048 \times 2048 \times 3$. Results (in Figure 2.2, typical case) show that the run time is nearly proportional to the scale, which indicates that our optimization has a high scalability.

The reason lies in the following facts: (1) Loop tiling has enhanced cache reuse and eliminated the requirements of larger size. Then, for Arrays B and C, their memory-access patterns are independent of the scale. (2) For Array A, its DMA latency is also proportional to the scale.

2.5.8 Other Computations

For the seven-point stencil computation ($512 \times 512 \times 3$), we test it on the core of the configuration of the best case; the DMA, SIMD, and the method setting cache attributes on the fly to avoid unnecessary memory accesses are also employed. Compared with the naïve version, results show that the performance has been increased by 218% and the energy consumption decreases by 32%.

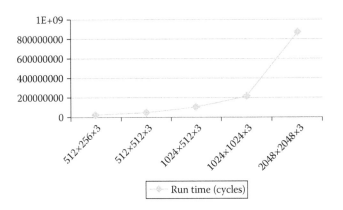

FIGURE 2.2 Emulation results of the scalability.

TABLE 2.8 Typical Case

	Cycles	Energy (pJ)
Seven-point stencil	11900015 (best case)	4354807686 (best case)
	37908504 (naïve case)	6388964111 (naïve case)
Matrix multiplication	358900856 (best case)	114735036704 (best case)
	604901600 (naïve case)	103352236824 (naïve case)
Vector inner products	1210861 (best case)	495103037 (best case)
	4647819 (naïve case)	832893033 (naïve case)
Vector scaling	1104176 (best case)	318991895 (best case)
	3960484 (naïve case)	660990168 (naïve case)

For dense matrix multiplication (512 × 512) using the same customization, the performance can also be increased by 41% and the energy consumption increases by only 11%. Tests show that, besides the common loop tiling technique, DMA transfer of the multiplicand matrix has remarkably improved the operation efficiency, because the latencies of those discontinuous data accesses can be hidden.

For vector inner products (512 × 512), the performance can be improved by 74% and the energy consumption decreases by only 40%. Compared with matrix multiplication, there is greater improvement for this case because there is no array transpose and then the locality of data accesses is better. Similarly, the improvements of vector scaling are 72% and 52%, respectively. Detailed data are listed in Table 2.8.

2.5.9 Test Summary

The test results show that, from the viewpoint of performance per watt, the simple architecture of customizable process is highly efficient: the performance per watt of the tiling case is the second highest (the first is the no-allocate case because it introduces almost no extra overhead). The absolute performance is not satisfying, so we use the DMA, SIMD, and other techniques to improve it by about 29%, while the energy consumption is only increased by 17%. Thus from the viewpoint of performance per energy, the best case is the highest.

Anyway, owing to the specific design, the relatively simple core can achieve an order of magnitude higher performance per watt, compared with the X86 core; its power efficiency is even comparable with the FPGA solutions.

Finally, tests for other computations have proved that those hardware customizations are common optimizations and can be widely used for other algorithms.

2.6 CONCLUSIONS AND FUTURE WORK

We present a systematic approach to enhance a preliminary customizable processor core with some common architecture features (not totally application-specific) to adapt to some high-performance computations, and we select stencil computation as the main application. Detailed evaluations are presented.

From the results, we can make the following conclusions:

1. The customizable core can obtain high power efficiency and high area efficiency even for some scientific calculations, owing to keeping the core simple while augmenting necessary architecture features. At the same time, the programming flexibility can be still maintained, which is the unique feature in contrast to the ASIC solution.

2. From the various aspects of architecture design (regardless of optimizing bandwidth or extending instructions), hardware and software codesign is an efficient means of improvement. Specifically, some data-reuse techniques like loop tiling and DMA can efficiently improve performance by increasing the data access speed; specific SIMD extensions can also offset its weakness on the computation capability of floating point data to a certain extent.

3. Last but not least, those hardware customizations are common optimization technologies. Thus we believe they can be widely used for more algorithms.

Now we are carrying out the development of the chip multiprocessor based on the tailored cores, as well as the corresponding parallel algorithms. We intend to embed some hardware supports of the parallel programming models (including one- and two-sided message passing) into the network-on-chip. In particular, the communication work will be offloaded to the specially designed NoC routers to a great degree, which is beneficial for overlapping the communication with computation for higher efficiency.

REFERENCES

1. Lawrence Berkeley National Laboratory, *Modeling and Simulation at the Exascale for Energy and the Environment*, Report on the Advanced Scientific Computing Research Town Hall Meetings on Simulation and Modeling at the Exascale for Energy, Ecological Sustainability and Global Security (E3).
2. J. Cong, V. Sarkar, G. Reinman, and A. Bui, 2011, Customizable domain-specific computing, *IEEE Design and Test of Computers*, vol. 28, no. 2, pp. 5–15.
3. Research: Custom Computing, http://cc.doc.ic.ac.uk.

4. F. Xia, Y. Dou, G. Lei, and Y. Tan, 2011, FPGA accelerator for protein secondary structure prediction based on the GOR algorithm, *Proceedings of the Ninth Asia Pacific Bioinformatics Conference*, Fort Lauderdale.

5. V. Mirian, K. P. Tang, P. Chow, and Z. Xing, 2009, Matrix multiplication based on scalable macro-pipelined FPGA accelerator architecture, *International Conference on Reconfigurable Computing and FPGAs*, Cancun, Mexico.

6. L. Ling, N. Oliver, C. Bhushan, et al., 2009, High-performance, energy-efficient platforms using in-socket FPGA accelerators, *Proceedings of the ACM/SIGDA International Symposium on Field Programmable Gate Arrays*.

7. J. Jeffers, *Intel many integrated core architecture: An overview and programming models*, Intel technical report, http://www.olcf.ornl.gov/wp-content/training/electronic-structure-2012/ORNL_Elec_Struct_WS_02062012.pdf.

8. M. Wehner, L. Oliker, and J. Shalf, 2008, Towards ultra-high resolution models of climate and weather, *International Journal of High Performance Computing Applications*, vol. 22, no. 2, pp. 149–165.

9. M. Wehner, L. Oliker, and J. Shalf, 2009, Green flash: Designing an energy efficient climate supercomputer, *IEEE Spectrum*.

10. D.E. Shaw, R.O. Dror, J.K. Salmon, et al., Millisecond-scale molecular dynamics simulations on anton, *Proceedings of the ACM/IEEE Conference on Supercomputing (SC09)*.

11. R. Hameed, W. Qadeer, M. Wachs, et al., 2010, Understanding sources of inefficiency in general-purpose chips, in *Proceedings of the 37th Annual International Symposium on Computer Architecture*, pp. 37–47.

12. Y. Zhang, P. Qu, Z. Qian, H. Wang, and W. Zheng, 2013, Software/hardware hybrid network-on-chip simulation on FPGA, *10th IFIP International Conference on Network and Parallel Computing (NPC 2013)*, Fort Lauderdale.

13. H. Wang, S. Lu, Y. Zhang, G. Yang, and W. Zheng, 2014, Customized network-on-chip for message reduction, *The 14th International Conference on Algorithms and Architectures for Parallel Processing*, Dalian, China.

14. C. Wang, X. Li, and X. Zhou, 2015, SODA: Software defined FPGA based accelerators for big data, *DATE*, pp. 884–887.

15. C. Wang, X. Li, P. Chen, A. Wang, X. Zhou, and H. Yu, 2015, Heterogeneous cloud framework for big data genome sequencing, *IEEE/ACM Transactions on Computational Biology and Bioinformatics*, vol. 12, no. 1, pp. 166–178.

16. A. Fidjeland, W. Luk, and S. Muggleton, 2008, A customisable multiprocessor for application-optimised inductive logic programming, *Proceeding of Visions of Computer Science—BCS International Academic Conference*, London, UK.

17. K. Atasu, W. Luk, O. Mencer, et al., 2012, FISH: Fast Instruction SyntHesisfor Custom Processors, *IEEE Transactions on Very Large Scale Integration (VLSI) Systems*, vol. 20, no. 1.

18. M. Grad and C. Plessl, 2010, Pruning the design space for just-in-time processor customization, *International Conference on Reconfigurable Computing and FPGAs (ReConFig)*, Cancun, Mexico.

19. M. Berger and J. Oliger, 1984, Adaptive mesh refinement for hyperbolic partial differential equations, *Journal of Computational Physics*, vol. 53, pp. 484–512.

20. P. Colella, 2004, Defining software requirements for scientific computing. *Slide of 2004 presentation included in David Patterson's 2005 talk*, http://www.lanl.gov/orgs/.

21. Y. Zhang and F. Mueller, 2012, Auto-generation and auto-tuning of 3D stencil codes on GPU clusters, *International Symposium on Code Generation and Optimization (CGO'2012)*, Hilton.

22. S. Kamil, K. Datta, S. Williams, L. Oliker, J. Shalf, and K. Yelick, 2006, Implicit and explicit optimizations for stencil computations, in *ACM SIGPLAN Workshop Memory Systems Performance and Correctness*, San Jose, CA.

23. K. Datta, M. Murphy, V. Volkov, S. Williams, J. Carter, L. Oliker, D. Patterson, J. Shalf, and K. Yelick, 2008, Stencil computation optimization and auto-tuning on state-of-the-art multi-core architectures, *Supercomputing 2008 (SC08)*, Austin, TX, November 18–20.

24. R. Membarth, F. Hannig, Jürgen Teich, et al., 2012, Towards domain-specific computing for stencil codes in HPC, *Proceedings of the 2nd International Workshop on Domain-Specific Languages and High-Level Frameworks for High Performance Computing (WOLFHPC)*, Salt Lake City, UT, November 16.

25. E. Phillips and M. Fatica, 2010, Implementing the himeno benchmark with CUDA on GPU clusters, in *Proceeding of IPDPS*, Atlanta, GA.

26. Y. Yang, H. Cui, X. Feng, and J. Xue, 2012, A hybrid circular queue method for iterative stencil computations on GPUs, *Journal of Computer Science and Technology*, vol. 27, pp. 57–74.

27. M. Araya-Polo et al., 2011, Assessing accelerator-based HPC reverse time migration, *IEEE Transactions on Parallel and Distributed Systems*, vol. 22, pp. 147–162.

28. X. Niu, Q. Jin, W. Luk, et al., 2012, Exploiting run-time reconfiguration in stencil computation, *22nd International Conference on Field Programmable Logic and Applications (FPL)*.

29. G. Rivera and C-W. Tseng, 2000, Tiling optimizations for 3D scientific computations, *ACM/IEEE 2000 Conference on Supercomputing*, Dallas, TX.

30. S. Coleman and K.S. McKinley, 1995, Tile size selection using cache organization and data layout, *Proceedings of the ACM Conference on Programming Language Design and Implementation*, La Jolla, CA.

31. H. Dursun, K-I. Nomura, W. Wang, et al., 2009, In-core optimization of high-order stencil computations, in *Proceedings of PDPTA*, pp. 533–538.

32. D. Kaushik et al., 2009, Optimization and performance modeling of stencil computations on modern microprocessors, *SIAM Review*, vol. 51, pp. 129–159.

33. U. Bondhugula, A. Hartono, J. Ramanujam, and P. Sadayappan, 2008, A practical automatic polyhedral parallelizer and locality optimizer, *SIGPLAN*, vol. 43, no. 6, pp. 101–113.

CHAPTER 3

Electromigration Alleviation Techniques for 3D Integrated Circuits

Yuanqing Cheng

Beihang University
Beijing, China

Aida Todri-Sanial, Alberto Bosio, Luigi Dilillo, Patrick Girard, and Arnaud Virazel

LIRMM, CNRS
Montpellier, France

Pascal Vivet and Marc Belleville
CEA-LETI
Grenoble, France

CONTENTS

Three-dimensional (3D) integration is considered to be a promising technology to tackle the global interconnect scaling problem for terascale integrated circuits (ICs). 3D ICs typically employ through-silicon vias (TSVs) to connect planar circuits vertically. Due to the immature fabrication process, several defects such as void, misalignment, and dust contamination may be introduced. These defects can increase current densities within TSVs significantly and cause severe electromigration (EM) effects, which can degrade the reliability of 3D ICs considerably. In this paper, we propose a novel method, TSV-SAFE, to mitigate the EM effect of the defective TSV. At first, we analyze various possible TSV defects and demonstrate that they can aggravate EM dramatically. Based on the observation that the EM effect can be alleviated significantly by balancing the direction of current flow within TSVs, we design an online self-healing circuit to protect defective TSVs, which can be detected during test procedures, from EM without degrading performance. To ensure that all defective TSVs are protected with low hardware overhead, we also propose a switch-network–based sharing structure such that the EM protection modules can be shared among TSV groups in neighborhood. Experimental results show that our proposed method can achieve over 10 times improvement on mean time to failure (MTTF) compared to the design without using such methods with negligible hardware overhead and power consumption.

3.1 ELECTROMIGRATION EFFECT IN 3D INTEGRATED CIRCUITS

The term *reliability* usually refers to the probability that a component or system will operate satisfactorily either at any particular instant at which it is required or for a certain length of time. Fundamental to quantifying reliability is a knowledge of how to define, assess, and combine probabilities. This may hinge on identifying the form of the variability which is inherent in most processes. If all components had a fixed known lifetime, there would be no need to model reliability.

3.1.1 EM Phenomenon and Related Work

With continuous technology scaling, chip integration density continues to increase sharply. Billions of transistors can be built within a single chip. As a consequence, chip power consumption has also skyrocketed. At the same time, the supply voltage has decreased gradually with each technology generation. Thus, the current density on chip has elevated quickly. High current density may induce a significant electromigration (EM) effect, which threatens chip operation reliability. It is caused by mass transport within metal interconnects. When current flows in the metal line, electrons collide with metal atoms and drag them away from their original positions. As a result, voids generate within the region where metal atoms are dragged away while hillocks forms where they aggregate together. Voids introduce open defects and hillocks cause shorts with the neighboring interconnects. As the technology node enters the deep submicron regime, EM is becoming a severe challenge for very large scale integration (VLSI) designers.

According to Ref. [1], there are mainly three types of interconnects within a chip, that is, unidirectional interconnects, bidirectional interconnects, and power grid interconnects. As unidirectional lines charge and discharge loading capacitance through one end, they are immune to EM. The bidirectional interconnects can charge through one end and discharge through the other end, causing current to flow continuously in one specific direction. Therefore, it may suffer from the EM effect. The DC current flows on power grid lines can only flow from the power supply to ground and also suffer from EM.

As early as the 1960s and 1970s, several researchers had already observed EM in aluminum metal lines. Belch et al. observed the eletrotransport phenomenon in aluminum metal lines [2]. In their experiments, voids or holes could form where electrons flowed along with the increasing temperature direction. Meanwhile, hillocks could generate where electrons flowed along with decreasing temperature direction. Black et al. proposed the famous mean time to failure (MTTF) formula considering the EM effect [3]. For the detailed EM failure mechanism, readers can refer to Ref. [4], which is a good survey of EM in aluminum metal lines. Starting in the 1980s, copper gradually replaced aluminum as the on-chip interconnect material. Due to its high melting point, the EM effect is alleviated significantly. However, as the current density increases sharply for deep submicron interconnects, the EM effect becomes a challenging issue again and is believed to be more severe as the technology node scales further. Hau-Riege investigated the EM phenomenon in copper metal lines and compared it with that of aluminum metal lines [5]. The author also suggested an EM assessment method for metal lines with different complex geometries. Gozalez et al. explored the relationship between metal line shape and EM effect [6]. They observed that metal lines with a right angle shape are more prone to suffer from the EM effect.

Due to the EM effect threatening the lifetime of the chip significantly, several papers in the literature have proposed effective techniques to mitigate it from various levels. Liew et al. considered EM related reliability issues at the register transfer level (RTL) level [7]. Through judiciously mapping control dataflow graph onto data busses, the MTTF considering EM effect can be improved significantly. Teng et al. proposed a hierarchical analysis method for EM diagnosis [8]. Firstly, the critical interconnections that may have EM problems are identified by the top component of the hierarchy. Then, a detailed analysis on these lines is performed by a circuit simulation tool to evaluate the EM impact on them. In Ref. [9], the authors observed that different current waveforms may cause different EM effects even if their magnitudes are the same. The DC current–induced EM effect is much more significant than AC pluses. This implies that the metal interconnects have self-healing abilities under AC flows. Todri et al. investigated the EM effect caused by the power-gating technique on power grid interconnects and proposed a grid line–sizing algorithm to solve this problem [10]. Based on the above research efforts, Abella et al. proposed a refueling microarchitecture to alleviate the EM effect and enhance the reliability of metal interconnects [11]. In our work, we also try to explore this property to prolong the lifetime of defective TSVs in terms of EM MTTF.

3.1.2 EM of 3D Integrated Circuits and Related Work

As the technology scales, power consumption becomes a severe problem for contemporary VLSI circuits. Meanwhile, the interconnect delay has already exceeded gate delay, becoming the performance bottleneck of processors. In order to reduce on-chip interconnect power consumption and delay, 3D integrated circuits (ICs) are proposed to deal with this issue [12]. A typical 3D IC structure is shown in Figure 3.1. The bonding style can be classified into face-to-face, face-to-back, and back-to-back bonding. Except the bottom tier, all tiers are thinned to be hundreds of microns thick. By stacking planar dies and connecting them with vertical through-silicon vias (TSVs), the global interconnect can be reduced from several millimeters to only tens of microns. Therefore, both interconnect power consumption and delay can be reduced dramatically. Additionally, 3D IC facilitates disparate technology process integration. As a result, it has become a promising integration technology for the next generation of ICs.

When the 2D design transforms to a 3D design, the critical data busses, such as those between the L1 and L2 caches, are usually implemented by TSVs to cut down the interconnect length and improve performance. The EM problem can still occur on a TSV due to the high thermomechanical stress gradient between TSVs and the bonding pad. Moreover, the TSV fabrication process may introduce defects such as void, particle contamination, and bonding misalignment, all of which can exacerbate the EM problem

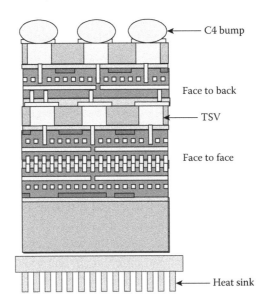

FIGURE 3.1   Illustration of a typical 3D integrated circuit structure.

by tens of orders of magnitude, as shown later in this chapter. Therefore, the TSVs, especially those with defects, threatened by EM effects should be protected against EM.

Tan et al. investigated TSV EM performance and evaluated different possible EM occurring sites on TSVs [13]. Pak et al. evaluated the EM impact on TSVs from the layout perspective and provided some guidelines for EM-robust TSV design [14]. Frank et al. explored the impact of EM on resistances of TSVs [15]. Zhao et al. investigated EM impact on power delivery networks and showed that EM can cause a large IR drop on power grid interconnects [16]. However, most work has focused on EM modeling on the TSV without any reliability enhancements, especially for defective TSVs.

In this chapter, we propose a framework called *TSV-SAFE* (TSV self-healing architecture for electromigration) from the architecture perspective to efficiently mitigate the EM effect for TSVs of 3D ICs. The framework provides a workflow for defective TSV identification and protection from EM. The rest of this chapter is organized as follows. Section 3.1.2 evaluates the EM effect on defective TSVs. Section 3.1.3 proposes the TSV-SAFE framework to identify defective TSVs and mitigate their EM effects online. Experimental results are shown in Section 3.1.4. Section 3.1.5 presents the conclusions. Cheng et al. proposed to take advantage of self-healing effect to mitigate EM effect on defective TSVs but their method introduces large area overhead and can not protect all defective TSVs from electromigration effectively [17].

3.2 ELECTROMIGRATION THREATS FOR DEFECTIVE TSVs

3.2.1 TSV EM MTTF Calculation

According to Ref. [3], the EM MTTF of the TSV can be estimated by the following formula:

$$\text{MTTF} = A.J^{-\eta} \cdot \frac{Q}{e\kappa \cdot T} \tag{3.1}$$

where A is a constant depending on the TSV fabrication technology, J is the TSV current density, Q is the activation energy for EM, κ is the Boltzmann's constant, and T is the temperature. The current density J can be expressed as follows:

$$J = \frac{C.V_{dd}}{S} \cdot f \cdot p \tag{3.2}$$

where C is the TSV capacitance, V_{dd} is the supply voltage, S is the cross-sectional area of TSV, f is the clock frequency, and p is the signal's switch activity transferred by TSV. Equations 3.1 and 3.2 are used to derive the EM MTTF of defective TSVs in the following simulations. In the evaluation, we assume the TSV diameter is 5 μm and its aspect ratio is 5:1, according to [18]. The filling material is copper, and silicon dioxide material isolates the copper from substrate. The size of the bounding pad is assumed to be 6 × 6 μm [18]. TSV is fabricated by the via-last process. Three common types of TSV defects, that is, TSV void, misalignment of TSV bonding pads, and dust contamination on the bonding surface shown in Figure 3.2, are examined in the following evaluations.

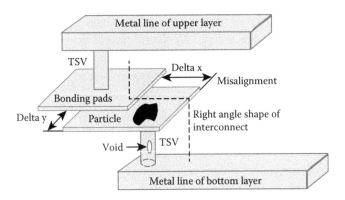

FIGURE 3.2 Through-silicon via defects: void, misalignment, and bonding surface contamination.

3.2.2 EM Occurrence due to Void

During the TSV filling process, due to anisotropic metal deposition on the sidewall and center of TSV, voids can be formed [19]. This reduces the effective cross-sectional area of TSV and increases the current density according to Equation 3.2. The increased current density can elevate the EM effect suffered by TSV. Therefore, the mean time to failure of TSVs with voids may degrade according to Equation 3.1.

Using the TSV feature size mentioned above, we calculate the TSV MTTF under different void sizes. The result is plotted in Figure 3.3. The x-axis denotes void size; the left y-axis denotes the corresponding MTTF value, which is normalized to that of TSV without void; and the right y-axis represents the TSV conductive area. The figure indicates that TSV MTTF decreases rapidly with increasing void size. For instance, when the void size exceeds 3.5 μm, the MTTF value decreases over 50%. Thus, void defects can degrade TSV immunity to EM significantly.

3.2.3 EM Occurrence due to Bonding Pad Misalignment

To stack tiers together, a bonding process is required for 3D ICs. In order to guarantee the bonding yield, each TSV is attached with a pad. TSVs of different tiers can be bonded

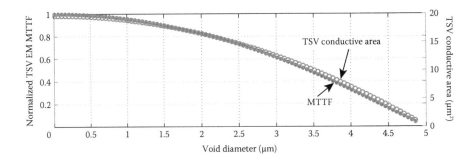

FIGURE 3.3 Normalized through-silicon via (TSV) electromigration (EM) mean time to failure (MTTF) and TSV conductive area variations with different void sizes.

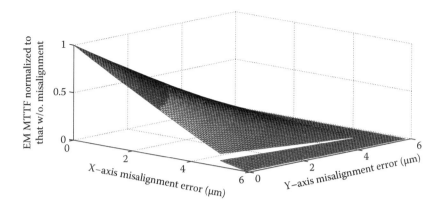

FIGURE 3.4   Normalized TSV EM MTTF versus misalignment error.

together using the pads. Taking the face-to-back bonding style as an instance, the bonding pads of TSVs in the upper tier will be matched with those in the bottom tier as shown in Figure 3.2. However, the bonding process may incur some errors on bonding positions due to the accuracy error of the bonding equipment. As a result, a TSV bonding pad from the upper tier may not be aligned very well with one from the lower tier [20]. Misalignment can reduce the conductive area of the TSV as shown in Figure 3.2. Therefore the current density increases and the EM MTTF decreases according to Equations 3.1 and 3.2. We calculated the TSV EM MTTF values based on different misalignment errors. The results are shown in Figure 3.4. In the figure, the $x(y)$-axis denotes a misalignment error in the $x(y)$ direction in units of μm. The z-axis represents the MTTF value, which is normalized to that of the TSV without misalignment defect. As shown in the figure, the MTTF decreases rapidly as the misalignment error increases. Note that the curved surface becomes discontinuous when the error exceeds the TSV diameter (e.g., 5 μm in our experiments) due to the formation of right-angle current flow as shown in Figure 3.5, which can aggravate the EM effect abruptly [6]. Therefore, misalignment-induced MTTF degradation should also be considered for reliability enhancement.

3.2.4 EM Occurrence due to Contamination

During TSV fabrication, dust particles in the environment may contaminate the bonding surface, which reduces the effective cross-sectional area of TSV and degrades the TSV MTTF, as indicated by Equations 3.1 and 3.2. We plot the normalized TSV EM MTTF versus the TSV conductive area with different dust particle sizes in Figure 3.6. It shows that the TSV EM MTTF reduces quickly with increasing dust particle size. When it exceeds 4.5 μm in our case, the MTTF decreases over 50%.

In summary, it shows that defective TSVs can suffer more severe EM effects than normal TSVs. Due to the bucket effect, the chip lifetime is determined by those defective TSVs instead of normal ones. Therefore, it is imperative to protect them from EM such that the chip reliability can be improved.

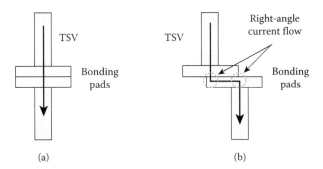

FIGURE 3.5 Right-angle current is formed due to misalignment errors: (a) without misalignment and (b) with misalignment.

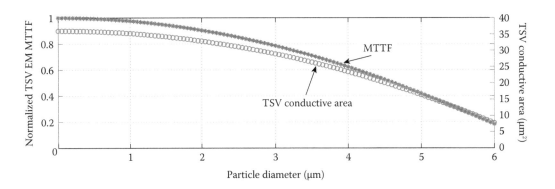

FIGURE 3.6 Normalized TSV EM MTTF/TSV conductive area versus particle size.

3.3 OUR PROPOSED FRAMEWORK TO ALLEVIATE THE EM EFFECT FOR 3D INTEGRATED CIRCUITS

In Ref. [21], the authors observed that bidirectional currents can alleviate the EM effect better than DC currents. In other words, AC flows can mitigate the EM effect they cause. Therefore, the reliability of the metal line can be enhanced effectively. Abella et al. exploits this phenomenon to enhance the bidirectional data busses suffering from EM [11]. In this section, we propose an EM mitigation framework to protect defective TSVs from the EM effect, taking advantage of the self-healing mechanism.

3.3.1 Overview of Our Framework

The workflow of our framework as shown in Figure 3.7 contains two stages, that is, offline identification of defective TSVs and an online EM mitigation module. In the first offline stage, we can take advantage of existing research efforts to identify defective TSVs and obtain the fault map. Then, an on-chip switch network connects defective TSVs to online EM mitigation modules. In the second stage, the EM mitigation modules monitor current flows within these TSVs and balance the current flow directions in time to alleviate EM by the self-healing mechanism.

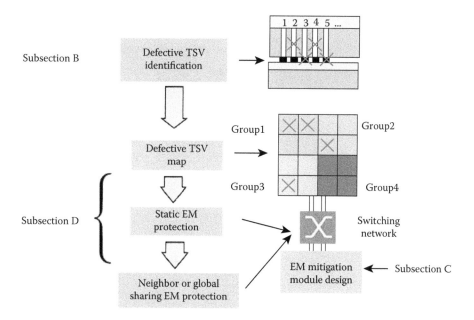

FIGURE 3.7   Workflow of the TSV-SAFE framework.

3.3.2 Defective TSV Identification

As voids may be introduced in the TSV during the metal filling process, we can expose this defect by burn-in or stress tests [22]. Then, the defective TSV can be identified through either capacitance or resistance sensing techniques. Since this defect occurs before the bonding process, we adopt the method proposed in Ref. [22] for defective TSV testing.

As shown in Figure 3.8, the TSV is treated as a DRAM cell. The test sequence is write "1", read "1", hold on, read "0". By charging and discharging the TSV capacitance through test sequence, the sensing circuit can sense the voltage variations between normal TSV and defective one within a prespecified time period, and defective TSVs can be identified.

The other two type defects (i.e., misalignment and bonding interface contamination) can only be detected after the TSV bonding stage. The resistance variations due to these defects are plotted in Figures 3.9 and 3.10, respectively.

As shown in Figure 3.9, when misalignment error exceeds 3.5 μm, the resistance increases by thousands of times. Similar trends can be observed in Figure 3.10, that is, the resistance increases significantly when particle size exceeds 4 μm in our case. As a result, we can identify these defects easily by online sensing circuit to detect TSV resistance variations.

We adopted the test structure proposed in Ref. [23] (shown in Figure 3.11). As shown in the figure, V_{ref} is set at a threshold voltage according to the normal TSV resistance value. Then, we can apply the voltage dividing principle to sense the potential difference between TSV under test and V_{ref}. If it exceeds the threshold voltage, the test result indicating a defective TSV will be latched to a scan register. Through both prebond and postbond testing, we can determine the fault map of TSVs, which will be used by our online EM mitigation circuit.

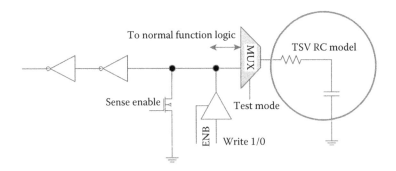

FIGURE 3.8   Test circuit of TSV with void defect before bonding stage [22].

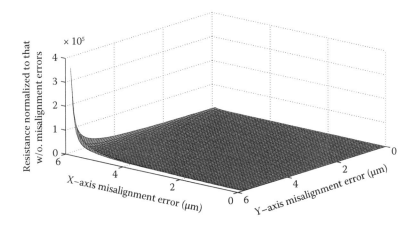

FIGURE 3.9   TSV resistance versus misalignment errors.

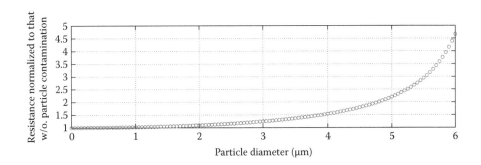

FIGURE 3.10   TSV resistance versus particle size.

3.3.3 Defective TSV Grouping and Crossbar Network Design

To protect defective TSVs from EM, an intuitive method can be adopted, described as follows. During the chip design stage, TSVs are divided into several groups. For each group, an EM mitigation circuit module is allocated. Note that the group size

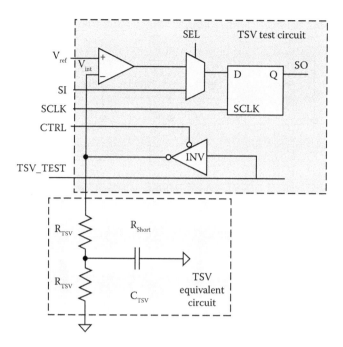

FIGURE 3.11   TSV test structure [23].

depends on TSV yield and is a trade-off between area overhead and EM MTTF. Smaller group size can protect more TSVs from the EM effect but also introduce larger area overheads. Taking five TSVs in one group as an example, each TSV is connected to the EM mitigation module allocated to this group through a crossbar-based switch network, as shown in Figure 3.12. The CTRL i controls which TSV should be connected to the EM mitigation circuit module. Although the switch network incurs some routing overhead, we can use the white space around TSV arrays and keep the TSV group size small to alleviate routing congestion.

Although the above method can protect one defective TSV for each group, it cannot tolerate more than one defective TSV in the group. If not all defective TSVs can be protected from the EM effect, the MTTF of the whole system may still be degraded due to unprotected defective TSVs. This problem can be solved by allocating more EM mitigation modules for each group. However, it will introduce huge hardware overhead. Moreover, considering the defective TSV generally only occupies a small fraction of the total TSV count, most of the allocated EM modules may not be used, causing a waste of hardware and area resources.

In order to handle the case with two or more defective TSVs in a group and improve EM mitigation module usage efficiency, we explore sharing EM mitigation modules among groups. Then, the possibility of all defective TSVs being protected can increase dramatically. All groups can be organized in a (Network-on-Chip) NoC-like topology as shown in Figure 3.13. Each group corresponds to one node in the topology. Not only the protection module allocated to this group but also the spare protection module in

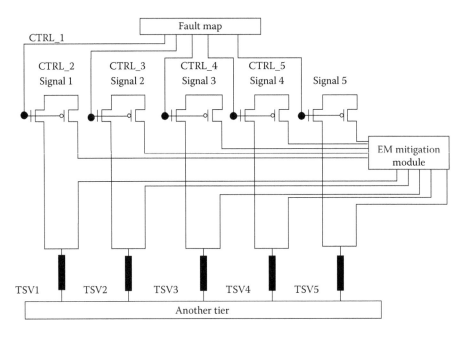

FIGURE 3.12   Switch network connecting the defective TSV to online EM mitigation circuit.

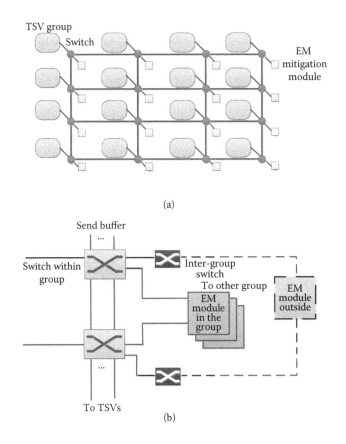

FIGURE 3.13   (a) Mesh-style EM mitigation module sharing architecture and (b) switch structure.

its direct neighborhood can be used for defective TSVs in the group. Depending on the fault map of each TSV group, we can determine which group's protection module can be shared by others. The reason for using only the direct neighboring EM mitigation module is that using distant spare modules would incur a large timing overhead, which may degrade the bus frequency.

The interconnect of defective TSVs and EM mitigation modules can be described as follows. Firstly, defective TSVs in each group are identified. The first defective TSV is connected to the module in the group. Secondly, if there are more defective TSVs to be protected, the direct neighbors of the group are searched. To avoid conflict sharing, the search order is fixed as north, east, south, west. If the corresponding neighboring group has a spare EM mitigation module, it will connect to the defective TSV in the group considered. Accordingly, the crossbar-based switching network in each group as shown in Figure 3.12 should be revised slightly. As at most five EM mitigation modules can be used in each group, the switching network should be converted to $5 \times N$, where N is the number of TSVs in each group. Since the defective rate is low, the protection rate by the proposed method can be much higher than that without sharing mechanism. The comparison of both methods will be illustrated in Section 3.4.

3.3.4 Online TSV EM Mitigation Circuit

The online EM mitigation circuit monitors the current flows within defective TSVs and tries to balance their directions such that EM effect can be alleviated by the self-healing effect [2] as previously mentioned. Assume the two ends of a TSV are A and B. Depending on the data transmitted previously and data to be transmitted, the current flow direction within TSV can be derived as shown in Table 3.1. The circuit used to identify the current flow direction of a TSV can be implemented by several logic gates and a decoder [11] as shown on the left side of the counter in Figure 3.14. The current direction balance circuit is also illustrated in Figure 3.14. When the chip is powered on, the counter loads a preset value, which is the mid-value of its range.

Referring to Table 3.1, if the current direction is from A to B (in our case, it means current flows from top tier to bottom tier), the counter increases by 1. The counter decreases by 1 if vice versa. If the counter overflows or approaches zero, it indicates that the current has flowed along a direction for a long time and needs to be reversed for self-healing.

TABLE 3.1   Relationship between Current Flow and Data Pattern

Original Bus State	Data Transmission	Current Flow
"0"	"1" $A \to B$	$A \to B$
	"1" $A \leftarrow B$	$A \leftarrow B$
	"0"	–
"1"	"0" $A \to B$	$A \leftarrow B$
	"0" $A \leftarrow B$	$A \to B$
	"1"	–

Source: Abella, J., Vera, X., Unsal, O.S., and Ergin, O., *IEEE Micro*, 28(6), 37–46, 2008.

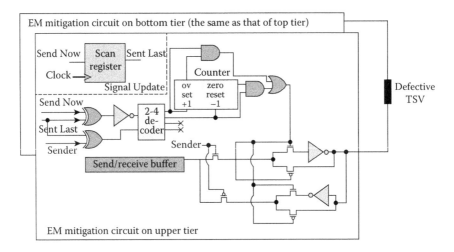

FIGURE 3.14   Online EM mitigation circuit structure.

Then, the output of OR gate enables the inverter to change the signal value such that the current flow direction is reversed. There is the same circuit module residing on the other layer, which is synchronous with it, such that the inverted signal can be recovered. The clock signal shown in Figure 3.14 is generated from a clock network on chip to provide a synchronous signal.

The counter monitors current flows within the TSV. The number of bits within the counter determines the time interval to activate self-healing. If it is small, the circuit is activated very often and can balance current flows in a short time interval but much power is consumed. Otherwise, more counter bits will result in longer time intervals and lower power consumption for self-healing but will incur a larger area overhead. In our case, we found that a 10-bit counter could achieve the optimal trade-off between area, power, and EM MTTF enhancement. Note that the transmitted signal only goes through two extra inverters (one on the top tier and the other one on the bottom tier) when the current direction needs to be reversed. Hence, the delay caused by our EM mitigation circuit is negligible compared to the clock cycle, which is in the nanosecond range.

3.4 EXPERIMENTAL RESULTS

3.4.1 Experimental Setup

To evaluate the effectiveness of our method, we simulated TSV data bus traffic between L1 and L2 caches based on SimpleScalar [24], as shown in Figure 3.15. The simulation target consisted of two dies. The top tier contained a CPU and L1 cache, and the bottom one contained an L2 cache. The memory was assumed to be off-chip. A heat sink was attached to the top CPU tier to facilitate heat dissipation. The cache block size was assumed to be 128 bytes, and the L1/L2 TSV bus width was set to 1024, such that a data block could be transferred within a cycle. The detail architecture parameters are listed in Table 3.2. SPEC2K benchmarks were used for our simulations.

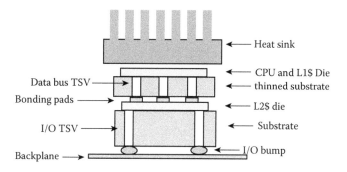

FIGURE 3.15   Illustration of the 3D target platform.

TABLE 3.2   Parameters of the Simulated 3D Platform

CPU	Alpha 21264 1.33 GHz
Predictor	Bimodal predictor, using a BTB with two-bit counter, three cycle miss prediction penalty
IFQ size/LSQ size	4/8
L1 D$/I$	32 KB, 128 B block size, two-way associative, LRU replacement write-back policy, one cycle hit latency
L2 Unified $	512 KB, 128 B block size, two-way associative, LRU replacement write-back policy, six cycle hit latency
ITLB/DTLB	64 entries/128 entries
TSV bus width	1024
TSV feature size	5 μm diameter, 25 μm depth
TSV pad size	6 μm × 6 μm

Note: BTB, Branch Target Buffer; DTLB, Instruction Translation Look-aside Buffer; IFQ, Instruction Fetch Queue; ITLB, Instruction Translation Look-aside Buffer; LRU, Least Recently Used; LSQ, Load/Store Queue.

3.4.2 Trade-Off between Group Partition and Hardware Overheads for Protecting Defective TSVs from EM

As stated previously, there are two choices for EM protection module allocation. The first one is to allocate one module to each group, and only the defective TSV within this group can use it. The second one is to allocate one module to each group, but the directly neighboring group can share the module if it is not used in the group. In order to evaluate the two strategies for the protection effectiveness of defective TSVs, we performed simulations under different defect rates (1%, 3%, and 5%). The distribution of defects was assumed to be uniform. For the second strategy, we checked the spare module in the following order: north → east → south → west. The search procedure would continue if there were defective TSVs left in the group until all the neighboring protection modules had been used. If there were nonprotected defective TSVs, then our protection scheme would be treated as failed.

Figure 3.16 shows a comparison of protection effectiveness between sharing neighboring protection module and that without sharing. The defective rate was assumed to be 3%.

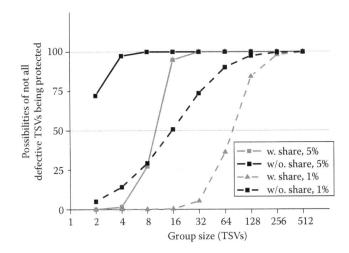

FIGURE 3.16 Possibilities of not all defective TSVs being protected. (The defect rates are assumed to be 5% [denoted by solid lines] and 1% [denoted by dashed lines].)

As shown in the figure, sharing EM protection modules among neighboring groups can protect all defective TSVs with much higher possibility, especially when the group size is less than 16. Then, we performed simulations assuming that the defect rates were 5% and 1%, respectively. The results are shown in Figure 3.16. The solid lines represent the case of a 5% defect rate, while the dashed line represents the case of a 1% defect rate. The results also show similar trends to that shown in Figure 3.16.

3.4.3 Reliability Enhancement by Our Method Considering EM

In this experiment, we assume the defects are distributed randomly within the TSV bundle and only 3% of all TSVs are defective and require being protected by our EM mitigation circuit. According to the TSV yield estimation in Ref. [20], 3% is a reasonable percentage considering the TSV yield. As shown in Figure 3.16, a group size of eight TSVs can ensure the possibility of all defective TSVs being protected approaching almost 100% when the sharing strategy is adopted. Note that our proposed technique can be applied to any defect rate of TSVs. The only modification is that the group size should be tuned accordingly to ensure that all defective TSVs can be protected.

At the beginning of the simulation, we fast-forwarded 10 million instructions to warm up the cache. Then, we ran 100 million instructions for cycle-accurate simulation. During every L1 cache read/write miss or write-back from the L1 cache to the L2 cache, we traced the data patterns between them. The current direction in every clock cycle can be derived based on Table 3.1. Subsequently, we were able to calculate the duty cycle of current waveforms over the simulation period. Once the current waveform was derived, we used Equation 3.2 and the relationship of the current pulse and EM MTTF proposed in Ref. [9] to obtain the current density of each TSV. Then, the TSV EM MTTF was calculated using Equation 3.1. The minimum TSV EM MTTF value among all 1024 data bus TSVs determined the lifetime of the whole chip.

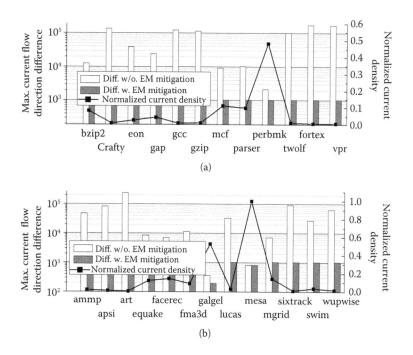

FIGURE 3.17   (a, b) Current flow direction differences and current density comparisons.

Figure 3.17 plots the current flow direction difference comparisons. As shown in the figure, current flow direction can be well balanced by our proposed EM mitigation technique for both SPECINT and SPECFP benchmarks. The figure also shows the current densities normalized to those without EM mitigation. The results show that current density can be dramatically reduced by our proposed technique for most applications.

Additionally, TSV EM MTTF comparisons are shown in Figure 3.18. Figure 3.18a shows the simulation results for SPEC2K integer benchmarks and Figure 3.18b shows those for SPEC2K floating point benchmarks. The y-axis denotes the EM MTTF achieved by our proposed method normalized to that without an EM mitigation circuit. It is shown that the EM MTTF of the chip can be improved dramatically for both benchmark suites, which implies that our proposed method can be effective for most applications. On average, the chip MTTF is enhanced by more than 100 times for the SPECINT benchmark suite, and 70 times for the SPECFP benchmark suite. However, depending on the characteristics of the applications, the effectiveness of our method is also different. Take bzip2 and ammp as examples. The MTTF improvement is improved by only less than 20 times for bzip2, while it is improved by 80 times for ammp. To explain the reason behind this phenomenon, we trace the differences between different current flow directions within TSV busses for the two applications and show them in Figure 3.19. The maximum difference between the alternative current directions of bzip2 is much smaller than that of ammp (max. 1.8×10^4 vs. max. 5×10^4), which means that bzip2 has better current flow balance property than ammp. Therefore, the effectiveness of EM mitigation is more significant for ammp.

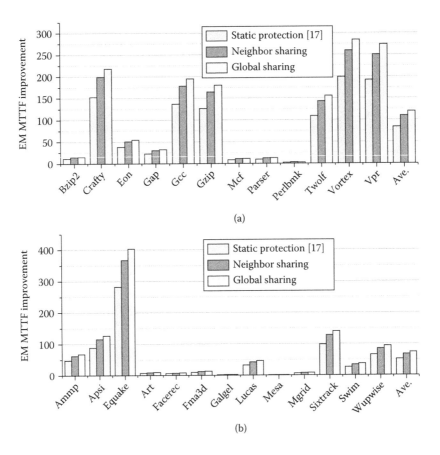

FIGURE 3.18   MTTF comparisons on (a) SPECINT and (b) SPECFP benchmarks.

3.4.4 Area and Performance Overhead

In our area evaluation, since the TSV resistance measurement and scan registers were reused from design-for-testability circuitry, we did not take their area overheads into account. The proposed EM mitigation circuit only introduces several primary logic gates, pass transistors, and a counter for each defective TSV. In our case, we assumed 3% of TSVs need protection. We estimated the chip area of our simulation target to be 1.6 mm × 1.6 mm using ST 90-nm technology. The Synopsys Design Compiler was used for circuit synthesis. The synthesized area of our EM mitigation circuit is 25536 μm², which is roughly 1% of the whole chip area. We also used Synopsys PrimeTime PX for power estimation of the EM mitigation circuit in vector-less mode. The average power consumption was 7.4 mW under the 3% defective TSV case. Compared to the chip power consumption, the power overhead caused by EM mitigation was also negligible. Additionally, as shown in Figure 3.14, the EM mitigation circuit works in parallel with signal transmission and is not located at the critical path. A transmission gate and an inverter connect in series with the send buffer and only introduce tens of picoseconds delay, which is negligible compared to 750 ps clock period (1.33 GHz).

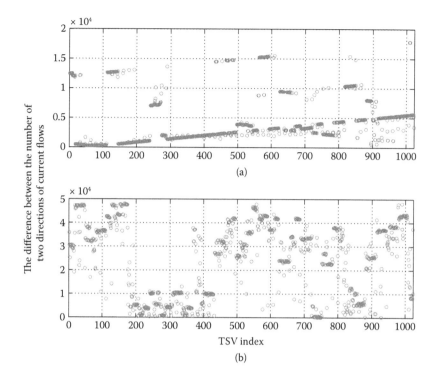

FIGURE 3.19 (a, b) Differences of reversing current directions within TSVs.

3.5 CONCLUSIONS

As integration density skyrockets with every technology generation, interconnect optimization becomes more intractable for 2D ICs. Consequently, 3D technology has emerged as an effective method to continue Moore's law. The reliability of 3D ICs, however, requires investigation to improve the fabrication yield and chip lifetime. Among them, the EM-induced reliability issue is of great concern. In this paper, we exploited the defect-induced EM of TSVs and analyzed the relationship between defects and EM reliability of 3D ICs. Then, we proposed a framework to enhance TSVs reliability by balancing current flows within TSVs. Through extensive experiments, we showed the effectiveness of our proposed method, which can improve the reliability significantly with negligible hardware overhead and power consumption.

REFERENCES

1. X. Vera and J. Abella, 2010, Electromigration for microarchitects, *ACM Computing Surveys (CSUR)*, vol. 42, no. 2, p. 9.
2. E.S. Meieran and I.A. Blech, 1967, Direct transmission electron microscope observation of electrotransport in aluminum thin films, *Applied Physics Letters*, vol. 11, no. 8, pp. 263–266.
3. J.R. Black, 1969, Electromigration failure modes in aluminum metallization for semiconductor devices, *Proceedings of the IEEE*, vol. 57, no. 9, pp. 1587–1594.
4. F.M. D'Heurle, 1971, Electromigration and failure in electronics: An introduction, *Proceedings of the IEEE*, vol. 59, no. 10, pp. 1409–1418.

5. C.S. Hau-Riege, 2004, An introduction to Cu electromigration, *Microelectronics Reliability*, vol. 44, no. 2, pp. 195–205.

6. A. Rubio and J.L. Gonzalez, 1997, Shape effect on electromigration in VLSI inter-connects, *Microelectronics and Reliability*, vol. 37, no. 7, pp. 1073–1078.

7. R. Karri and A. Dasgupta, 1996, Electromigration reliability enhancement via bus activity distribution, in *Proceedings of 33rd IEEE/ACM Design Automation Conference (DAC)*, June 3–7, Las Vegas, NV, pp. 353–356.

8. C.C. Teng, Y.K. Cheng, E. Rosenbaum, and S.M. Kang, 1996, Hierarchical electromigration reliability diagnosis for VLSI interconnects, in *Proceedings of 33rd IEEE/ACM Design Automation Conference (DAC)*, June 3–7, Las Vegas, NV, pp. 752–757.

9. C. Hu, B.K. Liew, and N.W. Cheung, 1990, Projecting interconnect electromigration lifetime for arbitrary current waveforms, *IEEE Electron Device Letters*, vol. 37, no. 5, pp. 1343–1351.

10. A. Todri, S.C. Chang, and M. Marek-Sadowska, 2007, Electromigration and voltage drop aware power grid optimization for power gated ICs, in *Proceeding of the IEEE/ACM International Symposium on Low Power Electronics and Design (ISLPED)*, August 27–29, Portland, OR, pp. 391–394.

11. J. Abella, X. Vera, O.S. Unsal, and O. Ergin, 2008, Refueling: Preventing wire degradation due to electromigration, *IEEE Micro*, vol. 28, no. 6, pp. 37–46.

12. K. Banerjee, S.J. Souri, P. Kapur, and K.C. Saraswat, 2001, 3-D ICs: A novel chip design for improving deep-submicrometer interconnect performance and systems-on-chip integration, *Proceedings of the IEEE*, vol. 89, no. 5, pp. 602–633.

13. Y.C. Tan, C.M. Tan, X.W. Zhang, T.C. Chai, and D.Q. Yu, 2010, Electromigration performance of through silicon via (TSV)—A modeling approach, *Microelectronics Reliability*, vol. 50, no. 9–11, pp. 1336–1340.

14. J. Pak, M. Pathak, S.K. Lim, and D.Z. Pan, 2011, Modeling of electromigration in through-silicon-via based 3D IC, in *Proceedings of 2011 IEEE Electronic Components and Technology Conference (ECTC)*, May 31–June 3, Lake Buena Vista, FL, pp. 1420–1427.

15. T. Frank, C. Chappaz, P. Leduc, L. Arnaud, F. Lorut, S. Moreau, A. Thuaire, R. El Farhane, and L Anghel, 2011, Resistance increase due to electromigration induced depletion under TSV, in *Proceedings of 49th IEEE International Reliability Physics Symposium (IRPS)*, April 10–14, Piscataway, NJ, pp. 347–352.

16. X. Zhao, Y. Wan, M. Scheuermann, and S.K. Lim, 2013, Transient modeling of TSV-wire electromigration and lifetime analysis of power distribution network for 3D ICs, in *Proceedings of the IEEE/ACM International Conference on Computer-aided Design (ICCAD)*, October 13–16, Florence, Italy, pp. 363–370.

17. Y. Cheng, A. Todri-Sanial, A. Bosio, L. Dillio, P. Girard, A. Virazel, P. Vevet, and M. Belleville, 2013, A novel method to mitigate TSV electromigration for 3D ICs, in *Proc. of IEEE Computer Society Annual Symposium on VLSI (ISVLSI'13)*, Augest 5–7, Natal, Brazil, pp. 121–126.

18. J. Van Olmen, J. Coenen, W. Dehaene, K. De Meyer, C. Huyghebaert, A. Jourdain, G. Katti, et al., 2009. 3D stacked IC demonstrator using hybrid collective die-to-wafer bonding with copper through silicon vias (TSV), in *Proceedings of 2009 IEEE International 3D Systems Integration Conference (3DIC)*, September 28–30, San Francisco, CA, pp. 1–5.

19. B. Kim, C. Sharbono, T. Ritzdorf, and D. Schmauch, 2006, Factors affecting copper filling process within high aspect ratio deep vias for 3D chip stacking, in *Proceedings of 2006 IEEE Electronic Components and Technology Conference (ECTC)*, May 30–June 2, San Diego, CA, pp. 838–843.

20. I. Loi, S. Mitra, T. H. Lee, S. Fujita, and L. Benini, 2008, A low-overhead fault tolerance scheme for TSV-based 3D network on chip links, in *Proceedings of 26th IEEE/ACM International Conference on Computer-Aided Design (ICCAD)*, November 10–13, San Jose, CA, pp. 598–602.

21. C. Hu, J. Tao, and N.W. Cheung, 1993, Metal electromigration damage healing under bidirectional current stress, *IEEE Electron Device Letters (EDL)*, vol. 14, no. 12, pp. 554–556.

22. P. Chen, C. Wu, and D. Kwai, 2009, On-chip TSV testing for 3D IC before bonding using sense amplification, in *Proceedings of 18th IEEE Aisan Test Symposium (ATS)*, November 23–26, Taichung, Taiwan, pp. 450–455.
23. M. Cho, C. Liu, D.H. Kim, S.K. Lim, and S. Mukhopadhyay, 2010, Design method and test structure to characterize and repair TSV defect induced signal degradation in 3D system, in *Proceedings of 28th IEEE/ACM International Conference on Computer-Aided Design (ICCAD)*, November 7–11, San Jose, CA, pp. 694–697.
24. D. Ernst, T. Austin, and E. Larson, 2002, Simplescalar: An infrastructure for computer system modeling, *IEEE Computer*, vol. 35, no. 2, pp. 59–67.

CHAPTER 4

A 3D Hybrid Cache Design for CMP Architecture for Data-Intensive Applications

Ing-Chao Lin, Jeng-Nian Chiou, and Yun-Kae Law

National Cheng Kung University
Tainan, Taiwan

CONTENTS

4.1 INTRODUCTION

With the advance of CMOS technology, CPU performance has been improved by increasing frequency. However, the performance improvement for a single-core processor has reached a bottleneck due to chip power and heat removal limitations. To overcome these problems, chip multiprocessors (CMPs) have gradually replaced single-core processors, and the number of cores in CMPs is expected to continue to grow. A processor integrating 80 cores has been demonstrated by Intel [1]. In CMP architecture, the last level cache (LLC) is shared by multi-core processors and has a significant influence on performance. Therefore, as the CMP architecture has become more widely used, LLC-related research has drawn increased attention.

In the CMP architecture, the LLC is typically composed of SRAM and shared by multiple processor cores. Recently, nonvolatile memory (NVM) technologies such as spin-transfer torque RAM (STT-RAM) and phase-change RAM (PRAM) have been considered as candidates for LLC design due to their low leakage and high density features. However, NVM suffers from write problems such as high write latency, high write energy consumption, and limited write endurance problems [2].

Table 4.1 compares SRAM, STT-RAM, and PRAM. Compared to PRAM, STT-RAM has higher access speed, lower read energy, and higher endurance. Thus, STT-RAM is more suitable for CMP LLC design. However, compared to SRAM, STT-RAM still has slow write time and high write energy. To mitigate these problems, Sun et al. [3] and Wu et al. [4] proposed a hybrid cache architecture that consists of SRAM and STT-RAM and an access-aware mechanism to mitigate the influence of the STT-RAM write problem.

However, the interference among competing processes leads to increased shared resource contention and conflict misses in LLC. Traditionally, the LLC is shared by multiple cores in CMP architecture. Therefore, these cores may compete for the cache resources. Figure 4.1 is an example of the nonuniform cache access (NUCA) architecture [5] that is widely used in CMP LLC design. The cache is divided into multiple cache banks with different access latency. In Figure 4.1a, all of the cache banks are shared by Cores 0 and 1, and both cores may compete for the same cache lines at the same time. To reduce the competition, a cache partitioning scheme was proposed [6,7], as shown in Figure 4.1b. Cache banks are divided into two partitions and each core is assigned their own private cache partition. A core is prohibited from accessing the cache banks owned by the other core. This scheme can effectively prevent cache competition between each core. However, in this partitioning scheme, the number of cache banks assigned to a core is fixed at design time and cannot be adjusted during run time. If the number of cache banks for each core is

TABLE 4.1 Comparison between SRAM and NVMs [2]

	SRAM	STT-RAM	PRAM
Density	1×	4×	16×
Read time	Very fast	Fast	Slow
Write time	Very fast	Slow	Very slow
Read energy	Low	Low	Medium
Write energy	Low	High	High
Leakage energy	High	Low	Low
Endurance	10^{16}	4×10^{12}	10^9

Note: NVM, nonvolatile memory; PRAM, phase-change RAM; SRAM, static RAM; STT-RAM, spin-transfer torque RAM.

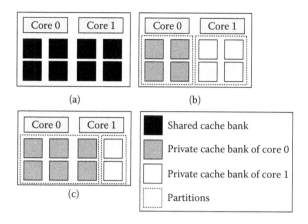

FIGURE 4.1   Three different cache partitioning schemes: (a) shared cache; (b) private cache (equally shared, fixed size); (c) dynamic partitioning cache.

determined without considering the workload executed on each core and the cache bank demand during the runtime, it may happen that a core that requires many cache banks to execute memory-intensive workloads only has a few cache banks. Similarly, a core that executes fewer memory access workloads may have many unused cache banks. The inefficient use of cache banks increases cache miss rate and decreases the system performance. Therefore, the dynamic partitioning cache scheme in Figure 4.1c was proposed [8–10]. The number of cache banks assigned to each core is determined at run time according to their workload execution status. Hence, the cache banks can be used more effectively.

Meanwhile, as the number of transistors integrated in a chip increases exponentially and the size of a chip increases, the global wire delay has become a critical limitation on the 2D chip performance. In order to reduce the wire latency of the system, a three-dimensional (3D) integration technology has been proposed. 3D integration can mitigate the on-chip interconnect delay problem by stacking multiple silicon layers on top of each other, and it uses direct vertical interconnects, called *through-silicon vias* (TSVs), to connect each vertical layer. Figure 4.2 is an example of 3D stacked LLC. Processor cores are allocated in Layer 1 and the L1 cache in each core is not shown in the figure. Multiple L2 (last level) cache die is stacked above the multicore die in Layer 2 and uses TSVs to communicate with each processor core.

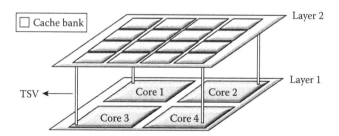

FIGURE 4.2   Three-dimensional integration technology applied in last-level cache design.

A 3D architecture with a SRAM/STT-RAM hybrid cache design has been proposed in some related works [3,11,12]. However, the hybrid cache in a 3D architecture still suffers from high access latency since STT-RAM has higher access latency. Therefore, in this chapter, we will focus on reducing the long access latency problem of 3D hybrid cache, and we adopt the 3D integration technique with hybrid cache, which contains three types of cache banks: a SRAM bank, an STT-RAM bank, and a hybrid STT-RAM/SRAM bank. In the meantime, an access-aware technique and dynamic partitioning algorithm are proposed for our 3D hybrid cache.

The contributions of this chapter can be summarized as follows:

- We propose a 3D stacked STT-RAM/SRAM hybrid cache for CMP to reduce the average latency and energy consumption. The local bank of a core is an STT-RAM/SRAM hybrid bank, which can reduce leakage power and cache miss rate when compared to a SRAM local bank.

- We propose an access-aware technique that redirects write traffic from STT-RAM to SRAM to reduce the access latency and improve STT-RAM endurance and moves frequently read data from SRAM to STT-RAM to keep more space in SRAM for write operations.

- We propose a dynamic cache partitioning algorithm for a proposed 3D hybrid cache that considers the cache access latency of banks in different layers and write pressure of each core to reduce the miss rate and access latency of proposed 3D hybrid cache.

- Experimental results show that our proposed 3D stacked hybrid cache with hybrid local banks can save energy at a rate of 60.4% and 18.9% when compared to 3D pure SRAM cache and 3D hybrid cache with SRAM local bank. With the proposed dynamic partitioning algorithm and access-aware technique, the proposed 3D hybrid cache reduces the miss rate by 7.7%, access latency by 18.2%, and energy delay product (EDP) by 18.9% on average.

The rest of this chapter is organized as follows. Section 4.2 introduces the STT-RAM background and the related work for the hybrid cache. Section 4.3 presents our proposed 3D stacked hybrid cache with the access-aware technique and the dynamic partitioning algorithm. Section 4.4 details the experimental setup and results. Section 4.5 concludes the chapter.

4.2 PRELIMINARIES

In this section, we first introduce the fundamentals of STT-RAM cell and then describe the NUCA architecture. Related works on hybrid cache design are presented.

4.2.1 STT-RAM Fundamentals

STT-RAM is a new generation of magnetoresistive random-access memory (MRAM). Figure 4.3 shows a conventional single-level cell STT-RAM, which uses a magnetic tunnel

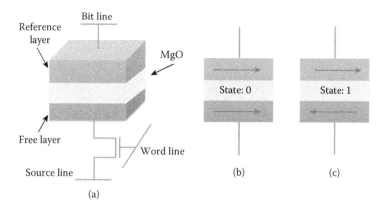

FIGURE 4.3   Overview of an STT-RAM cell: (a) schematic of one STT-RAM cell; (b) parallel low resistance, representing the 0 state; (c) antiparallel high resistance, representing the 1 state.

junction (MTJ) as the memory storage instead of electric charges. A MTJ consists of two ferromagnetic layers and one tunnel barrier layer. One of the ferromagnetic layers, which is called the *reference layer*, has a fixed magnetic direction. The other ferromagnetic layer, which is called the *free layer*, can change magnetic direction through a switching current. When the magnetic directions of reference and free layers are parallel, the resistance of MTJ is low, representing a 0 state. Conversely, when two layers have different magnetic direction (antiparallel), the resistance of MTJ is high, representing a 1 state. A low current is used to read the state of MTJ, while a high current of an appropriate polarity is used to change the magnetic state, which requires long write latency and high write energy consumption. Due to its high cell density and low leakage power [2], STT-RAM is considered as the candidate for the LLC design.

4.2.2 NUCA Cache Design

With an increase in chip capacity and area, the differences in cache bank access time in LLC increase significantly. If all cache banks use the same access latency, the performance will be limited by the cache banks that have the largest access latency. Therefore, NUCA [5] is proposed to improve the average access latency. In NUCA, the banks that are closer to the processor cores have lower access latency due to shorter wire delay. Since cache banks that are closer to processor cores are accessed more frequently, the average access latency is reduced. It can be classified into two categories:

- *Static NUCA (S-NUCA)*: the data in cache banks cannot be moved to other cache banks, which is shown in Figure 4.4a.

- *Dynamic NUCA (D-NUCA)*: since local banks have lower access latency, the frequently accessed data is moved to local banks to improve system performance, which is shown in Figure 4.4b.

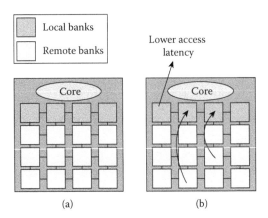

FIGURE 4.4 Two type of nonuniform cache access (NUCA) architecture: (a) static NUCA and (b) dynamic NUCA.

4.2.3 Related Works

In recent years, hybrid cache based on NUCA architecture has attracted considerable attention due to the advantage of low power and higher density. The concept of integrating NVMs with SRAM to construct hybrid cache was previously proposed [3,4,13–15]. Li et al. [14] integrated STT-RAM with SRAM and proposed a counter-based mechanism to migrate frequent write data from STT-RAM to SRAM to improve performance. Wu et al. [4] proposed a SRAM and STT-RAM hybrid cache architecture design. The cache was divided into read and write regions to improve cache performance. Syu et al. [15] proposed a hybrid cache architecture that contains three types of cache banks: a SRAM bank, an STT-RAM bank, and a hybrid STT-RAM/SRAM bank. In the meantime, two access-aware policies and a wearout-aware dynamic cache partitioning scheme are proposed to improve the endurance of the hybrid cache. Lee et al. [13] proposed a model that can evaluate the average memory access time, power consumption, and area of cache memory to evaluate the efficacy of the cache architecture. They also analyzed the hybrid cache architecture, considering the L1 SRAM cache and external memory.

In 3D architecture, Sun et al. [3] integrated the 3D integration technology with hybrid cache design, and proposed a 3D cache architecture that stacked MRAM-based LLC directly atop CMPs and two architectural techniques, read-preemptive write buffer and SRAM/STT-RAM hybrid LLC, to improve the performance issue due to the long write latency of MRAM.

There are also some related works investigating the LLC allocation mechanism in CMP architecture [10,11,16]. Qureshi and Patt [10] used utility-based cache partitioning to partition a shared cache depending on the reduction in cache misses that each application is likely to obtain for a given amount of cache resources. They also proposed a mechanism to monitor each application at run time using a cost-effective hardware circuit. Jung et al. [11] explored the designs of 3D-stacked NUCA cache, and proposed a run-time cache partitioning algorithm to improve system performance. Kadjo et al. [16] adopted the power gating technique to save power consumption and proposed a method that migrated the high temporal locality blocks to future active partition, which can mitigate the performance impact of power gating.

In this chapter, a 3D SRAM/STT-RAM hybrid cache for CMP is proposed to reduce the energy consumption and the access latency. Meanwhile, an access-aware technique and a dynamic partitioning algorithm are proposed to reduce the access latency and improve cache utility for the proposed 3D hybrid cache.

4.3 PROPOSED 3D HYBRID CACHE DESIGN

This section first proposes a 3D stacked SRAM/STT-RAM hybrid cache architecture for CMPs and proposes an access-aware technique for the architecture. This section then explains the details of the dynamic partitioning algorithm for the architecture. Finally, this section explains the address controlling mechanism that keeps record of the banks that a core can use.

4.3.1 3D Stacked SRAM/STT-RAM Hybrid Cache Architecture

STT-RAM is a good candidate for low power LLC design due to the high density and low leakage power. Meanwhile, to reduce wire delay and integrate heterogeneous components, a 3D architecture has been proposed and extensively investigated. In this work, we propose a 3D stacked hybrid cache architecture that uses SRAM and STT-RAM in the LLC. The NUCA architecture is used in the proposed 3D stacked hybrid cache architecture. The L2 cache is divided into many cache banks, and the cache banks that are closer to the processor cores have lower access latency.

Figure 4.5 shows the proposed architecture for four processors. The hybrid SRAM/STT-RAM L2 (last level) cache is stacked as 3D architecture. There are three layers in our hybrid cache architecture. The processor cores are placed in Layer 1, and the cache banks are placed in Layers 2 and 3. The communication between different layers is through TSVs. STT-RAM banks are used as the main part of the hybrid cache and some SRAM banks are added. Hence, write requests to STT-RAM banks can be redirected to SRAM banks to mitigate high write energy and latency problems of STT-RAM banks.

As for the local bank, since it normally receives a significant amount of write traffic from its core, if the write traffic on the local bank cannot be redirected, the high write pressure on the local bank may cause high access latency. Therefore, to reduce the write pressure of local banks, we use the SRAM/STT-RAM hybrid bank proposed in Ref. [15] as the local bank. Only the write traffic to the hybrid local bank can be redirected to the SRAM region in the hybrid local bank, reducing the write pressure of the STT-RAM region in the local bank.

4.3.2 The Proposed Access-Aware Technique

Since write operations in STT-RAM require longer latency and larger energy when compared to SRAM, if there is too much write traffic on STT-RAM, the system performance will degrade. To reduce the write pressure of STT-RAM, we propose an access-aware technique. The technique contains two algorithms. The first algorithm is a write-aware policy for STT-RAM that redirects the write request from STT-RAM to SRAM. The second algorithm is a read-aware policy for SRAM that migrates frequently read data from SRAM to STT-RAM.

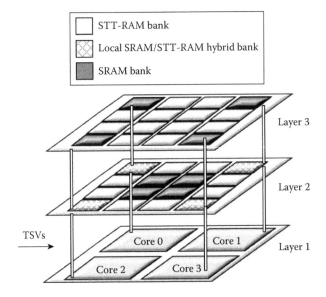

FIGURE 4.5 Proposed 3D stacked SRAM/STT-RAM hybrid cache architecture with hybrid local banks.

ALGORITHM 4.1   STT-RAM WRITE-AWARE POLICY

1. **if** a write request hit on a STT-RAM line {
2.   **if** there is an invalid line in a SRAM bank
3.   Redirect the write request to this SRAM line
4.   Invalidate this STT-RAM line
5.   **else** //there are no invalid lines in SRAM
6.   write this STT-RAM line
7. }
8. **else**{ //write request miss in a STT-RAM line
9.   **if** there is an invalid line in a SRAM bank
10.   Redirect the write request to this SRAM line
11.   Invalidate this STT-RAM line
12.   **else**
13.   Select a SRAM line as victim using LRU policy
14.   Write the SRAM line back to lower level memory
15.   Perform the write operation on this SRAM line
16. }

Algorithm 4.1 shows our write-aware policy for STT-RAM. When a write hit occurs on an STT-RAM line, if there is an invalid SRAM line, the write request will be redirected to this invalid SRAM line and the STT-RAM line is invalidated (Lines 2 to 4). If there is no invalid SRAM line, then the data will be written into the STT-RAM line (Lines 5 and 6).

Lines 8 to 15 describe the situation when a write miss occurs in the STT-RAM line. When a cache miss in STT-RAM lines occurs and there is an invalid SRAM line, the write request is redirected to the SRAM lines, and the original STT-RAM line is invalidated (Lines 9 to 11); otherwise, a SRAM line is selected as a victim based on Least-recently used (LRU) policy and the SRAM line is written back to the lower level memory. Then, the write operation is performed on this line (Lines 12 to 15).

Note that the SRAM lines in a hybrid bank can only receive the write request from the STT-RAM lines of the same hybrid bank in the proposed 3D hybrid cache.

In order to further increase the write utilization of SRAM, the less-written data on the SRAM lines should be moved to STT-RAM and more SRAM lines should be available for write operations. To obtain more space for write operations in SRAM banks, we propose a SRAM read-aware policy to move frequently read data from SRAM to STT-RAM.

Algorithm 4.2 shows our read-aware policy for SRAM. Each SRAM line has one read counter and one write counter to record the number of read and write operations that happen on this SRAM line. In Lines 1 to 6, when a write hit occurs on a SRAM line, if the read count number of this SRAM line is two times larger than the write count number, the data in this line will be regarded as the frequently read data and it would be better to move the data into STT-RAM. In this situation, if there is an invalid STT-RAM line, this data will be redirected to the STT-RAM line, the original SRAM line will be invalided, and both read and write counters of this SRAM line will be reset to zero. If there is no invalid line in STT-RAM, an STT-RAM line is selected as a victim based on LRU policy, and the victim is written back to lower level memory. Then the write request will be redirected to the victim line, the original SRAM line will be invalidated, and the read and write counter of the SRAM line will be reset to zero (Lines 7 to 12).

ALGORITHM 4.2   SRAM READ-AWARE POLICY

1. **if** a write request hit on a SRAM line {
2.   **if** read count is two times larger than write count
3.   **if** there are invalid lines in STT-RAM bank
4.   Redirect the write request to the SRAM line
5.   Invalidate the original SRAM line
6.   Reset the access counters
7.   **else** //there are no invalid lines in STT-RAM
8.   Select LRU STT-RAM line to be the victim
9.   Write the victim line back to lower level memory
10.   Perform the write operation on this line
11.   Invalidate the original SRAM line
12.   Rest the access counters
13.   **else** //less frequently read data are written to SRAM
14.   Write on this SRAM line
15. }

In Lines 13 and 14, if the read count number is smaller than two times the write count number, this means the data is less frequently read, and the data will be written in the SRAM line directly.

Through the above STT-RAM write-aware policy and SRAM read-aware policy, the frequently written data will be stored in SRAM, and the frequently read data will be stored in STT-RAM. As a result, the write pressure on STT-RAM can be mitigated, and the access latency of the L2 cache can be reduced.

Note that in this work each SRAM line has one read counter and one write counter. The counters used in our design are both 8-bit. In our architecture, there are eight 128 KB SRAM cache banks (16-way), and a SRAM bank has 2048 SRAM lines. The total required storage overhead for the read and write counters is less than 32 KB (= 2048 × 8 × 8 bit × 2). The storage overhead is 0.24% (= 32 KB/13 MB).

4.3.3 Dynamic Cache Partitioning Algorithm

As mentioned in Section 4.1, the LLC is traditionally shared by multiple cores, and these cores compete for the LLC. Figure 4.6 shows the unbalanced distribution of write operations among each core. It can be seen in the bodytrack benchmark, the write operations in Core 2 are over 50% of total write operations. The unbalanced write distributions among each core have a significant influence in performance.

Some cache partitioning algorithms have been proposed to determine the cache partition size dynamically for each core to improve the cache utility [9,10]. However, these algorithms are not suitable for 3D hybrid cache architecture since they do not consider the cache access latency of different cache banks in different layers and the long latency issues of STT-RAM.

In this work, we propose a dynamic cache partitioning algorithm for 3D hybrid cache and a framework for the proposed partitioning algorithm. Figure 4.7 illustrates the framework. There are four cores and each core has its own private L1 cache. A 3D hybrid L2 (last level) cache is shared by each core and L2 cache access information of each core is monitored by its corresponding monitor. We propose a dynamic partitioning algorithm to decide how to assign the cache banks to each core according to the collected information by monitors.

Algorithm 4.3 shows the proposed dynamic partitioning algorithm. There are two stages in the partitioning algorithm. In the first stage (Lines 1 to 5), the proposed algorithm determines how many STT-RAM banks should be assigned to each core to minimize the cache miss rate

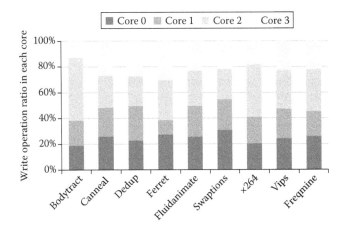

FIGURE 4.6 The unbalanced write count distribution among each core in chip multiprocessor architecture [15].

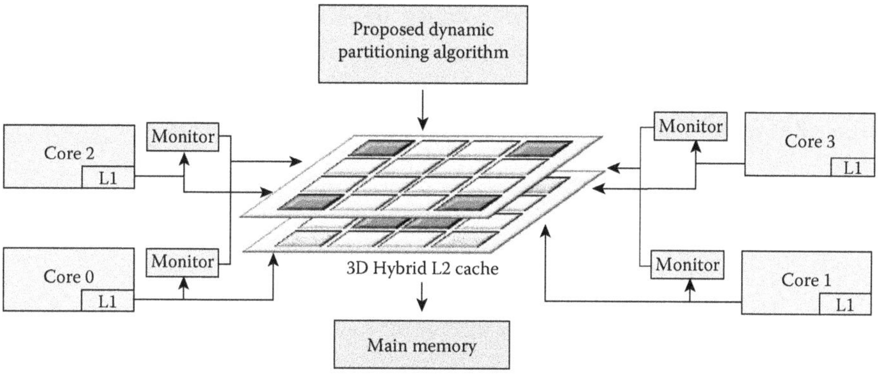

FIGURE 4.7   Framework for dynamic cache partitioning algorithm.

ALGORITHM 4.3   CACHE PARTITIONING ALGORITHM

Inputs : Number of cores : N
        Number of STT-RAM banks: T
        Number of SRAM banks: S
        The information of cache access of each core
Output : Cache bank allocation for each core
1. **for** (i = 0 to N–1) **do** //the beginning of the first stage
2.   Calculate WR_i and MR_i
3. $STTRAM\_ALLOC_i = [T \times WR_i]$;
4. $SRAM\_ALLOC_i = [S \times MR_i]$;
5. **end for** //the ending of the first stage
6. **for** i = 0 to N–1 //the beginning of the second stage
7. $temp=0$;
8.   **while** ($temp < STTRAM\_ALLOC_i$) **do**
9.   Find a STT-RAM bank j that has minimum access

latency to core i

10.   Assign STT-RAM bank j to core i
11. $temp++$;
12. **end while**
13. $temp=0$;
14. **while** ($temp < SRAM\_ALLOC_i$) **do**
15.   Find a SRAM bank j that has the minimum access latency to core i
16.   Assign SRAM bank j to core i
17. $temp++$;
18. **end while**
19. **end for**
20. **if** there are still some SRAM bank not assigned to core
21.   Assign a SRAM bank to the core with minimal number of SRAM bank every time until no SRAM left
22. **end if**
23. **if** there are still some STT-RAM banks not assigned to core
24.   Set unassigned STT-RAM banks as **shared bank**
25. **end if** //the ending of the second stage

and how many SRAM banks should be assigned to each core to afford the write pressure. In the beginning of each period, the cache access information for each core in the previous period is collected by monitors. In Line 2, the collected information is used to calculate the cache miss ratio (MR_i) and write count ratio (WR_i) of each core i. MR_i and WR_i are defined as follows:

$$MR_i = \frac{\#Miss_i}{\sum_{i=0}^{N-1} \#Miss_i}$$

$$WR_i = \frac{\#Write_i}{\sum_{i=0}^{N-1} \#Write_i}$$

$\#Miss_i$ and $\#Write_i$ represent the miss count and write count of each core i in the previous period, respectively.

Line 3 determines the number of STT-RAM assigned to each core in this period. The number of STT-RAM banks that should be assigned to core i in this time period, $STTRAM\_ALLOC_i$, is calculated by $[T \times WR_i]$, in which T is the total number of STT-RAM banks in the hybrid cache.

Line 4 determines the number of SRAM banks assigned to each core in this period. The number of SRAM banks that should be assigned to core i in this time period, $SRAM\_ALLOC_i$, is calculated by $[S \times WR_i]$, in which S is the total number of SRAM banks in the hybrid cache. Therefore, the core with higher miss count will be assigned more STT-RAM banks, and the core with higher write count will be assigned more SRAM banks to reduce write pressure.

After the number of SRAM banks and STT-RAM banks assigned to each core is determined, this algorithm decides which cache banks are actually assigned to which core according to the access latency of cache banks. The proposed algorithm considers the cache access latency in different banks and in different layers. Cache banks with lower access latency will be first chosen by a core. Note that in 3D architecture, the latency of horizontal wires and TSVs are different (shown in Table 4.2). When calculating the access latency of banks in different layers, it is necessary to consider the latency of both TSVs and horizontal wires.

In the first stage, the proposed algorithm determines how many STT-RAM and SRAM banks should be assigned to each core. In the second stage, based on the results obtained in the first stage, the proposed algorithm decides which SRAM banks and STT-RAM banks are actually assigned to which core, such that the access latency between the cache banks and the corresponding core is minimized.

Lines 6 to 25 describe the second stage of the partitioning algorithm. First, a temporary variable, *temp*, is initialized to 0 to indicate no STT-RAM banks have been assigned (Line 7). For each core i, the algorithm finds an STT-RAM bank j that has minimum access latency to core i (Line 9); then this STT-RAM bank is assigned to core i (Line 10), and

TABLE 4.2   System Configuration Used in Simulation

Processor	Four cores, 2 GHz
L1 I/D Cache	32/64 KB per core (private), four-way, two cycles latency, 64 B block size, write back
Hybrid L2 Cache	20 STT-RAM banks, 8 SRAM banks, 4 STT-RAM/SRAM hybrid banks, write back
Allocation for Layer 1	Four processor cores
Allocation for Layer 2	Four STT-RAM/SRAM hybrid local banks (for each core) Eight STT-RAM banks Four SRAM banks
Allocation for Layer 3	12 STT-ARM banks 4 SRAM banks
SRAM Bank	128 KB, 16-way set associative, 64 B block size
STT-RAM Bank	512 KB, 16-way set associative, 64 B block size
STT-RAM/SRAM Hybrid Bank	512 KB (480 KB + 32 KB), 16-way set associative, 64 B block size
L2 Cache Access Lat.	SRAM: Six cycles STT-RAM read/write: 6/23 cycles
Wire Lat.	Horizontal wire: two cycles (0.57394 ns) per hop TSV: one cycle (0.13297 ns) per hop
Coherence Mechanism	MESI directory protocol

Note: Lat. = Latency; MESI = Modified, Exclusive, Shared, Invalid.

temp is incremented (Line 11). The iteration in Lines 9 to 11 finishes when *temp* is equal to $STTRAM\_ALLOC_i$.

Next, the temporary variable, *temp*, is reinitialized to 0 to indicate no SRAM banks have been assigned (Line 13). For each core *i*, the algorithm finds a SRAM bank *j* that has minimum access latency to core *i* (Line 15); then this SRAM bank is assigned to core *i* (Line 16), and *temp* is incremented (Line 17). The iteration in Lines 15 to 17 finishes when *temp* is equal to $SRAM\_ALLOC_i$.

If there are still some SRAM banks not assigned to any core, the proposed algorithm will assign a SRAM bank at a time to the core with the minimal number of SRAM banks until all the SRAM banks are assigned. (Lines 20 to 22). However, if there are still some STT-RAM banks not assigned to any core, these STT-RAM banks are regarded as shared banks (Lines 23 to 25), which means these STT-RAM banks can be accessed by any core. This is because by sharing these STT-RAM banks by each core, the cache miss rate can be reduced. In addition, setting these banks as shared banks can avoid the situation that these banks are assigned to different cores in each period, resulting in cache bank flush and miss rate increase.

4.4 EXPERIMENTAL SETUP AND RESULTS

4.4.1 Experimental Setup

The Gem5 simulator [17] is used in our work to simulate a four-core CMP architecture running at 2 GHz. The classic cache model in Gem5 is modified to implement the hybrid L2

TABLE 4.3   Timing and Latency Parameters of SRAM, STT-RAM, and STT/SRAM Cache Banks

Bank Type	Tech.	Op.	Lat. (ns)	Dynamic Energy (nJ)	Leak. (W)
SRAM bank (128 KB)	SRAM	R/W	1.74	0.609	0.3691
STT-RAM bank (512 KB)	STT-RAM	R	2.99	0.598	0.0686
		W	11.41	4.375	
STT/SRAM Hybrid bank (1920/128 KB)	SRAM	R/W	1.57	0.219	0.0764
	STT-RAM	R	1.71	0.569	
		W	11.32	4.215	

Note: Lat. = Latency; Leak. = Leakage; Op. = Operation; Tech. = Technology.

cache with nonuniform access time, the proposed access-aware technique, and the partitioning algorithm described in Section 4.3. The PARSEC 2.1 benchmark suite [18] is used as the parallel workload to evaluate the proposed design and technique. In order to obtain a reasonable evaluation, all benchmarks are fast-forwarded to the beginning region of interest, and then the next 100 M instructions are considered as a warm-up period.

Figure 4.5 shows our proposed architecture, which includes a four-core CMP system with private L1 cache and 3D stacked hybrid L2 (last-level) cache. The private L1 cache in each core is not shown in the figure. The hybrid cache consists of 4 hybrid (SRAM + STT-RAM) local banks, 20 STT-RAM banks, and 8 SRAM banks. From Table 4.1, it can be seen that the density of the STT-RAM cache is about four times higher than the SRAM cache [2]. In order to achieve a similar area for each bank, the cache capacity of the STT-RAM and SRAM banks used in our work are 512 KB and 128 KB, respectively. Table 4.2 shows the system configuration used in the simulation, and Table 4.3 shows the average latency, dynamic energy, and leakage of read and write operations in each kind of cache banks. These parameters of SRAM cache are obtained from CACTI [19]. The NVSim simulator [20] and the model reported in Ref. [3] are used to the parameters for STT-RAM in 65 nm technology.

4.4.2 Normalized Miss Rate Comparison

Figure 4.8 compares the miss rate between 3D pure SRAM cache, 3D hybrid cache with SRAM local banks, and the proposed 3D hybrid cache with hybrid local banks.

Compared to 3D pure SRAM cache, it is evident that the average reduction of miss rate in the proposed 3D hybrid cache is up to 39.5% in the canneal benchmark, and 14.9% on average. This is because the capacity of the hybrid cache in the proposed architecture is about three times larger than that of the 3D pure SRAM cache and the miss rate is reduced due to the larger capacity.

When compared with the 3D hybrid cache with SRAM local banks, our proposed 3D hybrid cache with hybrid local bank can reduce the miss rate by up to 6.05% in the ×264 benchmark, and 2.9% on average. This is because the hybrid cache in the proposed architecture used hybrid banks as local banks instead of SRAM banks. Hybrid local banks have a larger capacity than SRAM local banks, reducing the miss rate.

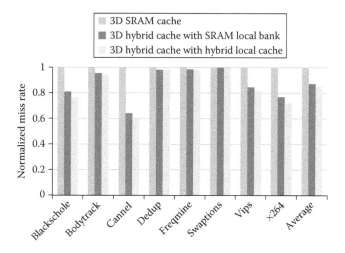

FIGURE 4.8 Normalized miss rate for 3D pure SRAM cache, 3D hybrid cache with SRAM local banks, and 3D hybrid cache with hybrid local banks.

4.4.3 Energy Comparison

Figure 4.9 compares the energy consumption of 3D cache with pure SRAM L2 cache, 3D hybrid L2 cache with SRAM local bank, and proposed 3D hybrid cache with hybrid local bank. The energy consumption is normalized to the maximum energy value in all benchmarks, which happens in the x264 benchmark.

When compared to the pure SRAM cache, our proposed hybrid cache with hybrid local banks can reduce the energy consumption up to 60.7% in the x264 benchmark and 60.3% on average. This is because in the LLC design, the static power takes a large proportion of the total cache energy consumption [2,21,22]. The total energy consumption is significantly reduced if many SRAM banks are replaced with STT-RAM banks.

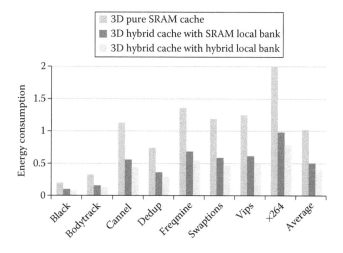

FIGURE 4.9 The comparison of normalized energy consumption for the pure SRAM cache, hybrid cache with SRAM local bank, and proposed hybrid cache (with hybrid local bank).

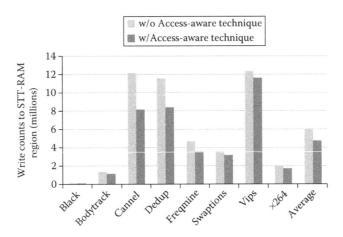

FIGURE 4.10 Comparison of write traffic to the STT-RAM region with and without the proposed access-aware technique.

When compared to a hybrid cache with SRAM local bank, our proposed hybrid cache with hybrid local bank can reduce energy consumption by up to 20.1% in the blackschole benchmark and 18.9% on average. The energy consumption reduction is mainly because the local SRAM banks are replaced with hybrid STT-RAM/SRAM banks. The miss rate reduction in the proposed hybrid cache with hybrid local banks can reduce energy consumption as well.

4.4.4 Write Count Comparison

Figure 4.10 compares the write count on STT-RAM regions with and without the proposed access-aware technique. The experiment is done in the proposed 3D hybrid cache with hybrid local banks. It is evident that with the proposed access-aware technique, the write pressure on STT-RAM regions can be reduced up to 33.03% in the canneal benchmark and 21% on average. This is because our proposed access-aware technique can effectively migrate write operations from STT-RAM to SRAM regions and migrate read data from SRAM to STT-RAM regions.

4.4.5 Average Access Latency Comparison

Figure 4.11 compares L2 cache access latency with and without the proposed access-aware technique. The experiment is done in the proposed 3D hybrid cache with hybrid local banks. It is evident that the proposed access-aware technique can reduce access latency by up to 30.7% in the bodytrack benchmark and by 13.4% on average. This is because our proposed technique can redirect write traffic from STT-RAM regions to SRAM regions; since SRAM has lower write latency than STT-RAM, when write traffic is redirected to SRAM, the average access latency is reduced.

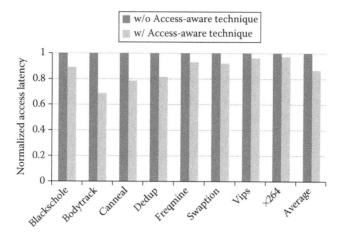

FIGURE 4.11 Comparison of normalized cache access latency with and without the proposed access-aware technique.

We also compare the proposed access-aware technique with the access-aware technique in Ref. [15], as shown in Figure 4.12. Compared to the access-aware technique in Ref. [15], it can be seen that the proposed access-aware technique can decrease access latency up to 11% in the blackschole benchmark and by 4.03% on average. This is because the access-aware technique used in Ref. [15] to migrate the less-written data from SRAM to STT-RAM is different. In Ref. [15], when a read hit occurs in SRAM, a read operation needs to be executed before migrating the data from SRAM to STT-RAM. However, the proposed technique migrates the less-written data from SRAM to STT-RAM when a write hit occurs in SRAM. Therefore, it can migrate the data without an additional read operation and extra latency overhead is avoided.

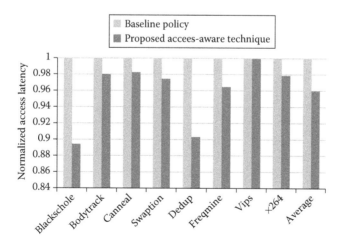

FIGURE 4.12 Comparison of access latency between baseline and the proposed access-aware technique.

4.4.6 Dynamic Partitioning Algorithm Comparison

As mentioned in Section 4.1, some partitioning algorithms have been proposed to improve the cache utility of each core. However, these algorithms are not suitable for the 3D hybrid cache, since they do not consider the write pressure on STT-RAM and the different cache access latency of each layer in the 3D hybrid cache. Both issues are considered in the proposed dynamic partitioning algorithm.

Figure 4.13 compares the normalized miss rate of the utility-based partitioning algorithm in Ref. [11] with the proposed dynamic partitioning algorithm. The proposed partitioning algorithm is implemented in two versions: one has the proposed access-aware technique, and the other does not.

Compared to utility-based partitioning, it can be seen that the miss rate can be reduced up to 7.39% in blackschole benchmark and 4.4% on average in the proposed portioning algorithm without the proposed access-aware technique. This is because in the utility-based partitioning in Ref. [11], some STT-RAM banks are frequently assigned to different cores in each period, and the data in these STT-RAM banks will be flushed, increasing the miss rate. However, our proposed dynamic partitioning sets some STT-RAM as shared banks to avoid this condition.

When combining the proposed dynamic partitioning algorithm and the proposed access-aware technique, the miss rate reduction is slightly improved by up to 13.4% in the freqmine benchmark and by 7.7% on average. The effect of the proposed access-aware technique is more significant for access latency.

Figure 4.14 compares the normalized access latency of the utility-based partitioning algorithm in Ref. [11] and the proposed partitioning algorithm. Two cases are implemented for the proposed partitioning algorithm. One has the proposed access-aware technique,

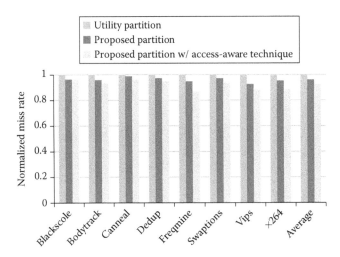

FIGURE 4.13 Comparison of the access miss rate for the last level cache between baseline and the proposed method.

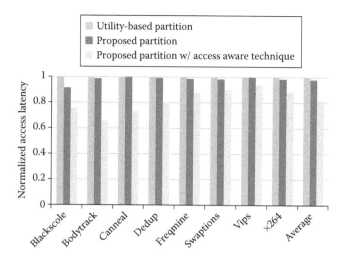

FIGURE 4.14 The access latency comparison for the last level cache between baseline and the proposed method.

and the other does not. It can be seen that when our proposed partitioning algorithm is used, the average latency can be reduced by up to 8.56% in the blackschole benchmark, and 2% on average. This is because the different cache access latencies of each layer are considered in the proposed partitioning algorithm and a bank is assigned to a core that can achieve less access latency.

Furthermore, when combining the proposed partitioning algorithm with the proposed access-aware technique, the access latency can be reduced by up to 34.1% in the body-track benchmark and 18.2% on average. This is because the write traffic can be migrated from STT-RAM banks to the SRAM banks through the proposed access-aware technique, reducing the access latency.

Figure 4.15 compares the normalized EDP of the utility-based partitioning in Ref. [11] with the proposed partitioning. Two cases are implemented for the proposed partitioning algorithm. One has the proposed access-aware technique, and the other does not.

Compared to the utility-based partitioning in Ref. [11], it can be seen that the EDP can be reduced up to 9.8% in the blackschole benchmark and 2.5% on average in the proposed portioning algorithm. The main reason is that the average access latency is reduced (see Figure 4.14).

Furthermore, when combining the proposed partitioning algorithm with the proposed access-aware technique, the EDP can be improved by up to 34.3% in the bodytrack benchmark, and 18.9% on average. The improvement is significant when combining the proposed dynamic partitioning algorithm and access-aware technique since the write pressure can be redirected from STT-RAM to SRAM. Since SRAM has lower write latency, the access latency can be reduced and EDP is improved.

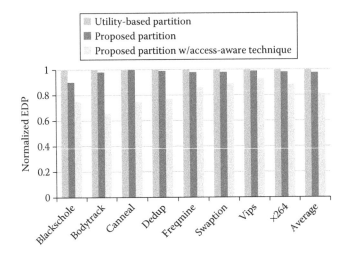

FIGURE 4.15   Comparison of the energy delay product between baseline and the proposed method.

4.4.7 Normalized Lifetime with and without the Access-Aware Technique

From Table 4.1, it can be seen that currently STT-RAM write cycles are limited by about 4×1012 [23], and reliable writes are not guaranteed if write cycles are higher [23]. It has been reported that when a medical image application, segmentation, is executed on a 4 GHz CPU with 32 KB L1 cache and 2 MB STT-RAM L2 cache continuously [24], the lifetime of a STT-RAM is only 2.17 years without any optimization applied. This issue is even more serious on multilevel cell STT-RAM, since its write current is higher than single-level cell STT-RAM [23,25]. Therefore, this work also investigates the benefit of the proposed access-aware technique on STT-RAM endurance.

Figure 4.16 compares the estimated lifetime of the proposed 3D hybrid cache with and without the proposed access-aware technique. A STT-RAM cell is regarded as faulty if its

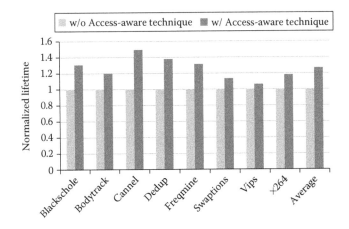

FIGURE 4.16   Comparison of lifetime with and without our proposed access-aware technique.

write count exceeds 4×1012 times. It can be seen that the hybrid cache with the proposed access-aware technique can increase the lifetime up to 49.3% in the canneal benchmark, and 26.5% on average. This is because the proposed technique can redirect the write traffic from STT-RAM to SRAM and reduce the write pressure to the STT-RAM region. Therefore, the lifetime of STT-RAM is increased.

4.5 CONCLUSIONS

In this chapter, we proposed a 3D hybrid cache to mitigate the energy consumption for CMP architecture. We also proposed an access-aware technique and dynamic partitioning algorithm to improve the access latency and cache utility for the proposed 3D hybrid cache.

The experimental results showed that our proposed 3D stacked hybrid cache can save 60.4% and 18.9% of energy compared to pure SRAM cache and hybrid cache with SRAM local bank, respectively. With the proposed dynamic partitioning algorithm and access-aware technique, our proposed 3D hybrid cache reduces the miss rate by 7.7% and access latency by 18.2%. Finally, the EDP can be reduced by 18.9%.

REFERENCES

1. S. Vangal, J. Howard, G. Ruhl, S. Dighe, H. Wilson, J. Tschanz, D. Finan, et al., 2008, An 80-tile sub-100-W TeraFLOPS processor in 65-nm CMOS, *IEEE Journal of Solid-State Circuits*, vol. 43, no. 1, pp. 29–41.
2. Y.-T. Chen, J. Cong, H. Huang, B. Liu, M. Potkonjak, and G. Reinman, 2012, Dynamically reconfigurable hybrid cache: An energy-efficient last-level cache design, in *Proceeding of DATE*, pp. 45–50.
3. G. Sun, X. Dong, Y. Xie, J. Li, and Y. Chen, 2009, A novel architecture of the 3D stacked Mram L2 cache for CMPs, in *Proceedings of IEEE International Symposium on High Performance Computer Architecture (HPCA)*, Raleigh, NC, pp. 239–249.
4. X. Wu, J. Li, E. Speight, and Y. Xie, 2009, Power and performance of read-write aware hybrid cache with non-volatile memories, in *Proceedings of Design, Automation and Test in Europe Conference and Exhibition (DATE)*, Nice, pp. 737–742.
5. C. Kim, D. Burger, and S. Keckler, 2002, An adaptive, non-uniform cache structure for wire-delay dominated on-chip caches, in *Proceedings of International Conference on Architectural Support for Programming Languages and Operating Systems (ASPLOS)*, San Jose, CA, pp. 211–222.
6. S. Kim, D. Chandra, and Y. Solihin, 2004, Fair cache sharing and partitioning in a chip multiprocessor architecture, in *Proceedings of Parallel Architecture and Compilation Techniques (PACT)*, Antibes, Juan-les-Pins, pp. 111–122.
7. B. Verghese, A. Gupta, and M. Rosenblum, 1998, Performance isolation : Sharing and isolation in shared-memory multiprocessors, in *International Conference on Architectural Support for Programming Languages and Operating Systems (ASPLOS)*, San Jose, CA, pp. 181–192.
8. K. Nesbit, M. Moreto, F. Cazorla, A. Ramirez, M. Valero, and J. Smith, 2008, Multicore resource management, *IEEE Micro*, vol. 28, no. 3, pp. 6–16.
9. G. Suo, X. Yang, G. Liu, J. Wu, K. Zeng, B. Zhang, and Y. Lin, 2008, IPC-based cache partitioning: An IPC-oriented dynamic shared cache partitioning mechanism, in *Proceedings of International Conference on Convergence and Hybrid Information Technology (ICHIT)*, Daejeon, pp. 399–406.
10. M. Qureshi, and Y. Patt, 2006, Utility-based cache partitioning: A low-overhead. High-performance, runtime mechanism to partition shared caches, in *Proceedings of IEEE/ACM International Symposium on Microarchitecture (MICRO)*, pp. 423–432.

11. J. Jung, K. Kang, and C.-M. Kyung, 2011, Design and management of 3D-stacked NUCA cache for chip multiprocessors, in *ACM Symposium on Great lakes on VLSI (GLSVLSI)*, pp. 91–96.
12. Y.-F. Tsai, F. Wang, Y. Xie, N. Vijaykrishnan, and M.-J. Irwin, 2008, Design space exploration for 3-D cache, *IEEE Transactions on Very Large Scale Integration Systems (TVLSI)*, vol 16, no. 4, pp. 444–455.
13. S. Lee, J. Jung, and C.-M. Kyung, 2012, Hybrid cache architecture replacing SRAM cache with future memory technology, in *Proceedings of International Symposium on Circuits and Systems (ISCAS)*, Seoul, pp. 2481–2484.
14. J. Li, C. Xue, and Y. Xu, 2011, STT-RAM based energy-efficiency hybrid cache for CMPs, in *Proceedings of IEEE/IFIP International Conference on VLSI and System-on-Chip (VLSI-SoC)*, Hong Kong, pp. 31–36.
15. S.-M. Syu, Y.-H. Shao, and I.-C. Lin, 2013, High-endurance hybrid cache design in CMP architecture with cache partitioning and access-aware policy, in *ACM Symposium on Great lakes on VLSI (GLSVLSI)*, Paris, pp. 19–24.
16. D. Kadjo, H. Kim, P. Gratz, J. Hu, and R. Ayoub, 2013, Power gating with block migration in chip-multiprocessor last-level caches, in *IEEE Conference on International Conference on Computer Design (ICCD)*, Asheville, NC, pp. 93–99.
17. N. Binkert, B. Beckmann, G. Black, S. Reinhardt, A. Saidi, A. Basu, J. Hestness, et al., 2011, The Gem5 Simulator, *ACM Computer Architecture News*, vol. 39, no. 2, pp. 1–7.
18. C. Bienia, S. Kumar, J. Singh, and K. Li, 2008, The Parsec benchmark suite: Characterization and architectural implications, in *Proceedings of International Conference on Parallel Architectures and Compilation Techniques (PACT)*, Toronto, ON, Canada, pp. 72–81.
19. CACTI: An integrated cache and memory access time, cycle time, area, leakage, and dynamic power model, Version 5.3, http://www.hpl.hp.com/research/cacti/ (Accessed on May 2015).
20. X. Dong, C. Xu, Y. Xie, and N. Jouppi, 2012, NVSim: A circuit-level performance, energy, and area model for emerging nonvolatile memory, *IEEE Transactions on Computer-Aided Design of Integrated Circuits and Systems (TCAD)*, vol. 31, no. 7, pp. 994–1007.
21. M.-T. Chang, P. Rosenfeld, S.-L. Lu, and B. Jocab, 2013, Technology comparison for large last-level caches (L3Cs): Low-leakage SRAM, low write-energy STT-RAM, and refresh-optimized eDRAM in *Proceedings of IEEE 19th International Symposium on High Performance Computer Architecture (HPCA)*, Fukuoka, pp. 23–27.
22. S. Li, K. Chen, J.-H. Ahn, J.-B. Brockman, and N.-P. Jouppi, 2011, CACTI-P: Architecture-level modeling for SRAM-based structures with advanced leakage reduction techniques, in *IEEE/ACM International Conference on Computer-Aided Design (ICCAD)*, San Jose, CA, pp. 649–701.
23. Y. Chen, W.-F. Wong, H. Li, and C.-K. Koh, 2011, Processor caches built using multi-level spin-transfer torque RAM cells, in *Proceedings of International Symposium on Low Power Electronics and Design (ISLPED)*, Fukuoka, pp. 73–78.
24. Y.-T. Chen, J. Cong, H. Huang, C. Liu, R. Prabhakar, and G. Reinman, 2012, Static and dynamic co-optimizations for blocks mapping in hybrid caches, in *Proceeding of the 2012 ACM/IEEE International Symposium on Low Power Electronics and Design (ISLPED)*, pp. 237–242.
25. L. Jiang, B. Zhao, Y. Zhang, and J. Yang, 2012, Constructing large and fast multi-level cell STT-MRAM based cache for embedded processors, in *Proceedings of the 49th Annual Design Automation Conference (DAC)*, San Francisco, CA, pp. 907–912.

II

Emerging Big Data Applications

CHAPTER 5

Matrix Factorization for Drug–Target Interaction Prediction

Yong Liu, Min Wu, and Xiao-Li Li

Institute of Infocomm Research (I2R)
A*STAR, Singapore

Peilin Zhao

Artificial Intelligence Department
Ant Financial Services Group, China

CONTENTS

5.1 INTRODUCTION

The drug discovery is one of the primary objectives of the pharmaceutical sciences, which is an interdisciplinary research field of fundamental sciences covering biology, chemistry, physics, statistics, etc. In the drug discovery process, the prediction of drug–target interactions (DTIs) is an important step that aims to identify potential new drugs or new targets for existing drugs. Therefore, it can help guide the experimental validation and reduce costs. In recent years, the DTI prediction has attracted vast research attention and numerous algorithms have been proposed [1,2]. Existing methods predict DTIs based on a small number of experimentally validated interactions in existing databases, for example, ChEMBL [3], DrugBank [4], KEGG DRUG [5], and SuperTarget [6]. Previous studies have shown that a fraction of new interactions between drugs and targets can be predicted based on the experimentally validated DTIs, and the computational methods for identifying DTIs can significantly improve the drug discovery efficiency.

In general, traditional methods developed for DTI prediction can be categorized into two main groups: docking simulation approaches and ligand-based approaches [7–9]. The docking simulation approaches predict potential DTIs, considering the structural information of target proteins. However, the docking simulation is extensively time-consuming, and the structural information may not be available for some protein families, for example, the G-protein coupled receptors (GPCRs). In the ligand-based approaches, potential DTIs are predicted by comparing a candidate ligand with the known ligands of the target proteins. This kind of approaches may not perform well for the targets with a small number of ligands.

Recently, the rapid development of machine learning techniques provides effective and efficient ways to predict DTIs. An intuitive idea is to formulate the DTI prediction as a binary classification problem, where the drug-target pairs are treated as instances, and the chemical structures of drugs and the amino acid subsequences of targets are treated as features. Then, classical classification methods [e.g., support vector machines (SVM) and regularized least square (RLS)] can be used for DTI prediction [10–16]. Essentially, the DTI prediction problem is a recommendation task that aims to suggest a list of potential DTIs. Therefore, another line of research for DTI prediction is the application of recommendation technologies, especially matrix factorization-based approaches [17–20]. The matrix factorization methods aim to map both drugs and targets into a shared latent space with low dimensionality and model the DTIs using the combinations of the latent representations of drugs and targets.

In this chapter, we introduce a DTI prediction approach, named neighborhood regularized logistic matrix factorization (NRLMF), which focuses on predicting the probability that a drug would interact with a target [21]. Specifically, the properties of a drug and a target are represented by two vectors in the shared low-dimensional latent space, respectively. For each drug-target pair, the interaction probability is modeled by a logistic function of the drug- specific and target-specific latent vectors. This is different from the kernelized Bayesian matrix factorization (KBMF) method [17] that predicts the interaction probability using a standard normal cumulative distribution function of the drug-specific and target-specific latent vectors [22]. In NRLMF, an observed interacting drug-target pair (i.e., positive observation) is treated as $c = (c \geq 1)$ positive examples, while an unknown pair (i.e., negative observation) is treated as a single negative example. As such, NRLMF assigns higher importance levels to positive observations than negatives. The reason is that the positive observations are biologically validated and thus usually more trustworthy. However, the negative observations could contain potential DTIs and are thus unreliable. This differs from previous matrix factorization-based DTI prediction methods [17–19] that treat the interaction and unknown pairs equally.

Furthermore, NRLMF also studies the local structure of the interaction data to improve the DTI prediction accuracy by exploiting the neighborhood influences from most similar drugs and most similar targets. In particular, NRLMF imposes individual regularization constraints on the latent representations of a drug and its nearest neighbors, which are most similar with the given drug. Similar neighborhood regularization constraints have also been added on the latent representations of targets. Note that this neighborhood regularization method is different from previous approaches that exploit the drug similarities and target similarities using kernels [12,13,15,23] or factorizing the similarity matrices [19]. Moreover, the proposed approach only considers nearest neighbors instead of all similar neighbors as used in previous approaches, avoiding noisy information, thus achieves more accurate results.

The performances of NRLMF were empirically evaluated on four benchmark data sets, compared with five baseline DTI prediction methods. Experimental results showed that NRLMF usually outperformed other competing methods on all data sets under different experimental settings, in terms of the widely adopted measures, that is, the area under the ROC curve (AUC) and the area under the precision-recall curve (AUPR). In addition, the practical prediction ability of NRLMF was also confirmed by mapping with the latest version of online biological databases, including ChEMBL [3], DrugBank [24], KEGG [5], and Matador [6].

The remaining parts of this chapter are organized as follows. Section 5.2 reviews existing DTI prediction methods. Section 5.3 introduces the details of the NRLMF model. Section 5.4 reports the experimental results conducted on real data sets. Finally, Section 5.5 draws the conclusion of this study.

5.2 RELATED WORK

This section reviews existing DTI prediction methods from two aspects: traditional classification-based methods and matrix factorization-based methods.

5.2.1 Classification-Based Methods

In the literature, DTI prediction is usually formulated as a binary classification problem and is solved by traditional classification models, such as SVM and RLS. For example, in [10], an SVM model was utilized to classify a given drug-target pair into interaction and noninteraction, considering the amino acid sequences of proteins, chemical structures, and the mass spectrometry data. Bleakley and Yamanishi developed a supervised approach for DTI prediction based on the bipartite local models (BLMs), where SVM was used to build the local models [11]. Xia et al. proposed a semisupervised DTI prediction approach named Laplacian regularized least square (LapRLS) and extended it to incorporate the kernel constructed from the known DTI network [12]. van Laarhoven et al. defined a Gaussian interaction profile (GIP) kernel to represent the interactions between drugs and targets, and they employed RLS with the GIP kernel for DTI prediction [13,14]. Cheng et al. developed three supervised inference methods for DTI prediction based on the complex network theory [25]. Mei et al. integrated BLM method with a neighbor-based interaction-profile inferring (NII) procedure to form a DTI prediction approach called BLM-NII, where the RLS classifier with GIP kernel was used as the local model [15]. Yuan et al. proposed an ensemble learning method called DrugE-Rank that combined multiple similarity-based DTI prediction methods to improve the prediction performance [26]. In addition, other auxiliary information has also been exploited. For example, in [27], Chen et al. utilized the data from public data sets to build a semantic linked network connecting drugs and targets. A statistical model was proposed to evaluate the association of drug-target pairs. Yamanishi et al. developed a web server called DINIES, which utilized supervised machine learning techniques, such as pairwise kernel learning and distance metric learning to predict unknown DTIs from different sources of biological data [16].

5.2.2 Matrix Factorization-Based Methods

DTI prediction is essentially a recommendation problem. Thus, the recommendation technologies have also been exploited for DTI prediction. In the literature, collaborative filtering-based approaches are the most widely adopted recommendation methods, which can be categorized into two main groups: memory-based collaborative filtering approaches and model-based collaborative filtering approaches [28]. As the most successful model-based approach, matrix factorization has been explored for DTI prediction in recent studies. For example, Gönen proposed a KBMF method, which combined the kernel-based dimensionality reduction, matrix factorization, and binary classification for DTI prediction [17]. Cobanoglu et al. utilized probabilistic matrix factorization to predict unknown DTIs [18]. The prediction accuracy was further improved by an active learning strategy. In [19], Zheng et al. introduced the multiple similarities collaborative matrix factorization (MSCMF) model, which exploited several kinds of drug similarities and target similarities to improve the DTI prediction accuracy. In [29], Ezzat et al. developed two graph regularized matrix factorization methods for DTI prediction and proposed a preprocessing step to enhance predictions in the "new drug" and "new target" cases by adding edges with intermediate interaction likelihood scores. In [30], Liao et al. developed a matrix completion method to predict potential DTIs. This method built an approximation matrix by minimizing the distance between the DTI matrix and its approximation subject that the values in the observed positions are equal to the known interactions at the corresponding positions. In [20], Lim et al. introduced a fast and accurate predication method, named REMAP, which used a dual regularized one-class matrix factorization to explore the continuous chemical space, protein space, and their interaction on a large scale. In [31], Lan et al. proposed a distributed and privatized framework for DTI prediction. In this approach, the distributed repositories are analyzed on local computers by matrix factorization technique and the local computers can exchange privatized information for improving prediction accuracy.

5.3 NEIGHBORHOOD REGULARIZED LOGISTIC MATRIX FACTORIZATION

This section introduces the details of the NRLMF model. The workflow of the NRLMF model is shown in Figure 5.1.

5.3.1 Problem Formalization

In this chapter, the set of drugs is denoted by $D = \{d_i\}_{i=1}^{m}$, and the set of targets is denoted by $T = \{t_j\}_{j=1}^{n}$, where m and n are the number of drugs and the number of targets, respectively. The interactions between drugs and targets are represented by a binary matrix $Y \in \mathbb{R}^{m \times n}$, where each element $y_{ij} \in \{0, 1\}$. If a drug d_i has been experimentally verified to interact with a target t_j, y_{ij} is set to 1; otherwise, y_{ij} is set to 0. The nonzero elements in Y are called "interaction pairs" and regarded as positive observations. The zero elements in Y are called

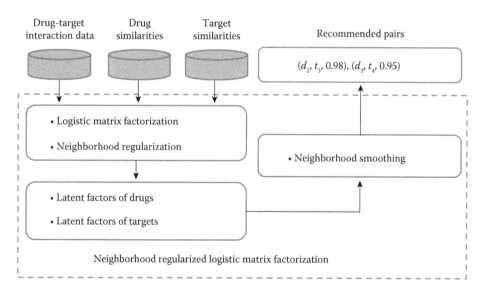

FIGURE 5.1   The workflow of the NRLMF model.

"unknown pairs" and regarded as negative observations. We define the set of positive drugs and targets as $D^+ = \left\{ d_i \left| \sum_{j=1}^{n} y_{ij} > 0, \forall 1 \le i \le m \right. \right\}$ and $T^+ = \left\{ t_j \left| \sum_{i=1}^{m} y_{ij} > 0, \forall 1 \le j \le n \right. \right\}$, respectively. Then, the set of negative drugs (i.e., new drugs without any known interaction targets) and negative targets (i.e., new targets without any known interaction drugs) is defined as $D^- = D \backslash D^+$ and $T^- = T \backslash T^+$ respectively. In addition, the drug similarities are represented by $S^d \in \mathbb{R}^{m \times m}$, where the (i, μ) element sd is the similarity between d_i and $d\mu$. The target similarities are described using $S^t \in \mathbb{R}^{n \times n}$, where the (j, v) element st is the similarity between t_j and t_v. The objective of this study is to first predict the interaction probability of a drug-target pair and subsequently rank the candidate drug-target pairs according to the predicted probabilities in descending order such that the top-ranked pairs are the most likely to interact.

5.3.2 Logistic Matrix Factorization

The matrix factorization technique has been successfully applied for DTI prediction in previous studies. In this work, we develop the DTI prediction model based on logistic matrix factorization (LMF) [32], which has been demonstrated to be effective for personalized recommendations. The primary idea of applying LMF for DTI prediction is to model the probability that a drug would interact with a target. In particular, both drugs and targets are mapped into a shared latent space, with a low dimensionality r, where $r \ll \min(m, n)$. The properties of a drug d_i and a target t_j are described by two latent vectors $\mathbf{u}_i \in \mathbb{R}^{1 \times r}$ and $\mathbf{v}_j \in \mathbb{R}^{1 \times r}$, respectively. Then, the interaction probability p_{ij} of a drug-target pair (d_i, t_j) is modeled by the following logistic function:

$$p_{ij} = \frac{\exp\left(u_i V_j^T\right)}{1 + \exp\left(u_i V_j^T\right)} \tag{5.1}$$

For simplicity, we further denote the latent vectors of all drugs and all targets by $U \in \mathbb{R}^{m \times r}$ and $V \in \mathbb{R}^{n \times r}$, respectively, where $\mathbf{u}_i$ is the ith row in $\mathbf{U}$ and $\mathbf{v}_j$ is the jth row in $\mathbf{V}$.

In DTI prediction tasks, the observed interacting drug-target pairs have been experimentally verified; thus, they are more trustworthy and important than the unknown pairs. For a more accurate modeling of DTI prediction, we propose the assignment of higher importance levels to the interaction pairs than to the unknown pairs. In particular, each interaction pair is treated as c ($c \ge 1$) positive training examples, and each unknown pair is treated as a single negative training example. Here, c is a constant used to control the importance levels of observed interactions and is empirically set to 5 in the experiments. This importance weighting strategy has been demonstrated to be effective for personalized recommendations [32–34]. However, to the best of our knowledge, it has not been explored for DTI prediction in previous studies. By assuming that all the training examples are independent, the probability of the observations is as follows:

$$p\left(Y|U,V\right)=\left(\prod_{1\le i\le m,\,1\le j\le n,\,y_{ij}=1}\left[p_{ij}^{y_{ij}}\left(1-p_{ij}\right)^{\left(1-y_{ij}\right)}\right]^{c}\right)$$

$$\times\left(\prod_{1\le i\le m,\,1\le j\le n,\,y_{ij}=0}p_{ij}^{y_{ij}}\left(1-p_{ij}\right)^{\left(1-y_{ij}\right)}\right). \tag{5.2}$$

Note that when $y_{ij}=1$, $c(1-y_{ij})=1-y_{ij}$, and when $y_{ij}=0$, $cy_{ij}=y_{ij}$. Hence, we can rewrite Equation 5.2 as follows:

$$p\left(Y|U,V\right)=\left(\prod_{1\le i\le m,\,1\le j\le n,\,y_{ij}=1}p_{ij}^{cy_{ij}}\left(1-p_{ij}\right)^{\left(1-y_{ij}\right)}\right)\times\prod_{i=1}^{m}\prod_{i=1}^{n}p_{ij}^{cy_{ij}}\left(1-p_{ij}\right)^{\left(1-y_{ij}\right)}.$$

$$\times\left(\prod_{1\le i\le m,\,1\le j\le n,\,y_{ij}=0}p_{ij}^{cy_{ij}}\left(1-p_{ij}\right)^{\left(1-y_{ij}\right)}\right) \tag{5.3}$$

In addition, we also place zero-mean spherical Gaussian priors on the latent vectors of drugs and targets as:

$$p\left(U|\sigma_{d}^{2}\right)=\prod_{i=1}^{m}N\left(u_{i}|0,\sigma_{d}^{2}I\right),\; p\left(V|\sigma_{t}^{2}\right)=\prod_{j=1}^{n}N\left(V_{j}|0,\sigma_{t}^{2}I\right), \tag{5.4}$$

where σ_{d}^{2} and σ_{t}^{2} are parameters controlling the variances of Gaussian distributions and I denotes the identity matrix. Hence, through a Bayesian inference, we have

$$p\left(U,V|Y,\sigma_{d}^{2},\sigma_{t}^{2}\right)\alpha p\left(Y|U,V\right)p\left(U|\sigma_{d}^{2}\right)p\left(V|\sigma_{t}^{2}\right). \tag{5.5}$$

The log of the posterior distribution is thus derived as follows:

$$\log p\left(U,V|Y,\sigma_{d}^{2},\sigma_{t}^{2}\right)=\sum_{i=1}^{m}\sum_{j=1}^{n}-\left(1+cy_{ij}-y_{ij}\right)\log\left[1+\exp\left(u_{i}v_{j}^{T}\right)\right]$$

$$+\sum_{i=1}^{m}\sum_{j=1}^{n}cy_{ij}u_{i}v_{j}^{T}-\frac{1}{2\sigma_{d}^{2}}\sum_{i=1}^{m}\|u_{i}\|_{2}^{2}-\frac{1}{2\sigma_{t}^{2}}\sum_{j=1}^{n}\|v_{j}\|_{2}^{2}+c, \tag{5.6}$$

where C is a constant term independent of the model parameters (i.e., **U** and **V**). The model parameters can then be learned by maximizing the posterior distribution, which is equivalent with minimizing the following objective function:

$$\min_{\mathbf{U},\mathbf{V}} \sum_{i=1}^{m}\sum_{j=1}^{n}\left(1+cy_{ij}-y_{ij}\right)\log\left[1+\exp\left(\mathbf{u}_i\mathbf{v}_j^{\mathrm{T}}\right)\right]-cy_{ij}\mathbf{u}_i\mathbf{v}_j^{\mathrm{T}}+\frac{\lambda_d}{2}\|\mathbf{U}\|_F^2+\frac{\lambda_t}{2}\|\mathbf{v}\|_F^2, \tag{5.7}$$

where $\lambda_d=\dfrac{1}{\sigma_d^2}, \lambda_t=\dfrac{1}{\sigma_t^2}$ and $\|\bullet\|_F$ denotes the Frobenius norm of a matrix.

The problem in Equation 5.7 can be solved by using an alternating gradient descent method [32].

5.3.3 Neighborhood Regularization

Through mapping both drugs and targets into a shared latent space, the LMF model can effectively estimate the global structure of the DTI data. However, LMF ignores the strong neighborhood associations among a small set of closely related drugs or targets. Thus, we propose to exploit the nearest neighborhood of a drug and that of a target to further improve the DTI prediction accuracy. For a drug d_i, we denote the set of its nearest neighbors by $|N(d_i) \in D\backslash d_i$, where $N(d_i)$ is constructed by choosing K_1 most similar drugs with d_i. Then, we construct the set $|N(t_j) \in T\backslash t_j$, which consists of the K_1 most similar targets with t_j. In the experiments, we empirically set K_1 to 5.

In this chapter, the drug neighborhood information is represented using an adjacency matrix **A**, where the (i, μ) element $a_{i\mu}$ is defined as follows:

$$a_{i\mu}\begin{cases} s_{i\mu}^d & \text{if } d_\mu \in N(d_i) \\ 0 & \text{otherwise.} \end{cases} \tag{5.8}$$

Similarly, the adjacency matrix used to describe the target neighborhood information is denoted by **B**, where its (j, v) element b_{jv} is defined as follows:

$$b_{jv}=\begin{cases} s_{j\mu}^t & \text{if } t_v \in N(t_j) \\ 0 & \text{otherwise.} \end{cases} \tag{5.9}$$

Note that the adjacency matrices **A** and **B** are not symmetric.

The primary idea of exploiting the drug neighborhood information for DTI prediction is to minimize the distance between d_i and its nearest neighbors $N(d_i)$ in the latent space.

This objective can be achieved by minimizing the following objective function:

$$\frac{\alpha}{2}\sum_{i=1}^{m}\sum_{\mu=1}^{m} = a_{i\mu}\left\|\mathbf{u}_i - \mathbf{u}_\mu\right\|_F^2$$

$$= \frac{\alpha}{2}\left[\sum_{i=1}^{m}\left(\sum_{\mu=1}^{m}a_{i\mu}\right)\mathbf{u}_i\mathbf{u}_i^{\mathrm{T}}\sum_{\mu=1}^{m}\left(\sum_{i=1}^{m}a_{i\mu}\right)\mathbf{u}_\mu\mathbf{u}_\mu^{\mathrm{T}}\right]_\mu^{\mathrm{T}}$$

$$-\frac{\alpha}{2}\mathrm{tr}\left(\mathbf{U}^{\mathrm{T}}\mathbf{A}\mathbf{U}\right)-\frac{\alpha}{2}\mathrm{tr}\left(\mathbf{U}^{\mathrm{T}}\mathbf{A}^{\mathrm{T}}\mathbf{U}\right)$$

$$= \frac{\alpha}{2}\mathrm{tr}\left(\mathbf{U}^{\mathrm{T}}\mathbf{L}^d\mathbf{U}\right), \tag{5.10}$$

where tr(.) is the trace of a matrix, $\left|\mathbf{L}^d = \left(\mathbf{D}^d + \tilde{\mathbf{D}}^d\right) - \left(\mathbf{A} + \mathbf{A}^{\mathrm{T}}\right)\right.$. $\mathbf{D}^d$ and $\tilde{\mathbf{D}}^d$ are two diagonal matrices, in which the diagonal elements are $D_{ij}^d = \sum_{\mu=1}^{m} a_{i\mu}$ and $\tilde{D}_{\mu\mu}^d = \sum_{i=1}^{m} a_{i\mu}$, respectively. Moreover, we also exploit the neighborhood information of targets for DTI prediction by minimizing the following objective function:

$$\frac{\beta}{2}\sum_{j=1}^{n}\sum_{v=1}^{n}b_{jv}^\mu\left\|\mathbf{v}_j - \mathbf{v}_v\right\|_F^2 = \frac{\beta}{2}\mathrm{tr}\left(\mathbf{V}^{\mathrm{T}}\mathbf{L}^t\mathbf{V}\right), \tag{5.11}$$

where $\mathbf{L}^t = \left(\mathbf{D}_t + \tilde{\mathbf{D}}^t\right) - \left(\mathbf{B} + \mathbf{B}^{\mathrm{T}}\right)$, $\mathbf{D}^t$ and $\tilde{\mathbf{D}}^t$ are two diagonal matrices, in which the diagonal elements are $\sum_{v=1}^{n} b_{jv}$ and $\tilde{D}_{vv}^d = \sum_{j=1}^{n} b_{jv}$. Note that the proposed neighborhood regularization only considers influences from the K_1 nearest neighbors of each drug and each target. It is different from the graph Laplacian constraints used in previous studies [35,36], which consider influences from all similar drugs and targets. Clearly, given a drug-target pair, we leverage their nearest neighbors, instead of all the neighbors that could potentially introduce noisy information, to enhance the prediction accuracy.

5.3.4 Combined Model

The final DTI prediction model can be formulated by considering the DTIs as well as the neighborhood of drugs and targets. By integrating Equations 5.10 and 5.11 into Equation 5.7, the proposed NRLMF model is formulated as follows:

$$\min_{\mathbf{U},\mathbf{V}}\sum_{i=1}^{m}\sum_{j=1}^{n}\left(1 + cy_{ij} - y_{ij}\right)\ln\left[1 + \exp\left(\mathbf{u}_i\mathbf{v}_j^{\mathrm{T}}\right)\right] - cy_{ij}\mathbf{u}_i\mathbf{v}_j^{\mathrm{T}}$$

$$+\frac{1}{2}\mathrm{tr}\left[\mathbf{U}^{\mathrm{T}}\left(\lambda_d\mathbf{I} + \alpha\mathbf{L}^d\right)\mathbf{U}\right]+\frac{1}{2}\mathrm{tr}\left[\mathbf{V}^{\mathrm{T}}\left(\lambda_t\mathbf{I} + \beta\mathbf{L}^t\right)\mathbf{V}\right]. \tag{5.12}$$

The optimization problem in Equation 5.12 can be solved by an alternating gradient ascent procedure. Denoting the objective function in Equation 5.12 by L, the partial gradients with respect to $\mathbf{U}$ and $\mathbf{V}$ are as follows:

$$\frac{\partial L}{\partial \mathbf{U}} = \mathbf{PV} + (c-1)(\mathbf{Y} \odot \mathbf{P})\mathbf{V} - c\mathbf{YV} + (\lambda_d \mathbf{I} + \alpha \mathbf{L}^d)\mathbf{U}$$

$$\frac{\partial L}{\partial \mathbf{V}} = \mathbf{P}^\mathrm{T}\mathbf{U} + (c-1)(\mathbf{Y}^\mathrm{T} \odot \mathbf{P}^\mathrm{T})\mathbf{U} - c\mathbf{Y}^\mathrm{T}\mathbf{U} + (\lambda_t \mathbf{I} + \beta \mathbf{L}^t)\mathbf{V}, \qquad (5.13)$$

where $\mathbf{P} \in \mathbb{R}^{m \times n}$, in which the (i, j) element is $p_{i,j}$ (see Equation 5.1), $\odot$ denotes the Hadamard product of two matrices. To accelerate the convergence of the gradient descent optimization methods, we use the AdaGrad algorithm [37] to adaptively choose the gradient step size. The details of the optimization algorithm for the proposed NRLMF model are described in Algorithm 5.1, where $\mathbf{U}$ and $\mathbf{V}$ are randomly initialized using a Gaussian distribution with mean 0 and standard deviation $\frac{1}{\sqrt{r}}$.

5.3.5 Neighborhood Smoothing

Once the latent vectors $\mathbf{U}$ and $\mathbf{V}$ have been learned, the probability associated with any unknown drug-target pair (d_i, t_j) can be predicted by Equation 5.1. However, in the training procedure, the latent vectors of drugs belonging to the negative drug set D^- and those of the targets belonging to the negative target set T^- are estimated solely based on negative observations (i.e., unknown pairs). As we know, some negative observations may be potential positive DTIs. Due to such uncertainty over negative observations, the learned latent vectors of the negative drugs and targets may not be accurate enough to describe their properties. One solution for this problem is to replace the latent vector of a negative drug/target by the linear combination of the latent vectors of its nearest neighbors in the positive set. For a drug $d_i \in D^-$, we denote the set of its K_2 nearest neighbors in D^+ by $N^+(d_i)$. Similarly, for a target $t_j \in T^-$, the set of its K_2 nearest neighbors in T^+ is denoted by $N^+(t_j)$. Note that $N^+(d_i)$ and $N^+(t_j)$ are built by using the same criteria as that used to construct the neighborhood in the training procedure. Then, the prediction of the interaction probability of a drug-target pair (u_i, v_j) is modified as

$$\hat{p}_{ij} = \frac{\exp\left(\tilde{u}_i \tilde{v}_j^\mathrm{T}\right)}{1 + \exp\left(\tilde{u}_i \tilde{v}_j^\mathrm{T}\right)}, \qquad (5.14)$$

where

$$\tilde{u}_i = \begin{cases} u_i & \text{if } d_i \in D^+ \\ \dfrac{1}{\sum_{\mu \in N+(d_i)} s_{i\mu}^d} \displaystyle\sum_{\mu \in N+(d_i)} s_{i\mu}^d \ u_\mu & \text{if } d_i \in D^-, \end{cases}$$

$$\tilde{v}_j = \begin{cases} v_j & \text{if } t_j \in T^+ \\ \dfrac{1}{\sum_{v \in N+(t_j)} s_{jv}^t} \displaystyle\sum_{v \in N+(d_j)} s_{jv}^t \ v_v & \text{if } t_j \in T^-. \end{cases} \qquad (5.15)$$

ALGORITHM 5.1: NRLMF OPTIMIZATION ALGORITHM

Input: Y, S^d, S^t, c, ,r, K_1, K_2, λ_d, λ_t, α, β, γ
Output: U, V

1. Initialize U and V randomly, and set $\varphi_{ik} = 0$, $\phi_{jk} = 0$, $\forall 1 \le i \le m$,
   $1 \le j \le n$, and $1 \le k \le r$;

2. Construct the adjacency matrices A and B according to Equations 5.8 and 5.9 respectively;

3. Compute the neighborhood regularization matrices L^d and L^t according to Equations 5.10 and 5.11, respectively;

4. **for** $t = 1, \dots,$ *maxiter* **do**
   // fix V and compute the gradient with respect to U

5. $G^d \leftarrow \dfrac{\partial L}{\partial U}$.

6.   for $i = 1, \dots, m$ **do**

7.   for $\kappa = 1, \dots, r$ **do**
   // g^d_{ik} and u_{ik} are the (i, k) elements in G^d and U.

8. $\varphi_{ik} \leftarrow \varphi_{ik} + g^d_{ik} \cdot g^d_{ik}$;
   // update each element of d_i's latent vector

9. $u_{ik} \leftarrow u_{ik} - \gamma \dfrac{g^d_{ik}}{\sqrt{\varphi_{ik}}}$;

   // fix U and compute the gradient with respect to V

10. $G^t \leftarrow \dfrac{\partial L}{\partial V}$;

11.   for $j = 1, \dots, n$ **do**

12.   for $k = 1, \dots, r$ **do**
   // g^j_{jk} and υ_{jk} are the (j, k) element in G^t and V.

13. $\phi_{jk} \leftarrow \phi_{jk} + g^t_{jk} \cdot g^t_{jk}$;
   // update each element of t_j's latent vector

14. $\upsilon_{jk} \leftarrow \upsilon_{jk} - \gamma \dfrac{g^t_{jk}}{\sqrt{\phi_{jk}}}$;

Note that Equation 5.15 shows a general case for smoothing the learned drug-specific and target-specific latent vectors. In the experiments, K_2 is empirically set to 5 to simplify the model.

5.4 EXPERIMENTAL RESULTS

Extensive experiments on the benchmark data sets have been performed to evaluate the performances of different DTI prediction methods.

5.4.1 Experimental Settings

The performances of DTI prediction algorithms are evaluated on four benchmark data sets, including Nuclear Receptors, G-Protein Coupled Receptors (GPCR), Ion Channels, and Enzymes. These data sets are originally provided by Yamanishi et al. [38] and are publicly available at http://web.kuicr.kyoto-u.ac.jp/supp/yoshi/drugtarget/. Table 5.1 summarizes the statistics of all four data sets. Each data set contains three types of information: (1) observed DTIs, (2) drug similarities, and (3) target similarities. Particularly, the observed DTIs are retrieved from public databases KEGG BRITE [39], BRENDA [40], SuperTarget [6], and DrugBank [4]. The drug similarities are computed based on the chemical structures of the compounds derived from the DRUG and COMPOUND sections in the KEGG LIGAND database [39]. For a pair of compounds, the similarity between their chemical structures is measured by the SIMCOMP algorithm [41]. The target similarities, on the other hand, are calculated based on the amino acid sequences of target proteins retrieved from the KEGG GENES database [39]. The sequence similarity between two proteins is computed by using the normalized Smith–Waterman score.

The cross-validation is adopted to evaluate the performances of DTI prediction methods. For NRLMF and other competing methods, 10-fold cross-validation is performed for five times, each with a different random seed. Following previous studies [14,15,19], the widely adopted measures (i.e., the AUC and the AUPR) are used as the evaluation metrics. In particular, an AUC score in each repetition of cross-validation is calculated, and a final AUC score that is the average over the five repetitions is reported. The AUPR is calculated using the same strategy.

The DTI matrix $Y \in R^{m \times n}$ had m rows for drugs and n columns for targets. We conducted CV under three different settings as follows [19,42]:

CVS1: CV on drug-target pairs—random entries in Y (i.e., drug-target pairs) are selected for testing.

CVS2: CV on drugs—random rows in Y (i.e., drugs) are blinded for testing.

CVS3: CV on targets—random columns in Y (i.e., targets) are blinded for testing.

These three settings CVS1, CVS2, and CVS3 refer to the DTI prediction for (1) new (unknown) interactions, (2) new drugs, and (3) new targets, respectively. In this chapter, the proposed NRLMF model is compared with the following DTI prediction methods, namely, NetLapRLS [12], KBMF2K [17], BLM-NII [15], WNN-GIP [14], and CMF [19], by testing their prediction capabilities under the above three settings.

TABLE 5.1   The Statistics of the Drug–Target Interaction Data Sets

Data set	# Drugs	# Targets	# Interactions
Nuclear Receptor	54	26	90
GPCR	223	95	635
Ion Channel	210	204	1476
Enzyme	445	664	2926

In the matrix factorization-based methods (i.e., KBMF2K, CMF, and NRLMF), the dimensionality of the latent space r is selected from $\{50, 100\}$ [19]. For NRLMF, λ_d is set to be the same with λ_t, and these two parameters are chosen from $\{2^{-5}, 2^{-4}, \cdots, 2^1\}$ (see Equation 5.7). The neighborhood regularization parameters α and β of NRLMF are selected from $\{2^{-5}, 2^{-4}, \cdots, 2^2\}$ and $\{2^{-5}, 2^{-4}, \cdots, 2^0\}$, respectively (see Equation 5.12), and the optimal learning rate γ is selected from $\{2^{-3}, 2^{-2}, \cdots, 2^0\}$ (see Algorithm 5.1). The parameters of the remaining methods (i.e., NetLapRLS, KBMF2K, BLM-NII, WNN-GIP, and CMF) are specified following the corresponding references. For each CV setting, the best AUC and the corresponding AUPR values of each method, obtained by different parameter combinations, are reported.

5.4.2 Performance Comparison

Table 5.2 shows the AUC and AUPR values obtained by various methods under the cross-validation setting CVS1. As shown in Table 5.2, NRLMF attains the best AUC values over all data sets. The final average AUC obtained by NRLMF is 0.974, which is 2.10% better than the second method BLM-NII. Moreover, NRLMF achieves the highest AUPR over three data sets (i.e., Nuclear Receptor, GPCR, and Enzyme) and obtains the second best AUPR on the Ion Channel data set, where CMF outperforms NRLMF (0.923 for CMF vs. 0.906 for NRLMF). The average AUPR obtained by NRLMF is 0.819, which is 4.73% higher than that obtained by the second best method CMF. In summary, under the cross-validation setting CVS1, NRLMF outperforms other competing methods, being statistically significant except two comparison cases with CMF at the significant level of 0.05 using t-test.

The results obtained under the setting CVS2 for new drugs are shown in Table 5.3. In particular, NRLMF outperforms the other methods over the Nuclear Receptor, GPCR, and Ion Channel data sets in terms of AUC. On the Enzyme data set, WNN-GIP

TABLE 5.2   The AUC and AUPR Obtained Under Cross-Validation Setting CVS1

	AUC			
	Nuclear Receptor	GPCR	Ion Channel	Enzyme
NetLapRLS	0.850±0.021*	0.915±0.006*	0.969±0.003*	0.972±0.002*
BLM-NII	<u>0.905</u>±0.023*	<u>0.950</u>±0.006*	<u>0.981</u>±0.002*	<u>0.978</u>±0.002*
WNN-GIP	0.901±0.017*	0.944±0.005*	0.959±0.003*	0.964±0.003*
KBMF2K	0.877±0.023*	0.926±0.006*	0.961±0.003*	0.905±0.003*
CMF	0.864±0.026*	0.940±0.007*	0.981±0.002*	0.969±0.002*
NRLMF	**0.950**±0.011	**0.969**±0.004	**0.989**±0.001	**0.987**±0.001
	AUPR			
	Nuclear Receptor	GPCR	Ion Channel	Enzyme
NetLapRLS	0.465±0.044*	0.616±0.015*	0.837±0.009*	0.789±0.005*
BLM-NII	<u>0.659</u>±0.039*	0.524±0.024*	0.821±0.012*	0.752±0.011*
WNN-GIP	0.589±0.034*	0.520±0.021*	0.717±0.020*	0.706±0.017*
KBMF2K	0.534±0.050*	0.578±0.018*	0.771±0.009*	0.654±0.008*
CMF	0.584±0.042*	<u>0.745</u>±0.013	**0.923**±0.006	<u>0.877</u>±0.005*
NRLMF	**0.728**±0.041	**0.749**±0.015	<u>0.906</u>±0.008	**0.892**±0.006

Note: In each column, the best results are in boldface and the second best results are underlined. The symbol * indicates NRLMF significantly outperforms the competitor with $p < 0.05$ using T-test.

TABLE 5.3   The AUC and AUPR Obtained Under Cross-Validation Setting CVS2

	AUU			
	Nuclear Receptor	**GPCR**	**Ion Channel**	**Enzyme**
NetLapRLS	0.789±0.039*	0.817±0.015*	0.757±0.025*	0.786±0.023*
BLM-NII	0.799±0.037*	0.838±0.016*	0.796±0.025	0.813±0.022*
WNN-GIP	<u>0.890</u>±0.023	<u>0.891</u>±0.010	0.797±0.028	**0.882**±0.015
KBMF2K	0.844±0.023*	0.839±0.020*	<u>0.799</u>±0.019	0.713±0.029*
CMF	0.818±0.036*	0.857±0.014*	0.743±0.029*	0.829±0.019*
NRLMF	**0.900**±0.021	**0.895**±0.011	**0.813**±0.027	<u>0.871</u>±0.017
	AUPR			
	Nuclear Receptor	**GPCR**	**Ion Channel**	**Enzyme**
NetLapRLS	0.417±0.048*	0.229±0.017*	0.200±0.026*	0.123±0.009*
BLM-NII	0.438±0.048*	0.315±0.022*	0.302±0.033	0.253±0.023*
WNN-GIP	<u>0.504</u>±0.056	0.295±0.025*	0.258±0.032*	<u>0.278</u>±0.037*
KBMF2K	0.477±0.049	**0.366**±0.024	<u>0.308</u>±0.038	0.263±0.033*
CMF	0.488±0.050	<u>0.365</u>±0.022	0.286±0.030*	0.229±0.020*
NRLMF	**0.545**±0.054	0.364±0.023	**0.344**±0.033	**0.358**±0.040

Note: In each column, the best results are in boldface and the second best results are underlined. The symbol * indicates NRLMF significantly outperforms the competitor with $p < 0.05$ using T-test.

achieves a little better AUC than NRLMF (0.882 for WNN-GIP vs. 0.871 for NRLMF). Over all data sets, NRLMF obtains the best average AUC value 0.870. For the AUPR metric, NRLMF achieves the best results on all data sets except the GPCR data set, where KBMF2K and CMF are slightly better than NRLMF. Overall, NRLMF achieves the best average AUPR 0.403, which is 13.84% higher than the second best method KBMF2K and 17.84% higher than the third best method CMF.

Furthermore, Table 5.4 summarizes the results obtained under the setting CVS3 for new targets. It is observed that WNN-GIP outperforms other methods on the Nuclear Receptor data set in terms of AUC and AUPR. On the other three data sets, the proposed NRLMF achieves the best AUC and AUPR values. Over all data sets, WNN-GIP achieves the highest average AUC value 0.940, which is 1.29% better than the second best method NRLMF. For AUPR, NRLMF achieves the best average AUPR 0.651, which is a 11.09% better than the second best method WNN-GIP.

The task under the setting CVS1 focuses on predicting the unknown pair (d_i, t_j), where at least one DTI is known for d_i and t_j, respectively, in the training data. However, the tasks under CVS2 and CVS3 focus on the predictions for new drugs and new targets, respectively, where no DTIs are observed for new drugs and new targets in the training data. Therefore, the task under CVS1 is easier than those under CVS2 and CVS3, and the AUC and AUPR values obtained by DTI prediction methods under CVS1 are higher than those obtained under CVS2 and CVS3 as expected. For all CV settings, the proposed NRLMF method achieves the best AUC values in 10 out of 12 scenarios (i.e., three CV settings on four data sets) by integrating LMF with neighborhood regularization. In the remaining two scenarios (i.e., CVS2 on Enzyme data set and CVS3 on Nuclear Receptor data set), WNN-GIP attains better AUC values than NRLMF.

TABLE 5.4 The AUC and AUPR Obtained Under Cross-Validation Setting CVS3

	AUC			
	Nuclear Receptor	**GPCR**	**Ion Channel**	**Enzyme**
NetLapRLS	0.655±0.046*	0.770±0.024*	0.914±0.012*	0.905±0.014*
BLM-NII	0.534±0.086*	0.778±0.025*	0.914±0.012*	0.909±0.014*
WNN-GIP	**0.935**±0.017	0.926±0.013	0.950±0.007*	0.947±0.008*
KBMF2K	0.668±0.060*	0.882±0.016*	0.938±0.008*	0.876±0.012*
CMF	0.680±0.066*	0.837±0.019*	0.905±0.012*	0.915±0.013*
NRLMF	0.851±0.027	**0.930**±0.012	**0.964**±0.007	**0.966**±0.005
	AUPR			
	Nuclear Receptor	**GPCR**	**Ion Channel**	**Enzyme**
NetLapRLS	0.449±0.074	0.334±0.025*	0.737±0.020*	0.669±0.021*
BLM-NII	0.402±0.083	0.341±0.034*	0.762±0.020	0.735±0.022*
WNN-GIP	**0.531**±0.073	0.550±0.047	0.696±0.035*	0.566±0.038*
KBMF2K	0.324±0.071	0.516±0.045	0.677±0.021*	0.565±0.023*
CMF	0.400±0.077	0.433±0.028*	0.620±0.027*	0.698±0.021*
NRLMF	0.449±0.079	**0.556**±0.038	**0.785**±0.028	**0.812**±0.018

Note: In each column, the best results are in boldface and the second best results are underlined. The symbol * indicates NRLMF significantly outperforms the competitor with $p < 0.05$ using T-test.

The results in these two scenarios can be interpreted as follows. For instance, under CVS2, the interactions for 10% of the drugs (i.e., the set of negative drugs D^-) have been blinded in the training phase. The latent vectors of D^- are learned solely based on negative observations and thus are not accurate. This may lead to the inaccuracies of the learned latent vectors of targets (see Equation 5.13). Especially, for the targets with only one interaction, the accuracies of the learned latent vectors may be drastically reduced. In NRLMF, the latent vectors of negative drugs and targets are smoothed using their nearest neighbors. However, there is no smoothing for the latent vectors of targets with only one interaction (see Equation 5.15). As such, the performances of NRLMF under CVS2 may be affected more on the data set with a higher percentage of targets that have only one interaction. Interestingly, over four data sets, the percentage of targets that have only one interaction is 30.77%, 35.79%, 11.27%, and 43.37%, for Nuclear Receptor, GPCR, Ion Channel, and Enzyme, respectively. Enzyme data set has the highest percentage of targets with only one interaction, and thus the performance of NRLMF on this data set under CVS2 is likely to be affected most. Similarly, the percentage of drugs with only one interaction is 72.22% for Nuclear Receptor, 47.53% for GPCR, 38.57% for Ion Channel, and 39.78% for Enzyme data sets. Thus, by blinding the interactions of 10% targets (i.e., under CVS3), the performance of NRLMF on Nuclear Receptor data set is the most likely to be affected. For the AUPR metric, NRLMF attains the best AUPR values in 9 out of 12 scenarios, which is generally expected, since the methods that optimize AUC are not guaranteed to optimize AUPR [43]. In addition, the target sequence similarity S^t is more reliable and informative than the drug chemical similarity S^d [13]. Hence, the information propagated from the neighbors to the new targets by the regularization term in Equation 5.11 will be more accurate than those to new drugs by the term in Equation 5.10. This explains the results well that various methods usually achieve higher AUC and AUPR under CVS3 than under CVS2.

5.4.3 Neighborhood Benefits

The NRLMF model incorporates neighborhood information for DTI prediction through the neighborhood regularization in training and the neighborhood smoothing in prediction. This section discusses how the neighborhood information benefits DTI prediction under cross-validation setting CVS1.

Figure 5.2a shows the AUC values obtained by NRLMF with respect to different settings of the neighborhood size K_1 used for the neighborhood regularization in the training procedure. As shown in Figure 5.2a, the optimal values of K_1 are 3, 5, 5, and 5, for four data sets, respectively. Under the setting CVS1, the average AUC of NRLMF is 0.958 when K_1 is set as 0 (i.e., without neighborhood regularization in training), while it is increased to 0.974 when K_1 is set as 5. Figure 5.2b illustrates the AUPR values with respect to different settings of K_1. It is observed that NRLMF achieves the best AUPR by setting K_1 as 7, 7, 9, and 3, respectively. When $K_1 = 0$, the average AUPR achieved by NRLMF without neighborhood regularization is 0.772, while it is increased to 0.818 by setting $K_1 = 5$. These results highlight that the neighborhood regularization is highly desirable for DTI prediction.

Furthermore, this section also discusses the impact of the neighborhood size K_2 used for neighborhood smoothing in the prediction procedure. Figure 5.3a and b plot the AUC and AUPR values obtained by NRLMF with respect to different settings of K_2. As shown in Figure 5.3a, NRLMF achieves best AUC via setting K_2 as 5, 3, 5, and 5, respectively. For AUPR measure, the best results are achieved by setting K_2 as 5, 3, 9, and 5, respectively. Over all data sets, when $K_2 = 0$ (i.e., without neighborhood smoothing in prediction), the average AUC and AUPR values obtained by NRLMF are 0.950 and 0.772, respectively, while these values are 0.974 and 0.819 when $K_2 = 5$. These observations demonstrate the effectiveness of using nearest neighbors to predict the interaction probability for a given drug-target pair. In addition, when K_1 and K_2 are set at 5, NRLMF can get reasonably good results for both AUC and AUPR, respectively.

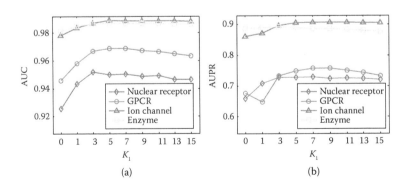

FIGURE 5.2 Performance trend of NRLMF measured by (a) AUC and (b) AUPR with different settings of K_1 under cross-validation setting CVS1.

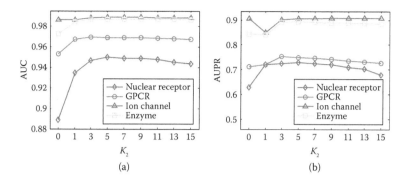

FIGURE 5.3   Performance trend of NRLMF measured by (a) AUC and (b) AUPR with different settings of K_2 under cross-validation setting CVS1.

5.4.4 Parameter Sensitivity Analysis

This section focuses on the sensitivity analysis for other two parameters, that is, the importance levels of observed DTIs c and the dimensionality of the latent space r, under the setting CVS1.

As shown in Figure 5.4a, when the importance level c is set as 1, NRLMF achieves the lowest AUC on all the data sets, and it is able to achieve the optimal AUC over all data sets with $c = 5$. Similarly, Figure 5.4b shows that NRLMF achieves better AUPR under the setting $c > 1$ than under the setting $c = 1$, on the GPCR, Ion Channel, and Enzyme data sets. On the Nuclear Receptor data set, NRLMF attains slightly better AUPR under the setting $c = 1$ than under the other settings. These observations demonstrate that assigning more importance to the observed interactions can boost the performance of NRLMF. However, when c is large enough, the performance of NRLMF tends to become saturated, where further increasing c has very limited improvement.

The impact of the dimensionality of the latent space r on the performance of NRLMF in terms of AUC and AUPR is shown in Figure 5.5a and b, respectively. It is found that larger r generally achieves better results. The two exceptions are the AUPR measure on Nuclear Receptor and Ion Channel data sets, where $r = 30$ leads to slightly better results than $r = 50$. Nevertheless, $r = 100$ achieves the best results or the second best results measured by AUC

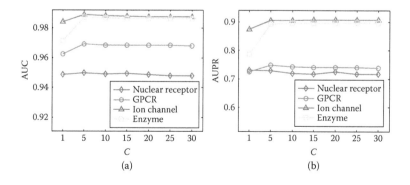

FIGURE 5.4   Performance trend of NRLMF measured by (a) AUC and (b) AUPR with different settings of c under cross-validation setting CVS1.

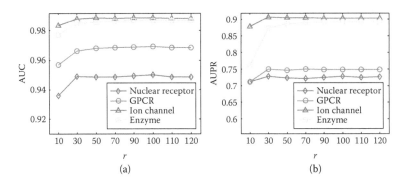

FIGURE 5.5 Performance trend of NRLMF measured by (a) AUC and (b) AUPR with different settings of r under cross-validation setting CVS1.

and AUPR on all data sets. Thus, the parameter r is recommended to be set in the range (50, 100), which is consistent with previous studies [19].

5.4.5 Predicting Novel Interactions

This section evaluates the practical ability of NRLMF on recommending novel interactions, which refer to interactions with high probabilities that do not occur in the benchmark data sets. Following similar settings in previous studies [11,13,17], four well-known biological databases, ChEMBL [3], Drug- Bank [24], KEGG [5], and Matador [6], are used as reference to verify whether the suggested new DTIs are true or not.

To conduct this study, the online profiles associated with the drugs and targets in each benchmark data set are crawled from the online reference databases, and the approved DTIs are collected. Over all benchmark data sets, there are 791 drugs and 986 targets, and 1999 novel interactions have been confirmed in one or more reference databases. The number of confirmed novel interactions in Nuclear Receptor, GPCR, Ion Channel, and Enzyme data sets is 21, 512, 1034, and 432, respectively. For each data set, the entire data set is used as a training set. The unknown interactions will be ranked based on the interaction probabilities predicted using the optimal parameters learned under cross-validation setting CVS1 instead of those learned under other two settings (i.e., CVS2 and CVS3). This is because that the objective is to suggest those novel likely DTIs, instead of focusing on a new drug or a new target. Then, the recommended novel interactions are the top-ranked unknown DTI pairs.

Table 5.5 summarizes the fractions of true DTIs among the top N (N = 10, 30, 50) predictions generated by various DTI methods using the optimal parameters learned under the cross-validation setting CVS1. It is observed that NRLMF is capable of achieving consistently accurate prediction results across all the data sets. For example, the fractions of true DTIs among the top 10 predicted interactions are 50%, 60%, 50%, and 90% for all data sets, respectively. Compared with other methods, NRLMF is capable of achieving comparable or even better prediction results across all the data sets. These observations indicate that the proposed algorithm is very effective for finding novel DTIs; thus, it may help biologists or clinicians significantly to reduce the cost of biological tests.

TABLE 5.5   The Fractions of True DTIs among the Predicted Top-N (N = 10, 30, 50) Interactions Under Cross-Validation Setting CVS1

Data set	Method	Top 10	Top 30	Top 50
	NetLapRLS	10%	23%	26%
	BLM-NII	30%	27%	16%
Nuclear Receptor	WNN-GIP	0%	20%	14%
	KBMF2K	40%	30%	22%
	CMF	10%	20%	24%
	NRLMF	50%	43%	28%
	NetLapRLS	40%	40%	46%
	BLM-NII	70%	60%	58%
GPCR	WNN-GIP	30%	43%	38%
	KBMF2K	90%	53%	52%
	CMF	50%	40%	36%
	NRLMF	60%	67%	60%
	NetLapRLS	60%	47%	38%
	BLM-NII	30%	30%	34%
Ion Channel	WNN-GIP	30%	43%	48%
	KBMF2K	100%	83%	84%
	CMF	0%	0%	6%
	NRLMF	50%	33%	34%
	NetLapRLS	70%	50%	40%
	BLM-NII	70%	60%	46%
Enzyme	WNN-GIP KBMF2K	70%	50%	40%
	CMF	20%	7%	4%
	NRLMF	90%	60%	44%

5.5 CONCLUSIONS

This chapter introduces a computational approach, namely, NRLMF, to predicting potential interactions between drugs and targets. The novelty of NRLMF comes from integrating logistic matrix factorization with neighborhood regularization to predict the interaction probability of a given drug-target pair. Specifically, both drugs and targets are mapped into a shared latent space, and the DTIs are modeled using the linear combinations of the drug-specific and target-specific latent vectors. In addition, higher importance level is assigned to positive observations (i.e., interaction pairs), while lower importance level is for negative observations (i.e., unknown pairs). Moreover, the neighborhood regularization based on the drug similarities and target similarities is utilized to further improve the prediction ability of the model.

To evaluate the performance of NRLMF, an extensive set of experiments was performed on four benchmark data sets, compared with five state-of-the-art DTI prediction methods. The promising results further validated the empirical efficacy of the proposed algorithm. For example, on average, NRLMF attains the best AUC values under CVS1 and CVS2, and the second best AUC value under CVS3. In terms of AUPR, NRLMF achieves the best averaged AUPR values over all data sets under all three CV settings. These results indicate that NRLMF outperforms the existing state-of-the-art methods in predicting new pairs and new drugs and is comparable or even better than existing methods in predicting new targets. However, on the data set with a large fraction of drugs that have only one interaction (e.g., 72.22% on the Nuclear Receptor data set), WNN-GIP may outperform NRLMF in predicting new targets. On the data set with a large fraction of targets that have only one interaction (e.g., 43.37% on the Enzyme data set), WNN-GIP may achieve better results than NRLMF in predicting new drugs. In addition, the high practical prediction ability of NRLMF has also been verified. For example, on the Enzyme data set, 90% of the top 10 novel DTIs predicted by NRLMF have been confirmed by the latest version of four well-known biological databases, including ChEMBL, DrugBank, KEGG, and Matador.

The optimization problem of NRLMF is solved using an alternating gradient descent optimization algorithm, the time complexity of which is $O(iter \cdot r \cdot m \cdot n)$, where $iter$ denotes the number of iterations. However, the time complexity of the solutions to the other two matrix factorization-based DTI prediction methods (i.e., KBMF2K and CMF) is $O(iter \cdot (r \cdot m^3 + r \cdot n^3 + r^3))$ and $O(iter \cdot (r^2 \cdot (m + n)^2 + r^3 \cdot (m + n)))$, respectively. Therefore, NRLMF is more efficient than KBMF2K and CMF.

In this chapter, the DTI prediction approach, that is, NRMF, only considers one type of similarity from drugs and targets. The drug similarities are calculated based on the chemical structures of compounds, and the target similarities are computed based on the amino acid sequences of the target proteins. However, there are various types of side information associated with drugs and targets. Thus, multiple types of drug similarities and target similarities can be computed, for example, the chemical structure similarity and ATC similarity for drugs and the genomic sequence similarity, protein-protein interaction network similarity, and gene ontology similarities for targets. Previous work [19] has also demonstrated that the DTI prediction accuracy can be significantly improved by considering multiple types of similarities defined based on different kinds of side information. As a part of future work, NRLMF will be extended to exploit multiple kinds of similarities via coupling the logistic matrix factorization technique with the multiple kernel learning technique [44]. Moreover, the DTI prediction is indeed a top-N recommendation problem, which can be solved by the ranking-based matrix factorization models. Another potential direction for future work is to utilize ensemble matrix factorization models, for example, the AdaBPR model in [45], which aims to directly optimize the ranking metrics for improving the prediction accuracy. Furthermore, we can also extend existing DTI prediction methods to the distributed computing platforms [46,47] to perform DTI prediction on large-scale biological data sets.

REFERENCES

1. H. Ding, I. Takigawa, H. Mamitsuka, and S. Zhu, 2014, Similarity-based machine learning methods for predicting drug–target interactions: A brief review, *Briefings in Bioinformatics*, vol. 15, no. 5, pp. 734–747.
2. Y.-F. Dai and X.-M. Zhao, 2015, A survey on the computational approaches to identify drug targets in the postgenomic era, *BioMed Research International*, vol. 2015, p. 9.

3. A. Gaulton, L. J. Bellis, A. P. Bento, J. Chambers, M. Davies, A. Hersey, Y. Light, S. McGlinchey, D. Michalovich, B. Al-Lazikani, and J. P. Overington, 2012, Chembl: A large-scale bioactivity database for drug discovery, *Nucleic Acids Research*, vol. 40, no. D1, pp. D1100–D1107.
4. D. S. Wishart, C. Knox, A. C. Guo, D. Cheng, S. Shrivastava, D. Tzur, B. Gautam, and M. Hassanali, 2008, Drugbank: A knowledgebase for drugs, drug actions and drug targets, *Nucleic Acids Research*, vol. 36, no. suppl 1, pp. D901–D906.
5. M. Kanehisa, S. Goto, Y. Sato, M. Furumichi, and M. Tanabe, 2012, Kegg for integration and interpretation of large-scale molecular data sets, *Nucleic Acids Research*, vol. 40, no. gkr988, pp. D109–D114.
6. S. Günther, M. Kuhn, M. Dunkel, M. Campillos, C. Senger, E. Petsalaki, J. Ahmed, et al., 2008, Supertarget and matador: Resources for exploring drug-target relationships, *Nucleic Acids Research*, vol. 36, no. suppl 1, pp. D919–D922.
7. S. L. Kinnings, N. Liu, N. Buchmeier, P. J. Tonge, L. Xie, and P. E. Bourne, 2009, Drug discovery using chemical systems biology: Repositioning the safe medicine comtan to treat multi-drug and extensively drug resistant tuberculosis, *PLoS Computational Biology*, vol. 5, no. 7, p. e1000423.
8. Y. Y. Li, J. An, and S. J. M. Jones, 2011, A computational approach to finding novel targets for existing drugs, *PLoS Computational Biology*, vol. 7, no. 9, pp. e1002139–e1002139.
9. K. Wang, J. Sun, S. Zhou, C. Wan, S. Qin, C. Li, L. He, and L. Yang, 2013, Prediction of drug-target interactions for drug repositioning only based on genomic expression similarity, *PLoS Computational Biology,* vol. 9, no. 11, p. e1003315.
10. N. Nagamine and Y. Sakakibara, 2007, Statistical prediction of protein–chemical interactions based on chemical structure and mass spectrometry data, *Bioinformatics,* vol. 23, no. 15, pp. 2004–2012.
11. K. Bleakley and Y. Yamanishi, 2009, Supervised prediction of drug–target interactions using bipartite local models, *Bioinformatics,* vol. 25, no. 18, pp. 2397–2403.
12. Z. Xia, L.-Y. Wu, X. Zhou, and S. T. C. Wong, 2010, Semi-supervised drug-protein interaction prediction from heterogeneous biological spaces, *BMC Systems Biology*, vol. 4, no. suppl 2, p. S6.
13. T. V. Laarhoven, S. B. Nabuurs, and E. Marchiori, 2011, Gaussian interaction profile kernels for predicting drug–target interaction, *Bioinformatics*, vol. 27, no. 21, pp. 3036–3043.
14. T. V. Laarhoven and E. Marchiori, 2013, Predicting drug-target interactions for new drug compounds using a weighted nearest neighbor profile, *PLoS One*, vol. 8, no. 6, p. e66952.
15. J.-P. Mei, C.-K. Kwoh, P. Yang, X.-L. Li, and J. Zheng, 2013, Drug–target interaction prediction by learning from local information and neighbors, *Bioinformatics*, vol. 29, no. 2, pp. 238–245.
16. Y. Yamanishi, M. Kotera, Y. Moriya, R. Sawada, M. Kanehisa, and S. Goto, 2014, Dinies: Drug–target interaction network inference engine based on supervised analysis, *Nucleic Acids Research*, vol. 42(W1), pp. W39–W45.
17. M. Gönen, 2012, Predicting drug–target interactions from chemical and genomic kernels using Bayesian matrix factorization, *Bioinformatics*, vol. 28, no. 18, pp. 2304–2310.
18. M. C. Cobanoglu, C. Liu, F. Hu, Z. N. Oltvai, and I. Bahar, 2013, Predicting drug–target interactions using probabilistic matrix factorization, *Journal of Chemical Information and Modeling*, vol. 53, no. 12, pp. 3399–3409.
19. X. Zheng, H. Ding, H. Mamitsuka, and S. Zhu, 2013, Collaborative matrix factorization with multiple similarities for predicting drug-target interactions, *Proceedings of the 19th ACM SIGKDD International Conference on Knowledge Discovery and Data Mining*, August 11–14, 2013, Chicago, IL, pp. 1025–1033.
20. H. Lim, A. Poleksic, Y. Yao, H. Tong, D. He, L. Zhuang, P. Meng, and L. Xie, 2016, Large-scale off-target identification using fast and accurate dual regularized one-class collaborative filtering and its application to drug repurposing, *PLoS Computational Biology*, vol. 12, no. 10, p. e1005135.

21. Y. Liu, M. Wu, C. Miao, P. Zhao, and X.-L. Li, 2016, Neighborhood regularized logistic matrix factorization for drug-target interaction prediction, *PLoS Computational Biology*, vol. 12, no. 2, p. e1004760.
22. M. Gönen and S. Kaski, 2014, Kernelized Bayesian matrix factorization, *IEEE Transactions on Pattern Analysis and Machine Intelligence*, vol. 36, no. 10, pp. 2047–2060.
23. L. Jacob and J.-P. Vert, 2008, Protein-ligand interaction prediction: An improved chemogenomics approach, *Bioinformatics*, vol. 24, no. 19, pp. 2149–2156.
24. C. Knox, V. Law, T. Jewison, P. Liu, S. Ly, A. Frol-kis, A. Pon, et al., 2011, Drug-bank 3.0: A comprehensive resource for 'omics' research on drugs, *Nucleic Acids Research*, vol. 39(suppl 1), pp. D1035–D1041.
25. F. Cheng, C. Liu, J. Jiang, W. Lu, W. Li, G. Liu, W. Zhou, J. Huang, and Y. Tang, 2012, Prediction of drug-target interactions and drug repositioning via network-based inference, *PLoS Computational Biology*, vol. 8, no. 5, p. e1002503.
26. Q. Yuan, J. Gao, D. Wu, S. Zhang, H. Mamitsuka, and S. Zhu, 2016, DrugE-rank: Improving drug–target interaction prediction of new candidate drugs or targets by ensemble learning to rank, *Bioinformatics*, vol. 32, no. 12, pp. i18–i27.
27. B. Chen, Y. Ding, and D. J. Wild, 2012, Assessing drug target association using semantic linked data, *PLoS Computational Biology*, vol. 8, no. 7, p. e1002574.
28. X. Su and T. M. Khoshgoftaar, 2009, A survey of collaborative filtering techniques, *Advances in Artificial Intelligence*, vol. 2009, p. 4.
29. A. Ezzat, P. Zhao, M. Wu, X. Li, and C. K. Kwoh, 2016, Drug-target interaction prediction with graph regularized matrix factorization, *IEEE/ACM Transactions on Computational Biology and Bioinformatics*, vol. 14(3), pp. 646–656, 2017.
30. Q. Liao, N. Guan, C. Wu, and Q. Zhang, 2016, Predicting unknown interactions between known drugs and targets via matrix completion, *Pacific-Asia Conference on Knowledge Discovery and Data Mining*, April 19–22, 2016, Auckland, New Zealand, pp. 591–604, Springer.
31. C. Lan, S. N. Chandrasekaran, and J. Huan, 2016, A distributed and privatized framework for drug-target interaction prediction, In *IEEE International Conference on Bioinformatics and Biomedicine*, December 15–18, 2016, Shenzhen, China, pp. 731–734.
32. C. C. Johnson, 2014, Logistic matrix factorization for implicit feed-back data, *NIPS 2014 Workshop on Distributed Machine Learning and Matrix Computations*.
33. Y. Hu, Y. Koren, and C. Volinsky, 2008, Collaborative filtering for implicit feedback datasets, *Proceedings of the 8th IEEE International Conference on Data Mining*, December 15–19, 2008, Pisa, Italy, pp. 263–272.
34. Y. Liu, W. Wei, A. Sun, and C. Miao, 2014, Exploiting geographical neighborhood characteristics for location recommendation, *Proceedings of the 23rd ACM International Conference on Information and Knowledge Management*, November 3–7, 2014, Shanghai, China, pp. 739–748.
35. T. Hwang, G. Atluri, M. Xie, S. Dey, C. Hong, V. Kumar, and R. Kuang, 2012, Co-clustering phenome–genome for phenotype classification and disease gene discovery, *Nucleic Acids Research*, vol. 40, no. 19, p. e146.
36. V. Gligorijević, V. Janjić, and N. Pržulj, 2014, Integration of molecular network data reconstructs gene ontology, *Bioinformatics,* vol. 30, no. 17, pp. i594–i600.
37. J. Duchi, E. Hazan, and Y. Singer, 2011, Adaptive subgradient methods for online learning and stochastic optimization, *Journal of Machine Learning Research*, vol. 12, pp. 2121–2159.
38. Y. Yamanishi, M. Araki, A. Gutteridge, W. Honda, and M. Kanehisa, 2008, Prediction of drug–target interaction networks from the integration of chemical and genomic spaces, *Bioinformatics*, vol. 24, no. 13, pp. i232–i240.
39. M. Kanehisa, S. Goto, M. Hattori, K. F. Aoki-Kinoshita, M. Itoh, S. Kawashima, T. Katayama, M. Araki, and M. Hirakawa, 2016, From genomics to chemical genomics: New developments in keg, *Nucleic Acids Research*, vol. 34, no. suppl 1, pp. D354–D357.

40. I. Schomburg, A. Chang, C. Ebeling, M. Gremse, C. Heldt, G. Huhn, and D. Schomburg, 2004, Brenda, the enzyme database: Updates and major new developments, *Nucleic Acids Research*, vol. 32, no. suppl 1, pp. D431–D433.

41. M. Hattori, Y. Okuno, S. Goto, and M. Kanehisa, 2003, Development of a chemical structure comparison method for integrated analysis of chemical and genomic information in the metabolic pathways, *Journal of the American Chemical Society*, vol. 125, no. 39, pp. 11853–11865.

42. T. Pahikkala, A. Airola, S. Pietilä, S. Shakyawar, A. Szwajda, J. Tang, and T. Aittokallio, 2015, Toward more realistic drug–target interaction predictions, *Briefings in Bioinformatics*, vol. 16, pp. 325–337.

43. J. Davis and M. Goadrich, 2006, The relationship between precision-recall and roc curves, *Proceedings of the 23rd International Conference on Machine Learning*, June 25–29, 2006, Pittsburgh, PA, pp. 233–240.

44. M. Gönen and E. Alpaydjn, 2011, Multiple kernel learning algorithms, *Journal of Machine Learning Research*, vol. 12, pp. 2211–2268.

45. Y. Liu, P. Zhao, A. Sun, and C. Miao, 2015, A boosting algorithm for item recommendation with implicit feedback, *Proceedings of the 24th International Conference on Artificial Intelligence*, July 28–August 1, 2015, Buenos Aires, Argentina, pp. 1792–1798.

46. C. Wang, X. Li, P. Chen, A. Wang, X. Zhou, and H. Yu, 2015, Heterogeneous cloud framework for big data genome sequencing, *IEEE/ACM Transactions on Computational Biology and Bioinformatics*, vol. 12, no. 1, pp. 166–178.

47. C. Wang, D. Dai, X. Li, A. Wang, and X. Zhou, 2016, Accelerating computation of large biological datasets using MapReduce framework, *IEEE/ACM Transactions on Computational Biology and Bioinformatics*, DOI: 10.1109/TCBB.2016.2550430.

CHAPTER 6

Overview of Neural Network Accelerators

Yuntao Lu, Chao Wang, Lei Gong, Xi Li,
Aili Wang, and Xuehai Zhou

University of Science and Technology of China

Hefei, China

CONTENTS

6.1 INTRODUCTION

In heterogeneous computer systems, features of neural networks applications, which are iterating rapidly and utilizing more and more hardware resources, brings serious challenges to construct the architecture and design the middleware and programming models. Recently, international researchers have focused on some aspects: ASIC heterogeneous deep learning accelerators, GPU neural network accelerators, FPGA heterogeneous neural network accelerators, modern storage accelerators, and parallel programming models and the middleware facing neural networks.

6.2 ARCHITECTURES OF HARDWARE ACCELERATORS

6.2.1 The ASIC Heterogeneous Accelerators of Deep Learning

As deep learning and neural networks have developed, smart chips and ASIC accelerators have become the hotspot of the computer architecture domain. The representative research contains a series of related works including DianNao [1], DaDianNao [2], and PuDianNao [3], and Cambricon which were proposed by the Institute of Computing Technology, Chinese Academy of Science, develop heterogeneous of machine learning and neural networks, and Nervana and other artificial intelligent specialized chips. Otherwise, several ASIC neural networks accelerators have emerged in international conferences such as International Symposium on Computer Architecture (ISCA), Annual IEEE/ACM International Symposium on Microarchitecture (MICRO), and so on. For example, Cnvlutin [4] proposed a deep neural network accelerator that eliminates ineffective neurons. Where the number of parameters is redundant for representing functions, neural networks have high sparsity. Cnvlutin proposed a method to eliminate ineffective neurons to design a neural networks accelerator, according to the value of operators. Instead of aiming at control flow, Cnvlutin separates and recombines instructions that contain zero operators from the rest of instructions, so as to decrease the usage of computing resources and accelerate memory access, optimizing performance and energy. Cambricon proposed a neural network instruction set when face processing neurons and synapses on a large scale; this means that the one instruction can process a group of neurons, and especially, support transfer of neurons and synapses onto the chip. EIE [5] proposed an efficient compressed deep neural network inference engine and compressed convolutional neural network hardware implementations. The cause of the high information redundancy and coefficients of compressed convolutional neural networks can depend totally on static random access memory (SRAM), which greatly decrease most access of dynamic random access memory (DRAM) in traditional convolutional neural network accelerators. Eyeriss [6] proposed a low power data structure for convolutional neural networks, at a high data transfer cost, especially the data transfer cost beyond data computing cost, though the SIMD GPU architecture satisfies the requirement of convolutional neural network massive computing. As a result, Eyeriss made an accelerator using modern data transfer mode Row-Stationary (RS) to replace the accelerator with single instruction multiple data (SIMD) or single instruction multiple threads (SIMT) GPU architecture. Neurocube [7] proposed a programmable neural network accelerator architecture using 3D stacking storage. The accelerator adopts modern 3D stacking storage technology as the basis of memory computing architecture, adds a computing unit at the deep layer of 3D stacking memory (logical layer), and accelerates neural network computing by specific logical modules to eliminate unnecessary data transfer while utilizing large internal memory bandwidth. Minerva [8] is a low power consumption and high accuracy deep neural network accelerators. In this chapter, they proposed an accelerator and optimized flow based on design space exploration, which decreased data complexity and bandwidth by neural networks pruning, and then lowered system power. RedEye [9] proposed an analog convolutional neural network image sensor architecture aiming at mobile vision, using the modularized column paralleling design idea to decrease the complexity of analog design and promote the reuse of physical design and algorithms. These studies fully demonstrate that neural network accelerators have become a hotspot and keystone in the computer architecture domain. A dataflow-based reconfigurable deep convolutional neural network hardware accelerator architecture in Ref. [10] adopts a typical specialized convolutional neural network accelerating engine integrating digital signal processor (DSP) general processors. The accelerator develops the computing parallelism between the accelerating engine and the DSP processor by making use of the accelerating engine to process convolutional operations which occupy the most operations of neural networks, and DSP to process the rest operations in the rectified linear unit (ReLU) function, pooling, and fully connected layers. D. Shin et al. [11] process an energy efficiency reconfigurable general processor for neural networks, which implements two independent architectures for computing and memory bottlenecks, especially for the encoding and decoding of long short term memory (LSTM) networks. The convolutional accelerating module convolution layer processor (CP) and recurrent neural network and long short term memory module full-connceted layer recurrent neural network processor (FRP) using distributed memory to ensure the data requirements of processing elements and computing cores. Aggregation core collects data and communicates with recurrent neural network computing modules. Whatmough et al. [12] designed a chip-based accelerator for sparse neural networks, adopting two measures to optimize the whole system. The first measure uses a number format of the sign magnitude to storage computing parameters, which increases the bit flipping rate of complement representation. The other measure is eliminating zero operators in computing. Price et al. [13] presented a circuit using limited network width and quantified sparse weight matrices for automatic speech recognition and voice activity detection to improve precision, programmability, and scalability. ENVISION [14] is a DVAFS-based adjustable convolutional neural network processor. With the requirements of computing and limited energy of embedded devices, ENVISION expands the dynamic voltage accuracy scalable method to a dynamic voltage accuracy frequency scalable (DVAFS) method, optimizes multipliers, and finally implements frequency adjustments. DVAFS implements the increasing value of all configurable parameters, such as activity, frequency, and voltage. Through high-bit and low-bit multiplication, two 8-bit multiplication can run on a 16-bit array that has a significant improvement throughput and resource utilization in different precision. Bong et al. [15] proposed an always-on, internet-of-things (IoT) application scenario, which uses CIS and convolutional neural networks to realize an system on chip (SoC) of much lower face recognition. According to the energy requirements in variable application scenarios, the architecture is different. The specific chip for IoT deep neural networks features four-level hierarchical cache memory in different types of speed and energy consumption.

Aiming at improving performance, energy efficiency, and taking advantage of FPGAs, we have proposed FPGA-based accelerators for deep learning and Big Data applications. Wang et al. [16] presented a software-defined FPGA-based accelerator named SODA for Big Data. The accelerator could reconstruct and reorganize for various requirements of data-intensive applications by decomposing complex applications into coarse-grained single-purpose RTL code libraries that perform specialized tasks in out-of-order hardware. Due to the layer-wise structure and the data dependency between layers, Zhao et al. [17] proposed a pipeline energy-efficient multi-FPGA–based accelerator PIE, which accelerates operations in deep neural networks by processing two adjacent layers in a pipeline. With the diversity and increasing size of deep learning neural networks for high accuracy, the authors of Refs. 19 and 20 designed accelerator architectures to improve the performance and adapt to the scalability of various neural networks. In Ref. [18], the authors presented a service-oriented deep learning architecture (SOLAR) by various accelerators such as GPU and FPGA-based approaches. In order to facilitate programming, SOLAR provides a uniform programming model that hides hardware design and scheduling. C. Wang et al. [19] present an accelerating unit for large scale deep learning networks based on field programmable gate array (FPGA). To improve the throughput and take full use of data locality for applications, the accelerator uses three pipelined processing units.

6.2.2 GPU Accelerators of Neural Networks

As a result of the fixed circuit, the long design and verification cycles of ASIC, and the high speed of model iterators and optimizations in neural network algorithms and application developing, designing future neural network ASIC specialized chips presents much difficulty and risk. However, heterogeneous GPU accelerators with a short design period and high bandwidth are the widely used solution to build quick prototype systems in the industry. Otherwise, in academia, there exist some neural network accelerators for GPU. For instance, with the research focusing on convolutional neural network computing efficiency, neglecting convolutional neural network internal memory efficiency, Li et al. [20] focus on the memory efficiency of different convolutional neural network layers, and demonstrate the effect of data layout and memory access mode on performance. B. Li et al. [21] proposed a high-efficiency GPU accelerator for large scale recurrent neural networks and demonstrated the scalability of this CPU implementation. Utilizing the potential parallel ability of recurrent neural networks, this work proposed a fine-grained two-stage pipeline. Park et al. [22] suggested that the executing time of processing deep neural networks depends on the number of convolutional operations and aimed to improve the performance of advanced convolution algorithms (Winograd convolutions) on GPU. Generally, convolutional neural networks have many zero weights; the research proposed a low latency and high-efficiency hardware mechanism to pass zero input multiplication and set zero as results of multiplications directly (ZeroSkip). Winograd convolutions with extra data conversions limit performance, but the data reuse optimizing of add operations (AddOpt) improves the utilization of local registers and then decreases the on-chip buffer accesses. The experimental results demonstrate that compared with the nonoptimized method, the method proposed by this work has a 58% improvement in performance. The authors of Ref. [23] compared open-source convolutional neural network GPU-based implementations and analyzed potential bottlenecks of system performance to suggest optimizing methods. The authors of Ref. [24] proposed two scheduling strategies to optimize object detection tasks and improve the system performance. One is to accelerate the convolutional neural network forward process utilizing an efficient image compositional algorithm; the other is a lightweight memory consumption algorithm to make it possible to train a convolutional neural network model of arbitrary size in limited memory conditions. Overall, the heterogeneous accelerating systems based on GPU are relatively mature, which can quickly iterate among GPU boards, neural network topology models, and algorithms.

6.2.3 The FPGA Heterogeneous Accelerators of Neural Networks

The ASIC and the GPU, the FPGA is also an important platform to implement heterogeneous hardware accelerators. Compared to the ASIC and the GPU, the FPGA has higher flexibility and lower energy consumption. Moreover, the current neural networks, such as deep neural networks and recurrent neural networks, have the ability to rapidly evolve. For example, utilizing the sparse methods (i.e., pruning) and simple data types (1–2 bits). However, the innovations of customized data types introduce irregular parallelism, result in hardness for GPU processing, while adapting for the FPGA customizable features.

In recent years, there has been a series of representative heterogeneous FPGA-based accelerators. For instance, ESE [25] proposed an efficient sparse long short term memory neural networks speech recognition engine by FPGA, which optimizes software and hardware simultaneously. The engine not only compresses neural networks into a small size, but also supports compressed deep learning algorithms in hardware. In software, this work comes up with a load-balance–aware pruning algorithm, which solves the load balance problems among different cores when multi-cores process computing in parallel. In hardware, ESE redesigned the hardware architecture supporting multiuser and recurrent neural networks. Nurvitadhi et al. [26] evaluated the difference between performance and power efficiency between the FPGA and the GPU when accelerating next-generation deep neural networks and concluded that the strong computing resources on GPU make it have natural parallelism with regular neural networks. Nevertheless, the pruning and compressing methods cause irregular access of memory and computations in neural networks, which impacts parallel computations of neural networks using GPU. To solve the above problems, the FPGA could use customized methods. With the increasing resources of the next-generation FPGA, the FPGA will become the choice of next-generation deep neural network accelerating platform. Nurvitadhi et al. [27] researched a variant of recurrent neural networks called gated recurrent unit (GRU) and proposed an optimized storage means to avoid partial dense matrix-vector multiplication (SEGMV). In addition, they evaluated implementations of the FPGA, the ASIC, the GPU, and the multicore CPU; the results demonstrated that compared with the other implementations, the FPGA performs with higher energy efficiency. On the one hand, DNNWeaver [28] designed an accelerator for specific models; on the other hand, it implements an auto-generated synthesizable accelerator framework according to the network topology and hardware resources.

From the optimizing perspective, loop unrolling, tiling, and switching or fine-tuning the fixed accelerator architecture and dataflow are general ways to optimize neural networks. Yufei Ma [29] proposed a quantitative multivariable-based analyzing and optimizing method to optimize convolution loops. The hardware accelerator not only searches configurations of design variables, but minimizes the number of memory access and data migration by a certain data flow, otherwise, maximizes the efficiency of hardware efficiency to gain better performance. Similarly, Jialiang Zhang et al. [30] proposed a performance analysis model for deeply analyzing the resource requirements of classification kernels in convolutional neural networks and resources provided from state-of-the-art FPGAs. The critical bottleneck is the memory bandwidth of chips. Therefore, the authors proposed a new core design that efficiently orientates the bandwidth-limited problems to optimally balance the computing, the on-chip memory access, and the off-chip memory access.

All of the above works demonstrate that constructing neural network hardware accelerators adopting the FPGA is feasible, while most of the research is limited by the bandwidth of the FPGA and could not fully solve the problems of optimizing memory access in computing. Hence, researching a computing and storing combination architecture should improve the FPGA hardware access bandwidth.

6.2.4 The Modern Storage Accelerators

In traditional computer systems, we adopt DRAM as a system memory, before processing, programs, and data are loaded into the main memory. Because of the speed of the data scale increasing faster than main memory, the bandwidth of traditional main memory cannot improve simultaneously. The challenge of the "storage wall" will become serious. Moreover, with the rapid development of modern storage technologies (such as 3D stacking technology [31]), researchers find novel materials thare are metal-oxide resistor random access memory (ReRAM), spin transfer torque magneto resistive random access memory (STT-RAM) and phase change memory. The three materials have ability to store data as well as execute operations. Hence, research on new storage neural networks accelerators has become more and more widespread.

PRIME [32] proposed that a neural network memory computer architecture with ReRAM, in the PRIME, partial ReRAM corssbar arrays implement as a neural network accelerator or main memory. Additionally, circuits, structures and software interfaces make the accelerator have abilities of dynamical reconfiguration changing from accelerators to main memory, as well as processing various neural networks. ISAAC [33] proposed a crossbar analog computations accelerators for convolutional neural networks. ISAAC uses eDRAM as a data register between pipeline stages to implement accelerating computing of different layers in neural networks in the way organized in pipelines, and designs analog data encoding types to decrease the overhead of analog-to-digital conversions. Although both PRIME and ISAAC use the ReRAM modern storage to accelerate neural network computing, they only accelerate the testing stage of neural networks; in the meanwhile, the training stage of neural networks adopts traditional methods as before. Therefore, PipeLayer [34] proposed an accelerator with the ReRAM, supporting both the testing stage and the training stage. PipeLayer analyzes the data dependency and weight updating problems in the training stage and designs pipelines to implement parallel computing in layers; moreover, [34] processes layers in parallel, which achieve a highly parallelism of weighs by tuning parallel granularity. Junwhan et al. [35] proposed an extensible accelerator called *Tesseract*, which performs graph data processing concurrently in main memory. It puts the computing unit in the 3D stacking DRAM; each vault of the HMC is responsible for processing different subgraph data, and a message-passing communication mechanism is used between vaults. To improve the utilization of memory bandwidth, Tesseract designed and implemented two prefetching mechanisms suitable to the memory access mode of graph data. Graphicionado [36] proposed a high performance and energy efficiency graph data analyzing accelerator with on-chip embedded DRAM (eDRAM). The accelerator processes graph data into two phases which contain processing and applying phrase implemented by pipelines. Additionally, Graphicionado as far as possible designed the following graph data access mode to decrease the number of random accesses. OSCAR [37] adopted STT-RAM as the last-level cache to relieve cache conflicts in the CPU-GPU heterogeneous architecture. OSCAR integrates the asynchronous batching scheduling mechanism and the priority-based allocation strategy to maximize the potential of STT-RAM based last-level cache. Hamdioui et al. [38] proposed a memristor-based architecture for data dense memory computing, which integrates storage and computing in a crossbar topology structure memristor. Tang et al. [39] proposed a ReRAM-based crossbar accelerator for the forward processing of binary convolutional neural networks. In the ReRAM-based computing system, this work adopts the low bit-level ReRAM and low bit-level analog-to-digital converter (ADC) or digital-to-analog converter (DAC) interfaces to more quickly realize read and write operations and achieve higher energy efficiency. When a crossbar is incapable of storing the total weights in a neural network layer, the accelerator designs a matrix partition type and a pipeline type to implement. RESPARC [40] proposed a memristor-based crossbar accelerator for spiking neural networks, which is reconfigurable and efficient. RESPAEC utilizes a highly energy-efficient crossbar to perform inner products and implements a layered reconfigurable design for spiking neural network (SNN) including a dataflow model; it is more important that for given crossbar technologies, RESPARC can map the topology of spiking neural networks to the most optimal scale crossbars.

All of the aforementioned works are based on modern storage to implement heterogeneous accelerators for typical neural network applications; however, as the restricted capacity of storage structures to employ logic, and methods to integrate current GPUs, FPGAs, and other computing units into an integration framework are still a domain requiring further research.

6.3 PARALLEL PROGRAMMING MODELS AND THE MIDDLEWARE OF NEURAL NETWORKS

Although the heterogeneous hardware accelerators have several advantages of performance, bandwidth, power, and other aspects, they often have problems with difficult programming and need to provide programming models to support development. For machine learning approaches, different kinds of open-source deep-learning frameworks at present are widely used in lots of domain, such as in computer version, speech recognition, natural language processing, and other domains. Recently, there have been mainly common open-source frameworks to processing kinds of neural networks, such as Theano [41], Torch [42], TensorFlow [43], Caffe [44], CNTK [45], Keras [46], SparkNet [47], Deeplearning4J [48], ConvNetJS [49], MxNet [50], Chainer [51], PaddlePaddle [52], DeepCL [53], and PyTorch [54].

Theano [41] is a Python library developed by École Polytechnique de Montréal in 2008. Users could define, optimize, and evaluate mathematical formulas, especially multidimensional arrays. Theano calls for GPU to realize large data problems compared to using C language, and this method can get better accelerating and performance. The subsequent significant open-source frameworks in academia and industry, such as Lasagne [55], Keras, and Blocks [56], were constructed by Theano. Keras is an advanced Python-based neural network library that runs on the TensorFlow or Theano frameworks and rapidly constructs prototype systems. This tool supports convolutional neural networks, recurrent neural networks, and arbitrary connecting strategies running on the CPU and the GPU. Torch is a scientific computing framework, which invokes the GPU first to widely support machine learning algorithms. The framework developed in Lua language is highly recommended by Facebook and Twitter; it can build complex, flexible neural networks and utilize multiple CPUs and GPUs in parallel. TensorFlow is a digital calculating open-source software library employing dataflow graph, which was developed using C++ by Google. Each node and edge in the dataflow graph represents a mathematical operation and a multidimension data between nodes which compose of a tensor, respectively. TensorFlow with its feasible architecture, which can migrate among variable platforms, supports multiple users to utilize different kinds of programming languages, and is continually being developed on distributed platforms, will then be migrated to the Spark platform called *TensorFlow on Spark*. Caffe, developed by Yangqing Jia of the University of California (Berkeley), features modularization to implement base structures and provide python interfaces at the top level. As well, it is flexible to allocate Caffe on clusters or mobile devices, and the distribute projects can be supported by Caffe on Spark. [45] is an open-source deep learning toolkit from Microsoft, which has now changed its name to the *Microsoft Cognitive Toolkit*; The framwork is developed by C++ language and integrates Python interfaces for users. In the CNTK, a directed graph is used to describe a series of operation steps in neural networks. Leaf nodes and the other nodes represent input data or neural networks parameters and matrix operations, respectively. SparkNet developed by AMPLab is a Spark-based framework for training deep neural networks, which contains a convenient interface to read data from Spark resilient distributed dataset (RDD), a Scala interface in the Caffe deep learning framework, and a lightweight multi-dimension tensor library. Deeplearning4J from Skymind Company, the first Java-based commercial open-source distributed deep learning library, integrates Hadoop and Spark and can be used on distributed CPUs and GPUs. The method through Keras interfaces imports neural network models from other deep learning frameworks, including TensorFlow, Caffe, Torch, and Theano. ConvNetJS is a browser plugin developed by Andrej Karpathy at Stanford University, which utilizes JavaScript library to train deep learning models in browsers. ConvNetJS supports general neural network modules, containing classification, logistical regression functions, and other essential structures without GPU participation. MxNet, a lightweight, feasibly distributed, C++-based, and mobile deep learning framework, was developed by researchers on the CXXNet [57], Minerva [8], and Purine2 [58] projects. It is embedded in host languages and integrates symbol representation and tensor computations. For users, the framework supplies automatic division to get gradients. The main features of the framework are computing and memory efficiency, running on variable heterogeneous platforms and even mobile devices. Chainer is a software framework developed by Preferred Networks based on the principle that the definition of neural networks is always dynamical while programs are running. Chainer provides feasible, visualized, and high-performance deep learning models, including models and changeable self-encoders at present. The C++-based PaddlePaddle is a deep learning framework created by Baidu, containing Python interfaces. Users configure a series of parameters to train traditional neural networks or more complex models. In emotion analysis, machine translations, image descriptions, and other domains, the frameworks have the best performance. DeepCL is an OpenCL library developed by Hugh Perkins that is used to train convolution neural networks. The framework supports training models and shared-memory multithread concurrency, adopting dynamic computing graph structure to construct the whole neural network rapidly.

6.4 LATEST DEVELOPMENTS AND CONCLUSIONS

6.4.1 Latest Developments

A survey of international conferences shows that neural networks, especially deep neural networks and recurrent neural networks, tend to rapidly evolve—for instance, their sparsity, simpler data types, and shorter data width make it more efficiency of algorithms. We focus on accelerating methods of deep learning algorithms whose data structures are sparse or compressed, as well as optimized methods of load balance caused by sparsity. Comparing performance and energy efficiency in GPUs and FPGAs, GPUs have significant advantages in processing regular neural networks in parallel, and FPGAs can be customized and reconfigured to process irregular pruned and compressed neural networks. As a result, the FPGA is a candidate for the next-generation deep neural network accelerating platform.

Another candidate for the next-generation deep neural network accelerating platform is specialized neural network chips. Accelerators implemented by specific neural network chips allocate convolutional layers which are computation intensive on accelerating engine, and the others, such as activation layers, pooling layers and full-connected layers on another module (i.e., DSP) to achieve processing computing in parallel. Additionally, we took sparsity and other features into consideration.

6.4.2 Conclusions

Analyzing the ASIC, GPU-based, and FPGA-based hardware neural network accelerators, the research on how to perform neural network applications has become a hot issue in industry and academia, and the related works have concentrated on the domains of optimizing memory access bandwidth, advanced storage devices, and programming models. However, researches of heterogeneous accelerators are still in a developing stage, and ultimately, will form mature application technologies that needs scientists to contribute more creative literature. The first critical problem is to describe the neural network features and memory access of applications. The second one is to design an architecture integrating computing and memory together. At last, tools supporting programmable frameworks and code conversions should be developed.

As neural networks are more widely used in a range of domains, such as computer vision, speech recognition, and natural language processing, more and more studies will develop new chips and software and hardware accelerating systems. Recently, there have been developments not only in software applications, algorithms, programming models, and topology structures but also in constructing hardware architectures. All these works provide a firm foundation to promote construction of new computer systems, artificial intelligence chips, and system industrialization.

6.5 ACKNOWLEDGMENTS

This work was supported by the National Science Foundation of China (No. 61379040), Anhui Provincial Natural Science Foundation (No. 1608085QF12), CCF-Venustech Hongyan Research Initiative (No. CCF-VenustechRP1026002), Suzhou Research Foundation (No. SYG201625), Youth Innovation Promotion Association CAS (No. 2017497), and Fundamental Research Funds for the Central Universities (WK2150110003).

REFERENCES

1. Chen Tianshi, Zidong Du, Ninghui Sun, Jia Wang, Chengyong Wu, Yunji Chen, and Olivier Temam. 2014, Diannao: A small-footprint high-throughput accelerator for ubiquitous machine-learning, *ACM Sigplan Notices*, 49(4):269–284, ACM.
2. Chen Yunji, Tao Luo, Shaoli Liu, Shijin Zhang, Liqiang He, Jia Wang, Ling Li, et al., 2014, Dadiannao: A machine-learning supercomputer, in *Proceedings of the 47th Annual IEEE/ACM International Symposium on Microarchitecture*, pp. 609–622, IEEE Computer Society.
3. Liu Daofu, Tianshi Chen, Shaoli Liu, Jinhong Zhou, Shengyuan Zhou, Olivier Teman, Xiaobing Feng, Xuehai Zhou, and Yunji Chen, 2015, Pudiannao: A polyvalent machine learning accelerator, *ACM SIGARCH Computer Architecture News*, 43(1):369–381, ACM.
4. Albericio Jorge, Patrick Judd, Tayler Hetherington, Tor Aamodt, Natalie Enright Jerger, and Andreas Moshovos, 2016, CnvlutIn: ineffectual-neuron-free deep neural network computing, in *43rd Annual International Symposium on Computer Architecture (ISCA), 2016 ACM/IEEE*, pp. 1–13, IEEE.
5. Han Song, Xingyu Liu, Huizi Mao, Jing Pu, Ardavan Pedram, Mark A. Horowitz, and William J. Dally, 2016, EIE: efficient inference engine on compressed deep neural network, in *Proceedings of the 43rd International Symposium on Computer Architecture*, pp. 243–254, IEEE Press, Hoboken, NJ.
6. Chen Yu-Hsin, Joel Emer, and Vivienne Sze, 2016, Eyeriss: A spatial architecture for energy-efficient dataflow for convolutional neural networks, in *43rd Annual International Symposium on Computer Architecture (ISCA), 2016 ACM/IEEE*, pp. 367–379, IEEE.
7. Kim Duckhwan, Jaeha Kung, Sek Chai, Sudhakar Yalamanchili, and Saibal Mukhopadhyay, 2016, Neurocube: A programmable digital neuromorphic architecture with high-density 3D memory, in *43rd Annual International Symposium on Computer Architecture (ISCA), 2016 ACM/IEEE*, pp. 380–392, IEEE.
8. Wang Minjie, Tianjun Xiao, Jianpeng Li, Jiaxing Zhang, Chuntao Hong, and Zheng Zhang, 2014, Minerva: A scalable and highly efficient training platform for deep learning, in *NIPS Workshop, Distributed Machine Learning and Matrix Computations*.
9. LiKamWa Robert, Yunhui Hou, Julian Gao, Mia Polansky, and Lin Zhong, 2016, RedEye: analog ConvNet image sensor architecture for continuous mobile vision, in *Proceedings of the 43rd International Symposium on Computer Architecture*, pp. 255–266, IEEE Press, Hoboken, NJ.

10. Desoli Giuseppe, Nitin Chawla, Thomas Boesch, Surinder-pal Singh, Elio Guidetti, Fabio De Ambroggi, Tommaso Majo, et al., 2017, 14.1 A 2.9 TOPS/W deep convolutional neural network SoC in FD-SOI 28nm for intelligent embedded systems, in *Solid-State Circuits Conference (ISSCC)*, pp. 238–239, IEEE, Hoboken, NJ.

11. Shin Dongjoo, Jinmook Lee, Jinsu Lee, and Hoi-Jun Yoo, 2017. 14.2 DNPU: An 8.1 TOPS/W reconfigurable CNN-RNN processor for general-purpose deep neural networks, in *Solid-State Circuits Conference (ISSCC)*, pp. 240–241, IEEE.

12. Whatmough Paul N., Sae Kyu Lee, Hyunkwang Lee, Saketh Rama, David Brooks, and Gu-Yeon Wei, 2017, 14.3 A 28nm SoC with a 1.2 GHz 568nJ/prediction sparse deep-neural-network engine with >0.1 timing error rate tolerance for IoT applications, in *Solid-State Circuits Conference (ISSCC)*, pp. 242–243, IEEE.

13. Price Michael, James Glass, and Anantha P. Chandrakasan, 2017, 14.4 A scalable speech recognizer with deep-neural-network acoustic models and voice-activated power gating, in *Solid-State Circuits Conference (ISSCC)*, pp. 244–245, IEEE.

14. B. Moons, et al., 2017, 14.5 Envision: A 0.26-to-10TOPS/W subword-parallel dynamic-voltageaccuracy-frequency-scalable Convolutional Neural Network processor in 28nm FDSOI, in *IEEE International Solid-State Circuits Conference (ISSCC), 2017*, IEEE.

15. Bong Kyeongryeol, Sungpill Choi, Changhyeon Kim, Sanghoon Kang, Youchang Kim, and Hoi-Jun Yoo, 2017, 14.6 A 0.62 mW ultra-low-power convolutional-neural-network face-recognition processor and a CIS integrated with always-on haar-like face detector, in *Solid-State Circuits Conference (ISSCC)*, pp. 248–249, IEEE.

16. Wang Chao, Xi Li, and Xuehai Zhou, 2015, SODA: Software defined FPGA based accelerators for big data, in *Design, Automation & Test in Europe Conference & Exhibition (DATE)*, pp. 884–887, IEEE.

17. Zhao Yangyang, Qi Yu, Xuda Zhou, Xuehai Zhou, Xi Li, and Chao Wang, 2016, PIE: A Pipeline Energy-Efficient Accelerator for Inference Process in Deep Neural Networks, in *IEEE 22nd International Conference on Parallel and Distributed Systems (ICPADS)*, pp. 1067–1074, IEEE.

18. Wang Chao, Xi Li, Qi Yu, Aili Wang, Patrick Hung, and Xuehai Zhou, 2016, SOLAR: Services-Oriented Learning Architectures, in *IEEE International Conference on Web Services (ICWS)*, pp. 662–665, IEEE.

19. Wang Chao, Lei Gong, Qi Yu, Xi Li, Yuan Xie, and Xuehai Zhou, 2017, DLAU: A scalable deep learning accelerator unit on FPGA, *IEEE Transactions on Computer-Aided Design of Integrated Circuits and Systems* 36(3): 513–517.

20. Li Chao, Yi Yang, Min Feng, Srimat Chakradhar, and Huiyang Zhou, 2016, Optimizing memory efficiency for deep convolutional neural networks on GPUs, in *SC16: International Conference for High Performance Computing, Networking, Storage and Analysis*, pp. 633–644, IEEE.

21. Li Boxun, Erjin Zhou, Bo Huang, Jiayi Duan, Yu Wang, Ningyi Xu, Jiaxing Zhang, and Huazhong Yang, 2014, Large scale recurrent neural network on GPU, in *International Joint Conference on Neural Networks (IJCNN)*, pp. 4062–4069, IEEE.

22. Park Hyunsun, Dongyoung Kim, Junwhan Ahn, and Sungjoo Yoo, 2016, Zero and data reuse-aware fast convolution for deep neural networks on gpu, in *International Conference on Hardware/Software Codesign and System Synthesis (CODES+ ISSS)*, pp. 1–10, IEEE.

23. Li, Xiaqing, Guangyan Zhang, H. Howie Huang, Zhufan Wang, and Weimin Zheng, 2016, Performance analysis of gpu-based convolutional neural networks, in *45th International Conference on Parallel Processing (ICPP)*, pp. 67–76, IEEE.

24. Li Shijie, Yong Dou, Xin Niu, Qi Lv, and Qiang Wang, 2017, A fast and memory saved GPU acceleration algorithm of convolutional neural networks for target detection, *Neurocomputing* 230:48–59.

25. Han Song, Junlong Kang, Huizi Mao, Yiming Hu, Xin Li, Yubin Li, Dongliang Xie, et al., 2017, ESE: Efficient speech recognition engine with sparse LSTM on FPGA, in *FPGA*, pp. 75–84.

26. Nurvitadhi Eriko, Ganesh Venkatesh, Jaewoong Sim, Debbie Marr, Randy Huang, Jason Ong Gee Hock, Yeong Tat Liew, et al., 2017, Can FPGAs Beat GPUs in Accelerating Next-Generation Deep Neural Networks? in *FPGA*, pp. 5–14.

27. Nurvitadhi Eriko, Jaewoong Sim, David Sheffield, Asit Mishra, Srivatsan Krishnan, and Debbie Marr, 2016, Accelerating recurrent neural networks in analytics servers: Comparison of FPGA, CPU, GPU, and ASIC, in *26th International Conference on Field Programmable Logic and Applications (FPL)*, pp. 1–4, IEEE.

28. Sharma Hardik, Jongse Park, Emmanuel Amaro, Bradley Thwaites, Praneetha Kotha, Anmol Gupta, Joon Kyung Kim, Asit Mishra, and Hadi Esmaeilzadeh, 2016, Dnnweaver: From high-level deep network models to fpga acceleration, in *the Workshop on Cognitive Architectures*.

29. Ma Yufei, Yu Cao, Sarma Vrudhula, and Jae-sun Seo, 2017, Optimizing Loop Operation and Dataflow in FPGA Acceleration of Deep Convolutional Neural Networks, in *Proceedings of the 2017 ACM/SIGDA International Symposium on Field-Programmable Gate Arrays*, pp. 45–54. ACM.

30. Zhang Jialiang and Jing Li, 2017, Improving the performance of openCL-based FPGA Accelerator for Convolutional Neural Network, in *FPGA*, pp. 25–34.

31. Loh Gabriel H., Yuan Xie, and Bryan Black, 2007, Processor design in 3D die-stacking technologies, *IEEE Micro* 27(3):31–48.

32. Chi Ping, Shuangchen Li, Cong Xu, Tao Zhang, Jishen Zhao, Yongpan Liu, Yu Wang, and Yuan Xie, 2016, Prime: A novel processing-in-memory architecture for neural network computation in reram-based main memory, in *Proceedings of the 43rd International Symposium on Computer Architecture*, pp. 27–39, IEEE Press, Hoboken, NJ.

33. Shafiee Ali, Anirban Nag, Naveen Muralimanohar, Rajeev Balasubramonian, John Paul Strachan, Miao Hu, R. Stanley Williams, and Vivek Srikumar, 2016, ISAAC: A convolutional neural network accelerator with in-situ analog arithmetic in crossbars, in *Proceedings of the 43rd International Symposium on Computer Architecture*, pp. 14–26, IEEE Press, Hoboken, NJ.

34. Song Linghao, Xuehai Qian, Hai Li, and Yiran Chen, 2017, PipeLayer: A pipelined ReRAM-based accelerator for deep learning, in *IEEE International Symposium on High Performance Computer Architecture (HPCA)*, pp. 541–552, IEEE.

35. Ahn Junwhan, Sungpack Hong, Sungjoo Yoo, Onur Mutlu, and Kiyoung Choi, 2015, A scalable processing-in-memory accelerator for parallel graph processing, in *42nd Annual International Symposium on Computer Architecture (ISCA), 2015 ACM/IEEE*, pp. 105–117, IEEE.

36. Ham Tae Jun, Lisa Wu, Narayanan Sundaram, Nadathur Satish, and Margaret Martonosi, 2016, Graphicionado: A high-performance and energy-efficient accelerator for graph analytics, in *49th Annual IEEE/ACM International Symposium on Microarchitecture (MICRO)*, pp. 1–13, IEEE.

37. Zhan Jia, Onur Kayıran, Gabriel H. Loh, Chita R. Das, and Yuan Xie, 2016, OSCAR: Orchestrating STT-RAM cache traffic for heterogeneous CPU-GPU architectures, in *49th Annual IEEE/ACM International Symposium on Microarchitecture (MICRO)*, pp. 1–13, IEEE.

38. Hamdioui Said, Lei Xie, Hoang Anh Du Nguyen, Mottaqiallah Taouil, Koen Bertels, Henk Corporaal, Hailong Jiao et al., 2015, Memristor based computation-in-memory architecture for data-intensive applications, in *Proceedings of the 2015 Design, Automation & Test in Europe Conference & Exhibition*, pp. 1718–1725, EDA Consortium.

39. Tang Tianqi, Lixue Xia, Boxun Li, Yu Wang, and Huazhong Yang, 2017, Binary convolutional neural network on RRAM, in *22nd Asia and South Pacific Design Automation Conference (ASP-DAC), 2017*, pp. 782–787, IEEE.

40. Ankit Aayush, Abhronil Sengupta, Priyadarshini Panda, and Kaushik Roy, 2017, RESPARC: A reconfigurable and energy-efficient architecture with memristive crossbars for deep spiking neural networks, in *Proceedings of the 54th Annual Design Automation Conference 2017*, p. 27, ACM.

41. Bergstra James, Olivier Breuleux, Frédéric Bastien, Pascal Lamblin, Razvan Pascanu, Guillaume Desjardins, Joseph Turian, David Warde-Farley, and Yoshua Bengio, 2010, Theano: A CPU and GPU math compiler in Python, in *Proc. 9th Python in Science Conf*, pp. 1–7.

42. Collobert Ronan, Koray Kavukcuoglu, and Clément Farabet, 2011, Torch7: A matlab-like environment for machine learning, in *BigLearn, NIPS Workshop, no. EPFL-CONF-192376*.

43. Abadi Martín, Ashish Agarwal, Paul Barham, Eugene Brevdo, Zhifeng Chen, Craig Citro, Greg S. Corrado et al., 2016, *Tensorflow: Large-scale machine learning on heterogeneous distributed systems*, arXiv preprint arXiv:1603.04467.

44. Jia Yangqing, Evan Shelhamer, Jeff Donahue, Sergey Karayev, Jonathan Long, Ross Girshick, Sergio Guadarrama, and Trevor Darrell, 2016, Caffe: Convolutional architecture for fast feature embedding, in *Proceedings of the 22nd ACM International Conference on Multimedia*, pp. 675–678, ACM.

45. Seide Frank and Amit Agarwal, 2016, CNTK: Microsoft's Open-Source Deep-Learning Toolkit, in *Proceedings of the 22nd ACM SIGKDD International Conference on Knowledge Discovery and Data Mining*, pp. 2135, ACM.

46. Chollet François, 2015, *Keras: Deep learning library for theano and tensorflow*, Available at: https://keras.io/k.

47. Moritz Philipp, Robert Nishihara, Ion Stoica, and Michael I. Jordan, 2015, *Sparknet: Training deep networks in spark*, arXiv preprint arXiv:1511.06051.

48. Team, D. J. D., 2016, *Deeplearning4j: Open-source distributed deep learning for the JVM*, Available at: https://github.com/deeplearning4j.

49. Karpathy Andrej, 2014, *ConvNetJS: Deep learning in your browser*, Available at: http://cs.stanford.edu/people/karpathy/convnetjs.

50. Chen Tianqi, Mu Li, Yutian Li, Min Lin, Naiyan Wang, Minjie Wang, Tianjun Xiao, Bing Xu, Chiyuan Zhang, and Zheng Zhang, 2015, *Mxnet: A flexible and efficient machine learning library for heterogeneous distributed systems*, arXiv preprint arXiv:1512.01274.

51. Tokui, Seiya, Kenta Oono, Shohei Hido, and Justin Clayton 2015, Chainer: A next-generation open source framework for deep learning in *Proceedings of Workshop on Machine Learning Systems (LearningSys) in the Twenty-Ninth Annual Conference on Neural Information Processing Systems (NIPS)*, vol. 5.

52. Baidu, 2016, *PaddlePaddle: Open and easy to use deep learning platform for enterprise and research*, Available at: http://www.paddlepaddle.org.

53. Hugh Perkins, 2016, *DeepCL: OpenCL library to train deep convolutional networks*, Available at: https://github.com/hughperkins/DeepCL.

54. PyTorch Core Team, 2017, *PyTorch: Tensors and Dynamic Neural Networks in Python with Strong GPU acceleration*, Available at: https://github.com/pytroch.

55. Sander Dieleman, Jan Schlüter, Colin Raffel, Eben Olson, Søren Kaae Sønderby, Daniel Nouri, Daniel Maturana, et al., 2015, *Lasagne: Lightweight library to build and train neural networks in Theano*, Available at: https://github.com/Lasagne.

56. Van Merriënboer, Bart, Dzmitry Bahdanau, Vincent Dumoulin, Dmitriy Serdyuk, David Warde-Farley, Jan Chorowski, and Yoshua Bengio, 2015, *Blocks and fuel: Frameworks for deep learning*, arXiv preprint arXiv:1506.00619.

57. Minerva and Purine, 2015, *CXXNet: A lightweight C++ based deep learning framework*, Available at: https://github.com/dmlc/cxxnet.

58. Lin Min, Shuo Li, Xuan Luo, and Shuicheng Yan, 2014, *Purine: A bi-graph based deep learning framework*, arXiv preprint arXiv:1412.6249.

CHAPTER 7

Acceleration for Recommendation Algorithms in Data Mining

Chongchong Xu, Chao Wang, Lei Gong,
Xi Li, Aili Wang, and Xuehai Zhou

University of Science and Technology of China

Hefei, China

CONTENTS

7.1 INTRODUCTION

With the rapid increase in information technology and the vigorous development of the Internet industry, people are gradually moving from the era of lack of information into the era of information explosion. Massive overloading makes people blind and helpless in the face of numerous choices. Finding content of interest to users quickly and accurately from a wide range of information has become a tremendous challenge. In response to this challenge, the recommendation algorithm is born. The recommendation algorithm can exploit potential associations in the history of user behavior, which further helps to recommend the information that is more interesting to users or generate a predictive score for a noncontact item.

In the field of recommendation algorithms, the recommended algorithm based on collaborative filtering [1] is the most typical recommendation algorithm. This algorithm can be divided into two types: the algorithm based on the neighborhood model and the algorithm based on the implicit semantic and matrix decomposition model. The algorithm based on the neighborhood model is the most basic mature algorithm, which mainly includes a user-based collaborative filtering recommendation algorithm (user-based CF) [2], item-based collaborative filtering recommendation algorithm (item-based CF) [3], and the SlopeOne recommendation algorithm [4]. Such algorithms mentioned above not only have detailed research but also have a very wide range of applications. The novel algorithms based on the implicit semantic and matrix decomposition model have been proposed, which mainly includes RSVD, Bias-RSVD, SVD++. This kind of algorithm is the most famous research in the field of recommendation algorithm and originally originated in the Netflix Prize Contest [5].

The scale of data is in rapid growth with the advent of the Big Data age. The most noticeable feature of the Big Data era is the large size of the data. For the recommendation system, it is directly reflected in the constant influx of new users and new items into the system and increasing user behavior or scoring of items. Whether for the collaborative filtering algorithms based on the neighborhood model or implicit semantic and matrix decomposition model, the ever-expanding data size makes the execution time of the algorithm longer and longer in the training stage and the forecasting stage. Moreover, the recommendation system has to take a longer time to generate referral information for the user. Therefore, to reduce the response time of the recommendation system and generate the recommendation information for the user in a timely manner, it is necessary to accelerate the execution of the recommended algorithm.

At present, there are three commonly used acceleration platforms for algorithm acceleration: multicore processor cluster, cloud computing platform, and general purpose graphics processor (GPGPU). The multicore processor cluster consists of multiple compute nodes, which are based on general-purpose CPU. It mainly uses MPI [6], OpenMP [7], or Pthread [8] to perform multiprocess/multithreading on the task-level/data-level parallelism. The cloud computing platform is also composed of a vast number of computing nodes, which are also based on general CPU. It mainly uses Hadoop [9], Spark [10], or other computing frameworks to perform task-level/data-level parallelism in MapReduce. For GPGPU, it consists of a large number of hardware threads, adopts multithreads to implement data-level parallelism, and mainly uses CUDA [11], OpenCL [12], and OpenACC [13].

For the collaborative filtering recommendation algorithm, there is much related research work using the above three platforms to accelerate. Although this work has indeed been productive, it also has some problems that cannot be ignored. For example, although the multicore processor cluster and cloud computing platform can be productive, computing efficiency while dealing with the recommended algorithm task for a single computing node based on general-purpose CPU architecture is relatively low and accompanied by high energy consumption. GPGPU has a high computational efficiency while dealing with recommended algorithm tasks due to its strengths on data-level parallelism but often results in higher energy consumption and run-time power overhead compared to general-purpose CPU.

In recent years, attempts have been made to exploit the use of specific-purpose integrated circuit chips (ASICs) and field programmable gate arrays (FPGAs) to study the design of hardware acceleration in order to increase the cost of energy while reducing performance. ASIC is a dedicated integrated circuit structure for specific areas of application, whose hardware structure cannot be changed after the chip is produced. However, FPGA has a reconfigurable hardware structure, which can customize different hardware structures for various applications. A front-end hardware design process is required whether using ASIC or FPGA, and the difference is in the final implementation. ASIC can obtain superior performance but with a high cost, while the implementation cost of FPGA is relatively low but it often gets less performance than ASIC. At present, there is a lot of excellent hardware acceleration design in the field of machine learning, especially in the field of deep learning. However, for the collaborative filtering recommendation algorithm, both the neighborhood model and the implicit semantic model, the related hardware acceleration research work is very sparse and there are still some limitations and problems, so it is very important to study the hardware acceleration for the proposed algorithm.

In this chapter, we mainly study hardware acceleration for the collaborative filtering recommendation algorithm. This research work is mainly based on the collaborative filtering recommendation algorithm of the neighborhood model. The primary consideration of the algorithm based on the neighborhood model rather than the implicit semantic and matrix decomposition model is that the latter has a wide range of applications and is the mainstream research direction in the field of future recommendation algorithms. However, for the latter, the calculation model for each algorithm instance is different, and it is a learning method in essence, which often needs to store the global data information for the iterative calculation to learn the optimal model parameters. These flexible computational models, repeated iterative computations, and access to global data will significantly increase the difficulty of storing and computing resources with the extremely limited hardware-accelerated structural design. The neighborhood-based algorithms are widely used in Amazon, Netflix, YouTube, Digg, Hulu, and other major Internet systems, which are based on the statistical process in essence and have a more common computing model, without the repeated iterative learning process. Also, it is very suitable to adopt hardware to implement, for the reason that this algorithm requires a small amount of global information. Therefore, this chapter focuses on the collaborative filtering recommendation algorithm based on the neighborhood model as the principal object of the hardware acceleration research.

The contributions of this chapter can be summarized as follows:

- We analyze the hotspots both in the training phase and prediction phase of the three recommendation algorithms mentioned above.

- We analyze five different similarities that are required in the training phase and prediction phase, respectively. Moreover, we design and implement dedicate a hardware structure on an FPGA platform, called a *training accelerator* and *prediction accelerator*, to speed up the execution of recommendation algorithms.

- We conduct experiments on ZYNQ ZedBoard, and our experimental results show that our accelerator gains an excellent acceleration effect with low power and less energy consumption at run time.

The rest of this chapter is organized as follows. Section 7.2 introduces the preliminaries of the recommendation algorithms. Section 7.3 presents the commonly used hardware acceleration principle and method. Section 7.4 analyzes the collaborative filtering recommendation algorithm based on the neighborhood model in detail. Section 7.5 presents the detailed hardware acceleration system hierarchy structure. Section 7.6 shows the experimental results and analysis. Section 7.7 concludes the chapter.

7.2 PRELIMINARIES

In this section, we first introduce the relevant concepts of the collaborative filtering recommendation algorithm based on the neighborhood model. In addition to that, we present two kinds of typical collaborative filtering recommendation algorithms based on the neighborhood model, the user-based CF algorithm and item-based CF algorithm.

7.2.1 Collaborative Filtering Recommendation Algorithm Based on the Neighborhood Model

With the rapid growth of data and information, people interested in mining information are more and more dependent on the help of the recommended system in the era of Big Data. According to the different requirements, the primary task of the recommended system can be divided into TopN recommendation and score prediction. TopN recommended tasks are mainly responsible for generating a recommendation list for items when the user does not have a historical record, and the score prediction task is mainly responsible for generating a specific interest rank for items that the user has not evaluated.

The collaborative filtering recommendation algorithm based on the neighborhood model [1] is a classical and mature algorithm. When generating a recommendation list or scoring prediction for a given user, this algorithm firstly searches for a specific neighborhood information set associated with users according to a certain condition and then uses historical record of the user, combined with the content of the neighborhood information set, to generate the recommendation of the list of designated user items or the degree of preference of a certain item. According to the type of neighborhood information set, the collaborative filtering algorithm based on the neighborhood model is mainly divided into user-based CF and item-based CF.

The user-based and item-based collaborative filtering recommendation algorithms can be divided into two stages of training and prediction. The training phase is often carried out offline, and the prediction stage often needs to be carried out online. In general, the former takes much more time than the latter.

Whether in the training phase or the prediction phase, users should use the historical records of the items, and these historical behavior records can often be presented by a matrix, as shown in Figure 7.1. In this matrix, each row represents a user and each column represents an item; the intersection of rows and columns represents a user's specific behavior record or ranking value of an item. The value of the intersection is empty only if a user has not yet contacted or evaluated an item, which is indicated by a dash in the figure. It can be seen that the row vector represents the set of items that a user has the historical behaviors or evaluations, and the column vector represents the set of users whose historical history or evaluation has been made for an item. For TopN recommended tasks, which tend to use implicit user behavior records, the matrix is called the *user-item behavior matrix*, and the value of each intersection is either empty or 1, which means that a user has access to a certain item. For a scoring task, it typically uses the explicit evaluation information of users, so the matrix is also called the *user-item scoring matrix*, where the value at each intersecting position is an integer or real number that is within a certain range and represents the ranking value for an item.

Figure 7.2 briefly describes the process of the collaborative filtering recommendation algorithm. For an item i_j that is not evaluated by the target user u_a, the algorithm will

	i_1	i_2	...	i_{j-1}	i_j	...	i_n
u_1	3	4		-	2.5		-
u_2	-	2		1	3		5
⋮							
u_{j-1}	2	5		-	-		2.5
u_j	3	-		2	4		3.5
⋮							
u_m	-	-		1.5	-		-

FIGURE 7.1   User–item score matrix.

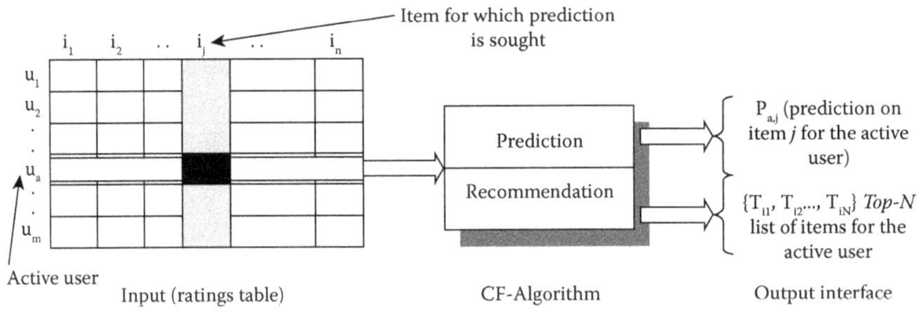

FIGURE 7.2 The execution process of the CF algorithm.

generate the interest or predictive score for i_j by using the data in the scoring table and the associated neighborhood information. For the score prediction task, the user u_a has obtained the score value of the item i_j. For the TopN recommendation task, the prediction value of the other item is also required, and then the list consists of the first N items, with the largest predicted value among all the items recommended to the user u_a.

7.2.2 User-Based Collaborative Filtering Recommendation Algorithm

The user-based CF algorithm is one of the most classic algorithms in the field of algorithms. In a sense, the birth of this algorithm also marks the birth of the recommendation system. Goldberg et al. proposed the user-based CF in 1992 and applied it to Tapestry [2]. Resnick et al. used this algorithm to build a news filtering system, GroupLens [14]. This algorithm was always the most well-known recommendation algorithm until the item-based CF appeared. At present, the user-based CF still exists in many recommended systems, such as Digg and so on.

The goal of the user-based CF recommendation algorithm is to find other users that have similar points of interest to the given user and then recommend the items that these other users have contacted or shown interest in to the given user.

User-based CF can perform either TopN recommendations or scoring tasks. The algorithm needs to go through the following two steps and stages regardless of the type of task:

- *Training phase*: To find and filter out the set that consists of K other users whose points of interest are most similar to the designated user, and the specific K value can be set based on different requirements or reference experience.

- *Prediction phase*: To find the collection of items that the designated user has not had historical activities in the collection of the items where all K other users have historical records and to generate the user's interest degree or score value (predicted value).

For the TopN recommendation task, it is necessary to sort the items according to the prediction value in descending order after the completion of the prediction phase and then recommend the first N items to the user.

In actual use, the training phase of user-based CF is often carried out offline. The recommendation system will first compute the similarity among all users in the user set and then sort the similarities between each user and the other users in reverse order. We can directly get the specified user's K size of the neighborhood collection for the online mode of operation in prediction phase, without having to repeat the operation.

The most important work in the training phase of user-based CF is to find the neighborhood collection that is most similar to other users. For the similarities, there are many metrics and methods: the Jaccard similarity coefficient (Jaccard coefficient), Euclidean distance, cosine similarity, and Pearson correlation coefficient, in which cosine similarity has two manifestations. It is necessary to perform the computation on the user's vector on the items evaluated by the two users regardless of which similarity is used. That is, i_1 and i_n of the user's vector u_{j-1} and u_j, which are circled in Figure 7.1.

The specific score values are not required in the computation of Jaccard similarity coefficient and cosine similarity, which means that these two metrics are often used in TopN recommended tasks. The computation of the similarity value of user vectors u and v in the Jaccard similarity coefficient is as shown in Equation 7.1:

$$w_{uv} = \frac{|N(u) \cup N(v)|}{|N(u) \cap N(v)|} \tag{7.1}$$

where the sets of items evaluated by users u, v are denoted by $N(u)$, $N(v)$, respectively. The Jaccard similarity coefficient needs to compute the size of intersection and union of two items.

The representation of the cosine similarity in the TopN recommendation is shown in Equation 7.2:

$$w_{uv} = \frac{|N(u) \cap N(v)|}{\sqrt{|N(u)||N(v)|}} \tag{7.2}$$

The specific scoring information is required in the computation of Euclidean distance, cosine similarity, and Pearson correlation coefficient, so they are often used in scoring tasks. Euclidean distance is as shown in Equation 7.3:

$$w_{uv} = \frac{1}{\sqrt{\sum_{i \in I} (r_{ui} - r_{vi})^2}} \tag{7.3}$$

where the set I represents the set of items that the user u, v collectively evaluates, i represents an item in the set, and r_{ui} and r_{vi} respectively represent the score of the user u, v on item i.

The representation of the cosine similarity in the scoring prediction is shown in Equation 7.4:

$$w_{uv} = \frac{\sum_{i \in I} r_{ui} * r_{vi}}{\sqrt{\sum_{i \in I} r_{ui}^2 \sum_{i \in I} r_{vi}^2}} \tag{7.4}$$

The definition of the Pearson correlation coefficient is shown in Equation 7.5:

$$w_{uv} = \frac{\sum\limits_{i \in I}\left(r_{ui} - \hat{r}_u\right) * \left(r_{vi} - \hat{r}_v\right)}{\sqrt{\sum\limits_{i \in I}\left(r_{ui} - \hat{r}_u\right)^2 \sum\limits_{i \in I}\left(r_{vi} - \hat{r}_i\right)^2}} \qquad (7.5)$$

where r_u and r_v, respectively, represent the user u, v in the item set I on their respective items' average score.

It is most important to use the similarity results of the training phase to generate the specified user's neighborhood set, then find the item collection that has not been contacted or evaluated and generate prediction values for each item in the neighborhood set. This process can also be expressed by a formula, which often uses the summed sum or weighted average to compute the final result value.

When the user-based CF executes the TopN recommendation, the prediction phase computes the user's interest in item i as shown in Equation 7.6:

$$P_{ui} = \sum\limits_{v \in S(u,K) \cap N(i)} w_{uv}, i \notin N(u) \qquad (7.6)$$

where $S(u, K)$ represents the set of neighborhoods of K other users that are most similar to user u. $N(i)$ represents all user sets that have a behavioral record of item i, v represents a group that does not belong to set $N(u)$, which combines to a user in the intersection of the sets $N(i)$ and $S(u, k)$, and w_{uv} is the similarity between users u and v.

The prediction stage not only takes into account the scoring information but also requires the weighted average of the results, compared to TopN's recommendation, as shown in Equation 7.7:

$$P_{ui} = \frac{\sum\limits_{v \in S(u,K) \cap N(i)} w_{uv} * r_{vi}}{\sum\limits_{v \in S(u,K) \cap N(i)} |w_{uv}|}, i \notin N(u) \qquad (7.7)$$

7.2.3 Item-Based Collaborative Filtering Recommendation Algorithm

The item-based CF recommendation algorithm is one of the most widely used algorithms in the industry and is widely used in systems such as Amazon, Netflix, Hulu, and YouTube. Sarwar et al. proposed item-based CF [3]. Linden et al. applied the algorithm to the Amazon product system [15]. Compared with user-based CF, item-based CF can not only have more accurate recommendation results but also can overcome the shortcomings that make user-based CF inefficient at a larger user scale and unable to explain the results of the recommendation.

We can summarize the goal of the item-based CF recommendation algorithm as recommending the items to the specified user. The items are most similar to those items that previous accessed by the user. The item-based CF algorithm does not adopt the contents of the property as a standard but analyzes the user's historical records of the items to compute the similarity of two items.

Item-based CF can also perform TopN recommended tasks and scoring tasks, and it also needs to go through the following two steps:

1. *Training phase*: To compute the similarity values among all the items in the collection and sort the similarity values between each item and other items in reverse order.

2. *Prediction phase*: To find the neighborhood set made up of K items that the specified user has not contacted or evaluated and then compute the predicted value for each item in the all-item neighborhood set.

These two phases can perform the scoring prediction tasks, while the process sorts the interest degree of item sets in descending order after the prediction phase for TopN tasks and then recommends the first N items to users. The item-based CF training phase is carried out offline, and the prediction phase is often carried out online.

The main task of item-based CF in the training phase is to compute the similarity between each item in the entire collection of items. For the similarity standard, the five similarities (e.g., Jaccard coefficient, Euclidean distance, cosine similarity, etc.) mentioned in user-based CF are most commonly used. The computation of item's vector occurs on the users that commonly evaluate these two items regardless of which kind of similarity is used, regardless of which kind of similarity is used, such as the circled items i_{j-1}, i_j and the users u_2, u_j in Figure 7.1.

There are some differences in presentation for those five similarities described above between user-based CF and item-based CF. For the Jaccard similarity coefficient, the method for computing the similarity of two user vectors i and j is shown in Equation 7.8:

$$w_{ij} = \frac{|N(i) \cap N(j)|}{|N(i) \cup N(j)|} \tag{7.8}$$

where $N(i)$ represents the set of all users who have accessed to or evaluated item i, and $N(j)$ represents the set of all users who have evaluated the item.

Cosine similarity, used in TopN recommendation, is shown in Equation 7.9:

$$w_{ij} = \frac{|N(i) \cap N(j)|}{\sqrt{|N(i)||N(j)|}} \tag{7.9}$$

The Euclidean distance is shown in item-based CF as shown in Equation 7.10:

$$w_{ij} = \frac{1}{\sqrt{\sum_{u \in U} (r_{ui} - r_{uj})^2}} \tag{7.10}$$

where the set U represents the user's collection that collectively evaluates the items i, j; u represents a user in the collection; and r_{ui}, r_{uj} respectively represent the score of the user u on items i, j.

Cosine similarity is used for the scoring prediction, which is shown in Equation 7.11:

$$w_{ij} = \frac{\displaystyle\sum_{u \in U} r_{ui} * r_{uj}}{\sqrt{\displaystyle\sum_{u \in U} r_{ui}^2 \sum_{u \in U} r_{uj}^2}} \tag{7.11}$$

The definition of the Pearson correlation coefficient is shown in Equation 7.12:

$$w_{ij} = \frac{\displaystyle\sum_{u \in U} \left(r_{ui} - \hat{r}_i\right) * \left(r_{uj} - \hat{r}_j\right)}{\sqrt{\displaystyle\sum_{u \in U} \left(r_{ui} - \hat{r}_i\right)^2 \sum_{u \in U} \left(r_{uj} - \hat{r}_j\right)^2}} \tag{7.12}$$

where r_i, r_j represent the average of the scores of all the users i, j in the user set U, respectively.

The main task of the prediction phase in item-based CF is to find the collection of K items, which are most similar to the given item and have not been evaluated by the specified user, by using the similarity results obtained in the training phase and then to generate predictions for each item in the neighborhood of all items. Likewise, this process can be expressed by the formula, which tends to use the cumulative sum or weighted average to calculate the final predicted value.

To get the TopN recommendation by item-based CF, the degree of interest of user u on item j will be computed in the prediction phase, which is shown in Equation 7.13:

$$P_{uj} = \sum_{i \in S(j,K) \cap N(u)} w_{ij}, j \notin N(u) \tag{7.13}$$

where $S(j, K)$ represents the neighborhood of the K other items that are most similar to item j; $N(u)$ represents the set of items in which user u has an activity record; item i represents the item that belongs to the intersection of the set $N(u)$ and $S(u, K)$; and w_{ij} is the similarity between items i and j.

Compared to TopN's recommendation, the prediction phase of score prediction requires not only the score information but also the final weighting of the results, as shown in Equation 7.14:

$$P_{uj} = \frac{\displaystyle\sum_{i \in S(j,K) \cap N(u)} w_{ij} * r_{ui}}{\displaystyle\sum_{i \in S(j,K) \cap N(u)} \left| w_{ij} \right|}, j \notin N(u) \tag{7.14}$$

7.2.4 SlopeOne Recommendation Algorithm

The SlopeOne recommendation algorithm is not a new class of algorithms in essence but a variant of the type of collaborative filtering recommendation algorithm based on items, which can be called a *special item-based CF algorithm*. Compared with the traditional item-based CF algorithm described earlier, the SlopeOne recommendation algorithm has the advantages of easy implementation and maintenance, fast response, and high accuracy.

The SlopeOne recommendation algorithm is mainly used for scoring prediction tasks and of course can also be used for TopN recommendation. However, while implementing the TopN recommendation, the SlopeOne algorithm often requires Boolean information that utilizes explicit user ratings rather than implicit user behavior. Figure 7.3 shows an example of the principle of the SlopeOne recommendation algorithm.

SlopeOne will first compute the average difference between all other items and items *J*. The specific method of computing the average difference degree is to subtract the score value on each of the two items, then add the result, and divide the number of components. In Figure 7.3, the other items are only item *I* and the common component is only user *A*, $(1.5 - 1)/1 = 0.5$. It is worth noting that the position of the two operands in the subtraction operation should be consistent. Then, for the predicted score of the user *B* to the item *J*, SlopeOne adds the score value of each item that the user has evaluated to the difference values between this item and item *J*, adds all the added results, and divides by the number of items that have been evaluated by the user. In this example, it is $(2 + 0.5)/1 = 2.5$.

From the above example, we can see that the SlopeOne recommendation algorithm can be divided into two stages of training and prediction:

1. *Training phase*: To compute the average difference of all the items in the collection.

2. *Prediction phase*: For an item has not been evaluated by the specified user. This phase computes the prediction values by using the scores of all items evaluated by the user and combining them with the average difference from the training phase.

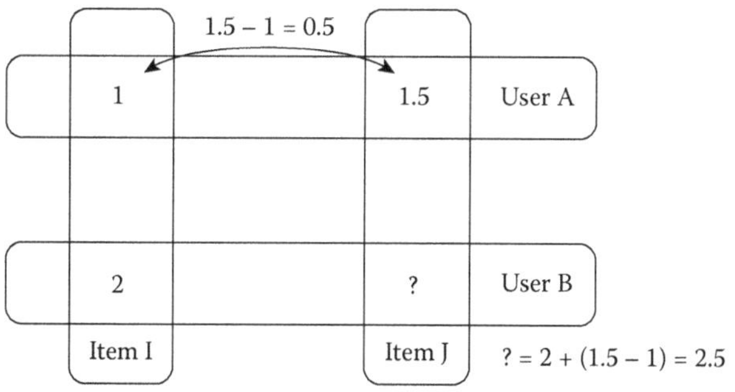

FIGURE 7.3   An example of the SlopeOne recommendation algorithm.

The main work of the SlopeOne algorithm in the training phase is to calculate the average difference between each item in the item set. The computation of average difference between items i and j is shown in Equation 7.15:

$$w_{ij} = \frac{\sum_{u \in U}(r_{ui} - r_{uj})}{|U|} \tag{7.15}$$

where the set U represents the set of users who collectively evaluate the items i, j; u represents a user in the set U; and w_{ij} represents the average difference between items i and j.

The SlopeOne algorithm uses the user item score information and evaluates the difference value to generate a predicted score for an item in the prediction phase. For user u, the predictor for item j is shown in Equation 7.16:

$$P_{uj} = \frac{\sum_{i \in R(u,j)}(w_{ij} + r_{ui})}{|R(u,j)|}, \quad j \notin N(u) \tag{7.16}$$

$$R(u,j) = \{i \in N(u), N(i) \cap N(j) \neq \varphi\}$$

where $N(u)$ represents the set of all the items that have been evaluated by the user u; $N(j)$ represents the set of all users who have evaluated the item j; $R(n)$ represents the set of all the items evaluated by the user u; $R(u, j)$ represents the set of items satisfying a certain condition in which each item i in this set belongs to the set $N(u)$ and satisfies the condition that the intersection of the user set $N(i)$ that corresponds to the item and the user set $N(j)$ of item j cannot be empty at the same time.

7.3 HARDWARE ACCELERATION PRINCIPLE AND METHOD

7.3.1 Hardware Acceleration Principle

The principle of hardware acceleration, in the general sense, is to assign those tasks, which are not suitable to CPUs, to the dedicated hardware accelerator. Thereby, it will reduce the workload of the CPU and in general enhance the system operating efficiency through the hardware to accelerate the efficient processing of the structure. At present, the most widely used hardware acceleration is the use of graphics processor GPU to speed up graphics and image processing tasks.

The general purpose CPU is essentially a Very Large Scale Integrated Circuit designed for general purpose tasks. It has a lot of computing units, control units, and storage units, which can process data by executing the user-written instruction stream (program). The versatile hardware design architecture allows the CPU to behave very well in dealing with most tasks, but there are also some tasks that are not suitable to process on CPUs due to their unique characteristics, which further reduces the efficiency of CPUs.

A typical case that is not suitable for CPU processing is image processing. In an image processing task, each pixel in the image involves a large number of the same floating-point operations, and each picture has at least hundreds of pixels. For the general CPU, its internal often only has two to four cores; even taking into account the super thread technology, the real number of hardware threads is only about four to eight, and these hardware threads run in MIMD(Multiple Instruction Stream Multiple Data Stream). Therefore, the parallelism of CPU is relatively small, and it appears powerless to deal with the parallel tasks when there is a large amount of repeated work. However, GPU is dedicated to graphics and image processing and has specifically designed hardware processor architecture. The general purpose GPU has hundreds of thousands of stream processors, and each stream processor has a strong floating point computing power, which is equivalent to having hundreds of thousands of hardware threads. These hardware threads run in SIMD (Single Instruction Stream Multiple Data Stream). Therefore, GPU has a strong parallel granularity and floating point computing power, which makes it very suitable for dealing with the graphics image processing type of task.

The GPU has the ability to handle other nongraphical image tasks thanks to the promotion and development of CUDA [11], OpenCL [12], OpenACC [13], and other programming techniques and frameworks. In general, GPU has a large number of computing unit components, so its running power is often more than the same level of CPU. Due to the characteristics of its hardware architecture, GPU is suitable to process the tasks that are easy to perform data-level parallelism. For some tasks that are easy to perform data-level parallelism but do not require too many floating-point computations, the utilization of GPU can improve efficiency but at the same time have a lot of unnecessary energy consumption.

In recent years, for some tasks or algorithms that are widely used and not suitable for CPU or GPU parallel processing, or for GPU parallel processing but at a great energy cost, people began to use ASIC and FPGA design dedicated hardware acceleration structure in an effort to reduce the power and energy consumption as much as possible while achieving the purpose of accelerating the acceleration effect. For example, SODA [16] presented a software defined FPGA-based accelerator for Big Data that could reconstruct and reorganize the acceleration engines according to the requirements of the various data intensive applications and was able to achieve up to 43.75× average speedup at 128 node application.

At present, the research of hardware accelerator for deep learning has become the hotspot, and a representative example is DianNao [17], which was proposed by Chen et al. DianNao is essentially a frequency of 1 GHz ASIC chip, which is specifically customized for the deep learning algorithm and adopts parallel and pipeline and other acceleration methods. Compared to a 2 GHz SIMD CPU, DianNao achieves 117.87× average speedup while reducing the energy consumption by 21.08× for the same task. In the same year, Chen et al. also improved and expanded DianNao, forming a new acceleration chip, DaDianNao [18]. A system with 64 DaDianNao accelerating chips achieves an acceleration ratio of 450.65× and a 150.31× reduction in power consumption compared to the high-end Nvidia Tesla K20M GPU. DLAU [19] presented a scalable deep learning accelerator unit on FPGA. The DLAU accelerator employs three pipelined processing units to improve the throughput and utilizes tile techniques to explore locality for deep learning applications. Experimental results on the state-of-the-art Xilinx FPGA board demonstrate that the DLAU accelerator is able to achieve up to 36.1 average speedup compared to the Intel Core 2 processors, with the power consumption at 234 mW.

For the collaborative filtering recommendation algorithm based on the neighborhood model, there has been relatively little research on the related hardware acceleration. Although there is not much relevant work, much of the hardware acceleration technology itself has a strong universality, and a method used in a particular algorithm can also be applied to other hardware acceleration implementation. Therefore, this design recommendation algorithm hardware acceleration structure will learn from research work related to other algorithms.

7.3.2 Commonly Used Hardware Acceleration Method

This section investigates and summarizes the research on hardware acceleration of machine learning algorithms. The research object mainly includes SVM [20,21], Apriori [22], k-means [23–25], DTC [26], deep learning [17,18,27], similarity calculation [28,29] of the algorithm's dedicated hardware acceleration architecture, and Refs. 30 and 31, which both have the ability to accelerate multiple machine learning algorithms of the general hardware acceleration structure.

Upon examination, we find that most of the hardware acceleration research work will first look for the computation of hotspots and common features, then select the parts for hardware acceleration, and finally use a variety of methods and means for common features and calculation of hotspots to design hardware accelerated structure.

This section summarizes the hardware acceleration methods that are frequently used in the above research work. These methods are mainly divided into two aspects: speeding up the computation process and reducing the communication cost. For accelerating the computation process, commonly used techniques include parallel computing, pipelining, approximation, and a variety of mixed techniques. For reducing communication overhead, data utilization techniques are often used.

7.3.2.1 Parallel Computing

Parallel computing is one of the most commonly used methods in hardware acceleration. For some tasks with high parallelisms, such as array addition and matrix multiplication, the execution time of the task can be greatly reduced by parallel computing.

In the related hardware acceleration research using parallelization technology, it is often seen that the hardware acceleration structure has multiple processing elements (PEs); each PE is responsible for a part of the whole task, and multiple PEs are in parallel to complete the entire task. In the case of two arrays of length L, for example, we assume that there are N PEs. Each PE is responsible for adding two components of a certain dimension of the array. If the operation takes up to C cycles, then $(L/) * C$ clock cycles are needed to complete the whole task. Compared to nonparallel $L * N * C$ cycles, the parallelization of the way does reduce the time overhead.

7.3.2.2 Pipeline Technology

Pipeline technology is also one of the most commonly used methods in hardware acceleration. Suppose there is a task with three computational stages, each corresponding to a

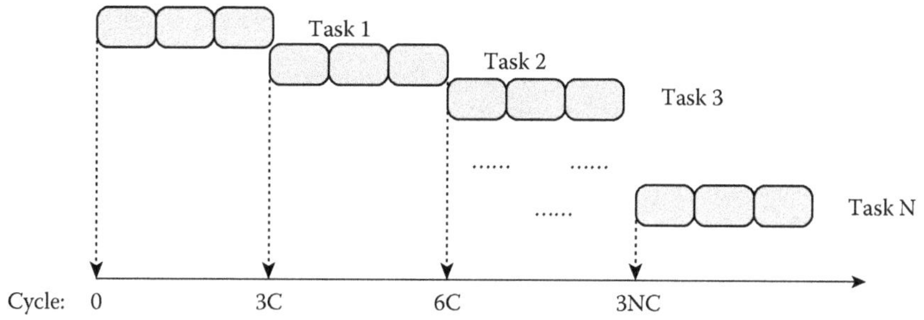

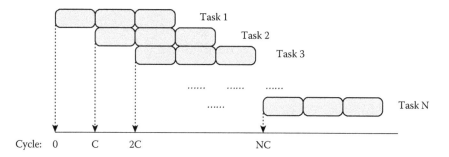

FIGURE 7.4   The time and space diagram of the nonpipeline mode execution case task.

FIGURE 7.5   The time and space diagram of the pipeline mode execution case task.

computation component; each execution time of these three components is C cycles. If the pipelined approach does not apply, and this will be able to perform a task until performing the next task, the period is $3 * N * C$, as shown in Figure 7.4.

If there is a completely pipelined design, then the implementation of multiple tasks, the new task does not have to wait for the completion of the former task. There are multiple tasks running on a different stage at the same time. For the case task in Figure 7.4, there are up to three tasks executing at the same time, and for N tasks it takes only $N * C + 2C$ clock cycles to complete the computation. Therefore, there is near 3× performance compared to the nonpipelined method, which is shown in Figure 7.5.

7.3.2.3 Approximate Computation

There are tasks such as the recommended algorithm, the deep learning, etc., that are involved in a large number of real operations during the execution time. However, at the same time, the real number are in a certain range, and the results of this task are the estimated value, or the accuracy requirements are not strict, which allows the existence of a certain range of errors.

For this type of task, in the design of the hardware acceleration structure, we can replace floating-point operations with fixed-point operations. The computation time of floating-point operation is longer than that of fixed-point operation. If the floating-point operation is replaced by a fixed-point operation in a task involving a large number of real numbers, a lot of time overhead will be reduced. The accuracy of fixed-point computing is not as good

```
1 movl    $0×1, %eax  ;  eax = a = 1
2 movl    $0×2, %edx  ;  edx = b = 2
3 addl    %edx, %eax  ;  eax = a + b = 3
4 imul    $0×3, %eax  ;  eax = (a + b) * c = 9
5 movl    $0×1, %ecx  ;  ecx = a = 1
6 subl    %edx, %ecx  ;  ecx = a - b = -1
7 movl    %ecx, %esi  ;  esi = ecx = -1
8 idiv    %esi        ;  eax = eax / esi = ((a + b) * c) / (a - b) = -9
```

FIGURE 7.6   Case task corresponding to the X86 CPU assembler.

as that for floating-point operations, so there will be some errors in the final computation of the task, compared to the floating point.

7.3.2.4 Mixing Technology

Most of the hardware acceleration work is often not a single use of the acceleration technology but will mix a variety of acceleration technology to achieve the greatest performance improvement. Let's take a hypothetical specific task example, which is calculated as $(a + b) * c / (a - b)$.

When input 1, 2, 3, the corresponding AT&T format assembly code is shown in Figure 7.6 for the X86_64 CPU. It can be seen that the CPU needs to execute eight instructions when the task is completed. Assuming that the instructions can be executed in a complete pipeline (one cycle to complete one instruction), and the CPU still needs at least eight clock cycles to complete the task. If the task needs to be computed n times, it will take at least $8n$ cycles.

We can use the parallel and pipeline technology in the design of the hardware to accelerate the structure of the task. The designed hardware structure is shown in Figure 7.7. It can be seen that the hardware accelerator structure can calculate $a + b$, $a - b$ in parallel and is a three-stage pipeline structure as a whole. If each level of hardware can be executed in full pipelining (one cycle produces one calculation result), for n tasks, if the number of cycles spent by a divide operation is t, then the structure only needs to cost about $n + t$ clock cycles.

7.3.2.5 Reduce Communication Overhead

The above methods are mainly focused on the optimization and improvement of the computation process. However, data communication optimization is also another area of hardware acceleration.

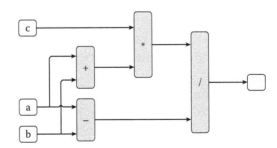

FIGURE 7.7   The task structure corresponding to the hardware implementation structure.

In most of the research designs, hardware accelerators often play a complementary role, as a coprocessor with the host CPU to handle the task. Hardware accelerators need to obtain relevant data when processing tasks. These data are usually stored in the main memory. The cost of access to the main memory based on AXI4, PCI-e, and other buses is often much higher than that of CPU direct access to main memory. Therefore, it is necessary to lower the data communication cost.

The main way to reduce the data overhead is to use data localization technology to tap the inherent nature of the task. Data that is frequently used should be resident in the hardware accelerator, thereby improving the data reuse rate and reducing the number of memory accesses. In addition, most accelerators have a storage hierarchy like the CPU cache, which can further reduce the cost of memory access.

7.4 ANALYSIS OF COLLABORATIVE FILTERING RECOMMENDATION ALGORITHM BASED ON THE NEIGHBORHOOD MODEL

7.4.1 Analysis of Training Phase

This section will analyze the training phase of these three algorithms: user-based CF, item-based CF, and SlopeOne, which will further mine the computational hotspots and common features.

As described in Section 7.2, user-based CF and item-based CF mainly include similarity computations and reverse order of similarity values in the training phase. SlopeOne contains only the average difference computation during the training phase. We used the ml-100k [32] data set to analyze the training stages of the three recommended algorithms. The results are shown in Table 7.1. It can be seen that the similarity/average difference computation takes more than 97% of the total time and is, therefore, a hotspot in the training phase.

User-based CF computes the similarity between two users when computing the similarity/average difference. Item-based CF computes the similarity between the two items. SlopeOne computes the average difference degree between the two items.

TABLE 7.1   Three-Recommendation Algorithm for the ml-100k Data Set Training Section Hotspot Analysis

Training	Metric	Similarity/Difference Calculation	Similarity Sort
User-based CF	Jaccard	98.99%	1.01%
	CosineIR	98.68%	1.32%
	Euclidean	98.82%	1.18%
	Cosine	98.73%	1.27%
	Pearson	98.79%	1.21%
Item-based CF	Jaccard	97.74%	2.26%
	CosineIR	97.43%	2.57%
	Euclidean	97.55%	2.45%
	Cosine	97.52%	2.48%
	Pearson	97.53%	2.47%
SlopeOne	SlopeOne	100.00%	–

Note: CF, collaborative filtering.

It can be found that the computational behavior of user-based CF and item-based CF is very similar and can share the five similarity computation standards described above. The only difference is that the former is oriented to the user and the latter is oriented to the item, essentially because of the difference in input data. SlopeOne is oriented to the computation of the average difference for items and has a relatively fixed computation mode.

The Jaccard similarity coefficient, Euclidean distance, two kinds of cosine similarity, and Pearson correlation coefficient can also be used to compute the two user vector or item vector. In this chapter, x, y represents two user and item vectors, respectively.

According to the Equations 7.1 and 7.8, the Jaccard similarity coefficient needs to know the number of vectors x, y, their nonempty scores N_x, N_y, and the vector x, y of the common number of scores N_{xy}, where N_x, N_y can often be obtained directly from the original data, so we only need to compute N_{xy}, using the formula shown in Equation 7.17:

$$w_{xy} = \frac{|N(x) \cap N(y)|}{|N(x) \cup N(y)|} = \frac{N_{xy}}{N_x + N_y - N_{xy}} \tag{7.17}$$

N_x, N_y, and N_{xy} are also required to be known when computing cosine similarity calculations for TopN recommended tasks according to Equations 7.2 and 7.9, as shown in Equation 7.18:

$$w_{xy} = \frac{|N(x) \cap N(y)|}{\sqrt{|N(x)||N(y)|}} = \frac{N_{xy}}{\sqrt{N_x * N_y}} \tag{7.18}$$

According to Equations 7.3 and 7.10, the computation of Euclidean distance needs to know the sum of the squares of squares $S_{(x-y)^2}$, where M is the collection of users or items for which both these vectors have historical behavior or evaluation record and m is a member of the set M, as shown in Equation 7.19:

$$w_{xy} = \frac{1}{\sqrt{\sum_{m \in M}\left(r_{xm} - r_{ym}\right)^2}} = \frac{1}{\sqrt{S_{(x-y)^2}}} \tag{7.19}$$

According to Equations 7.4 and 7.11, it is necessary to know the squared sums S_x^2, S_y^2 of the self-score at the two vector-common offset positions and the multiplied sum S_{xy} when computing vectors x, y by using the cosine similarity in score predictions, as shown in Equation 7.20:

$$w_{xy} = \frac{\sum_{m \in M} r_{xm} * r_{ym}}{\sqrt{\sum_{m \in M} r_{xm}^2 \sum_{m \in M} r_{ym}^2}} = \frac{S_{xy}}{\sqrt{S_{x^2} * S_{y^2}}} \tag{7.20}$$

According to the formula in Equations 7.5 and 7.12, the Pearson correlation coefficient is necessary in addition to the need for S_x^2, S_y^2, S_{xy}, but we also need to know the vector x,

y common score number N_{xy}, and their own in the common offset position and S_x, S_y. The simplified formula is as shown in Equation 7.21:

$$w_{xy} = \cfrac{\sum_{m \in M} r_{xm} * r_{ym} - \cfrac{\sum_{m \in M} r_{xm} * \sum_{m \in M} r_{ym}}{|M|}}{\sqrt{\left(\sum_{m \in M}(r_{xm})^2 - \cfrac{\left(\sum_{m \in M} r_{xm}\right)^2}{|M|}\right) * \left(\sum_{m \in M}(r_{ym})^2 - \cfrac{\left(\sum_{m \in M} r_{ym}\right)^2}{|M|}\right)}}$$

(7. 21)

$$= \cfrac{S_{xy} - \cfrac{S_x * S_y}{N_{xy}}}{\sqrt{\left(S_{x^2} - \cfrac{(S_x)^2}{N_{xy}}\right) * \left(S_{y^2} - \cfrac{(S_y)^2}{N_{xy}}\right)}}$$

The SlopeOne algorithm is used in the training phase of the formula as shown in Equation 7.15. It can be seen that SlopeOne needs to know S_{x-y}, the sum of difference at the common offset position, and N_{xy} when computing the two user vectors x, y, as shown in Equation 7.22:

$$w_{xy} = \frac{\sum_{m \in M}(r_{xm} - r_{ym})}{|M|} = \frac{S_{(x-y)}}{N_{xy}}$$

(7. 22)

The computation of two input vectors x, y under those six similarity criteria are related to 10 scalar values: N_x, N_y, N_{xy}, S_x, S_y, S_x^2, S_y^2, S_{xy}, $S_{(x-y)}$, and $S_{(x-y)}^2$. After the computation of this scalar information, the only need is to perform addition, subtraction, multiplication, prescribing, and the last step of the division of the operation to obtain the similarity or average difference.

For the original user–item behavior/score data, the application will often reorganize the structure of data after reading, and the organization is similar to the hash table structure [33]. Take the user–item score matrix in Figure 7.8 as an example. For user-based CF, the organization is shown in Figure 7.8a. The head node holds the number of items evaluated by a user. The linked node holds the item's number and the user's ranking value on the item. The organization of item-based CF and SlopeOne is as shown in Figure 7.8b; the head node saves the number of an item evaluated by the user, while the linked list node saves the user's number and the score of item.

According to the above data organization, the scalar N_x, N_y values can be obtained directly from the head node information, and the remaining scalar values need to be obtained after the vector x, y computation is completed. In the calculation of scalar N_{xy}, S_x,

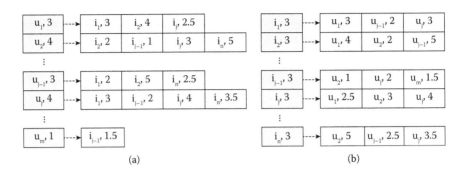

FIGURE 7.8   (a, b) Two ways of reorganizing the user–item scoring matrix shown in Figure 7.1.

TABLE 7.2   Hotspot Analysis of TopN Tasks in Three Predictors of the ml-100k Data Set

Prediction	Metric	Prediction Value Calculation	TopN Item ($N = 10$)
	Jaccard	93.37%	6.63%
User-based	CosineIR	95.14%	4.86%
CF	Euclidean	91.69%	8.31%
(neighbors: 80)	Cosine	91.54%	8.46%
	Pearson	91.86%	8.14%
	Jaccard	99.25%	0.75%
Item-based	CosineIR	98.83%	1.17%
CF	Euclidean	99.23%	0.77%
(neighbors: 80)	Cosine	99.26%	0.74%
	Pearson	99.23%	0.77%
SlopeOne	SlopeOne	99.23%	0.77%

S_y, S_x^2, S_y^2, S_{xy}, $S_{(x-y)}$, and $S_{(x-y)}^2$, we first need to perform the corresponding operations on the two components at each common position of the vector; then all of the partial results of the operation should be summed.

7.4.2 Analysis of the Prediction Phase

The user-based CF, item-based CF, and SlopeOne algorithms in the prediction phase according to the different types of tasks have different computing behaviors. For the scoring task, these three algorithms only need to calculate the predicted value of the undetected or evaluated items of the specified user in the prediction stage. For the TopN recommendation task, in addition to the need for computing the predictive values of the item, it is also necessary to select N items with the largest forecast for the designated user. We also use the ml-100k data set to perform TopN recommendations on the three algorithms in the prediction phase. The results are shown in Table 7.2. It can be seen that the cost of the calculation of the item is more than 90% of the total time spent, so it is the calculation hotspot of the prediction phase.

There are two computation methods, including cumulative and weighted average, to perform the prediction by user-based CF and item-based CF. SlopeOne has a fixed calculation mode when calculating the predicted value. The cumulative calculation is relatively simple; it can be considered a special case of weighted average calculations and is therefore not discussed.

7.5 HARDWARE ACCELERATION SYSTEM HIERARCHY

The hierarchical structure of the hardware acceleration system for the collaborative filtering recommendation algorithm based on the neighborhood is shown in Figure 7.9. We can see that the whole system runs in the Linux operating system environment and is divided into three levels, the hardware layer, the operating system kernel layer, and the operating system user layer.

The hardware layer is the most important layer of the hardware acceleration system, mainly including the training accelerator, predictive accelerator, DMA, and other equipment. At run time, the host CPU notifies the DMA to initiate a data transfer, and the hardware accelerator acquires the data by DMA.

The operating system kernel layer mainly includes the driver of hardware accelerator, DMA, and other devices in the Linux operating system environment. The driver typically encapsulates the interface of the hardware device control register and creates the device file in the file system. Users can control the hardware device through the read and write device files directly.

The top layer is the user layer, which includes the run-time library and application layer. Although the user can read and write hardware registers to control the hardware device to complete an operation directly, this approach is relatively cumbersome and requires the

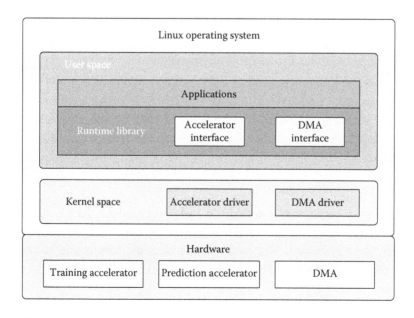

FIGURE 7.9   Hardware accelerator system hierarchy.

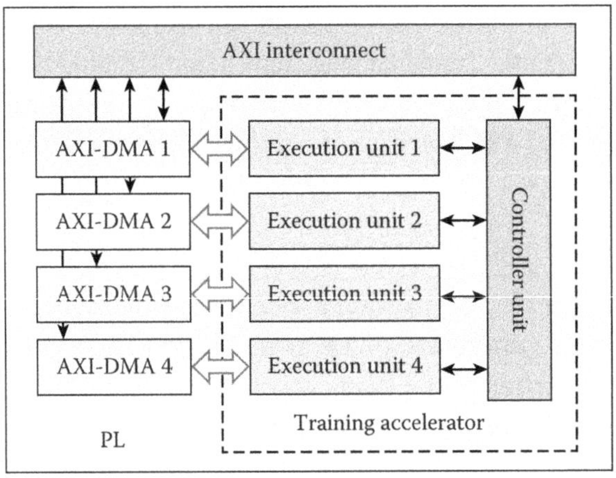

FIGURE 7.10 The overall structure of the training accelerator prototype.

user to have enough understanding of the device. For the convenience of the user, the run-time library encapsulates the register read and write operations required by the accelerator, DMA functions, and provides the upper interface for the user to invoke.

7.5.1 Training Accelerator Prototype Implementation

Figure 7.10 shows the implementation of the training accelerator prototype, which has four execution units and one control unit, where DMA adopts AXI-DMA IP cores provided by Xilinx. In each execution unit, the maximum supported vector length of the cache module is 8192. There are 32 PEs in the multifunction operation unit of the accumulation module, with five layers. AXI-DMA is connected with the memory controller in PS by AXI4 data bus, while host CPU controls the training accelerator control unit and AXI-DMA by AXI4-Lite bus.

7.5.2 Predictive Accelerator Prototype Implementation

Figure 7.11 shows the implementation of the predictive accelerator prototype, which also has four execution units, and DMA also uses AXI-DMA. In each execution unit, the maximum supported vector length of the cache module is 8192. The host CPU, AXI-DMA, and predictive accelerator execution unit are connected to the same bus in the training accelerator prototype.

7.5.3 Device Driver Implementation

Xilinx offers a Linux kernel that is optimized and optimized for the ZYNQ platform [34]. Digilent has further refined Xilinx's ZYNQ Linux kernel and added support for the ZedBoard development board. The hardware accelerator system selects Digilent-Linux 3.6 as a Linux kernel, based on ARM Ubuntu 14.10 Linaro 14.10 as the operating system root file system.

The training accelerator control unit, predictive accelerator execution unit controller, and AXI-DMA device drivers are implemented as mentioned above. Given the implementation

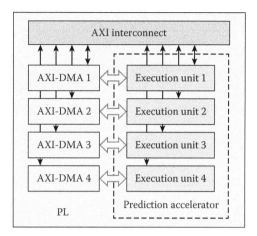

FIGURE 7.11 Predicted overall structure of the accelerator prototype.

of the details, due to the selection of the AXI4-Lite control bus and AXI-DMA, the number of accelerator control units and AXI-DMA registers is more than previously designed, and the driver needs to support read/write operations for the extra registers.

The implementation of the AXI-DMA character device driver is based on memory map. The DMA buffer adopts the reserve physical memory—that is, it modifies the device tree file and assigns the highest 64 MB memory on-board to four AXI-DMA before the start of ZedBoard. Therefore, each AXI-DMA has 16 MB for read/write operations. The drive module corresponding to the AXI-DMA will be mapped into the kernel space.

In order to verify the effect of this AXI-DMA driver module implementation, we implement the AXI-DMA driver in a traditional way and test the differences in performance between programs through two DMA drivers using the ArrayAdd IP core for adding two input arrays. The corresponding structure of the project is shown in Figure 7.12.

For two float arrays of length 1024, the single-core ARM CPU itself takes 4454 cycles. Taking into account the time for transferring the data between the main memory and IP core, for the AXI-DMA driver implemented in a traditional way, the ArrayAdd IP core needs to spend 6172 cycles to complete the task. However, it only needs to spend 2840 cycles to achieve the AXI-DMA driver by memory map. It can be seen that the use of memory mapping technology to achieve the DMA driver can indeed reduce data transmission costs.

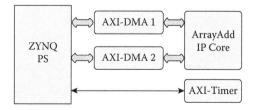

FIGURE 7.12 Test of the hardware engineering structure used by the two driver implementations of AXI-DMA.

7.6 EXPERIMENTAL RESULTS AND ANALYSIS

7.6.1 Acceleration Ratio of Training Accelerator

We use the ml-100k, which contains 943 users, 1682 items, and 100,000 data scores, to obtain the time spent on the operation of the five different platforms by calculating the similarity/average difference degree of the three algorithms in the training phase. We measure the acceleration ratio among the training accelerator, CPU, and GPU, where the time of the training accelerator includes the time of the accelerator calculation and the time of data transmission of the AXI-DMA. The CPU time contains only the calculation time. The time of the GPU includes the calculation time of the GPU and the data transfer copy time between the main memory and the GPU explicit memory.

The acceleration between the training accelerator and the same level of ARM CPU is shown in Figure 7.13. The leftmost column represents the ratio of the single-threaded CPU program to itself. The ratio is always 1, mainly as a benchmark. The middle column represents the speed ratio of the double-threaded CPU program compared to the single-threaded CPU program. The rightmost column represents the acceleration ratio of the training accelerator compared to the single-threaded CPU program. CosineIR ignores the score of the cosine similarity.

It can be seen that the acceleration ratio of the training accelerator and the single-threaded ARM CPU is around 35× for user-based CF. For item-based CF and SlopeOne, the acceleration ratio is around 16×. The speed of user-based CF is higher than that of item-based CF and SlopeOne because the former is the user vector and the latter is the item vector. The length of the user vector is 1682, and the length of the item vector is 943. When dealing with two vectors, the complexity of the CPU program is $O(n_x*\log n_y)$, where n_x, n_y denote the actual number of two vectors, and often in a positive correlation with the vector length n. The implementation of the training accelerator by using a parallel pipeline whose complexity is $O(n/32)$ will be more effective. Therefore, the longer the vector length, the higher the score in each vector, and the better the acceleration effect of the training accelerator.

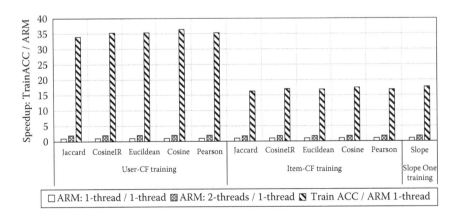

FIGURE 7.13 Acceleration ratio between the training accelerator and the ARM CPU under the ml-100k data set.

The acceleration between the training accelerator and the Intel Core 2 CPU is shown in Figure 7.14. It can be seen that the speed ratio of the training accelerator compared to the single-threaded Intel Core 2 CPU is around 4.3× for user-based CF. For item-based CF and SlopeOne, the acceleration ratio is around 2.1×. Since the performance of Intel Core 2 CPU(2.66 GHz) is higher than the ARM Cortex A9(677 MHz), the speedup of training accelerator has dropped significantly, compared to CPU.

The acceleration between the training accelerator and the Intel Core i7 CPU is shown in Figure 7.15. It can be seen that the training accelerator is only about 2.3× the acceleration ratio for the user-based CF. For the item-based CF, the training accelerator has no acceleration performance, the acceleration ratio is only about 1.1×, and the single-threaded CPU program performance is flat. Since the frequency of the Intel Core i7 CPU is 40 times faster than the training accelerator prototype, and the prototype has only four parallel execution units, there is not much advantage in the speedup.

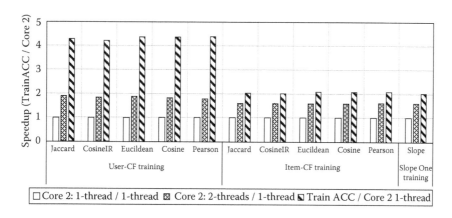

FIGURE 7.14 Acceleration ratio between the training accelerator and the Intel Core 2 CPU under the ml-100k data set.

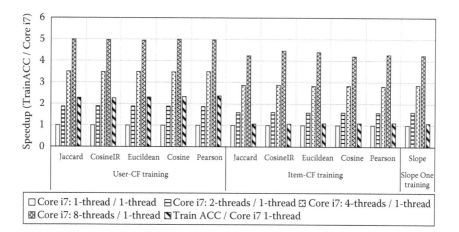

FIGURE 7.15 Acceleration ratio between the training accelerator and the Intel Core i7 CPU in the ml-100k data set.

The acceleration of the training accelerator and the NVIDIA Tesla K40C GPU is shown in Figure 7.16. The GPU program adopts 128 thread blocks, and each thread block has 128 threads, a total of 16,384 threads. Each thread is responsible for pairs of similarity/ average difference calculation. The Tesla K40C supports 2880 hardware threads. The peak running frequency of each hardware thread is 875 MHz; both parallelism and frequency are much higher than those of the training accelerator. When the two vectors are processed, the time taken by the GPU's single thread is O(n), while the training accelerator is on the order of O($n/32$), and this advantage is not helpful. In summary, the training accelerator prototype compared to the Tesla K40C without any acceleration effect is also reasonable. Thus, if the main consideration is performance factors, GPU is indeed an excellent platform.

7.6.2 Power Efficiency

The power efficiency of the Intel Core i7 CPU, Nvidia Tesla K40C GPU, and the training accelerator is shown in Figure 7.17. It can be seen that the CPU running time power

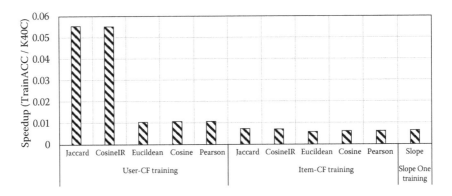

FIGURE 7.16 Acceleration ratio between the training accelerator and the NVIDIA Tesla K40C GPU in the ml-100k data set.

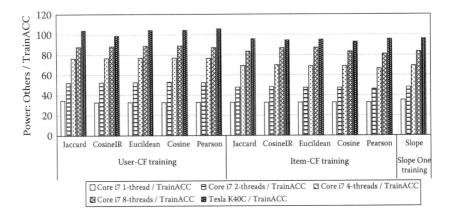

FIGURE 7.17 The power ratio between the contrast platform and the training accelerator in the ml-100k data set.

increases with the number of threads, about 33×–88× of the training accelerator prototype; the GPU's running power is about 100× that of the prototype.

7.6.3 Energy Efficiency

The energy consumption of the Intel Core i7 CPU compared to the training accelerator is shown in Figure 7.18a. For user-based CF, energy consumption is around 41×. For item-based CF and SlopeOne, energy consumption is around 21×. Thus, the training accelerator prototype compared to the CPU has a great energy saving advantage.

The energy consumption of the Nvidia Tesla K40C compared to the training accelerator is shown in Figure 7.18b. For user-based CF, energy consumption is around 5.5× for

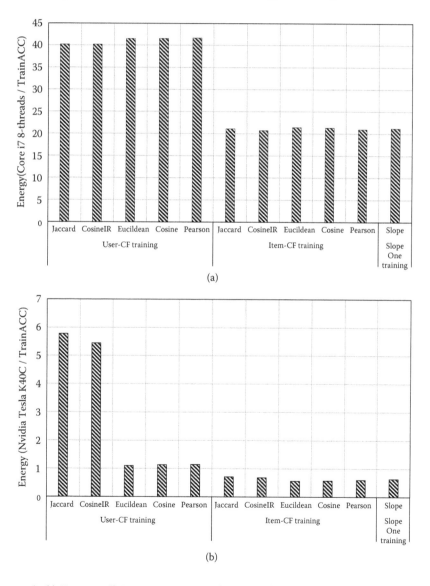

FIGURE 7.18 (a, b) Energy efficiency comparison between the contrast platform and the training accelerator in the ml-100k data set.

Jaccard and CosineIR and 1.1× for other standards. For item-based CF and SlopeOne, energy consumption is around 0.67×; the training accelerator is not dominant in energy-efficiency due to that the runtime of GPU is too short, which further results in the lower energy consumption.

7.7 CONCLUSIONS

In this chapter, the training accelerator and predictive accelerator structure and instruction set were designed for the training phase and prediction stage of user-based CF, item-based CF, and SlopeOne, three neighborhood-based algorithms. Both accelerators operate as a coprocessor under the control of the host CPU, and the training accelerator supports five different similarity calculation criteria required for user-based CF and item-based CF during the training phase. In addition, it supports the difference calculation criterion, which is required in the training phase of SlopeOne. The prediction accelerator supports the summing and weighted averaging operations required by the three algorithms in the prediction phase. Moreover, we design the interconnection among the host CPU, memory, accelerator, and DMA.

This chapter designs the device drivers for training accelerators, prediction accelerators, and DMA devices in the Linux operating system environment. We design the device driver for the training accelerator control unit and the predictor accelerator execution unit controller by using the Linux character device driver framework model. For the DMA device driver, we also adopt the character device driver framework model and memory mapping technique.

For the convenience of users, this chapter designs and encapsulates the operating system user-layer interface for hardware accelerator and DMA. It mainly involves the training accelerator control unit, prediction accelerator execution unit controller, and the user-layer interface of DMA.

Finally, this chapter carried out a performance experiment and appraisal to realize the hardware acceleration system prototype. The experimental results show that our hardware accelerator has an excellent acceleration effect and low run-time power and energy consumption.

7.8 ACKNOWLEDGMENTS

This work was supported by the National Science Foundation of China (No. 61379040), Anhui Provincial Natural Science Foundation (No. 1608085QF12), CCF-Venustech Hongyan Research Initiative (No. CCF-VenustechRP1026002), Suzhou Research Foundation (No. SYG201625), Youth Innovation Promotion Association CAS (No. 2017497), and Fundamental Research Funds for the Central Universities (WK2150110003).

REFERENCES

1. J. B. Schafer, D. Frankowski, J. Herlocker, and S. Sen, 2007, Collaborative filtering recommender systems, in *The adaptive web*, Springer, Berlin, pp. 291–324.
2. D. Goldberg, et al., 1992, Using collaborative filtering to weave an information tapestry, *Communications of the ACM*, vol. 35, no. 12, pp. 61–s70.

3. B. Sarwar, G. Karypis, J. Konstan, and J. Riedl, 2001, Item-based collaborative filtering recommendation algorithms, in *Proceedings of the 10th international conference on World Wide Web*, ACM, pp. 285–295.

4. D. Lemire, and A. Maclachlan, 2005, Slope one predictors for online rating-based collaborative filtering, in *Proceedings of the 2005 SIAM International Conference on Data Mining*, Society for Industrial and Applied Mathematics, pp. 471–475.

5. Y. Zhou, D. Wilkinson, R. Schreiber, and R. Pan, 2008, Large-scale parallel collaborative filtering for the netflix prize, *Lecture Notes in Computer Science*, vol. 5034, pp. 337–348.

6. P. S. Pacheco, 1997, *Parallel programming with MPI*, Morgan Kaufmann, MSan Francisco, CA.

7. L. Dagum and R. Menon, 1998, OpenMP: An industry standard API for shared-memory programming, *IEEE Computational Science and Engineering*, vol. 5, no. 1, pp. 46–55.

8. W. R. Stevens, and S. A. Rago, 2013, *Advanced programming in the UNIX environment*, Addison-Wesley.

9. T. White, 2012, *Hadoop: The definitive guide*, O'Reilly Media, Inc.

10. M. Zaharia, M. Chowdhury, M. J. Franklin, S. Shenker, and I. Stoica, 2010, Spark: Cluster computing with working sets, *HotCloud*, vol. 10, no. 10–10, p. 95.

11. C. U. D. A. Nvidia, 2007, *Compute unified device architecture programming guide*.

12. J. E. Stone, D. Gohara, and G. Shi, 2010, OpenCL: A parallel programming standard for heterogeneous computing systems, *Computing in Science & Engineering*, vol. 12, no. 3, pp. 66–73.

13. S. Wienke, P. Springer, C. Terboven, and an Mey, D. 2012, OpenACC—first experiences with real-world applications. In *Euro-Par 2012 Parallel Processing*, pp. 859–870.

14. P. Resnick, N. Iacovou, M. Suchak, P. Bergstrom, and J. Riedl, 1994, GroupLens: An open architecture for collaborative filtering of netnews, in *Proceedings of the 1994 ACM Conference on Computer Supported Cooperative Work*, ACM, pp. 175–186.

15. G. Linden, B. Smith, and J. York, 2003, Amazon. com recommendations: Item-to-item collaborative filtering, *IEEE Internet Computing*, vol. 7, no. 1, pp. 76–80.

16. C. Wang, X. Li, and X. Zhou, 2015, SODA: Software defined FPGA based accelerators for big data, in *Design, Automation & Test in Europe Conference & Exhibition (DATE)*, IEEE, pp. 884–887.

17. T. Chen, Z. Du, N. Sun, J. Wang, C. Wu, Y. Chen, and O. Temam, 2014, Diannao: A small-footprint high-throughput accelerator for ubiquitous machine-learning. *ACM Sigplan Notices*, vol. 49, no. 4, pp. 269–284.

18. Y. Chen, T. Luo, S. Liu, S. Zhang, L. He, J. Wang, . . . and O. Temam, 2014, Dadiannao: A machine-learning supercomputer, in *Proceedings of the 47th Annual IEEE/ACM International Symposium on Microarchitecture*, IEEE Computer Society, pp. 609–622.

19. C. Wang, L. Gong, Q. Yu, X. Li, Y. Xie, and X. Zhou, 2017, DLAU: A scalable deep learning accelerator unit on FPGA, *IEEE Transactions on Computer-Aided Design of Integrated Circuits and Systems*, 36(3), 513–517.

20. S. Cadambi, I. Durdanovic, V. Jakkula, M. Sankaradass, E. Cosatto, S. Chakradhar, and H. P. Graf, 2009, A massively parallel FPGA-based coprocessor for support vector machines, in FCCM'09. 17th IEEE Symposium on Field Programmable Custom Computing Machines, IEEE, pp. 115–122.

21. M. Papadonikolakis and C.-S. Bouganis, 2012, Novel cascade FPGA accelerator for support vector machines classification, *IEEE Transactions on Neural Networks and Learning Systems*, vol. 23, no. 7, pp. 1040–1052.

22. Z. K. Baker and V. K. Prasanna, 2005, Efficient hardware data mining with the Apriori algorithm on FPGAs, in *13th Annual IEEE Symposium on Field-Programmable Custom Computing Machines, 2005. FCCM*, IEEEE, pp. 3–12.

23. H. M. Hussain, K. Benkrid, A. T. Erdogan, and H. Seker, 2011, Highly parameterized K-means clustering on FPGAs: Comparative results with GPPs and GPUs, in *2011 International Conference on Reconfigurable Computing and FPGAs (ReConFig)*, IEEE, pp. 475–480.

24. H. M. Hussain, et al., 2012, Novel dynamic partial reconfiguration implementation of k-means clustering on FPGAs: Comparative results with GPPs and GPUs, *International Journal of Reconfigurable Computing*, vol. 2012, p. 1.
25. F. Jia, C. Wang, X. Li, and X. Zhou, 2015, SSAKMA: Specialized FPGA-based accelerator architecture for data-intensive K-means algorithms, in *International Conference on Algorithms and Architectures for Parallel Processing*, Springer, Cham, pp. 106–119.
26. R. Narayanan, D. Honbo, G. Memik, A. Choudhary, and J. Zambreno, 2007, Interactive presentation: An FPGA implementation of decision tree classification., in *Proceedings of the Conference on Design, Automation and Test in Europe*, EDA Consortium, pp. 189–194.
27. Q. Yu, C. Wang, X. Ma, X. Li, and X. Zhou, 2015, A Deep Learning prediction process accelerator based FPGA, in 2015 *15th IEEE/ACM International Symposium on Cluster, Cloud and Grid Computing (CCGrid)*, IEEE, pp. 1159–1162.
28. D. G. Perera and K. F. Li, 2008, Parallel computation of similarity measures using an fpga-based processor array, in *AINA 2008. 22nd International Conference on Advanced Information Networking and Applications*, IEEE, pp. 955–962.
29. N. Sudha, 2005, A pipelined array architecture for Euclidean distance transformation and its FPGA implementation, *Microprocessors and Microsystems*, vol. 29, no. 8, pp. 405–410.
30. S. Cadambi, A. Majumdar, M. Becchi, S. Chakradhar, and H. P. Graf, 2010, A programmable parallel accelerator for learning and classification, in *Proceedings of the 19th International Conference on Parallel Architectures and Compilation Techniques*, ACM, pp. 273–284.
31. D. Liu, T. Chen, S. Liu, J. Zhou, S. Zhou, O. Teman, . . . and Y. Chen, 2015, Pudiannao: A polyvalent machine learning accelerator, *ACM SIGARCH Computer Architecture News* Vol. 43, No. 1, pp. 369–381.
32. MovieLens Datasets. http://grouplens.org/datasets/movielens/.
33. T. Segaran, 2007, *Programming Collective Intelligence: Building Smart Web 2.0 Applications.* O'Reilly Media, Inc.
34. Kernel. https://github.com/Xilinx/linux-xlnx, X.L.

CHAPTER 8

Deep Learning Accelerators

Yangyang Zhao, Chao Wang, Lei Gong,
Xi Li, Aili Wang, and Xuehai Zhou

University of Science and Technology of China

Hefei, China

CONTENTS

8.1 INTRODUCTION

The artificial neural network (ANN), a layer-wise structure, is proposed based on the fact that the human brain recognizes things step by step, as depicted in Figure 8.1. ANNs with more network layers perform better in recognition accuracy and reduction of the curse of dimensionality [1]. Nevertheless, with the depth of networks increasing, local optimum, gradient diffusion, and other critical problems have arisen, leading to the regression of ANN performance [2]. Therefore, how to train multilayer neural networks has been a challenge.

Geoffrey Hinton proposed an unsupervised network model called *deep belief networks* (DBNs) and a new training method to train deep neural networks like DBNs [3]. The new

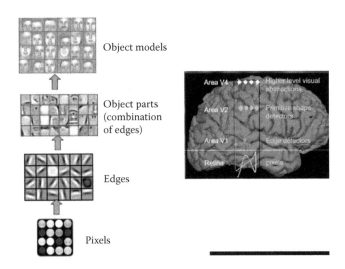

FIGURE 8.1 The abstract workflow of the human brain level by level.

method employs greedy layer-wise pretraining to solve the local optimum and other problems existing in ANNs. Afterward, the depth of neural networks could increase to seven layers, even more. Moreover, other deep neural network models are proposed, such as deep neural networks (DNNs), convolutional neural networks (CNNs), and recurrent neural networks (RNNs). Since then, the floodgates to deep learning have been opened, and Hinton has been honored as the godfather of deep learning.

Deep learning has been applied in image identification [4,5], automatic speech recognition [6–8], and other AI fields [9]. In the era of Big Data, the volume and scale of data are increasing sharply, leading to large-scale networks. In addition, deep learning applications are computing-intensive and data-intensive. When processing large-scale data, the number of parameters grows exponentially. As a result, the performance of deep learning is restricted by massive computing resources, computing time, and energy. Therefore, there is a strong demand for high-performance implementations of deep learning.

There are many research works on speeding up deep learning applications on parallel acceleration platforms. Zhang et al. [10] achieved the distributed learning for restricted Boltzmann machines (RBMs) using the MapReduce parallel framework on the Hadoop platform. Raina et al. [11] leveraged the abundant parallel resources in general purpose graphic processing units (GPGPUs) to speed up the computation of unsupervised DBNs. Although such platforms show high computing performance, the computing efficiency is rather low while costing fairly high energy due to their generality. These drawbacks can be alleviated on customized hardware platforms, such as application specific integrated circuit (ASIC) and field programmable gate arrays (FPGAs). Table 8.1 compares popular parallel acceleration platforms from various characters. FPGAs combine the advantages of general-purpose computing and special-purpose computing. The hardware structure of FPGAs enables high computing performance close to

TABLE 8.1   Comparison of Different Parallel Platforms

Platform	GPGPU	ASIC	FPGA
Generality	General purpose	Custom-built	Semi-custom
Resource–utility ratio	Low	High	High
Performance	Good	Top	Good
Energy cost	High	Low	Low
Development cost	Low	High	Middle

the performance of ASIC, while the reconfigurability of FPGAs allows the flexibility to change the hardware circuits to adapt to various applications, leading to a reduction in computing energy.

Since the high performance and energy-efficiency, accelerations for deep learning on hardware accelerators have sprung up in recent years. Chen et al. designed a high-throughput hardware accelerator for deep learning called *DianNao* on an ASIC ship [12] and achieved a speedup of 117.87× compared with a 2GHz SIMD processor. Then DaDianNao [13] was proposed to process large-scale deep learning applications by 64 ASIC chips, costing 450× less time than the GPU implementation. To apply to more machine learning applications, they designed PuDianNao [14], which is suitable for speeding up seven representative machine learning techniques, including *k*-means, support vector machine, DNN, and so on. Afterward, ShiDianNao [15], a CNN accelerator placed next to a sensor, was presented for visual applications on mobile ends and wearable devices, saving 30× the time and 4700× the energy compared with the GPU.

As for FPGA-based accelerators, there are many studies. Byungik Ahn proposed a novel neurocomputing architecture called Neuron Machine on an FPGA chip [16]. Neuron Machine speeds up the large-scale neuron computing by computing a number of connections in parallel and pipeline. Zhang et al. implemented an FPGA-based accelerator designed for CNN inference and achieved a peak performance of 61.62 Giga Floating-Point Operations Per Second (GFLOPS) under 100 MHz by full utilization of FPGA resources [17]. Ly and Chow studied accelerations of RBMs on single-FPGA, Quad-FPGA, and virtualized FPGA accelerators [18–20], which achieved a speedup of approximately 35×–85×. Kim et al. designed accelerators for RBMs on single FGPA [21] and multiple FPGAs [22] as well. They illustrated a scalable ring-connected multi-FPGA system that supports sparse networks with dense regions of connections and achieves a speedup of 46×–112× over an optimized single-core CPU implementation. Wang et al. designed a scalable deep-learning accelerator unit, called *DLAU* [23], for the kernel computational parts of deep learning algorithms. DLAU achieves up to 36.1× speedup compared to the Intel Core 2 processor. SODA, proposed by Wang et al., is a software-defined FPGA-based accelerator capable of reconstructing the acceleration engines according to the compute-intensive application requirements [24]. They also proposed a services-oriented learning framework, SOLAR [25], to speed up deep learning by the coordination of various CPU, GPU, and FPGA-based accelerators. Experimental results indicate that SOLAR shows significant speedup comparing to the conventional Intel i5 processors.

In this chapter, we introduce the FPGA-based accelerations for deep learning from three aspects as below:

- *Introduction to deep learning.* We describe the concept and components of deep learning, firstly. Then we introduce popular deep-learning models.

- *Introduction to FPGA-based accelerations.* We introduce the primary structure of FPGA, firstly. Then we detail the developing flow of designing FPGA-based accelerators. Afterward, we introduce the acceleration technologies commonly employed in hardware accelerations.

- *Introduction to FPGA-based systems.* Taking the inference algorithm of fully connected networks as an example, we first analyze the computing-intensive part of the algorithm and find out the parallel inside. Next, we propose an accelerating system on both a single FPGA chip and multiple FPGA chips.

The rest of this chapter is organized as follows. Section 8.2 introduces deep-learning structures and widely employed deep-learning models. Section 8.3 presents the structure of FPGA and hardware acceleration methods. Section 8.4 presents the FPGA-based accelerating systems we proposed.

8.2 DEEP LEARNING OVERVIEW

In this section, we first introduce the basic structure and components of deep-learning neural networks. Then we give a brief introduction of three widely employed neural networks: deep neural networks, convolutional neural networks, and recurrent neural networks.

8.2.1 Brief Introduction

Deep learning builds computational models and simulates the human neuron network mechanism to interpret text, images, speech, and other complex data. *Deep* indicates that deep-learning neural networks consist of multiple layers, while *learning* refers to improving the computational performance by continuous learning, as human brains do.

Figure 8.2 shows the basic structure of deep-learning neural networks. Deep-learning nets are made up of multiple bottom-up processing layers. Output features of the lower layer are the inputs of its upper layer. After abstracting features layer by layer, high-level features are represented to recognize or classify the sample data.

Inside layers, there are plenty of neuron units in charge of feature calculations, represented by circles in Figure 8.2. Similar to biological neurons, a deep-learning neuron owns one or more dendrites to accept input information from other neurons and exactly one axon with multiple terminals to send information to other neurons. Connections between axon terminals and dendrites, also called *synapses*, are the information carriers between neurons, shown as connecting lines in Figure 8.2.

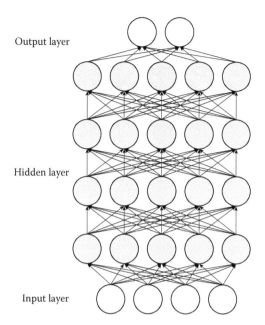

FIGURE 8.2   Deep learning structure.

Neurons are primary computation units in deep-learning neural networks, the computational process of which is shown in Figure 8.3. The neuron receives data from input neurons and calculates with corresponding synapse weights. The weighted result is added with a bias value, and then the activation function reads the sum to produce the final output. The computation of the neuron can be represented as $f(\sum_{i=1}^{n} x_i * w_i + b)$, where $x_1, x_2, \ldots, x_n$ are the input neuron values; $w_1, w_2, \ldots, w_n$ are the weight values between input neurons and the current neuron indicating the intensity of inputs; f is the activation function and controls the output amplitude; and b is the bias value to tune the input of f properly. In general, synapse weights and bias values are the main parameters to train during the learning process.

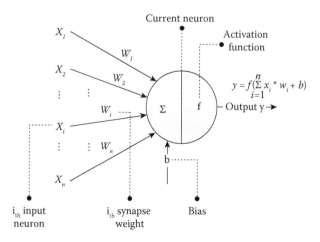

FIGURE 8.3   Deep-learning neuron processing diagram.

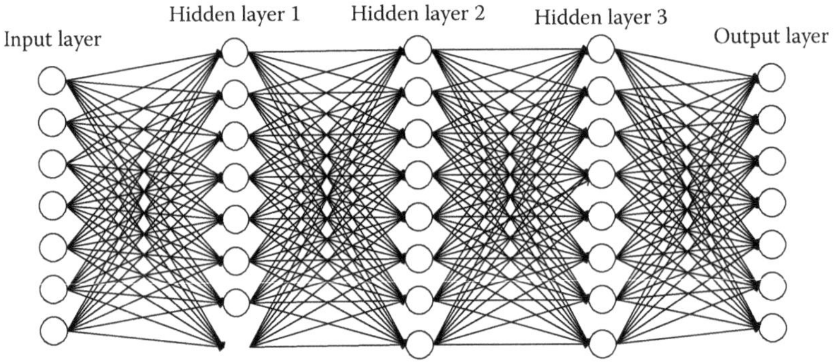

FIGURE 8.4   Deep neural network diagram.

8.2.2 Deep Neural Networks

The DNN, a primary neural network type of deep learning, is composed of an input layer, an output layer, and multiple hidden layers. Figure 8.4 illustrates the structure of DNNs.

Neuron values of the lower layer are the input data of the upper layer. Within DNNs in a narrow sense, neurons of adjacent layers are fully connected by individual synaptic weights, while neurons in the same layer or nonadjacent layers are not connected. The number of neurons in the input layer is equal to the scale of input data, and the number of categories decides the number of neurons in the output layer. Differently, the depth of the network, the number of neurons in hidden layers, weight parameters, and bias parameters are decided by the learning process. Neuron quantities in every layer, values of weights, and values of bias parameters determine the final structure of DNNs.

Due to the fully connected structure of DNNs, the number of parameters increases exponentially with the increment of data scales and neuron numbers, leading to a boost in computation quantity and cost.

8.2.3 Convolutional Neural Networks

Figure 8.5 is a CNN structure diagram called *DeepID* proposed by Sun Yi et al. [26] for face recognition. CNNs contain four kinds of neural layers: input layers, convolutional layers, pooling layers, and classifier layers. DeepID consists of one input layer, four convolutional layers, three max-pooling layers, and one classifier layer. Convolutional layers and max-pooling layers, placed alternatively, contain several feature maps each to extract features hierarchically. The classifier layer is a fully connected layer to identify classes finally.

CNNs leverage the locality of image data and replace the global full connections in DNNs with local full connections in the convolutional layers and pooling layers. Neurons in the same convolutional feature maps share a set of weights and are convolved with a local convolutional kernel to extract a feature. Multiple kernels are used to extract various features and significantly reduce the scale of parameters thereby. Pooling layers maximum, minimum, or average results from the previous convolutional layer by local

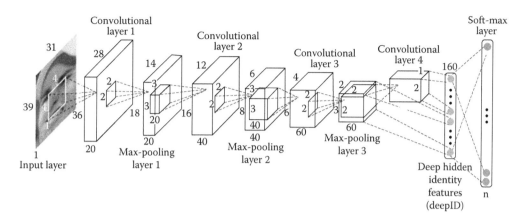

FIGURE 8.5   Convolutional neural network diagram [28].

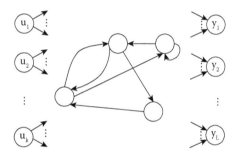

FIGURE 8.6   Recurrent neural network diagram.

windows. Classifier layers are fully connected layers with individual weights to learn localized features and global features.

8.2.4 Recurrent Neural Networks

DNNs and CNNs are feed-forward neural networks, while RNNs take the output from a previous time step as feedback input of the current time step. Figure 8.6 represents the recurrent structure of RNNs.

RNNs are known as network models with memory and are capable of modeling variations of time series, which is quite hard for feed-forward neural networks. RNNs show excellent performance when processing sequential applications, such as phone recognitions, natural language processing, and gene processing.

8.3 FPGA-BASED ACCELERATION

This section demonstrates the structure of FPGAs at first, and then introduces the design flow of FPGA-based reconfigurable accelerators. Next, key techniques for optimizing accelerator performance are presented, to reduce the computation time and communication cost.

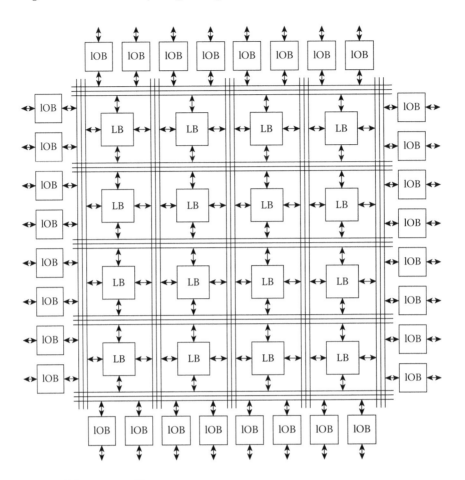

FIGURE 8.7   FPGA structure diagram.

8.3.1 FPGA Overview

Hardware acceleration means mapping the whole algorithm or compute-intensive part to hardware devices and speeding up the computation with the help of the inherent parallel in hardware devices. FPGA is one of the most popular hardware acceleration platforms, benefitting from its reconfigurability and high energy efficiency. According to different applications, FPGAs can be configured to different circuit layouts to fit application characteristics. FPGAs contain abundant parallel computational resources, which is the key for high-performance implementations. Figure 8.7 illustrates the structure of FPGAs, including input–output blocks, configurable logic block, and programmable interconnect. As they evolve, some FPGA chips have integrated embedded softcore or hardcore, on-chip memory, and digital signal processing.

FPGA-based accelerators are designed using hardware/software co-design technique, mapping the compute-intensive and logic-simple part onto FPGA and the other onto the host processor. The design flow is represented in Figure 8.8 with the following steps.

1. *Algorithm analysis.* Analyze the application algorithm, then get the compute-intensive module and control module.

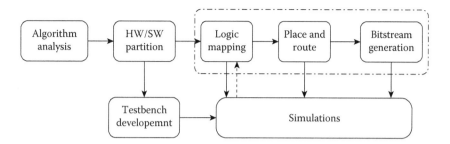

FIGURE 8.8 The design flow of FPGA-based hardware accelerators.

2. *HW/SW partition.* Assign the control flow or sequential part to the host processor, but put the parallel compute-intensive part onto FPGA devices.

3. *Logic mapping.* According to the parallel existing in the compute-intensive part, design the hardware logic units. Use hardware description languages like Verilog, VHDL to describe the hardware structures and behaviors. For the ease of software developers, Xilinx and Intel Altera proposed High-Level Synthesis and OpenCL, respectively, to program FPGA devices.

4. *Test bench development, synthesis, and simulation.* The test bench is developed to simulate the software function of the host processor. Interpret with test bench; simulate and verify if the hardware logic is correct. If not, return to Step c to modify the hardware code.

5. *Generating Intellectual Property (IP) core, placement, and routing.* Assign computational resources and memory resources and generate IP core from the hardware code. Then connect IP core with other system modules.

6. *Generating bitstreams.* Generate bitstreams, which are the configuration of FPGA. Then download bitstreams to the FPGA device by JTAG-USB or other interfaces.

7. *Test.* Run applications on the FPGA accelerator to test the correctness of memory interface, computational results, and input/output data. If not, return to Step c to modify the hardware code.

8.3.2 Optimization Techniques

To optimize the performance of FPGA accelerators, we consider two aspects: one is to speed up the computation process, the other is to reduce communication costs. For computation acceleration, parallel computing and pipeline computing are the conventional techniques, while for reduction of transmission costs, we apply local storage and data prefetching.

1. Parallel computing, a popular means in hardware accelerations, cuts down the computing time by running multiple processing elements (PEs) in parallel. Single instruction, multiple data (SIMD) is the principal method used in parallel computing. As a result, there must be no data dependence among parallel computations.

In this way, multiple parallel PEs calculate different data by the same computing operations. The performance improvement benefited from parallel computing is decided by the degree of parallelism, namely the number of PEs. Assuming there are D data in a computational task, and the computing time for each data point is t, the total sequential computing time is $D \times t$. If we employ parallel computing with P PEs, omitting the extra cost, the total parallel computing time is $D \times t/P$. Ideally, parallel computing saves nearly P times computing time.

2. Pipeline computing, a common technique in computer architecture design, is also widely used in the design of FPGA and ASIC accelerators. Essentially, pipeline computing leverages the time parallel to improve the throughput. In parallel computing, a computing task is divided into several subtasks without data hazards and structure hazards, so that each subtask can run with other subtasks in parallel. Figure 8.9 shows the difference between serial computing and pipeline computing. Pipeline computing realizes the parallel execution of computing tasks. When PE i finishes the subtask i of task K, subtask $i+1$ of task K starts in PE $i+1$; meantime, PE i computes the subtask i of task $K+1$. Different tasks are in different subtask phases at the same time. In the ideal case, every pipeline stage consumes the same computing time. When processing a mass of computing tasks, pipeline computing achieves a speedup near to the

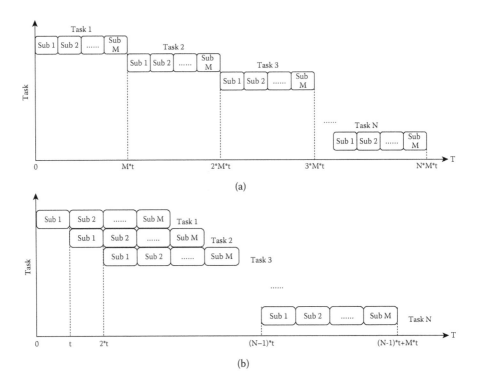

FIGURE 8.9 Comparison of serial computing and pipeline computing: (a) serial computing and (b) pipeline computing.

number of pipeline stages. In practice, the time of different pipeline stages is different in most cases. In such condition, the stage of the most time becomes the performance bottleneck of the pipeline and the key factor of pipeline speedup.

3. In the FPGA-based accelerating system, there are plenty of transmissions between the accelerator and host processor to transfer input data and computing results. If we did not optimize the transmissions, the time and energy of communications would be significant. Local storage is to leverage the data locality among computations and buffer the frequently used data locally inside the accelerator. After the related calculations are done, the data is replaced by new reuse data. The transmission overhead can be significantly reduced by reusing, which also results in the reduction of communication cost and energy consumption.

4. Data prefetching is to read the data needed into FPGA in advance, so as to cover up the transmission time by continuous computing. Such a pipeline of communication and computation weakens the influence of communications to the execution time. We apply a duplicate buffer to realize data prefetching. Two buffers play the role of producer and consumer alternatively. When a PE reads the data stored in Buffer A, the following data is written into Buffer B. In the next time calculation, the PE reads data from Buffer B and new data is transferred into Buffer A. A duplicate buffer can avoid the read/write conflicts of the single buffer and realize continuous computation without stalls. However, the premise is that the producing time is no more than the consuming time. Hence, we need to trade off the transfer volume and buffer size, to guarantee that the filling time of the buffer is no more than the interval time of data reading.

8.4 PROPOSED ACCELERATING SYSTEM

This section takes the inference process of fully connected networks as an example to introduce accelerating systems based on FPGAs. First, the inference algorithm is analyzed to find out the parallel within a single layer and among multiple layers. Then accelerating systems on single FPGA and multiple FPGAs are proposed in detail.

8.4.1 Algorithm Analysis

Computations of deep learning applications include two procedures, the learning and inference processes. Compared with the training process, the calculation of the inference process is more regular. As a consequence, accelerations of the inference process are more important for applications with great practical significance.

As Figure 8.3 shows, the calculation in a neuron includes three steps. First, input data from the lower layer neurons are read in and weighted with their synapse weights. Next, the weighted result is added with the bias. Then, the activation function reads the sum as input and computes the final output result. Supposing input data from the lower layer neurons are $(x_1, x_2, ..., x_n)$, weight values are $(w_1, w_2, ..., w_n)$, the bias is b, the activation function is f, and the output is y, then the computation of the neuron can be formulated as Equation 8.1. In our work, the activation function is the sigmoid function, as Equation 8.2 depicts.

$$y = f(\sum_{i=1}^{n} x_i * w_i + b) \tag{8.1}$$

$$f(x) = \frac{1}{1 + e^{-x}} \tag{8.2}$$

If we regard the inputs as a row vector and weights as a column vector, the weighted computation can be regarded as the inner product of a row vector $\vec{x}$ and a column vector $\vec{w}$. Equation 8.1 is simplified as Equation 8.3:

$$y = f(\vec{x} \cdot \vec{w} + b) \tag{8.3}$$

The inference algorithm of fully connected networks is a bottom-up feed-forward process. Assuming there are D sample data, the depth of net is L, and the lth layer contains N_l neurons with N_{l-1} inputs. In the lth layer, we represent inputs as X_l, outputs as Y_l, weights as W_l, and the bias as B_l. Moreover, the activation f is the sigmoid function. The computation in the lth layer can be represented by Equation 8.4:

$$Y_l = f(X_l * W_l), \quad (l = 1, 2, \ldots, L) \tag{8.4}$$

where

$$X_l = \begin{bmatrix} 1 & x_{11}^l & x_{12}^l & \cdots & x_{1N_{l-1}}^l \\ 1 & x_{21}^l & x_{22}^l & \cdots & x_{2N_{l-1}}^l \\ \vdots & \vdots & \vdots & \ddots & \vdots \\ 1 & x_{D1}^l & x_{D2}^l & \cdots & x_{DN_{l-1}}^l \end{bmatrix} \tag{8.5}$$

$$W_l = \begin{bmatrix} b_1^l & b_2^l & \cdots & b_{N_l}^l \\ w_{11}^l & w_{12}^l & \cdots & w_{1N_l}^l \\ w_{21}^l & w_{22}^l & \cdots & w_{2N_l}^l \\ \vdots & \vdots & \ddots & \vdots \\ w_{N_{l-1}1}^l & w_{N_{l-1}2}^l & \cdots & w_{N_{l-1}N_l}^l \end{bmatrix} \tag{8.6}$$

Based on the above, the inference process is divided into two parts: one is the matrix multiplication, the other is activation computing. There are plenty of parallelizable operations in matrix multiplications. There are two common operation orders of a single matrix multiplication, as Figure 8.10 depicts.

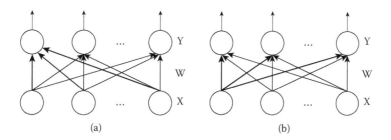

FIGURE 8.10 Different operation orders of matrix multiplications: (a) based on inner products and (b) based on scalar products.

The first operation order is dividing computations into a set of inner products of row vectors and column vectors. Every inner product result is an element of the result matrix. Bold lines in Figure 8.10a indicate one inner product. Among the matrix multiplication by inner products, there are two parallelizable computing. In the inner product of a row vector and a column vector, different groups of element multiplications can be processed in parallel. On the other hand, different inner products can be parallel processed as well. Moreover, the same row vector can be reused to multiply with various column vectors.

Figure 8.10b shows the second operation order that is dividing computations into a set of scalar products of an element with a row vector. Every scalar product produces an intermediate vector of the result vector in the result matrix. After all intermediate vectors are obtained, the final results are found by adding all intermediate vectors. The bold lines in Figure 8.10b indicate one scalar product. There are two operations which can be processed in parallel in the matrix multiplication by scalar products. In the scalar products, there is no data dependency between element multiplications, which can be computed in parallel. Likewise, multiplications of different elements and different row vectors are parallelizable.

Based on the parallel analysis within a single layer computation, we find the inherent parallel between two adjacent neural layers. Figure 8.11 illustrates the pipeline computing of two adjacent layers. Assuming Layer0 is the input layer, Layer1 and Layer2 are two adjacent hidden layers. The lower layer (Layer1) computes in the inner product manner, while the upper layer (Layer2) in the scalar product manner. As soon as Layer1 produces a neuron output result, Layer2 reads it in as an input and starts the scalar products by the input data. At the same time, Layer1 starts the computation of the next neuron by inner product computations. In this way, computations of Layer1 and Layer2 are processed in the pipeline. One thing to note is that the results produced in Layer2 every time are temporal results of all the neurons in Layer2, while the upper layer of Layer2 cannot start its computations until computations in Layer2 is done. Therefore, only two adjacent layers can be processed in the pipeline. Taking two adjacent layers as a group, calculations among different groups are executed in sequential order. Such a pipeline computing method has been applied to speed up the inference process of deep neural networks [27].

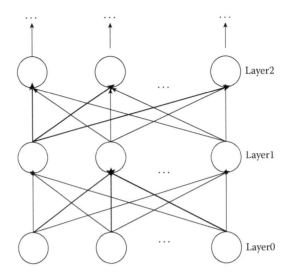

FIGURE 8.11 Pipeline computations of two adjacent neural layers.

8.4.2 Single FPGA System

Upon the parallel analysis in the last section, we propose a Pipeline Inference Engine (PIE) on a single FPGA to speed up the inference computation of fully connected networks. Figure 8.12 shows the structure of PIE. The host CPU controls the inference algorithm progress, distributes associated data, and configures the FPGA accelerator. Data needed are stored in the memory on-board and transferred by DMA into on-chip buffers. There are three groups of buffers, one each for input data, weights, and temporal data. Each group contains several sets of buffers for prefetching data into the accelerator to cover the transmission time. PE0 ~PEn is the main computing core to accomplish the inference calculations

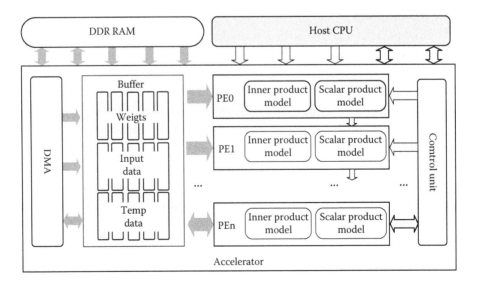

FIGURE 8.12 PIE system architecture diagram.

by parallel transfer and parallel computations. Each PE may contain an inner product model, a scalar product model, or both. To realize the pipeline between adjacent layers, the inner product model, and scalar product model must be placed alternately. Excluding the limitation of resources and bandwidth, putting more PEs in the accelerator would increase the degree of parallel and improve the performance. While considering the resources and bandwidth, it is essential to trade off the number of PEs and the internal structure of PEs.

Figure 8.13 indicates the structure of IP cores in PIE. Figure 8.13a is the IP core for the inner product model, applying multiple multipliers and adder tree to do multiply-accumulation (MAC) operations of inner products in parallel and pipeline. After MAC operations are done, the sigmoid unit computes the final results, which is realized approximately by piecewise linear interpolation activation function. Figure 8.13b illustrates the IP core for the scalar product model. The scalar products are processed by multiple multipliers, while vector additions of temporal results are processed by multiple adders. At the end of the IP core for scalar products, a piecewise linear interpolation activation function is also applied to accomplish the activation operations.

8.4.3 Scalable Multi-FPGA System

Since there are more computation and storage resources in a multi-FPGA platform, the accelerator obtains higher parallelism. Figure 8.14 is the system architecture based on multiple FPGAs. There are $F+1$ FPGA chips on a hardware accelerator card, including a control FPGA and F compute FPGA. The control FPGA plays the role of broker between host CPU and FPGAs in charge of data or signal transmissions and partial calculation work. In this way, frequent communication between CPU and FPGAs is avoided. Compute FPGAs undertake most of the calculation work of the inference algorithm, connecting with the control FPGA respectively and with each other in a ring topology. Moreover, there is a dedicated buffer and DDR for each FPGA to store input data, weights, and temporal results.

A key question in the multi-FPGA system is how to partition the computation of the whole network onto multiple FPGAs. We propose two partition methods: one is the division between layers (DBL) and the other is the division inside layers (DIL).

DBL means to divide the neural network by layers so that every FPGA calculates one neural layer separately. To realize the pipeline between computing FPGAs, we refer to the pipeline method of adjacent layers in PIE. Assuming F_i means the ith compute FPGA, when $i \bmod 2 = 1$ (i is odd), F_i computes the layer i by inner products. When $i \bmod 2 = 0$ (i is even), F_i calculates the Layeri in the scalar product manner. Thus, F_i and F_{i+1} (i is odd) are viewed as a group and compute the same task in the pipeline. Similar to PIE, DBL realizes a pipeline computation of two adjacent layers. Different groups compute the same task in serial but process multiple tasks in pipeline as Figure 8.15 shows. Considering the case that the depth of the network is larger than the number of compute FPGAs, DBL first finishes the first F layer computations of all data in pipeline, then starts the next F layers in the pipeline, and so on.

DIL means dividing the neural network into chunks so that every compute FPGA is in charge of a part of the same layer at the same time. Control FPGA partitions the data

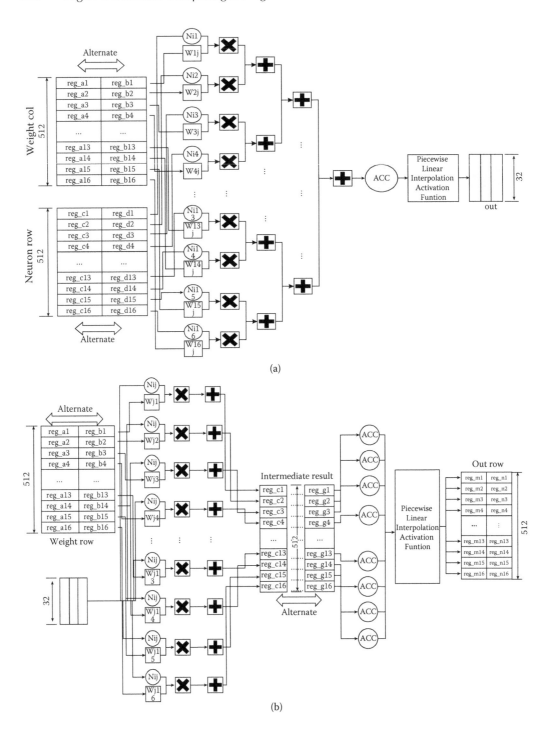

FIGURE 8.13 IP core design of the pipeline inference engine: (a) IP core structure of the inner product model (b) IP core structure of the scalar product model.

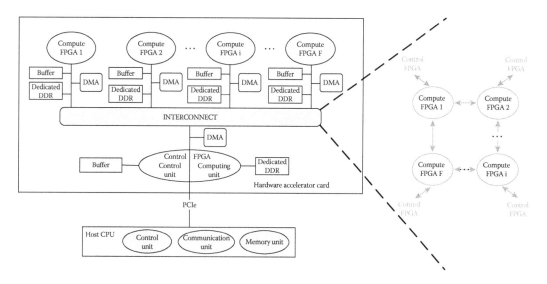

FIGURE 8.14   Multi-FGPA system architecture diagram.

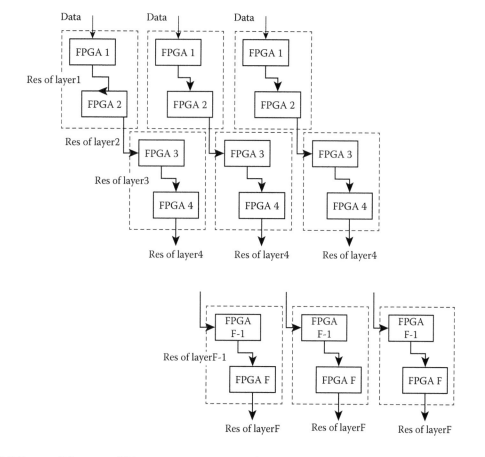

FIGURE 8.15   Diagram of Division Between Layers (DBL).

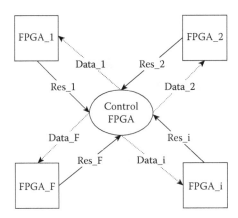

FIGURE 8.16   Diagram of Division Inside Layers (DIL).

into chunks and scatters to various computing nodes on FPGAs. In inner product, FPGAs finish their tasks in parallel, which is a partial task of the whole layer computation. After that, control FPGA gathers all temporal results from computing FPGAs and integrates them to get the final results. DIL realizes a parallel calculation of the single layer with a higher degree of parallel by multiple FPGAs but a sequential computation of different layers, which is quite different from DBL, which is shown in Figure 8.16.

8.5 CONCLUSIONS

In this chapter, we first introduced the computation of deep learning. We also presented the design flow and optimization techniques of the FPGA-based accelerating system. Moreover, taking the inference process of fully connected neural networks, for example, we studied the parallel existing in the inference algorithm and proposed a novel accelerating method to realize a pipeline computation of two adjacent layers. On this basis, we proposed accelerating systems on both a single FPGA and multiple FPGAs and discussed how to partition the computation onto multiple FPGAs.

8.6 ACKNOWLEDGMENTS

This work was supported by the National Science Foundation of China (No. 61379040), Anhui Provincial Natural Science Foundation (No. 1608085QF12), CCF-Venustech Hongyan Research Initiative (No. CCF-VenustechRP1026002), Suzhou Research Foundation (No. SYG201625), Youth Innovation Promotion Association CAS (No. 2017497), and Fundamental Research Funds for the Central Universities (WK2150110003).

REFERENCES

1. S. C. Wang, 2003, Artificial neural network. In Interdisciplinary Computing in Java Programming, pp. 81–100, Springer US.
2. Y. Bengio and O. Delalleau, 2011. On the expressive power of deep architectures. In Algorithmic Learning Theory, pp. 18–36, Springer, Berlin.

3. G. E. Hinton, S. Osindero, and Y. W. Teh, 2006, A fast learning algorithm for deep belief nets, *Neural Computation*, vol. 18, no. 7, pp. 1527–1554.
4. V. Nair and G. E. Hinton, 2009, 3D object recognition with deep belief nets. In *Advances in neural information processing systems*, pp. 1339–1347.
5. H. Lee, R. Grosse, R. Ranganath, and A. Y. Ng, 2009, Convolutional deep belief networks for scalable unsupervised learning of hierarchical representations. In Proceedings of the 26th Annual International Conference on Machine Learning, pp. 609–616, ACM.
6. A. Mohamed, G. Dahl, and G. Hinton, 2009, Deep belief networks for phone recognition, *Nips Workshop on Deep Learning for Speech Recognition and Related Applications*, vol. 1, no. 9, p. 39.
7. A. R. Mohamed, T. N. Sainath, G. Dahl, B. Ramabhadran, G. E. Hinton, and M. A. Picheny, 2011, Deep belief networks using discriminative features for phone recognition. In Acoustics, Speech and Signal Processing (ICASSP), 2011 IEEE International Conference on, pp. 5060–5063, IEEE.
8. T. N. Sainath, B. Kingsbury, B. Ramabhadran, P. Fousek, P. Novak, and A. R. Mohamed, 2011, Making deep belief networks effective for large vocabulary continuous speech recognition. In Automatic Speech Recognition and Understanding (ASRU), 2011 IEEE Workshop on, pp. 30–35, IEEE.
9. R. Salakhutdinov and G. Hinton, 2009, Semantic hashing, *International Journal of Approximate Reasoning*, vol. 50, no. 7, pp. 969–978.
10. K. Zhang and X. Chen, 2014, Large-scale deep belief nets with mapreduce, Access, *IEEE*, vol. 2, pp. 395–403.
11. R. Raina, A. Madhavan, and A. Y. Ng, 2009, Large-scale deep unsupervised learning using graphics processors. In Proceedings of the 26th Annual International Conference on Machine Learning, pp. 873–880, ACM.
12. T. Chen, Z. Du, N. Sun, J. Wang, C. Wu, Y. Chen, and O. Temam, 2014, Diannao: A small-footprint high-throughput accelerator for ubiquitous machine-learning, *ACM Sigplan Notices*, vol. 49, no. 4, pp. 269–284.
13. Y. Chen, T. Luo, S. Liu, S. Zhang, L. He, J. Wang, . . . and O. Temam, 2014, Dadiannao: A machine-learning supercomputer. In Proceedings of the 47th Annual IEEE/ACM International Symposium on Microarchitecture, pp. 609–622, IEEE Computer Society.
14. D. Liu, T. Chen, S. Liu, J. Zhou, S. Zhou, O. Teman, . . . and Y. Chen, 2015, Pudiannao: A poly-valent machine learning accelerator, *ACM SIGARCH Computer Architecture News*, vol. 43, no. 1, pp. 369–381.
15. Z. Du, R. Fasthuber, T. Chen, P. Ienne, L. Li, T. Luo, . . . and O. Temam, 2015, ShiDianNao: Shifting vision processing closer to the sensor, *ACM SIGARCH Computer Architecture News*, vol. 43, no. 3, pp. 92–104.
16. J. B. Ahn, 2012, Neuron machine: Parallel and pipelined digital neurocomputing architecture. In Computational Intelligence and Cybernetics (CyberneticsCom), 2012 IEEE International Conference on, pp. 143–147, IEEE.
17. C. Zhang, P. Li, G. Sun, Y. Guan, B. Xiao, and J. Cong, 2015, Optimizing fpga-based accelerator design for deep convolutional neural networks. In Proceedings of the 2015 ACM/SIGDA International Symposium on Field-Programmable Gate Arrays, pp. 161–170, ACM.
18. D. L. Ly, and P. Chow, 2009, A high-performance FPGA architecture for restricted boltzmann machines. In Proceedings of the ACM/SIGDA International Symposium on Field Programmable Gate Arrays, pp. 73–82, ACM.
19. D. L. Ly, and P. Chow, 2009, A multi-fpga architecture for stochastic restricted boltzmann machines. In Field Programmable Logic and Applications, 2009. FPL 2009. International Conference on, pp. 168–173, IEEE.
20. D. Le Ly and P. Chow, 2010, High-performance reconfigurable hardware architecture for restricted Boltzmann machines, *IEEE Transactions on Neural Networks*, vol. 21, no. 11, pp. 1780–1792.

21. S. K. Kim, L. C. McAfee, P. L. McMahon, and K. Olukotun, 2009, A highly scalable restricted boltzmann machine fpga implementation. In Field Programmable Logic and Applications, 2009. FPL 2009. International Conference on, pp. 367–372, IEEE.
22. S. K. Kim, P. L. McMahon, and K. Olukotun, 2010, A large-scale architecture for restricted boltzmann machines. In Field-Programmable Custom Computing Machines (FCCM), 2010 18th IEEE Annual International Symposium on, pp. 201–208, IEEE.
23. C. Wang, L. Gong, Q. Yu, X. Li, Y. Xie, and X. Zhou, 2017, DLAU: A scalable deep learning accelerator unit on FPGA, *IEEE Transactions on Computer-Aided Design of Integrated Circuits and Systems*, vol. 36, no. 3, pp. 513–517.
24. C. Wang, X. Li, and X. Zhou, 2015, SODA: software defined FPGA-based accelerators for big data, in Design, Automation and Test in Europe Conference & Exhibition (DATE), 2015, pp. 884–887, IEEE.
25. C. Wang, X. Li, Q. Yu, A. Wang, P. Hung, and X. Zhou, 2016, SOLAR: Services-oriented learning architectures. In Web Services (ICWS), 2016 IEEE International Conference on, pp. 662–665, IEEE.
26. Y. Sun, X. Wang, and X. Tang, 2014, Deep learning face representation from predicting 10,000 classes. In Proceedings of the IEEE Conference on Computer Vision and Pattern Recognition, pp. 1891–1898.
27. Y. Zhao, Q. Yu, X. Zhou, et al., 2016, PIE: A pipeline energy-efficient accelerator for inference process in deep neural networks. In 2016 IEEE 22nd International Conference on Parallel and Distributed Systems (ICPADS), pp. 1067–1074, IEEE.
28. Y. Sun, X. Wang, and X. Tang, 2014, Deep learning face representation from predicting 10,000 classes. In Proceedings of the IEEE Conference on Computer Vision and Pattern Recognition, pp. 1891–1898.

CHAPTER 9

Recent Advances for Neural Networks Accelerators and Optimizations

Fan Sun, Chao Wang, Lei Gong,

Xi Li, Aili Wang, and Xuehai Zhou

University of Science and Technology of China

Hefei, China

CONTENTS

9.1 INTRODUCTION

In the last few years, with the continuous popularity of the neural network, in the field of computer architecture and hardware, there have been a large number of neural network papers for chip design and optimization. Moreover, the research of neural network has extended to the electronic design automation (EDA) field. In this chapter, we integrate the 2016 EDA Conference (DAC, ICCAD, DATE) and the recently held DATE 2017 neural network papers, then classify and analyze the key technology in each paper. Finally, we give some new hot spots and research trends of the neural network.

9.2 THE NEURAL NETWORKS IN EDA

The neural network is a computation-intensive and storage-intensive application. And in the design of neural network accelerators, there are many contradictions, so in 2016 EDA and 2017 DATE, most of the papers are from the perspective of optimizing calculation, optimizing storage, and optimizing the area and power consumption to design the neural network accelerator; others apply the neural network to specific problems.

9.2.1 Optimizing Calculation

Although the most advanced CNN accelerators can deliver high computational through-put, the performance is highly unstable. Once changed to accommodate a new network with different parameters like layers and kernel size, the fixed hardware structure may no longer match the data flows well. Consequently, the accelerator will fail to deliver high performance due to the underutilization of either logic resource or memory bandwidth. To overcome this problem, C-Brain [1] proposes a novel deep-learning accelerator, which offers multiple types of data-level parallelism: interkernel, intrakernel, and hybrid. The interkernel is part of the input feature map in different layers of parallel data processing; the intrakernel is the same layer of input feature map for parallel processing. The design can adaptively switch among the three types of parallelism and the corresponding data tiling schemes to dynamically match different networks or even different layers of a single network. No matter how we change the hardware configurations or network types, the proposed network mapping strategy ensures the optimal performance and energy efficiency. Caffeine [2] first pointed out that the convolution layer of CNN is computation-intensive, and the fully connected layer is communication-intensive. When CNN is accelerated on the FPGA, the convolution layer cannot be accelerated only. Otherwise, the operation of the fully connected layer will become a new bottleneck. Then the authors analyzed and studied the uniform representation of the neural network for the convolution layer and the fully connected layer (as shown in Figures 9.1 and 9.2) to reduce the amount of intermediate data generated. Finally, they designed a hardware and software co-designed library to accelerate the entire CNN on FPGAs efficiently and optimize the bandwidth of the accelerator. Spiking neural network as the third generation of the artificial neural network has appeared in more and more applications. When the network scale rises to the order of cells in the human visual cortex, the spiking neural network also faces severe computational efficiency problems. AxSNN [3] applies the approximate calculation method to select the neuron, based on the static and dynamic information of the neuron's average spiking frequency, the current internal state, and the connected synaptic weight in the calculation of the spiking neural network. It then selectively skips the pulse reception and pulse output that does not affect the output of these neurons, thereby reducing the redundancy calculation, improving the calculation efficiency. In the experiment, the spiking neural network based on approximate calculation is implemented in software and hardware. Compared with the optimized network, the scalar computation is reduced by 1.4–5.5 times on average, and the energy consumption is reduced by 1.2–3.62 times and 1.26–3.9 times in hardware and software energies, respectively. The computational process of the convolution neural network is complex; a huge amount of data movement between

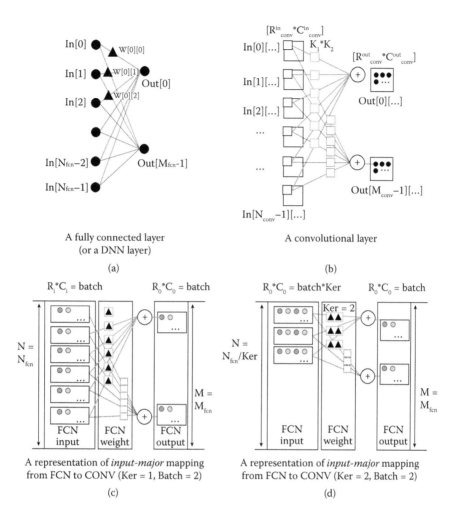

FIGURE 9.1 (a–d) Input-major mapping from the fully connected (FCN) layer to the convolution (CONV) layer.

the computational processor core and memory hierarchy occupies the majority of the power consumption. Chain-NN [4] focuses on the hardware calculation process of the convolution operation concerning multiplexing the input data and designs the convolution neural network accelerator Chain-NN based on the one-dimensional chain architecture. Chain-NN consists of dedicated dual-channel process engines (PE); the overall structure can be configured according to the structural parameters of the network to improve the overall resource utilization. The experimental results show that the accelerator can achieve 84%–100% of the internal resource utilization rate when dealing with the commonly used convolution neural network. Under the TSMC 28-nm structure, it can reach 806.4 giga operations per second (GOPS) throughput with 700 MHz operating frequency, and power efficiency is at least 2.5× to 4.1× times better than the state-of-the-art works. Ref. [5] presents a novel method to double the computation rate of convolutional neural network accelerators by packing two multiply-and-accumulate (MAC) operations into one DSP block of

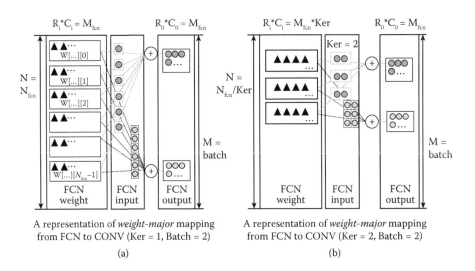

A representation of *weight-major* mapping from FCN to CONV (Ker = 1, Batch = 2)

(a)

A representation of *weight-major* mapping from FCN to CONV (Ker = 2, Batch = 2)

(b)

FIGURE 9.2 (a, b) Weight-major mapping from the FCN layer to the CONV layer.

off-the-shelf FPGAs. The same feature of the multiplier coincides with the computational model corresponding to the parallel processing of multiple output neurons, thus improving the computational efficiency and resource utilization of the network. The experimental results show that this approach not only increases the computation throughput of a CNN layer by twice with the same resource, the network performance also improves by 14%~84% over a highly optimized state-of-the-art accelerator solution, based on the fact that massive zero values of synapses in CNN degrade the computational efficiency. Ref. [6] proposes a novel hardware accelerator for CNNs exploiting zero weights and activations. Unlike most CNN accelerators that use a synchronous parallel computing model, the accelerator uses finer granular program element internally, and each program element uses a weak synchronous mode of operation that can independently detect and skip computations associated with zero weight/activation. In addition, the authors also reported a zero-induced load imbalance problem, which exists in zero-aware parallel CNN hardware architectures, and presented a zero-aware kernel allocation as a solution. The simulation results show that the proposed architecture running two real deep CNNs pruned AlexNet and VGG-16 offers 4×/1.8× (AlexNet) and 5.2×/2.1× (VGG-16) speedup compared with state-of-the-art zero-agnostic/zero-activation-aware architectures. The inherent approximation in neural network calculations can be used to simplify the computational process. LookNN [7] proposed a new simplified processing strategy, by using the similarity idea and the fault-tolerant properties of the neural network. All the floating-point multiplication operations in the neural network are transformed into a query operation based on the look-up table. Then, the quick search operation in the calculation process is realized by adding the associated memory for the quick retrieval of the calculation result in the GPU. The experimental results showed that this strategy can achieve energy saving by 2.2 times and performance improvement by 2.5 times in the absence of additional calculation errors. When the additional error of 0.2% is allowed, energy consumption is reduced by three times and the performance is improved by 2.6 times.

9.2.2 Optimizing Storage

Ref. [8] presented two techniques, factorization and pruning, that not only compress the models but also maintain the form of the models for the execution on neuromorphic architectures. The authors also proposed a novel method to combine the two techniques. The proposed method shows significant improvements in reducing the number of model parameters over the standalone use of each method while maintaining the performance. The experimental results showed that the proposed method can achieve a 31× reduction rate without loss of accuracy for the largest layer of AlexNet. In mobile devices and other embedded devices to deploy the machine learning accelerator, due to power consumption and area and other factors, accelerator on-chip storage capacity is very limited. To avoid frequent off-chip access, the network weights need to be compressed, and the traditional sparse matrix compression method of random access and online coding and decoding will make the calculation of logical throughput limited. To overcome this problem, Ref. [9] proposes an efficient on-chip memory architecture for CNN inference acceleration. The accelerator uses the k-means and base-delta method to encode the weight data online, greatly reducing the weight data storage. The accelerator memory subsystem provides a fast mechanism for decoding encoded data to ensure the throughput of the computational logic while compressing the weights. At the same time, the storage subsystem encodes the intermediate results of the output between the layers in the network by using a shorter index to replace the output of a large number of values 0, thus reducing the cost of storing intermediate results. Moreover, before storing data into the calculation logic, the storage subsystem can detect and skip the calculation of the operand of 0 to increase the computational speed. The results of the experiment showed that an accelerator using the proposed storage subsystem can reduce storage capacity by 8.7 times compared with an accumulator with large storage capacity on the common platform. Energy consumption was reduced by four times, which makes it possible for mobile phones and other small embedded devices to use the accelerator for efficient calculation on CNN. Large-scale artificial neural networks have shown significant promise in addressing a wide range of classification and recognition applications. However, their large computational requirements stretch the capabilities of computing platforms. The core of a digital hardware neuron consists of multiplier, accumulator, and activation functions. Multipliers consume most of the processing energy in the digital neurons and thereby in the hardware implementations of artificial neural networks. Ref. [10] proposed an approximate multiplier that utilizes the notion of computation sharing and exploits the error resilience of neural network applications to achieve improved energy consumption. The authors also proposed multiplier-less artificial neuron for even greater improvement in energy consumption and adapted the training process to ensure minimal degradation in accuracy. The experimental results showed 35% and 60% reduction in energy consumption, for neuron sizes of 8 bits and 12 bits, respectively, with a maximum of ~2.83% loss in network accuracy, compared to a conventional neuron implementation. Neural networks require significant memory capacity and bandwidth to store a large number of synaptic weights. Ref. [11] presented an application of JPEG image encoding to compress weights by exploiting spatial locality and smoothness of the weight matrix.

To minimize the loss of accuracy due to JPEG encoding, the authors proposed to adaptively control the quantization factor of the JPEG algorithm depending on the error-sensitivity (gradient) of each weight. With the adaptive compression technique, the weight blocks with higher sensitivity are compressed less for higher accuracy. The adaptive compression reduces the memory requirement, which in turn results in higher performance and lower energy of neural network hardware. The simulation for inference hardware for multilayer perceptron with the MNIST data set shows up to 42× compression with less than 1% loss of recognition accuracy, resulting in 3× higher effective memory bandwidth.

9.2.3 Optimizing the Area and Power Consumption

The emerging metal-oxide resistive random-access memory (RRAM) and RRAM crossbar have shown great potential on neuromorphic applications with high energy efficiency. However, the interfaces between analog RRAM crossbars and digital peripheral functions, namely analog-to-digital converters (ADCs) and digital-to-analog converters (DACs), consume most of the area and energy of RRAM-based CNN design due to the large amount of intermediate data in CNN. Ref. [12] proposed an energy-efficient structure for RRAM-based CNN. Based on the analysis of data distribution, a quantization method is proposed to transfer the intermediate data into 1 bit and eliminate DACs. An energy-efficient structure using input data as selection signals is proposed to reduce the ADC cost for merging results of multiple crossbars. The experimental results show that the proposed method and structure can save 80% area and more than 95% energy while maintaining the same or comparable classification accuracy of CNN on MNIST. Ref. [13] proposed using the metal-insulator-transition based two-terminal device as a compact oscillation neuron for the parallel read operation from the resistive synaptic array. The weighted sum is represented by the frequency of the oscillation neuron. Compared to the complex CMOS integrate-and-fire neuron with tens of transistors, the oscillation neuron achieves significant area reduction, thereby alleviating the column pitch matching problem of the peripheral circuitry in resistive memories. Finally, through the comparison of the circuit level benchmark, at the level of the single neuron node, oscillating neurons compared to CMOS neurons, the area decreased by 12.5 times. At the array level of 128×128, the oscillating neurons are used to reduce the total area by 4%; the delay is reduced by more than 30%, the energy consumption is saved five times, and the leakage power is reduced by 40 times, demonstrating the advantages of oscillating neuron integration. Because the number of synapses in ANN is much greater than the number of neurons, synaptic read and write operations also occupy a large part of the power consumption, so from the perspective of digital circuits, Ref. [14] proposed to reduce the voltage to improve the energy efficiency. However, the traditional 6T static random access memory (SRAM) with the voltage drop shows instability, easily leading to reduced computational accuracy. In this paper, the memory structure is optimized, using a stable 8T SRAM to replace part of the traditional 6T SRAM (as shown in Figure 9.3) to calculate the more important data stored, which can ensure the accuracy of the calculation and further reduce the voltage, to achieve the purpose of improving energy efficiency. At the same time, to reduce the power consumption while minimizing the use of the area, according to the importance of different network layers on the calculation results, change

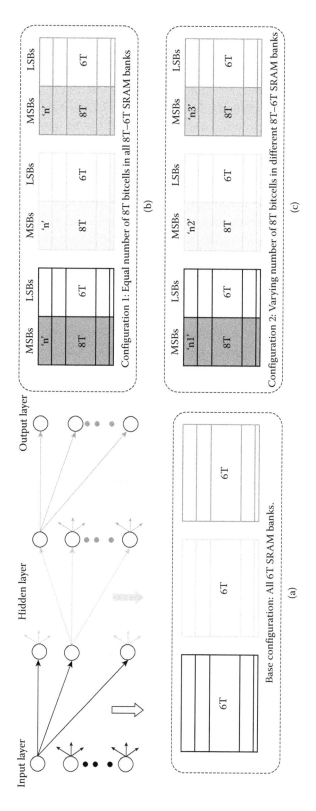

FIGURE 9.3 Synaptic memory configurations under study: (a) all 6T SRAM; (b) significance–driven hybrid 8T-6T SRAM; (c) synaptic-sensitivity–driven hybrid memory architecture.

the different layers of synaptic weights stored in 8T SRAM most significant bit number. To alleviate the computational energy efficiency problem in the neural network, Ref. [15] proposed a technical scheme, NNCAM, which can be used to calculate the neural network based on content addressable memory for GPU platform. First of all, NNCAM approximately models the basic computations of neural networks, stores frequent patterns, and searches for the closest similarity to reuse the results. Second, layer-based associative update and selective approximation techniques are used in NNCAM to improve computational efficiency and accuracy. The NNCAM module is integrated into AMD's Southern Island GPU for experimental evaluation. The results show that the new technology can reduce the energy consumption by 68%, improve the performance by 40%, at the cost of less than 2% accuracy loss. Neural associative memory (AM) is one of the critical building blocks for cognitive workloads such as classification and recognition. One of the key challenges in designing AM is to extend memory capacity while minimizing power and hardware overhead. However, prior arts show that memory capacity scales slowly, often logarithmically or in root with the total bits of synaptic weights. This makes it prohibitive in hardware and power to achieve large memory capacity for practical applications. Ref. [16] proposed a synaptic model called *recursive synaptic bit reuse*, which enables near-linear scaling of memory capacity with total synaptic bits. Also, the model can handle input data that are correlated, more robustly than the conventional model. The experiment was conducted in Hopfield neural networks (HNN), which contains the total synaptic bits of 5–327 kB and finds that the model could increase the memory capacity as large as 30× over conventional models. The authors also studied hardware cost via VLSI implementation of HNNs in a 65 nm CMOS, confirming that the proposed model can achieve up to 10× area savings at the same capacity over the conventional synaptic model. The standard CMOS-based artificial neuron designs to implement nonlinear neuron activation function typically consist of a large number of transistors, which inevitably causes large area and power consumption. There is a need for a novel nanoelectronic device that can intrinsically and efficiently implement such complex nonlinear neuron activation function. Magnetic skyrmions are topologically stable chiral spin textures due to Dzyaloshinskii-Moriya interaction in bulk magnets or magnetic thin films. They are promising next-generation information carriers owing to their ultrasmall size, high speed with ultralow depinning current density, and high defect tolerance compared to conventional magnetic domain wall motion devices. Ref. [17] was the first to propose a threshold-tunable artificial neuron based on magnetic skyrmions. Meanwhile, the authors propose a skyrmion neuron cluster (SNC) to approximate nonlinear soft-limiting neuron activation functions, such as the most popular sigmoid function. The device to system simulation indicates that the proposed SNC leads to 98.74% recognition accuracy in a deep-learning convolutional neural network with MNIST handwritten digits data set. Moreover, the energy consumption of the proposed SNC is only 3.1 fJ/step, which is more than two orders lower than that of its CMOS counterpart.

9.2.4 Programming Framework

The FPGA-based hardware accelerator design process is complex; the upper application developers may lack understanding of the underlying neural network structure, and as a result accelerator design is more difficult. To simplify the design process, Ref. [18] proposed a design automation tool, DeepBurning (as shown in Figure 9.4), allowing application developers to build from scratch learning accelerators that target their specific neural network (NN) models with custom configurations and optimized performance. DeepBurning includes an RTL-level accelerator generator and a coordinated compiler that generates the control flow and data layout under the user-specified constraints. The results can be used to implement FPGA-based NN accelerator or help generate chip design for early design stage. In general, DeepBurning supports a large family of NN models, and greatly simplifies the design flow of NN accelerators for the machine learning or AI application developers. The evaluation shows that the generated learning accelerators burnt to our FPGA board exhibit great power efficiency compared to state-of-the-art FPGA-based solutions. The framework makes it possible for the upper application designers to use FPGA to accelerate the computation of neural networks as easily as Caffe, which greatly improves the applicability of FPGA in this field. Ref. [2] first analyzed and studied a uniformed convolutional matrix multiplication representation for both computation-intensive convolutional layers and communication-intensive fully connected layers, then designed and implemented Caffeine (as shown in Figure 9.5), in the portable high-level synthesis and provide various hardware/software definable parameters for user configurations. Finally, Caffeine was integrated into the industry-standard software deep learning framework Caffe. Compared to traditional CPU and GPU, the accelerator has considerable performance and energy efficiency improvement. The question of how to best design an accelerator for a given CNN has not been answered yet, even on a very fundamental level. Ref. [19] addressed that challenge, by providing a novel framework that can universally and accurately evaluate and explore various architectural choices for CNN accelerators on FPGAs. The exploration framework is more extensive than that of any previous work concerning the design space and takes into account various FPGA resources to maximize performance including DSP resources, on-chip memory, and off-chip memory bandwidth. The experimental results using some

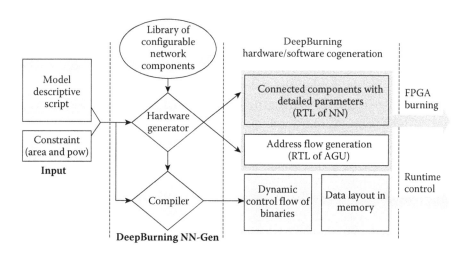

FIGURE 9.4　Neural network accelerator development framework—DeepBurning [18].

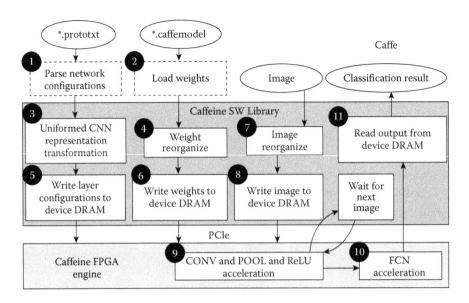

FIGURE 9.5   Caffe-Caffeine.

of the largest CNN models, including one that has 16 convolutional layers, demonstrate the efficacy of our framework, as well as the need for such a high-level architecture exploration approach to finding the best architecture for a CNN model.

9.2.5 The New Method Applied to Neural Network

Ref. [20] presented an efficient DNN design with stochastic computing (as shown in Figure 9.6). Observing that directly adopting stochastic computing to DNN has some challenges including random error fluctuation, range limitation, and overhead in accumulation, the authors address these problems by removing near-zero weights, applying weight-scaling, and integrating the activation function with the accumulator. The approach allows an easy implementation of early decision termination with a fixed hardware design by exploiting the progressive precision characteristics of stochastic computing, which was not easy with the existing approaches. The experimental results showed that the approach outperforms the conventional binary logic in terms of the gate area, latency, and power consumption. Ref. [21] also simplifies the computation of deep convolution neural networks (DCNNs) by stochastic computing (SC). In this paper, eight feature extraction designs for DCNNs using SC in two groups are explored and optimized in detail from the perspective of calculation precision, where the authors permute two SC implementations for inner-product calculation, two down-sampling schemes, and two structures of DCNN neurons. The experimental results showed that through exploration and optimization, the accuracies of SC-based DCNNs are guaranteed compared with software implementations on CPU/GPU/binary based ASIC synthesis, while area, power, and energy are significantly reduced by up to 776×, 190×, and 32,835×. Ref. [22] developed a highly energy-efficient hardware implementation of a class of sketching methods based on random projections, known as Johnson–Lindenstrauss (JL) transform. At the same time, it showed how to explore the

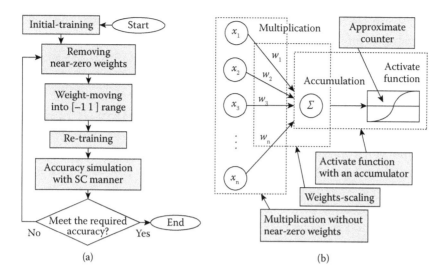

FIGURE 9.6 (a) Training procedure for deep neural networks using stochastic computing (SC) with 32-bit floating-point computation; (b) SC neurons are operated with SC exploiting the suggested solutions in testing phase.

randomness of the mapping matrix to build efficient machine-learning applications. It defined a random matrix construction method to explore the special sparse structure and thus efficiently use hardware to optimize the conversion on the FPGA. The proposed design of JL transform can achieve an up to 2× speedup with a 17% area reduction. Applying the JL transform to the problem of KNN classification and PCA achieves an up to 7× latency and energy improvement. More importantly, the ability of averaging accumulation error allows the design to use a 1-bit multiplier instead of a 4-bit used KNN algorithm, which results in a further 6% energy saving and 50% area reduction. Ref. [23] proposed a robust and energy-efficient analog implementation of the spiking temporal encoder. The authors patterned the neural activities across multiple timescales and encoded the sensory information using time-dependent temporal scales. The concept of iteration structure was introduced to construct a neural encoder that greatly increases the information process ability of the proposed temporal encoder. Integrated with the iteration technique and operational-amplifier-free design, the error rate of the output temporal codes is reduced to an extremely low level. A lower sampling rate accompanied by additional verification spikes is introduced in the schemes, which significantly reduces the power consumption of the encoding system. The simulation and measurement results show the proposed temporal encoder exhibits not only energy efficiency but also high accuracy deep neural networks (DNNs) with many convolutional layers and different parameters in terms of input/output/kernel sizes as well as input stride. Design constraints usually require a single design for all layers of a given DNN. Thus a key challenge is how to design a common architecture that can perform well for all convolutional layers of a DNN, which can be quite diverse and complex. Ref. [24] presented a flexible yet highly efficient 3D neuron array architecture that is a natural fit for convolutional layers. The authors also presented the technique to optimize its parameters including on-chip buffer sizes for a given set of resource constraint for modern FPGAs. The experimental results targeting a Virtex-7 FPGA demonstrated that the proposed technique can generate DNN accelerators that can outperform the state-of-the-art solutions by 22% for 32-bit floating point MAC implementations and are far more scalable in terms of computing resources and DNN size. A memristor-based neuromorphic computing system provides a promising solution to significantly boost the power efficiency of the computing system. However, a memristor-based neuromorphic computing system simulator that can model the system and realize an early-stage design space exploration is still missing. Ref. [25] developed a memristor-based neuromorphic system simulation platform (MNSIM, as shown in Figure 9.7). MNSIM proposes a general hierarchical structure for the memristor-based neuromorphic computing system and provides a flexible interface for users to customize the design. MNSIM also provides a detailed reference design for large-scale applications. MNSIM embeds estimation models of area, power, and latency to simulate the performance of the system. To estimate the computing accuracy, MNSIM proposes a behavior-level model between computing error rate and crossbar design parameters considering the influence of interconnect lines and nonideal device factors. Experimental results show that MNSIM achieves more than 7000 times speedup compared with SPICE and obtains reasonable accuracy. Aiming at a large number of dot product operation in neural network computation, Ref. [26] presented and experimentally validated 3D-DPE, a general-purpose dot-product engine, which is ideal for accelerating artificial neural networks (ANNs). 3D-DPE is based on a monolithically integrated 3D CMOS–memristor hybrid circuit and performs a high-dimensional dot-product operation (a recurrent and computationally expensive operation in ANNs) within a single step, using analog current-based computing. 3D-DPE is made up of two subsystems, namely a CMOS subsystem serving as the memory controller and an analog memory subsystem consisting of multiple layers of high-density memristive crossbar arrays fabricated on top of the CMOS subsystem. Their integration is based on a high-density area-distributed interface, resulting in much higher connectivity between the two subsystems, compared to the traditional interface of a 2D system or a 3D system integrated using through silicon via. As a result, 3D-DPE's single-step dot-product

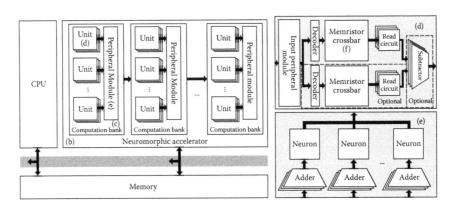

FIGURE 9.7 The architecture of Memristor-based neuromorphic system simulation platform.

operation is not limited by the memory bandwidth, and the input dimension of the operations scales well with the capacity of the 3D memristive arrays. Recently, memristor crossbar arrays are utilized in realizing spiking-based neuromorphic system, where memristor conductance values correspond to synaptic weights. Most of these systems are composed of a single crossbar layer, in which system training is done off-chip, using computer-based simulations, then the trained weights are preprogrammed to the memristor crossbar array. However, multilayered, on-chip trained systems become crucial for handling the massive amount of data, and to overcome the resistance shift that occurs to memristors over time. Ref. [27] proposed a spiking-based multilayered neuromorphic computing system capable of online training. The experimental results showed that the overall performance of the system was improved by 42% while ensuring the accuracy of the calculation. The resistance variations and stuck-at faults in the memristor devices, however, dramatically degrade not only the chip yield but also the classification accuracy of the neural networks running on the RRAM crossbar. Existing hardware-based solutions cause enormous overhead and power consumption, while software-based solutions are less efficient in tolerating stuck-at faults and large variations. Ref. [28] proposed an accelerator-friendly neural network training method, by leveraging the inherent self-healing capability of the neural network, to prevent the large weight synapses from being mapped to the abnormal memristors based on the fault/variation distribution in the RRAM crossbar. Experimental results show the proposed method can pull the classification accuracy (10%–45% loss in previous works) up close to ideal level with less than 1% loss.

9.2.6 Applications Using Neural Network

Artificial Neural Networks provide a suitable mechanism for fault-detection and fault-tolerance in critical domains like automotive systems. However, ANNs are inherently computationally intensive, and the precision requirements in harsh automotive environments mean large networks are required, making software implementations impractical. Ref. [29] presented a hybrid electronic control units (ECU) approach, based on the Xilinx Zynq platform, which integrates an ANN-based prediction system that doubles up as a replacement sensor in the case of persistent faults (as shown in Figure 9.8). The ANN network is completely contained within a partially reconfigurable (PR) region integrated with parallel sensor acquisition interfaces, a fault detection system, data processing engine, and a network interface. PR region allows seamless migration from the fault-detection ANN network (under normal operation) to the fault-tolerant mode with a larger, more complex and accurate network that effectively replaces the faulty sensor, by reusing hardware resources. The proposed parallel architecture enables the ANN to be evaluated in a predictable short latency of under 1 us, even for the larger prediction network. Deep convolutional networks (ConvNets) are currently superior in benchmark performance, but the associated demands on computation and data transfer prohibit straightforward mapping on energy-constrained wearable platforms. The computational burden can be overcome by dedicated hardware accelerators, but it is the sheer amount of data transfer and level of utilization that determines the energy-efficiency of these implementations. Ref. [30] presented the Neuro Vector Engine (NVE), an SIMD accelerator of ConvNets for visual object classification, targeting

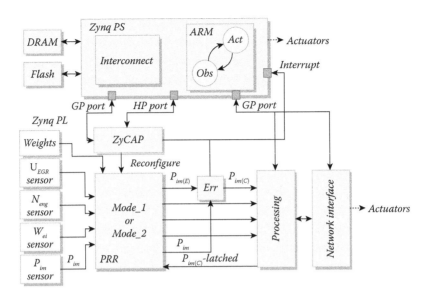

FIGURE 9.8   Proposed hybrid fault-tolerant electronic control units (ECU) model on Zynq.

portable and wearable devices. The proposed accelerator is very flexible due to the usage of very long instruction word (VLIW)instruction set architecture (ISA), at the cost of instruction fetch overhead. The authors showed that this overhead is insignificant when the extra flexibility enables advanced data locality optimizations and improves HW utilization over ConvNet vision applications. By co-optimizing the accelerator architecture and algorithm loop structure, 30 Gops is achieved with a power envelope of 54 mW and only 0.26 mm² silicon footprint at TSMC 40 nm technology, enabling high-end visual object recognition by portable and even wearable devices. Ideally, systems would employ near-sensor computation to execute these tasks at sensor end points to maximize data reduction and minimize data movement. However, near-sensor computing presents its own set of challenges such as operating power constraints, energy budgets, and communication bandwidth capacities. Ref. [31] proposed a stochastic binary hybrid design that splits the computation between the stochastic and binary domains for near-sensor NN applications. In addition, the proposed design uses a new stochastic adder and multiplier that are significantly more accurate than existing adders and multipliers. The authors also showed that retraining the binary portion of the NN computation can compensate for precision losses introduced by shorter stochastic bit-streams, allowing faster run times at minimal accuracy losses. The evaluation shows that proposed hybrid stochastic-binary design can achieve 9.8× energy efficiency savings, and application-level accuracies within 0.05% compared to conventional all-binary designs, which makes it possible to locally process the convolutional neural network at the sensor end. Deep Neural Networks (DNN) is generally difficult to deploy on resource-constrained devices, some existing attempts mainly focus on the client–server computing paradigm or DNN model compression, which require either infrastructure supports or special training phases, respectively. Ref. [32] proposed MoDNN—a local distributed mobile computing system for DNN applications. MoDNN can partition already-trained DNN models onto several mobile devices to accelerate DNN computations by alleviating device-level computing cost and memory usage. Two model partition schemes were also designed to minimize nonparallel data delivery time, including both wakeup time and transmission time. Experimental results showed that when the number of worker nodes increases from two to four, MoDNN can accelerate the DNN computation by 2.17×–4.28×. Bidirectional Long Short-Term Memory Neural Networks have shown a superior performance in character recognition with respect to other types of neural networks. Ref. [33] proposed the first hardware architecture of Bidirectional Long Short-Term Memory Neural Network with Connectionist Temporal Classification for Optical Character Recognition. Based on the new architecture, the authors presented an FPGA hardware accelerator that achieves 459 times higher throughput than the state of the art. Visual recognition is a typical task on mobile platforms that usually use two scenarios: either the task runs locally on an embedded processor or it is offloaded to a cloud to be run on a high-performance machine. The authors showed that computationally intensive visual recognition tasks benefit from being migrated to their dedicated hardware accelerator and outperform high-performance CPU in terms of run time while consuming less energy than low power systems with negligible loss of recognition accuracy.

9.2.7 Others

In addition to the above papers, there is some exploratory and optimized content that deserves our attention. Many neural networks are calculated by using hardware units with different data bits at different energy consumption and precision requirements. However, there is a lack of comprehensive research on the required input data and weight data bits in the neural network. Ref. [34] quantifies the impact of floating-point data and fixed-point data on network precision, memory footprint, power consumption, energy consumption, and design area for different bit widths in the network analysis. The author concluded that under the same hardware resources one can reduce the data bit width to deploy a more large-scale network, in order to achieve the network accuracy, energy consumption optimization. TrueNorth design has the issue of limited precision of synaptic weights. The current workaround is running multiple neural network copies in which the average value of each synaptic weight is close to that in the original network. Ref. [35] theoretically analyzed the impacts of low data precision in the TrueNorth chip on inference accuracy, core occupation, and performance and presented a probability-biased learning method to enhance the inference accuracy through reducing the random variance of each computation copy. The experimental results proved that the proposed techniques considerably improve the computation accuracy of TrueNorth platform and reduce the incurred hardware and performance overheads. In order to improve the performance as well to maintain the scalability, Ref. [36] presented SOLAR, a services-oriented deep learning architecture using various accelerators like GPU and FPGA-based approaches. SOLAR provides a uniform programming model to users so that the hardware implementation and the scheduling are invisible to the programmers. Ref. [37] presented a software-defined FPGA-based accelerator for Big Data, named SODA, which could reconstruct and reorganize the acceleration engines according to the requirement of the various data-intensive applications.

SODA decomposes large and complex applications into coarse-grained single-purpose RTL code libraries that perform specialized tasks in out-of-order hardware. The experiment results show that SODA is able to achieve up to 43.75× speedup at 128 node application. Ref. [38] used FPGA to design a deep learning accelerator, which focuses on the implementation of the prediction process, data access optimization, and pipeline structure. In order to improve the performance as well as to maintain the low power cost, Ref. [39] designed a deep-learning accelerator unit (DLAU), which is a scalable accelerator architecture for large-scale deep learning networks. The DLAU accelerator employs three pipelined processing units to improve the throughput and utilizes tile techniques to explore locality for deep learning applications. The experimental results on the state-of-the-art Xilinx FPGA board demonstrate that the DLAU accelerator is able to achieve up to 36.1× speedup comparing to the Intel Core2 processors, with the power consumption of 234 mW. After realizing two adjacent layers in different calculation orders, the data dependency between layers can be weakened. Ref. [40] proposed a pipeline energy-efficient accelerator named *PIE* to accelerate the DNN inference computation by pipelining two adjacent layers. As soon as a layer produces an output, the next layer reads the output as an input and starts the parallel computation immediately in another calculation method. In such a way, computations between adjacent layers are pipelined.

9.3 CONCLUSION AND DEVELOPMENT TRENDS

In Figure 9.9, we count the number of papers related to neural networks and the number of published papers from the 2016 EDA Conference (DAC, ICCAD, DATE) and DATE 2017. As can be seen from the figure, in 2016, there are only 5, 6, and 7 related papers in DAC, ICCAD and DATE, respectively, but in 2017 DATE alone, there are 22 related papers on the neural network which reflects that the neural network is the hot spot of current scientific research.

From the above research, the optimization of the neural network is mainly focused on improving the localization of data, mining the parallelism of data, reducing the storage space of weight data, and reducing the power consumption and area of the chip. From the

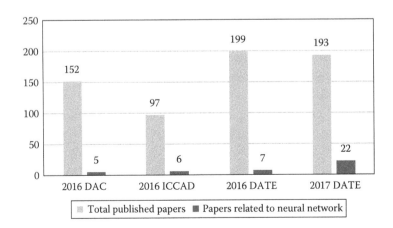

FIGURE 9.9 Number of papers related to neural networks and total number of papers published.

technology they use, there are pruning, weight compression, data sharing, data parallel, approximate calculation. At the same time, we also see a lot of researchers that migrate the methods of other areas to the neural network, and the application of new materials in neural network design. As the research continues, I believe we will see more and more such similar work in 2017, designing a new chip and hardware and software systems. In addition, it cannot be ignored that the neural network has a wide range of applications. At 2016 DATE, we saw the possibility of the neural network being used in automotive systems, in sensor-end, in the embedded system; later we will see more successful applications based on neural networks in other areas.

In general, the research on computer architecture and EDA has been close to each other, and the research on new applications has become a hot spot in recent years. In 2016, we were pleased to see a great degree of development in the field of hardware architecture, in the software application and algorithm levels, in the neural network topology, programming. We have also seen considerable progress on the construction of new computer systems, which promote the industrialization of artificial intelligence chips and systems to provide a very strong foundation.

REFERENCES

1. L. Song, Y. Wang, Y. Han, X. Zhao, B. Liu, and X. Li, 2016, *C-Brain: A deep learning accelerator that tames the diversity of CNNs through adaptive data-level parallelization*, in *Design Automation Conference (DAC), 2016 53nd ACM/EDAC/IEEE*, IEEE.
2. C. Zhang, Z. Fang, P. Zhou, P. Pan, and J. Cong, 2016, *Caffeine: Towards uniformed representation and acceleration for deep convolutional neural networks*, in *Proceedings of the 35th International Conference on Computer-Aided Design*, ACM.
3. S. Sen, S. Venkataramani, and A. Raghunathan, 2017, *Approximate computing for spiking neural networks*, in *Design, Automation & Test in Europe Conference & Exhibition (DATE), 2017*, IEEE.
4. S. Wang, D. Zhou, X. Han, and T. Yoshimura, 2017, *Chain-NN: An energy-efficient 1D chain architecture for accelerating deep convolutional neural networks*, in *Design, Automation & Test in Europe Conference & Exhibition (DATE)*, IEEE.
5. D. Nguyen, D. Kim, and J. Lee, 2017, *Double MAC: Doubling the performance of convolutional neural networks on modern FPGAs*, in *Design, Automation & Test in Europe Conference & Exhibition (DATE)*, IEEE.
6. D. Kim, J. Ahn, and S. Yoo, 2017, *A novel zero weight/activation-aware hardware architecture of convolutional neural network*, in *Design, Automation & Test in Europe Conference & Exhibition (DATE), 2017*, IEEE.
7. M. S. Razlighi, M. Imani, F. Koushanfar, and T. Rosing, 2017, *LookNN: Neural Network with No Multiplication*, in *Design, Automation & Test in Europe Conference & Exhibition (DATE), 2017*, IEEE.
8. J. Chung and T. Shin, 2016, *Simplifying deep neural networks for neuromorphic architectures*, in *Design Automation Conference (DAC), 2016 53nd ACM/EDAC/IEEE*, IEEE.
9. Y. Wang, H. Li, and X. Li, 2016, *Re-architecting the on-chip memory sub-system of machine-learning accelerator for embedded devices*, in *Proceedings of the 35th International Conference on Computer-Aided Design*, ACM.
10. S. S. Sarwar, S. Venkataramani, A. Raghunathan, and K. Roy, 2016, *Multiplier-less artificial neurons exploiting error resiliency for energy-efficient neural computing*, in *Design, Automation & Test in Europe Conference & Exhibition (DATE), 2016*, IEEE.

11. J. H. Ko, D. Kim, T. Na, J. Kung, and S. Mukhopadhyay, 2017, *Adaptive weight compression for memory-efficient neural networks*, in *Design, Automation & Test in Europe Conference & Exhibition (DATE), 2017*, IEEE.

12. L. Xia, T. Tang, W. Huangfu, M. Cheng, X. Yin, B. Li, Y. Wang, and H. Yang, 2016, *Switched by input: Power efficient structure for RRAM-based convolutional neural network*, in *Proceedings of the 53rd Annual Design Automation Conference*, ACM.

13. P.-Y. Chen, J.-s. Seo, Y. Cao, and S. Yu, 2016, *Compact oscillation neuron exploiting metal-insulator-transition for neuromorphic computing*, in *IEEE/ACM International Conference on Computer-Aided Design (ICCAD), 2016*, IEEE.

14. G. Srinivasan, P. Wijesinghe, S. S. Sarwar, A. Jaiswal, and K. Roy, 2016, *Significance driven hybrid 8T-6T SRAM for energy-efficient synaptic storage in artificial neural networks*, in *Design, Automation & Test in Europe Conference & Exhibition (DATE), 2016*, IEEE.

15. M. Imani, D. Peroni, Y. Kim, A. Rahimi, and T. Rosing, 2017, *Efficient neural network acceleration on GPGPU using contents addressable memory*, in *Design, Automation & Test in Europe Conference & Exhibition (DATE), 2017*, IEEE.

16. T. Guan, X. Zeng, and M. Seok, 2017, *Extending memory capacity of neural associative memory based on recursive synaptic bit reuse*, in *Design, Automation & Test in Europe Conference & Exhibition (DATE), 2017*, IEEE.

17. Z. He and D. Fan, 2017, *A tunable magnetic Skyrmion neuron cluster for energy efficient artificial neural network*, in *Design, Automation & Test in Europe Conference & Exhibition (DATE), 2017*, IEEE.

18. Y. Wang, J. Xu, Y. Han, H. Li, and X. Li, 2016, *Deepburning: Automatic generation of fpga-based learning accelerators for the neural network family*, in *Design Automation Conference (DAC), 2016 53nd ACM/EDAC/IEEE*, IEEE.

19. A. Rahman, S. Oh, J. Lee, and K. Choi, 2017, *Design space exploration of FPGA accelerators for convolutional neural networks*, in *Design, Automation & Test in Europe Conference & Exhibition (DATE), 2017*, IEEE.

20. K. Kim, J. Kim, J. Yu, J. Seo, J. Lee, and K. Choi, 2016, *Dynamic energy-accuracy trade-off using stochastic computing in deep neural networks*, in *Proceedings of the 53rd Annual Design Automation Conference*, ACM.

21. Z. Li, A. Ren, J. Li, Q. Qiu, B. Yuan, J. Draper, and Y. Wang, 2017, *Structural design optimization for deep convolutional neural networks using stochastic computing*, in *Design, Automation & Test in Europe Conference & Exhibition (DATE), 2017*, IEEE.

22. Y. Wang, C. Caramanis, and M. Orshansky, 2016, *Exploiting randomness in sketching for efficient hardware implementation of machine learning applications*, in *IEEE/ACM International Conference on Computer-Aided Design (ICCAD), 2016*, IEEE.

23. C. Zhao, J. Li, and Y. Yi, 2016, *Making neural encoding robust and energy efficient: An advanced analog temporal encoder for brain-inspired computing systems*, in *IEEE/ACM International Conference on Computer-Aided Design (ICCAD), 2016*, IEEE.

24. A. Rahman, J. Lee, and K. Choi, 2016, *Efficient FPGA acceleration of convolutional neural networks using logical-3D compute array*, in *Design, Automation & Test in Europe Conference & Exhibition (DATE), 2016*, IEEE.

25. L. Xia, B. Li, T. Tang, P. Gu, X. Yin, W. Huangfu, P.-Y. Chen, S. Yu, Y. Cao, and Y. Wang, 2016, MNSIM: Simulation platform for memristor-based neuromorphic computing system. in *Design, Automation & Test in Europe Conference & Exhibition (DATE), 2016*, IEEE.

26. M. A. Lastras-Montano, B. Chakrabarti, D. B. Strukov, and K.-T. Cheng, 2017, *3D-DPE: A 3D high-bandwidth dot-product engine for high-performance neuromorphic computing*, in *Design, Automation & Test in Europe Conference & Exhibition (DATE), 2017*, IEEE.

27. A. M. Hassan, C. Yang, C. Liu, H. H. Li, and Y. Chen, 2017, *Hybrid spiking-based multi-layered self-learning neuromorphic system based On memristor crossbar arrays*, in *Design, Automation & Test in Europe Conference & Exhibition (DATE), 2017*, IEEE.

28. L. Chen, J. Li, Y. Chen, Q. Deng, J. Shen, X. Liang, and L. Jiang, 2017, *Accelerator-friendly neural-network training: Learning variations and defects in RRAM crossbar*, in *Design, Automation & Test in Europe Conference & Exhibition (DATE), 2017*, IEEE.

29. S. Shreejith, B. Anshuman, and S. A. Fahmy, 2016, *Accelerated artificial neural networks on FPGA for fault detection in automotive systems*, in *Design, Automation & Test in Europe Conference & Exhibition (DATE), 2016*, IEEE.

30. M. Peemen, R. Shi, S. Lal, B. Juurlink, B. Mesman, and H. Corporaal, 2016, *The neuro vector engine: Flexibility to improve convolutional net efficiency for wearable vision*, in *Design, Automation & Test in Europe Conference & Exhibition (DATE), 2016*, IEEE.

31. V. T. Lee, A. Alaghi, J. P. Hayes, V. Sathe, and L. Ceze, 2017, *Energy-efficient hybrid stochastic-binary neural networks for near-sensor computing*, in *Design, Automation & Test in Europe Conference & Exhibition (DATE), 2017*, IEEE.

32. J. Mao, X. Chen, K. W. Nixon, C. Krieger, and Y. Chen, 2017, *MoDNN: Local distributed mobile computing system for deep neural network*, in *Design, Automation & Test in Europe Conference & Exhibition (DATE), 2017*. IEEE.

33. V. Rybalkin, N. Wehn, M. R. Yousefi, and D. Stricker, 2017, *Hardware architecture of bidirectional long short-term memory neural network for optical character recognition*, in *Design, Automation & Test in Europe Conference & Exhibition (DATE), 2017*, IEEE.

34. S. Hashemi, N. Anthony, H. Tann, R. I. Bahar, and S. Reda, 2017, *Understanding the impact of precision quantization on the accuracy and energy of neural networks*, in *Design, Automation & Test in Europe Conference & Exhibition (DATE), 2017*, IEEE.

35. H.-P. Cheng, W. Wen, C. Wu, S. Li, H. H. Li, and Y. Chen, 2017, *Understanding the design of IBM neurosynaptic system and its tradeoffs: A user perspective*, in *Design, Automation & Test in Europe Conference & Exhibition (DATE), 2017*, IEEE.

36. C. Wang, X. Li, Q. Yu, A. Wang, P. Hung, and X. Zhou, 2016, *SOLAR: Services-oriented learning architectures*, in *IEEE International Conference on Web Services (ICWS), 2016*, IEEE.

37. C. Wang, X. Li, and X. Zhou, 2015, *SODA: Software defined FPGA based accelerators for big data*, in *Design, Automation & Test in Europe Conference & Exhibition (DATE), 2015*, IEEE.

38. Q. Yu, C. Wang, X. Ma, X. Li, and X. Zhou, 2015, *A deep learning prediction process accelerator based FPGA*, in *15th IEEE/ACM International Symposium on Cluster, Cloud and Grid Computing (CCGrid), 2015*, IEEE.

39. C. Wang, L. Gong, Q. Yu, X. Li, Y. Xie, and X. Zhou, 2017 *Dlau: A scalable deep learning accelerator unit on fpga*, IEEE Transactions on Computer-Aided Design of Integrated Circuits and Systems, 2017, vol. 36 no. 3, pp. 513–517.

40. Y. Zhao, Q. Yu, X. Zhou, X. Zhou, X. Li, and C. Wang, 2016, *PIE: A pipeline energy-efficient accelerator for inference process in deep neural networks*, in *IEEE 22nd International Conference on Parallel and Distributed Systems (ICPADS), 2016*, IEEE.

CHAPTER 10

Accelerators for Clustering Applications in Machine Learning

Yiwei Zhang, Chao Wang, Lei Gong,
Xi Li, Aili Wang, and Xuehai Zhou

University of Science and Technology of China

Hefei, China

CONTENTS

10.1 INTRODUCTION

Clustering analysis plays an increasingly important role in our work and life. Presently, it is applied in many different fields, such as market research, pattern recognition, data analysis and image processing, customer segmentation, web document classification, and so on. With the rapid development of the Internet and e-commerce, the collected or accumulated data in different fields presents mass growth. Vast amounts of data greatly slow down the efficiency of clustering analysis and the study of accelerating algorithms has been an important topic.

Different application areas or different types of data sets need to adopt different clustering algorithms to achieve good performance. It is necessary to accelerate different clustering algorithms. Currently, the main platforms to accelerate clustering algorithms are cloud computing platforms and hardware acceleration. The cloud platform firstly partitions the application and then maps each partitioned application to each computer. Each computer calculates the respective application and then returns the result to the main computer. This platform needs many computers, so the cost is very high. What is more, the network bandwidth limits the performance of the cloud computing platform. There are three acceleration algorithms for hardware acceleration, the graphics processing unit (GPU), the field-programmable gate array (FPGA), and the application-specific integrated circuit (ASIC). Hardware acceleration accelerates an algorithm by adopting the parallel or pipeline method, except for the hardware features. Compared with the cloud computing platform, it has little cost, and the performance will not be limited by network bandwidth. So, hardware acceleration is an effective method to accelerate algorithms.

Currently, most hardware accelerators are designed for a single specific algorithm; research aiming at versatility and flexibility of hardware acceleration is rare. Although GPUs provide straightforward solutions, their energy efficiencies are limited due to their excessive supports for flexibility. The FPGA may achieve better energy efficiencies, but each accelerator based on FPGA often accommodates one algorithm [1]. If the hardware accelerator is designed only for one single algorithm, the accelerator cannot work for other algorithms, which greatly limits the versatility and flexibility. Can we design one hardware accelerator accommodating multiple clustering algorithms?

In this chapter, we design a hardware accelerator platform based on FPGA by the combination of hardware and software. The hardware accelerator accommodates four clustering algorithms, namely the k-means algorithm, PAM algorithm, SLINK algorithm, and DBSCAN algorithm. Each algorithm can support two kinds of similarity metrics, Manhattan and Euclidean. Through locality analysis, the hardware accelerator presented a solution to address the frequent off-chip memory access and then balanced the relationship between flexibility and performance by finding the same operations. To evaluate the performance of the accelerator, the accelerator is compared with both the CPU and GPU and then it gives the corresponding speedup and energy efficiency. Last but not the least, we present the relationship between data sets and the speedup.

The rest of this chapter is organized as follows. Section 10.2 introduces the clustering background and the related work for the accelerators. Section 10.3 presents the hardware accelerator for the clustering algorithm. Section 10.4 details the experimental setup and results. Finally, Section 10.5 concludes the chapter.

10.2 BACKGROUND

The clustering algorithm is a kind of unsupervised machine learning algorithm [2], which is widely used in various fields such as market research, pattern recognition, data mining, image processing, customer segmentation, web document classification [3], and so on. According to the different ways, the commonly used clustering algorithm can be divided into the following categories: division method, hierarchical method, density-based method, grid-based method and model-based method [4–6], and so on. In different application areas and the processing of various types of data, there is a need to use different clustering algorithms for clustering analysis to get a better clustering effect. For example, the k-means algorithm's [7] principle is simple, running time is short, and it can handle the spherical distribution of data. However, for the k-means algorithm, it's hard to obtain better clustering results. Especially in some data sets with severe noise, the k-means algorithm is often difficult to meet people's needs, and the DNSCAN algorithm [8] can achieve a good clustering effect.

With the rapid development of the Internet and e-commerce, the data collected, accumulated, or urgently needing to be processed by various trades show massive growth—the size and dimensions of the data are continually expanding [9]. Massive high-dimensional data substantially slow down the efficiency of cluster analysis, severely restricting the development of all walks of life. Especially in this fast-growing information age, the speed of information extraction has become a key factor affecting success. The importance of clustering algorithms and the importance of information extraction speed makes the acceleration of clustering algorithm important, accelerating clustering algorithms has become an urgent need for today's society.

The main current accelerating methods of the clustering algorithm include cloud computing platform [10] acceleration and hardware acceleration [11,12]. Most cloud computing platform accelerations use the Hadoop [13] or Spark [14] tools to partition functions and data sets for applications and then assign the assigned tasks or data to each PC node. Each PC node processes the task and returns the result to the host. There are many applications of cloud computing platform acceleration, such as the acceleration of gene sequencing applications [15], matrix computing acceleration [16], and so on. Hardware acceleration methods include GPU [17], FPGA [18], and ASIC [19]. They use hardware instead of software or CPU to achieve specific functional logic by utilizing the hardware's fast features, and a large number of built-in hardware logic components make hardware acceleration can accelerate the implementation of the algorithm by better use of parallel and pipeline. In summary, hardware acceleration is a more efficient method of acceleration.

In the hardware acceleration techniques, GPU, FPGA, and ASIC have their characteristics and application areas. GPU is mainly used in the field of graphics processing; it has a large number of parallel processing units and utilizes data-level parallel mode to accelerate the implementation of various applications, such as matrix multiplication and image processing. However, because of the existence of a vast number of parallel devices and the support for versatility and flexibility, GPU has a higher power consumption than FPGA. ASIC is a dedicated integrated circuit for custom circuit acceleration; it's fast but has poor flexibility; it's not reconfigurable. People favor FPGA because of its stability, relatively low cost, high degree of parallelism, and reconfigurable features [20]; there are more and more applications that use it to achieve acceleration, such as large data application acceleration [21], depth learning acceleration [22], recommended algorithm acceleration [23], k-means algorithm acceleration [24], and so on. FPGA makes the idea of changing the hardware function logic without adding hardware become reality.

At present, the design of hardware accelerators is mostly for a single particular algorithm; there is little research on the versatility and flexibility of the accelerator. While the GPU provides a way to solve versatility and flexibility, FPGAs achieve better energy savings due to the support for versatility and flexibility of GPU, resulting in high power consumption. However, FPGA-based accelerators are currently designed for specific algorithms by creating a particular hardware acceleration module, making the hardware accelerator only support one algorithm, significantly limiting the hardware accelerator versatility and flexibility [25]. Can an FPGA-based hardware accelerator be designed to support multiple clustering algorithms? This is the problem that this article aims to solve.

10.2.1 Research Status at Home and Abroad

As can be seen from the research background, it is important to accelerate a variety of clustering algorithms, and hardware acceleration is an efficient means of acceleration. At present, most of the research at home and abroad is to design a hardware accelerator for a single algorithm, and there is little research on the versatility and flexibility of the accelerator. The research is still in the exploratory stage. Most of the currently designed accelerators can only support a single particular algorithm; once the algorithm changes the accelerator cannot work properly, only redesigning the accelerator can meet the requirements, which significantly reduces the accelerator versatility and flexibility. In addition, some algorithms have significant similarity, or the key code of the algorithms are same; designing hardware accelerator for a single algorithm will make a lot of repeating work, wasting the time and effort of developers.

In 1998, MY Niamat connected some FPGAs to achieve acceleration of a hierarchical clustering algorithm, including the SLINK and CLINK algorithms. Since he accelerated the entire hierarchical clustering algorithm, the distance matrix must be stored inside the FPGA to speed up the execution of the algorithm, so it uses multiple FPGA interconnects to solve the problem [26].

In 2011, Hussain accelerated the *k*-means algorithm by using FPGA. He divided the whole algorithm into blocks, carrying out a similar design for each block; the whole algorithm was implemented in the hardware, and ultimately he developed five IP Core and achieved a 51.7× acceleration ratio [27]. In 2012, Zhongduo Lin achieved *k*-means acceleration of the high-density data set on FPGA based on triangular inequality [28]. In 2015, I created a solution aiming at the problem of frequent off-chip access in the *k*-means algorithm and counted the relationship between the various factors and the acceleration effect of the accelerator [24].

In 2013, KR Kurte used the GPU to accelerate the PAM algorithm and achieved a 30× acceleration ratio [29]. As the memory requirements of PAM algorithm are high, and FPGA memory is very limited, the FPGA-based PAM algorithm accelerator design is more complex. The current research in this area is not very mature.

In 2014, N Scicluna and CS Bouganis designed the DBSCAN algorithm based on FPGA by utilizing parallel hardware structure. The accelerator is designed for the entire algorithm, using multiple processing units in parallel when searching indirect neighbors. The entire data set is stored in the double data rate (DDR) memory setting up an internal arbitration mechanism to determine whether neighbors and the number of neighbors of the data object meet the requirements and also setting up a number of arrays used to store information. The final accelerator for the CPU achieved a 32× acceleration ratio [30].

The speeding up of these algorithms is less concerned with the effect of memory bandwidth on the acceleration effect. When the amount of data is small, the data can be stored in the block ram (BRAM) inside the FPGA, but when the amount of data is vast, it cannot be entirely stored inside the FPGA, so part of the data must be stored outside the FPGA, and the speed of off-chip accessing is much slower than the rate of the hardware calculation, which will significantly affect the acceleration performance of the hardware accelerator. Second, the previous acceleration scheme was designed as an accelerator for a single clustering algorithm, focusing on accelerator acceleration and energy consumption, and did not consider the versatility and flexibility of accelerator. Research on the general acceleration platform based on the FPGA of the clustering algorithm is still incomplete.

In 2015, a team led by Chen Yunji, a researcher at the Institute of Computing Technology, Chinese Academy of Sciences, proposed a new attempt when studying the acceleration of machine learning algorithms [31]. His work team did a corresponding analysis of seven machine learning algorithms, analyzing the locality of its key code and algorithm, extracted the same function of the algorithm (public operator), and then designed the shared hardware logic, implementing good support for seven machine learning algorithms in an accelerator. This design significantly expanded the accelerator of the versatility and flexibility. In the same year, a team led by Professor Zhou Xuehai and Wang Chao, in the Embedded System Laboratory at the University of Science and Technology of China, designed a hardware accelerator that could support multiple recommended algorithms [32,33]. These results give us a great deal of inspiration. By analyzing the hot-spot code of the four kinds of algorithms and the locality of each algorithm, we want to extract the same functional logic (public operator), use FPGA to harden this functional logic, and then build a support for the four types of clustering algorithms (k-means, PAM, SLINK, DBSCAN) to accelerate the platform through cooperation with the CPU processor.

10.3 ALGORITHM AND HARDWARE ACCELERATION TECHNOLOGY

10.3.1 Introduction to Algorithms

The clustering algorithm [34] is an algorithm for unsupervised types commonly used in machine learning and data mining. It is a division of the original data set; the similar data objects are divided into a cluster, so that the data objects in one cluster have a high degree of similarity, and the data objects in different clusters have significant differences [35].

10.3.1.1 k-Means Algorithm

The k-means algorithm is the simplest and most widely used algorithm of all clustering algorithms [36].

Algorithm input: The data set to be divided D = $\{d_1, d_2, d_3......, d_n\}$; Cluster of labels C = $\{c_1, c_2, c_3......, c_k\}$; d_i (1 < = i < = n) represents a data object, c_t (1 < = t < = k) represents a cluster label. *Algorithm output:* The set of cluster labels corresponding to the data object ID =$\{id_1, id_2, id_3......, id_n\}$, id_t (1 < = t < = n) represents the cluster number of the cluster that contains data object d_t, and the range of id_t is C = $\{c_1, c_2, c_3......, c_k\}$. The basic principles of the algorithm are as follows:

1. Arbitrarily select the k data objects in the original data set in the original data set as the center of the original cluster, and give it a different label c_t to represent different clusters.

2. For each data object d_i in the original data set, do the following:

   a. Calculate the distance between d_i and all clusters.

   b. Find the minimum value of the distance value from Operation a, give the cluster number of the center of the cluster which the distance value corresponds to, then divide the data object d_i into the specified cluster.

3. Do the following for each cluster:

   a. Summarize the sum of each data object in the cluster.

   b. Divide the summarized sum value in Step a by the number of data objects in the cluster; the resulting data is the new center of the cluster.

4. Repeat Steps 2 and 3 until the number of iterations reaches the convergence threshold or the data object in the cluster no longer changes.

From the above k-means algorithm it can be seen that the algorithm is simple and efficient, and the data in the k clusters determined by the algorithm has the smallest square error, but there are also the following several shortcomings:

1. The algorithm needs to know in advance that the data object set is divided into k different clusters, and in real life, many applications do not know the number of clusters.

2. The algorithm needs to set the initial cluster center, but if the center of the cluster is not selected, the result of the whole algorithm will be not ideal.

3. The algorithm uses the arithmetic mean when updating the cluster, which is not very sensitive to the effect of noise and isolated points and will lead to the bad effect of clustering.

4. The algorithm has a good effect on the data processing of the spherical distribution, but the effect of the clustering analysis of the data distribution with irregular distribution is very poor.

10.3.1.2 PAM Algorithm

Another clustering algorithm, the k-medoid algorithm, also known as the PAM algorithm [37], is proposed on the basis of the k-means algorithm. The PAM algorithm and k-means algorithm have similar ideas; the only difference is the operation of updating the center of the cluster.

Algorithm input: The data set to be clustered $D = \{d_1, d_2, d_3......, d_n\}$; cluster of labels $C = \{c_1, c_2, c_3......, c_k\}$; d_i ($1 < = i < = n$) represents a data object, c_t ($i < = t < = k$) represents a cluster label. *Algorithm output:* The set of cluster labels corresponding to the data object $ID = \{id_1, id_2, id_3......, id_n\}$, id_t ($1 < = t < = n$) represents the cluster number of the cluster that contains data object d_t and the range of id_t is $C = \{c_1, c_2, c_3......, c_k\}$. Specific steps are as follows.

1. Arbitrarily select the k data objects in the original data set as the center of the original cluster, and give it a different label c_t to represent different clusters.

2. For each data object d_i in the original data set, do the following:

    a. Calculate the distance between d_i and all clusters.

    b. Find the minimum value of the k distance values from Operation a, give the cluster number of the center of the cluster that the distance value corresponds to, then divide the data object d_i into the specified cluster.

3. Do the following for each cluster c_t:

    a. Do the following for each data object d_t:

        i. Calculate the distance between d_t and c_{ti} where c_{ti} represents the ith element in cluster c_t.

        ii. Accumulate the distance obtained in Step i, and get the sum of the distances.

b. Find the minimum value of the distance amounts in Operation a, the data object to which this minimum corresponds is the center point of the cluster c_t required for the next iteration operation.

4. Repeat Steps 2 and 3 until the number of iterations reaches the convergence threshold or the data object in the cluster no longer changes.

The PAM algorithm can solve the impact of noise or isolated points, but the algorithm still has the following shortcomings:

1. Since the operation of the center of the cluster is time-consuming, it is not suitable for large data sets.

2. The algorithm needs to know in advance that the data object set is divided into k different clusters, and in real life, many applications do not know the number of clusters.

3. It is necessary to set the initial cluster center, but the choice of the center point will affect the final data set clustering results. The clustering analysis of the data of the spherical distribution is more effective, but the clustering effect is very poor for the randomly distributed data set.

10.3.1.3 SLINK Algorithm

The k-means and PAM algorithms are clustering algorithms based on the division strategy, which need to know the number of clusters before cluster analysis, but in real life, many applications do not know the number of clusters. To circumvent this flaw, the SLINK algorithm came into being. The SLINK algorithm is a single link hierarchical clustering algorithm [38]. Its basic principle is as follows: data set D = $\{d_1, d_2, d_3......, d_n\}$ each of the data objects has a label for its own cluster, as a collection ID = $\{Id_1, Id_2, Id_3, Id_4...... Id_n\}$, the distance threshold is R.

1. Calculate the distance matrix DM for the data set D, matrix elements DM(i, j) represent the distance between the data object d_i and d_j in D, that is the distance between Idi and Idj, and DM is also called the distance matrix between clusters.

2. Calculate the minimum value in the row and the column corresponding to the minimum value for each row L_i (0 < i < = n, i rounding) of the distance matrix DM, and store the minimum value in the LineMin[i] array, The subscript of the corresponding column is stored in the Min_NB[i] array. The order of looking for the minimum value of each row is from the diagonal position of each line to the end of each line.

3. Find the minimum for the LineMin array, assuming it is LineMin[s]; the label of the corresponding column of this minimum value is Min_NB[s], which means the minimum is the distance between d_s and $d_{Min\_NB[s]}$.

4. Modify the LineMin array and the Min_NB array: The minimum value in the LineMin is changed to the maximum value of the floating-point type to ensure that it will not be selected at the next minimum value seeking; change values of the elements in Min_NB whose value is Min_NB[s] to s.

5. Update the distance matrix DM, change the minimum value in the matrix to the maximum value of the floating point type, prevent the data from being used for the second time, and then update the distance matrix between clusters by using the following formula:

$$DM_{[s][j]} = Min\left\{DM_{[s][j]}, DM_{[Min\_NB_{[s]}][j]}\right\}, Min\_NB_{[s]} \le j \le n. \qquad (10.1)$$

6. Merge s and Min_NB[s] to form a new cluster, update the ID set, and change the values of the elements whose label is Min_NB [s] to s.

7. Find the minimum value of the s line and the subscript of the corresponding column, store its value in LineMin [s] and Min_NB [s], and then repeat Steps 3 to 6 until the minimum distance between the two clusters is larger than R.

From the principle of the algorithm, we can see that the SLINK algorithm does not need to know the number of clusters, and the distribution of the clustering data sets is not required. However, compared with the first two algorithms, this algorithm is time-consuming, and a singular value will have an impact on the clustering results.

10.3.1.4 DBSCAN Algorithm

The DBSCAN algorithm is based on the density; the basic principle is to find high-density distribution areas where data points distribution are more dense, from different density distribution areas; and we call the sparse areas the *partition area* [39]. The original data objects are divided into three types:

1. *Core point data*: The points that contain more than min_num neighbors in radius R.

2. *Boundary point data*: The number of neighbors included in radius R is less than min_num, but its distance from one or more core points is less than R.

3. *Noise point data*: Except for core point data and boundary point data, there are few neighbors of this class of data objects. And there is no core point data in the neighbors.

R and min_num are the two thresholds that are used to define the high-density region, that is, the area where the radius R contains more than min_num data objects centered on a particular point.

Algorithm input: The data set to be clustered D = {d_1, d_2, d_3, d_4...... d_n}, radius R, threshold min_num and the data object corresponds to the label of the cluster C = {−1, −1, −1 ... ... −1},

d_i ($1 <= i <= n$) represents the data object, -1 means that the data object is not assigned to any cluster before clustering. *Algorithm output:* C = {$c_1, c_2, c_3......, c_k$}; there will be many elements in C having the same values other than -1, which represent these data objects belonging to the same cluster. The specific steps of the algorithm are as follows:

1. Calculate the distance matrix DM for the data set D. The distance between the data object d_i and d_j in D is represented by the matrix element DM(i, j) [3].

2. For each row in DM, count the number of elements whose distance values are less than R. If the number is larger than min_num, mark the point as the core point and record the neighbor node of the core point.

3. Read an unrecognized data in D in sequence, and determine whether the data is the core data. If it is the core point, create a cluster label, add the cluster label to the core point and its neighbor node, and set the processed tag for the data object that has been divided. Then proceed to Operation 4. Otherwise, perform the operation in Step 3 until all the data objects are processed.

4. Check the neighbor node of the core point in sequence to find whether there are core points:

   a. If it is the core point, and the core point has not been set to the mark which means it had been processed, add cluster labels to all the neighbor nodes of the core point, and set the processed tag for these neighbor nodes, then recursively call Operation 4.

   b. If it is not the core, the next neighbor node is checked in sequence. If the next neighbor node satisfies the condition in Step a, the operation in Step a is executed; otherwise the operation in Step b is performed until all the neighbor nodes have completed the judgment and then return to the previous level.

5. Repeat Operations 3, 4 until all the data objects in D are judged, which means the entire data set has completed density-based clustering.

The advantage of this algorithm is that the tolerance of noise is excellent, and it has a good clustering effect for any distributed data set. The disadvantage is that the algorithm is cumbersome to operate, and it involves recursive operation and high time complexity.

10.3.2 Hardware Acceleration Technology Introduction

Hardware acceleration is utilizing the natural hardware features and replacing the software algorithm or CPU with hardware to achieve the corresponding functional logic. Conventional hardware acceleration technologies include ASIC, FPGA, and GPU [40]. ASIC's processing speed is very fast, but because it is a proprietary integrated circuit, it is not flexible enough. GPU meets the support for flexibility and versatility requirements, but GPU acceleration power is very high. FPGA uses a look-up table structure, meaning that

FPGA can be reconstructed, to solve the ASIC custom circuit deficiencies, and built-in dedicated DSP module makes FPGA power consumption very low. In this chapter, we use FPGA (Figure 10.1) to implement a design for an acceleration platform that supports four clustering algorithms.

FPGA is designed to solve the custom circuit and is the product of programmable hardware development. It is mainly composed of the lookup table, configurable logic block, clock resource and clock management unit, block memory RAM, interconnected resources, dedicated DSP blocks, input and output blocks, gigabit transceivers, PCI-E modules, and XADC modules [38]. The main principle of FPGA work is by setting the status of the RAM on the chip, that is, the programming of RAM to set different functional logic.

FPGA acceleration methods include parallel computing, pipeline design and data locality, and so on. Parallel computing is mainly based on the characteristics of the algorithm; the algorithm can be part of the parallel distribution to a different hardware logic unit to perform. Parallel computing is divided into data parallel and computed parallel. *Data parallelism* refers to the fact that some of the data in the algorithm are unrelated, and these separate data are allocated to the same hardware execution unit PE with the same logic function. The calculation of parallel means that the data is not segmented but directly input to a hardware execution unit PE. The PE itself has the features of parallel computing, such as hardware logic unit addition tree, vector subtraction,

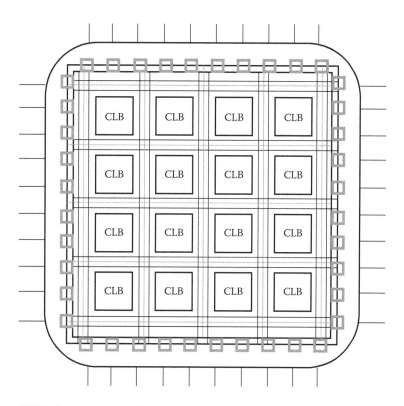

FIGURE 10.1 FPGA basic structure diagram.

vector multiplication, and so on. The pipeline design is another conventional parallel optimization method for FPGAs. By dividing a functional logic block into multiple logical blocks, the time delay of the entire functional logic block is reduced by setting multiple register banks. Ideally, the pipeline will perform a functional logic calculation in each cycle, giving the FPGA an excellent throughput, and the whole acceleration effect is very impressive. *Data locality* refers to the characteristics of the algorithm if the algorithm is localized between the data. The FPGA internal cache data can be used to improve data utilization and reduce the number of off-chip data access, so as to achieve the purpose of acceleration.

10.3.3 Summary

This section focuses on the basics knowledge and techniques, including the principle and advantages and disadvantages of each clustering algorithm and hardware acceleration technology. By analyzing the working principle of k-means, PAM, SLINK, and DBSCAN algorithms, this chapter also gives the advantages and disadvantages of each algorithm and the application fields of each algorithm. At the end of this chapter, we have introduced the structure of the FPGA, the working principle, and the entire FPGA acceleration program.

10.4 THE HARDWARE AND SOFTWARE DIVISION OF THE ACCELERATION SYSTEM

The work in the rest of the chapter has two important aspects: (1) the hardware and software division of the acceleration system—the key code of the algorithm is achieved in the hardware accelerator; (2) analyze the functional logic and locality of the key code of each algorithm and extract the same function code (public operator). The reason for the hardware and software division of the accelerating system is that the accelerator must be able to support four kinds of clustering algorithms well. Moreover, the FPGA hardware resources are limited; it is impossible to realize the four algorithms entirely at the FPGA side, so it can only accelerate the key code of the algorithm. The primary method is analyzing the time-consuming key code in each algorithm through some analysis tools and then achieving these key code in the FPGA side, to improve the efficiency of the entire algorithm. The second part of the work is to balance contradictions between the accelerator generality and performance, accelerator versatility improved, the performance will inevitably be affected. FPGA hardware resources are limited; if we design the corresponding hardware logic for each algorithm, the same code function will lead to a lot of hardware logic to repeat and waste. By extracting the same function code, the accelerator only implements one such hardware logic that shared by different algorithms, which significantly reduces the hardware resources used by the FPGA. The saved hardware resources can be used to speed up other code of the algorithm, and accelerator performance is also improved. The particular method is to refine the hotspot code of each algorithm until you find the same function and then extract the details of these functions, as the basic function of the accelerator logic unit. At the end of the chapter, the local analysis of the algorithm is given, which reveals the existence of the data in the algorithm and the use of the algorithm for the local use of the data.

10.4.1 Design Flow of Hardware and Software Collaborative Design

The rest of this chapter mainly uses the combination of hardware and software to achieve a universal acceleration platform for the four types of clustering algorithm. The design of the acceleration platform is divided into software subsystem design and hardware accelerator design. When the acceleration platform handles the specific application, it will call the particular clustering algorithm through the CPU interface. The algorithm calls the hardware accelerator to deal with the time-consuming key code through the corresponding driver. The accelerator accelerates the hotspot code and returns the calculation result to the CPU. Then the processor continues to run the calculation results until the entire algorithm is completed. The software subsystem design work includes the preparation of accelerator hardware driver and user-oriented acceleration platform interface design. The design of the hardware accelerator includes the design of the accelerator frame, the choice of the accelerator scheme, the design of the accelerator instruction set, and the implementation of the fragmentation technique [39].

The implementation of the entire acceleration system is completed by the hardware and software co-processing. The concrete steps of the whole process of the accelerator hardware and software design are as follows.

1. Analyze the application, find the hotspot code in the application by using profiling technology [40]; use the hardware description language [33] to describe the hardware behavior, data structure, and dataflow and simulate the functional logic of the hotspot code.

2. Design the RTL (register-transfer level) hardware code according to the hardware description language, the designed RTL code generates configurable stream files via hardware compiler and hardware integrator. This streaming file runs in Xilinx ISIM or ModelSim simulation environments to verify the accuracy of behavior and timing. At present, to speed up the production of the RTL code rate, there have been high-level integrated development tools, such as Vivado and LegUP.

3. If the behavior and timing do not meet the requirements, it is necessary to use the hardware description language HDL to redesign the hardware logic of the hotspot code. If the requirements are met, the hardware is packaged. Hardware is divided into two types, namely static module and reconfigurable module. *Static modules* include microprocessors, memory, buses, peripherals, etc.; *reconfigurable modules* mainly refers to the encapsulated IP Core components. For the corresponding hardware platform, the two components are integrated and built into a board-level support package (BSP) and netlist at the FPGA requirements. The netlist is used to generate the hardware bitstream, and the BSP is used to describe the essential environment in which the hardware runs.

4. Migrate the operating system to the development board, then install the tools for managing heterogeneous resources in the operating system, such as cross-compilers, and finally load the generated hardware bitstream files into the operating system.

5. At the SDK side, according to the BSP information, the application is compiled and linked into an executable file, and the operating system runs the executable program and calls the designed hardware resource execution application at the hotspot code.

6. Debug collaboratively at the same time as the program is executed. If the experimental results meet the requirements, it will generate some file sets, hardware, including hardware bitstream files and RTL code; the software is mainly ELF executable file. Otherwise it will optimize the operation and redesign the entire process.

Based on the above hardware and software collaborative design process, the design workflow of this chapter is as follows:

1. Find the key code of the clustering algorithm by the technique of hot spot analysis.

2. Refine the functional logic of the algorithm and find out the same functional logic unit (common operator).

3. Design the hardware accelerator IP Core; this part of the work includes the choice of acceleration program, instruction set design, and the realization of each hardware logic unit.

4. Design and develop accelerator kernel drivers.

5. Design a software subsystem to achieve the coordination of hardware and software.

6. Evaluate the performance of the accelerator: acceleration ratio, energy efficiency ratio.

10.4.2 Hot Code Analysis

This chapter chooses the profile tool to count the running time of each function of the algorithm in Linux. A GNU profiler is often used to analyze and test the time of various functions or operations in the Linux program, so as to find more time-consuming code or function.

10.4.2.1 Hotspot Analysis of k-Means Algorithm

The *k*-means algorithm consists of three critical operations: distance calculation, finding the minimum of the distance, and updating the center of the cluster. As shown in Table 10.1, Cal_Dist in the table represents a function of distance calculation, Find_Min represents a function that looks for the minimum value from the distance array, and Update_Centroid represents a function for cluster center point updates. Different data sets, the number of different clusters will affect the time-proportion distribution of various functions in the entire algorithm.

TABLE 10.1   Time Proportional Distribution of Functions Occupied by the *k*-Means Algorithm

Data Size	Cal_Dist (%)	Find_Min (%)	Update_Centroid (%)
Size = 3000, d =14, k = 5	60.09	22.03	18.03
Size = 3000, d=14, k = 10	75.70	19.08	4.17
Size = 3000, d=22, k = 5	68.76	20.93	10.46
Size = 3000, d=22, k = 10	87.78	7.96	4.19
Size = 3000, d=32, k = 10	90.19	6.09	3.32
Size = 10000, d = 32, k = 10	82.35	10.34	7.29

We tested the time proportion of the various functions of the Kmeans algorithm under the conditions of different data sets and different clusters. According to the data in the table, we can reach the following conclusions:

1. The distance calculation function Cal_Dist occupies a large proportion of time in the whole algorithm.

2. In the case of the same size of the data, the greater the number of clusters, the higher the proportion of time the distance calculation function Cal_Dist takes.

3. When the size of the data set and the number of clusters are determined, the proportion of the distance calculation function Cal_Dist increases as the data dimension increases.

It can be seen from the table that the time proportion of the distance calculation function is 60.09% ~ 90.19%, finding the minimum value is 6.09% ~ 22.03%, and the Update_Centroid function accounts for 3.32% ~ 18.03%. If you only accelerate the distance calculation function Cal_Dist or cluster partition operation, the performance of the accelerator will be significantly affected; from Amdahl's law we can see that the accelerator's best speedup ratio is 5× ~ 10 × or so. After general consideration, the algorithm should be the entire operation of the hardware implementation.

10.4.2.2 PAM Algorithm Hotspot Analysis

The PAM algorithm mainly includes cluster partition and cluster update. The main operation of cluster partition is calculating the distance between the point and the center of all the clusters and finding the minimum value of the cluster. The primary operation of the cluster update is calculating the distance between the data objects in the cluster and calculating the accumulated value of the distance. Through the analysis we can see that the whole algorithm can be divided into three functions: the distance calculation function Cal_Dist, distance minimum search function Fnd_MIN, and distance cumulative sum function Accumulate. The time-proportion ratio of each function in the PAM algorithm is shown in Table 10.2. The amount of data and the number of clusters also affect the time proportional distribution of each function in the PAM algorithm.

TABLE 10.2 Time Proportional Distribution of Each Function in PAM Algorithm

Data Size	Cal_Dist (%)	Accumulate (%)	Fnd_MIN (%)
Size = 3000, d = 14, k = 5	88.52	10.61	0.82
Size = 3000, d = 14, k = 20	90.02	8.85	0
Size = 3000, d = 22, k = 5	89.26	11.08	0
Size = 3000, d = 22, k = 20	87.25	13.09	0
Size = 3000, d = 32, k = 10	94.88	4.70	0.78
Size = 10,000, d = 32, k = 10	94.70	5.36	0

From the results shown in Table 10.2, we can see that the distance calculation function Cal_Dist occupies a large proportion of time in the PAM algorithm, which is about 88.52% ~ 94.88%. The time ratio of the accumulative sum function Accumulate is 4.70% ~ 13.09%. Since the distance calculation function is called to be executed in the cluster partitioning and cluster update operations, it is considered that the entire algorithm should be accelerated. However, because FPGA cannot store the entire data set to be divided, we need hardware and software collaboration to complete the whole algorithm of an iterative operation. First, call the accelerator to complete the cluster partition operation and make the results pass to the CPU side, and then the CPU side to transfer data to the FPGA according to the results of the division, and the accelerator performs the cluster update operation.

10.4.2.3 Hot Analysis of SLINK Algorithm

The SLINK algorithm is a single-link hierarchical clustering algorithm; the main operation is to calculate the distance matrix, find the minimum in the each row, update the cluster label, update the minimum array of rows, and update the distance matrix. In this chapter, the profiling analysis of the algorithm is carried out according to this granularity. Table 10.3 shows the time distribution ratio of each function.

From the time scale distribution of each function in the table, it can be seen that the distance calculation function Cal_Dist takes a large proportion of about 61.65% ~ 89.05%. Obviously, this function is the hot code in the SLINK algorithm. However, if only the Cal_Dist function is accelerated, the SLINK algorithm has the best theoretical value between 2.5× and 10×. And the time ratio of other functions in this algorithm is more

TABLE 10.3 Time Proportional Distribution of Individual Functions in SLINK Algorithm

Time Ratio	Size = 3000 Dim = 14 Radius = 10	Size = 3000 Dim = 14 Radius = 1000	Size = 3000 Dim = 22 Radius = 10	Size = 3000 Dim = 22 Radius = 1000	Size = 3000 Dim = 32 Radius = 1000	Size = 10000 Dim = 32 Radius = 1000
Cal_Dist	89.05	61.65	92.06	72.68	77.56	78.11
Up_SM	0	12.84	0	1.96	8.08	4.81
Cal_SM	7.42	7.71	5.42	3.93	3.23	3.11
Fnd_Min	0	5.14	0	5.89	3.23	3.11
Up_LMin	0	5.14	0	13.75	3.23	1.70
GetID	0	2.57	0	0	0	1.13
Up_CID	0	2.57	0	1.96	3.23	2.97
FndLMin	3.71	2.57	2.71	0	1.62	5.24

TABLE 10.4   Time Proportional Distribution of Each Function in the DBSCAN Algorithm

Data Size	Cal_Dist (%)	Fnd_Key (%)	Get_Neighbors (%)	Cluster (%)
Size=3000, d=14, W	69.34	7.70	15.41	7.70
Size=3000, d=14, B	77.90	7.42	14.84	0
Size=3000, d=22, W	71.54	9.54	11.92	7.15
Size=3000, d=22, B	90.38	4.89	4.89	0

dispersed, so the entire algorithm should be accelerated. However, because the FPGA internal resources are very limited, it is not possible to store the distance matrix into the FPGA, so the distance matrix update operation can only be achieved on the CPU side. From the table it is evident that the function that calculates the minimum value is only 0% ~ 5.24%. If the function uses FPGA to accelerate, it needs to transfer the entire line of data to the FPGA. Data transfer is time-consuming, so it is considered that this part is also achieved on the CPU side. Also, another code of the SLINK algorithm is implemented by using FPGA, that is, FPGA will achieve more than 90% of the entire algorithm work.

10.4.2.4 Hotspot Analysis of DBSCAN Algorithm

The DBSCAN algorithm is based on density. It can be seen from the introduction that the first step is to calculate the distance matrix, the second step is to count the core point and record neighbor nodes of the core node, and the last step is a recursive way to cluster. The percentage of time occupied by each part of the algorithm is shown in Table 10.4. In the table, W represents the condition that the distance calculation function Cal_Dist occupies the minimum proportion of the data size, and B represents the condition that the distance calculation function Cal_Dist occupies the maximum proportion of the data size. From the data in the table it can be seen that the size of the data will also affect the time-proportional distribution of various functions in the DBSCAN algorithm.

The distance calculation function Cal_Dist is the hot code in the SLINK algorithm, occupying the proportion of time from 69.34% to 90.38%; the function of the statistical core points accounts for 4.89% ~ 7.70%, the statistical core points occupy 4.89% ~ 15.41%, iterative clustering accounts for 0% ~ 7.70%. The iterative operation is not suitable for implementation on the FPGA, so the iterative clustering process is implemented on the CPU side. Because the FPGA hardware resources are very limited, the hardware cannot store the distance matrix or record the core node of the neighbor nodes, so searching the core point from distance matrix and recording the neighbor point of the core point cannot be achieved on the FPGA. In summary, only the distance matrix calculation in the DBSCAN algorithm is implemented by using FPGA. The key code occupies 69.34% ~ 90.38% of the entire algorithm, and the best acceleration effect is 3.3× ~ 10×.

10.4.2.5 Algorithm Hardware and Software Division of the Results

The analysis of the above hot code has given the time ratio of each function in each algorithm, and simply gives the hardware and software partition results of the acceleration system. The whole k-means algorithm is implemented on the FPGA side. The PAM algorithm is divided into two parts, the partitioning of the cluster and the update operation

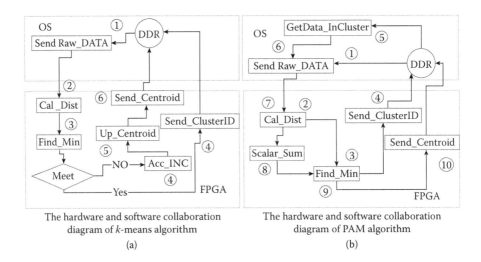

The hardware and software collaboration diagram of k-means algorithm

(a)

The hardware and software collaboration diagram of PAM algorithm

(b)

FIGURE 10.2 Diagram of accelerated system hardware and software collaboration under the (a) k-means and (b) PAM algorithms.

of the cluster. Both of them are implemented on the FPGA, but the CPU is required to cooperate with each other because the FPGA cannot store the large-scale data sets. The data needed for cluster update operations must be transferred from the CPU side. The SLITE algorithm updating the distance matrix and searching the minimum value runs at the CPU side; the other operations is implemented on the FPGA. The DBSCAN algorithm's calculating distance matrix is performed at the FPGA side, and the rest of the algorithm is executed on the CPU side.

Figure 10.2a shows the flow chart of collaboration between operating system and accelerator to accelerate the k-means algorithm; the full set of steps is as follows:

1. Under the operating system, the CPU reads data from the DDR and transfers the data to the BRAM of the FPGA.

2. The FPGA receives data and performs distance calculation operations.

3. It performs a lookup operation to find the minimum distance within the FPGA and divides the data into different clusters.

4. Determine whether the number of iterations within the FPGA meets the threshold. If satisfied, transfer the label of the cluster that includes the data object to DDR under the operating system, and the algorithm completes the calculation; otherwise, add the data object and cluster data and perform Operations 5 and 6.

5. Use the average method to update the center of the cluster inside the FPGA.

6. FPGA will transfer the new center point to DDR under the operating system and complete an iteration of the algorithm, and then repeat Steps 1 to 6.

Figure 10.2b shows the flow chart of collaboration between operating system and accelerator to accelerate the PAM algorithm; the full set of steps is as follows:

1. Under the operating system, the CPU reads data from the DDR and transfers the data to the BRAM of the FPGA.

2. The FPGA receives the data and performs distance calculation operations.

3. Performs a lookup operation to find the minimum distance within the FPGA and divides the data into different clusters.

4. The FPGA transfers the results to the DDR in the operating system.

5. Under the operating system, the CPU reads data from the DDR and counts the data objects in each cluster.

6. The CPU transfer the data objects in each cluster to the inside of the FPGA.

7. The FPGA receives data and performs distance calculation operations.

8. It performs a cumulative operation of distance within the FPGA.

9. The FPGA finds the smallest element, which is the new center of the cluster from the summed array.

10. The information of the center point of each cluster is transferred to the DDR under the operating system, an iteration operation of the algorithm is completed, and then the operations in Steps 1 to 10 are iterated until the number of iterations reaches the convergent threshold.

Figure 10.3a shows the flow chart of collaboration between operating system and accelerator to accelerate DBSCAN algorithm; the full steps are as follows:

1. The CPU reads data from the DDR and transfers the data to the BRAM of the FPGA.

2. The FPGA receives the data and performs distance calculation operations.

3. The calculated distance matrix is transferred to DDR.

4. The CPU acquires the distance matrix from DDR and counts the core point data.

5. It counts the neighbor node of the core point.

6. It performs the clustering operation and completes the division of the data object.

7. The results of the clustering are stored in DDR.

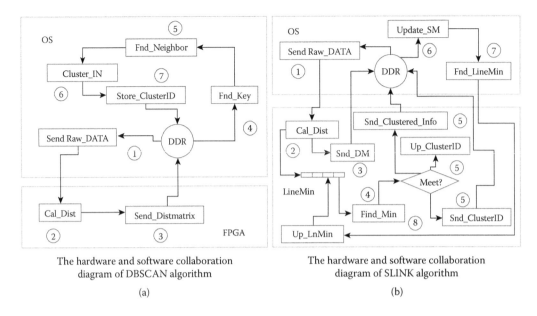

The hardware and software collaboration
diagram of DBSCAN algorithm

(a)

The hardware and software collaboration
diagram of SLINK algorithm

(b)

FIGURE 10.3   Diagram of hardware and software collaboration to accelerate the system in the (a) DBSCAN and (b) SLINK algorithms.

Figure 10.3b shows the flow chart of collaboration between operating system and accelerator to accelerate the SLINK algorithm; the full steps are as follows:

1. The CPU reads data from the DDR and transfers the data to the BRAM of the FPGA.

2. The FPGA receives data and performs distance calculation operations.

3. The calculated distance matrix is transferred to the DDR.

4. Look for the minimum value within the minimum row array inside FPGA.

5. Determine whether the minimum value meets the stop condition. If satisfied, transfer the label of the cluster that includes the data object to the DDR; otherwise, the information of the cluster will be transmitted to the DDR. Update the cluster in FPGA, and then perform the operations in Steps 6 through 8.

6. The CPU obtains the clustered information from the DDR and updates the cluster's distance matrix.

7. Calculate the minimum value of the rows that need to be updated and transfer the data to the FPGA.

8. Update the minimums of rows inside FPGA and repeat the operations in Steps 4 to 8.

10.4.3 The Same Code Extraction and Locality Analysis

10.4.3.1 Extraction of the Same Code

The analysis of the hotspots of the algorithms is shown in Figures 10.2 and 10.3, which shows the results of the hardware and software partitioning of the accelerating system. To make more efficient use of hardware resources to improve the performance of the accelerator, the key code of each algorithm needs to be analyzed and refined to extract the same functional logic unit (public operator) in the key code. Table 10.5 shows the functional logic elements of the key code refinement of each algorithm: Vector_Sub, Vector_ul, Vector_Mul, Scalar_Sum, Fnd_Min, Vector_Add, Vector_Div, SQRT, and Up_Vector represent the subtraction operation of the vector, the vector absolute value operation, the vector multiplication operation, the scalar sum operation, the minimum value search operation, the vector addition operation, the vector division operation, prescribing operation, and vector update operation, respectively.

From Figures 10.2 and 10.3 we can see that the same functional logic of each algorithm is distance calculation, searching the minimum value. However, since the distance calculation uses the standard of Manhattan and Euclidean's similarity measures, and the calculation of the two similarity metrics contains the same functional logic, the distance calculation is finely financed when the common operator is extracted, as shown in Table 10.5. The Manhattan distance formula includes vector subtraction, the vector for absolute value, scalar summation; Euclidean distance formula contains vector subtraction, vector multiplication, scalar summation, and prescribing operation. This fine-grained partition not only allows the hardware logic between the algorithms to be shared, but also the same functional logic unit can be shared between the two similarity metrics in each algorithm, significantly improving the utilization of hardware resources. The distance calculation is a common function of four algorithms but also the key code of each algorithm; it should give priority to the design of this part of the code to accelerate. For each functional logic unit unique to the algorithm, the accelerator needs to develop a separate hardware logic unit for each algorithm.

10.4.3.2 Locality Analysis

By analyzing, we know that calculating the distance is the functional logic common to all algorithms and that it is a very time-consuming key code. We give a partial analysis of the distance calculation [44], and the optimization operation is described in Chapter 4. The distance calculation between the k-means algorithm and the PAM algorithm refers

TABLE 10.5　The Functional Logic Unit of Each Function Whose Key Code Refined

Algorithm	Functional Logic Unit
k-Means	Vector_Sub, Vector_Fab, Vector_Mul, Scalar_Sum, Fnd_Min, Vector_Add, Vector_Div, SQRT
PAM	Vector_Sub, Vector_Fab, Vector_Mul, Scalar_Sum, Fnd_Min, SQRT
SLINK	Vector_Sub, Vector_Fab, Vector_Mul, Scalar_Sum, Fnd_Min, Up_Vector, SQRT
DBSCAN	Vector_Sub, Vector_Fab, Vector_Mul, Scalar_Sum, SQRT

to the distance between the *n* data objects and the center points of the *m* clusters. The distance calculation in the DBSCAN and SLINK algorithms is the distance between any two data objects. Although the data objects in each algorithm are somewhat different, these data objects have the same type; that is, the dimensions of the data are same, so the data in each algorithm can be stored in the same array, that is, it is not required for each algorithm to store the respective data on its own. In the FPGA side with two vector array can be stored, thus reducing the use of hardware resources in the storage, to provide a degree of protection for optimizing the functional logic.

Algorithm 10.1 shows the *k*-Means pseudo-code for distance calculation in cluster partitioning operations.

ALGORITHM 10.1:   ORIGINAL DISTANCE CALCULATION ALGORITHM

Input: N is Data Size
Input: M is Number of Clusters
Output: Dist[X,Y] denotes the Distance Array

```
1 : for i<−0 to N do
2 :    for j<−0 to M do
3 :       Read_Obj(i;&Objects[i])
4 :       Read_Means(j;&Centroid[j])
5 :       Dist[i; j] = Dist_Cal(Objects[i];Means[j])
6 :    end for
7 : end for
```

As can be seen from Algorithm 10.1, the center point data of each cluster is repeated *N* times. However, the FPGA hardware resources are limited, and sometimes the number of clusters *m* is vast, FPGA cannot completely store it in the BRAM, most of the data will be stored in the off-chip. Because each data object in the code is associated with *m* clusters, multiple off-chip accesses are required to process each data object, and the bandwidth of the data transfer will be a bottleneck in accelerator performance. The original code structure did not make good use of the principle of data locality, the data is out of the cache before used, resulting in frequent off-chip access. The fourth chapter of this chapter will use the chip technology to give frequent off-chip access as the solution.

10.5 PERFORMANCE TESTING AND ANALYSIS OF ACCELERATED PLATFORM

10.5.1 Lab Environment

Hardware platform: To assess the accelerated performance of the accelerated platform, we set up an experimental platform and accelerated system platform for testing. The main indicator of the assessment is speed and energy consumption of the accelerated platform; the contrast platform is the CPU and GPU. The hardware platform is the ZedBoard development board (Figure 10.4), which is a development board based on the ZYNQ-7000 architecture and embedded with the xc7z020clg484-1 FPGA chip provided by Xilinx [46].

FIGURE 10.4   Schematic diagram of the ZedBoard hardware platform.

The entire ZedBoard development board is divided into three: PS, PL, and peripherals. PS is the *processing system* for short; it includes two ARM Cortex-A9 Core clocked at 667 MHz and 512 M of off-chip memory. It is the key for the accelerator to achieve the hardware and software coordination, that is, the entire algorithm is scheduled by the PS to complete the scheduling. The PL (programmable logic) block is filled with programmable FPGA hardware logic, so it is the core of the entire accelerator because the hardware logic required to design the accelerator is derived from the PL. Peripherals are about PS and PL; it includes a lot of hardware devices, such as serial port, gigabit Ethernet port, display lights, switches, etc., and the core of each hardware device has been achieved, which can be used directly. The entire development board can work in standalone mode or under Linux OS; changing the development board jumper connection mode can achieve two methods of switching.

Comparison platform: To more comprehensive evaluation of the performance of the accelerated platform, this chapter selected CPU and GPU as two different platforms as target platforms to assess the accelerator acceleration effect. The CPU platform uses two kinds of processors: the Intel Xeon E5 processor, clocked at 2.33 GHZ and equipped with 4G memory, and the Intel Core i7-4790K processor, clocked at 4.0 GHz, 8 G memory, and equipped with 256 G solid-state hard drive. GPU is GeForce GTX 750, with 512 processors, the theoretical calculation of the peak value of 1.04 TFLOPs.

Experimental data set: The experimental data set chosen in this chapter is the KEGG metabolic reaction in the UCI data set [47]. It has 65,554 vectors, and each vector has 29 data dimensions. It is mainly used to test the acceleration effect and energy consumption of accelerator of each algorithm. In this chapter, we use a widely used pseudo-random number generator, Mason Blower [48], which produces some random vector synthesis data sets.

Development tools: The development tools used throughout the experimental environment are Xilinx's toolchains, including Vivado HLS, Vivado, Vivado SDK, and Vivado ISE, version 2014.2. The development tool has a fast synthesis, validation, integration features, can transform standard C or C++ language algorithm into RTL code, and package IP after passing the integration test, which significantly accelerated the hardware design and development cycle, and also reduces the difficulty of hardware development. The test tool for energy consumption under the CPU is the PAPI tool [49], which uses Intel's Running Average Power Limit (RAPL) to obtain power data. The RAPL uses the MSR kernel module to read model specific registers from the user space. The tool can count the processor's dynamic power consumption, processor core power consumption, and memory-related power consumption. The GPU power consumption test tool is the NVIDIA nvprof tool [50]; this tool can calculate the dynamic power consumption of an algorithm running on the GPU.

10.5.2 Accelerator Performance Evaluation

The performance evaluation of the accelerator includes both the speedup ratio and the energy efficiency ratio. The speedup ratio describes how fast the accelerator processing speed is; it is a ratio that divides the running time of the algorithm on the control platform by the running time of the algorithm on the accelerated platform. The energy efficiency ratio describes the performance of the accelerator regarding energy consumption, which divides the energy consumption of control platform by the energy consumption of accelerated platform. Equations 10.1 and 10.2 give the definition of the two indicators:

$$\text{Speedup ratio} = \frac{\text{running time of the algorithm on the control platform}}{\text{running time of the algorithm on the accelerated platform}} \quad (10.1)$$

$$\text{Energy efficiency ratio} = \frac{\begin{array}{c}\text{running time of the algorithm on the control}\\ \text{platform when the algorithm is completed}\end{array}}{\begin{array}{c}\text{running time of the algorithm on the accelerated}\\ \text{platform when the algorithm is completed}\end{array}} \quad (10.2)$$

10.5.3 Hardware Accelerator Acceleration Effect

From the overall frame of the accelerator, it can be seen that the accelerator is operating in the SIMD state, that is, multiple identical execution units can be configured to execute the same instruction on different data sets. If the hardware resources in the PL are sufficient, we can set multiple execution units within the IP Core to increase the degree of parallelism of the accelerator. But because the hardware platform resources are limited, only one execution unit is implemented in the designed IP Core, and the execution unit contains the hardware logic for each instruction. To save the hardware resources, in the design we

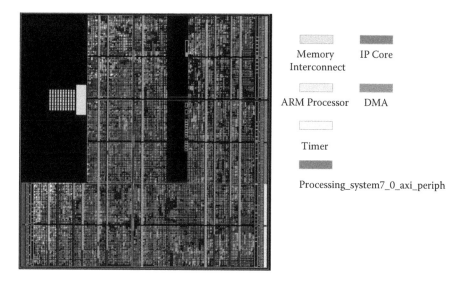

Memory

IP Core

Interconnect

ARM Processor

DMA

Timer

Processing_system7_0_axi_periph

FIGURE 10.5   Resource layout of each hardware logic after accelerator cabling.

use a fixed-point processing to deal with floating-point number. The maximum degree of parallelism supported by the entire accelerator is 32; the frequency of the accelerator is 100 MHz.

As the IP Core only has to achieve one executable unit, for the sake of fairness, the CPU platform algorithm also ran in single-threaded mode. Figure 10.5 shows the resource layout of the entire accelerator cabling. The different gray scale in the figure represent the resources occupied by various hardware logic.

In the test accelerator acceleration effect, the used data set is KEGG data set; we count the running time of the accelerator and CPU and GPU, respectively, and then give the acceleration effect of accelerator compared to different platforms by calculating it.

Figure 10.6 shows the acceleration effect of the accelerator compared to the Intel® Core™ i7-4790k CPU @ 4.00 GHz CPU. When the number of clusters is 600, the accelerator achieves the acceleration ratios of 4.38× and 6.47× for the k-means algorithm using the Manhattan and the Euclidean distance formulas, respectively. For the PAM algorithm, the Manhattan distance formula and the Euclidean distance formula are used to obtain the acceleration ratios of 4.62× and 7.32× respectively. The SLINK and DBSCAN algorithms use the Manhattan distance formula to achieve acceleration ratios of 0.73× and 0.69×, respectively. The acceleration ratio of the accelerator is 1.7× and 1.23× when the Euclidean distance formula is used. The average accelerating ratio of the k-means, PAM, SLINK, and DBSCAN algorithms are 5.43×, 5.97×, 1.22×, 0.96× respectively. The average acceleration of the accelerator is 2.61× when using the Manhattan similarity standard. The average of the acceleration when using the Euclidean similarity metric is 4.18×, and the average speedup of the entire accelerator is 3.34×. It is also possible to see that the acceleration of the accelerator is better when using the Euclidean distance formula. It can be seen from the figure that the acceleration effect of the SLINK and

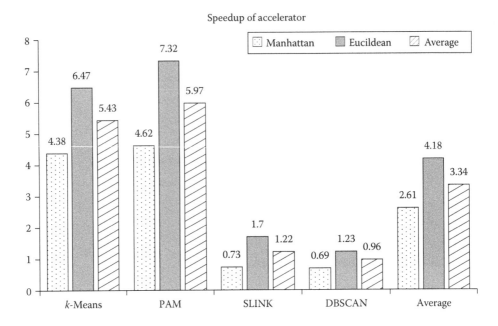

FIGURE 10.6   Accelerator compared to the Intel® Core™ i7-4790k CPU.

DBSCAN algorithms is not ideal because the experiment only allows the speeding up of some key codes of the algorithm, and some of the code is run by the CPU. According to Amdahl's Law, the speed of the algorithm is not very high; and the experimental platform processor frequency is only 667 MHz, while the comparison of the CPU platform frequency is 4 GHz, which in turn leads to a decline in the speed ratio. If the frequency of the experimental platform processor is as high as the frequency of the CPU platform, the entire acceleration ratio will be significantly improved.

10.5.4 Accelerator Energy Consumption Assessment

To more fully evaluate the performance of the accelerator, this chapter also gives the energy performance of the accelerator. As shown in Figure 10.7, the static power consumption is 0.154 w; the dynamic power consumption is 1.513 w, in which the dynamic power consumption includes ARM processor PS7, and IP Core, DMA, and other hardware resources. From the figure, we can see that the dynamic power consumption accounts for 91% of the total on-chip power consumption, representing the energy consumption of the entire accelerator level. Because this article uses the combination of hardware and software to achieve the algorithm to accelerate, so the calculation of energy consumption should use dynamic power consumption, instead of IP Core power consumption. And in the test of CPU and GPU power consumption, the test tool also counts dynamic power consumption. In summary, this chapter selects dynamic power as the basis for comparison of energy efficiency.

In this chapter, we use RAPL tools to analyze CPU power consumption information, because the processor model requirements of the tool are high, so it can only test the Intel®

Summary

Total On-Chip Power: **1.667 W**
Junction Temperature: **44.2 °C**
Thermal Margin: 40.8 °C (3.4 W)
Effective ɜJA: 11.5 °C/W
Power supplied to off-chip devices: 0.121 W

On-Chip Power

Dynamic:	**1.513 W**	**(91%)**
Clocks:	0.080 W	(5%)
Signals:	0.069 W	(5%)
Logics:	0.044 W	(3%)
BRAM:	0.011 W	(1%)
DSP:	0.001 W	(<1%)
PS7:	1.307 W	(85%)
Device Static:	**0.154 W**	**(9%)**

FIGURE 10.7   Power consumption profile of the accelerator.

Core™ i7-4790k model CPU energy consumption. Since energy consumption is the product of power and time, a new energy efficiency formula can be obtained:

$$\text{Energy efficiency ratio} = \frac{\text{CPU power consumption} * \text{CPU running time}}{\text{Accelerator power consumption} * \text{Accelerator run time}}$$
$$= \frac{\text{CPU power consumption}}{\text{Accelerator power consumption}} * \text{Speedup ratio} \tag{10.3}$$

It is easy to calculate the energy efficiency of each algorithm compared to the Intel® Core™ i7-4790k by Equation 10.3. Figure 10.8 shows the results of the test.

It can be seen from the figure that the k-means algorithm uses the Manhattan and Euclidean distance formulas to obtain the energy efficiency ratio of 83.78× and 128.79×, respectively. The PAM algorithm can achieve the energy efficiency ratio of 91.79× and 149.05×, respectively, by two different distance calculation formulas. The SLINK and DBSCAN algorithms use the Manhattan distance formula to obtain the energy efficiency ratios of 13.51× and 13.27×, respectively, and the energy efficiency ratio of 33.93× and 24.31× is achieved when the Euclidean distance formula is used. The average energy efficiency ratio of the k-means, PAM, SLINK, and DBSCAN algorithms are 108.29×, 120.42×, 23.72×, and 18.79×, respectively. The average efficiency ratio of the entire accelerator is 50.59× when using the Manhattan similarity standard, and the average efficiency ratio of the accelerator when using the Euclidean similarity metric is 84.02×; the average effectiveness of the entire accelerator is 67.81×. It can be seen from the comparison that the

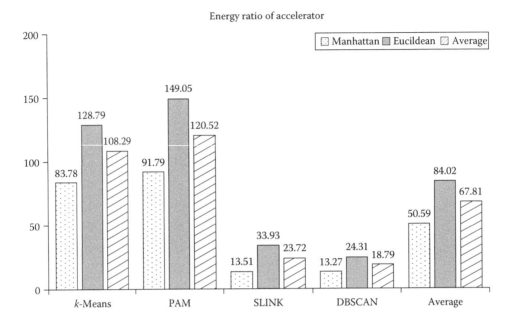

FIGURE 10.8 Energy efficiency ratio of each algorithm under accelerator and Intel® Core™ i7-4790k platform.

accelerator uses the Euclidean distance formula to achieve better energy efficiency than the Manhattan distance formula! This is because of the Manhattan distance formula and the Euclidean distance formula; although the acceleration ratio is very different, the power consumption is not much different. So the accelerator can achieve a better energy efficiency by using the Euclidean distance formula.

The power test under GeForce GTX 750 platform is provided by using the nvprof tool nvprof-system-profiling to complete. The energy efficiency of the accelerator and the GPU platform can be calculated, and Figure 10.9 gives detailed test results. It can be seen from the figure that the k-means algorithm uses the Manhattan and Euclidean distance formulas to obtain the energy efficiency ratios of 7.52× and 9.27×, respectively. The PAM algorithm can achieve an energy efficiency ratio of 10.62× and 13.88×, respectively, by two different distance calculation formulas. The SLINK and DBSCAN algorithms obtained the energy efficiency ratios of 5.18× and 3.38×, respectively, by using the Manhattan distance formula, and the energy efficiency ratios of 6.28× and 4.92× have been achieved by using the Euclidean distance formula. The average energy efficiency ratio of the k-means, PAM, SLINK, and DBSCAN algorithms are 8.4×, 12.25×, 5.73×, and 8.45× respectively. When using the Manhattan similarity criterion, the average efficiency ratio of the accelerator is 6.68×, and the average efficiency ratio is 8.58× when the Euclidean similarity metric is used. The average effectiveness of the entire accelerator is 8.71×. It can be seen from the comparison that the accelerator uses the Euclidean distance formula to achieve better energy efficiency than the Manhattan distance formula!

Through the above experimental results, we can see that comparing the accelerator to the Intel® Core™ i7-4790k platform, both the acceleration or energy performance of the

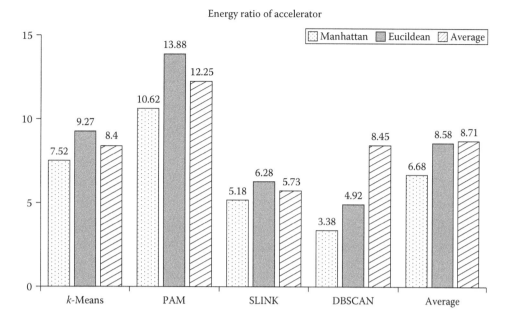

FIGURE 10.9 Energy efficiency ratio of each algorithm under accelerator and GeForce GTX 750 platform.

overall performance is better. Compared with the GPU, the speedup effect of the accelerator is not as good as the GeForce GTX 750 because of its limited hardware resources, but its energy performance is superior to the GPU. The above experimental results verify that the accelerator designed in this chapter has high performance.

10.6 CONCLUSIONS

The clustering algorithm is becoming more and more widely used in various fields, but the high latitude data makes the processing of clustering applications slower and slower, so the acceleration of clustering application has become a hot research topic. There are two ways to accelerate clustering applications: cloud computing platform acceleration and hardware acceleration. Cloud computing platform acceleration needs a significant maintenance overhead, and its single node computing is weak. Hardware acceleration can utilize the hardware's characteristics of fast-to-use hardware instead of software or CPU to implement a particular functional logic, and a large number of built-in hardware logic components make it such that hardware acceleration can better use parallel and pipelined ways to speed up the execution of the algorithm. In summary, the clustering algorithm needs to be accelerated, and hardware acceleration is an efficient means of acceleration.

In practical applications, different applications will need to use different clustering algorithms for processing, so acceleration is necessary for a variety of clustering algorithms. The current hardware acceleration is designed for a single specific algorithm; the support for flexibility and versatility of the accelerator is weak. While the GPU provides a way to solve versatility and flexibility, FPGAs achieve better energy savings because the versatility and flexibility of the GPU causes high power consumption. However, FPGA-based accelerators are currently designing specific hardware acceleration modules for specific algorithms. The hardware accelerator only supports one algorithm, which significantly limits the versatility and flexibility of hardware accelerators. This chapter presents a design scheme for this problem and develops a hardware acceleration platform that can support four kinds of clustering algorithms such as k-means, PAM, SLINK, and DBSCAN. Moreover, the accelerator can use two different similarity measure methods to accelerate each algorithm, which significantly expands the flexibility and versatility of the accelerator.

The main features of this work are as follows:

1. We use the tile layer method to segment the data, which improves the localities of the data to reduce the number of off-chip access.

2. The balance between accelerator versatility and speedup is achieved by analyzing and hardware design of the same functional logic of the algorithm.

3. In the DMA data transmission, we use the mapping mechanism to achieve the DMA driver, which reduces the number of copies of the data to improve the performance of the accelerator.

10.7 ACKNOWLEDGMENTS

This work was supported by the National Science Foundation of China (No. 61379040), Anhui Provincial Natural Science Foundation (No.1608085QF12), CCF-Venustech Hongyan Research Initiative (No. CCF-VenustechRP1026002), Suzhou Research Foundation (No. SYG201625), Youth Innovation Promotion Association CAS (No. 2017497), and Fundamental Research Funds for the Central Universities (WK2150110003).

REFERENCES

1. C. Wang, X. Li, and X. -H. Zhou, 2015, SODA: Software defined FPGA based accelerators for big data. in *Design, Automation & Test in Europe Conference & Exhibition (DATE)*, IEEE, pp. 884–887.
2. M. Annavaram, E. Grochowski, and J. Shen, 2005, Mitigating Amdahl's Law through EPI Throttling, in *Proc. of the 32nd Ann. Int. Symp. on Comp. Architecture (ISCA)*, pp. 298–309.
3. N. Binkert, B. Beckmann, G. Black, S. Reinhardt, A. Saidi, A. Basu, and J. Hestness, 2011, The gem5 simulator, *ACM SIGARCH Computer Architecture News*, vol. 39, no. 2, pp. 1–7.
4. C. Bienia, S. Kumar, J. Singh, and K. Li, 2008, The PARSEC benchmark suite: Characterization and architectural implications, in *Proceedings of the 17th International Conference on Parallel Architectures and Compilation Techniques*, ACM, pp. 72–81.
5. Y.-T. Chen, J. Cong, H. Huang, B. Liu, M. Potkonjak, and G. Reinman, 2012, Dynamically reconfigurable hybrid cache: An energy-efficient last-level cache design, in *Proceedings of the Conference on Design, Automation and Test in Europe*, EDA Consortium, pp. 45–50.
6. Y.-T. Chen, J. Cong, H. Huang, C. Liu, R. Prabhakar, and G. Reinman, 2012, Static and dynamic co-optimizations for blocks mapping in hybrid caches, in *Proceedings of the 2012 ACM/IEEE International Symposium on Low Power Electronics and Design*, ACM, pp. 237–242.
7. J. Cong, K. Gururaj, H. Huang, C. Liu, G. Reinman, and Y. Zou, 2011, An energy-efficient adaptive hybrid cache, in *Proceedings of International Symposium on Low Power Electronics and Design (ISLPED)*, IEEE, pp. 67–72.

8. M.-T. Chang, P. Rosenfeld, S.-L. Lu, B. Jocab, 2013, Technology comparison for large last-level caches (L3Cs): Low-leakage SRAM, low write-energy STT-RAM, and refresh-optimized eDRAM, in *Proceedings of IEEE 19th International Symposium on High Performance Computer Architecture (HPCA)*, IEEE, pp. 23–27.

9. Y. Chen, W.-F. Wong, H. Li, and C. Koh, 2011, Processor caches with multi-level spin-transfer torque ram cells, in *Proceedings of the 17th IEEE/ACM International Symposium on Low-Power Electronics and Design*, IEEE Press, pp. 73–78.

10. Y. Chen, X. Wang, W. Zhu, H. Li, Z. Sun, G. Sun, and Y. Xie, 2010, Access scheme of multi-level cell spin-transfer torque random access memory and its optimization, in *2010 53rd IEEE International Midwest Symposium on Circuits and Systems (MWSCAS)*, IEEE, pp. 1109–1112.

11. Z. Diao, Z. Li, S. Wang, Y. Ding, A. Panchula, E. Chen, L.-C. Wang, and Y. Huai, 2007, Spin-transfer torque switching in magnetic tunnel junctions and spin-transfer torque random access memory, *Journal of Physics: Condensed Matter*, vol. 19, no. 16, p. 165209.

12. X. Dong, C. Xu, Y. Xie, and N. Jouppi, 2014, NVSim: A circuit-level performance, energy, and area model for emerging nonvolatile memory, *IEEE Transactions on Computer-Aided Design of Integrated Circuits and Systems (TCAD)*, vol. 31, no. 7, pp. 994–1007.

13. A. Jadidi, M. Arjomand, and H. Sarbazi-Azad, 2011, High-endurance and performance-efficient design of hybrid cache architectures through adaptive line replacement, in *Proceedings of the 17th IEEE/ACM International Symposium on Low-Power Electronics and Design*, IEEE Press, pp. 79–84.

14. J. Jung, K. Kang, and C.-M. Kyung, 2011, Design and management of 3D-stacked NUCA cache for chip multiprocessors, in *Proceedings of the 21st Edition of the Great Lakes Symposium on VLSI*, ACM, pp. 91–96.

15. J. W. Joyner, P. Zarkesh-Ha, and J. D. Meindl, 2001, A stochastic global net-length distribution for a three-dimensional system-on-a-chip (3D-SoC), in *Proceedings of 14th Annual IEEE International ASIC/SOC Conference, 2001*, IEEE, pp. 147–151.

16. L. Jiang, B. Zhao, Y. Zhang, and J. Yang, 2012, Constructing large and fast multi-level cell STT-MRAM based cache for embedded processors, in *Proceedings of the 49th Annual Design Automation Conference*, ACM, pp. 907–912.

17. C. Kim, D. Burger, and S.W. Keckler, 2002, An adaptive, non-uniform cache structure for wire-delay dominated on-chip caches, in *ACM Sigplan Notices*, ACM, pp. 211–222.

18. S. Kim, D. Chandra, and Y. Solihin, 2004, Fair cache sharing and partitioning in a chip multiprocessor architecture, in *Proceedings of the 13th International Conference on Parallel Architectures and Compilation Techniques*, IEEE Computer Society, pp. 111–122.

19. D. Kadjo, et al., 2013, Power gating with block migration in chip-multiprocessor last-level caches, in *2013 IEEE 31st International Conference on Computer Design (ICCD)*, IEEE, pp. 93–99.

20. S. Li, et al., 2011, CACTI-P: Architecture-level modeling for SRAM-based structures with advanced leakage reduction techniques, in *2011 IEEE/ACM International Conference on Computer-Aided Design (ICCAD)*, IEEE, pp. 649–701.

21. S. Lee, J. Jung, and C.-M. Kyung, 2012, Hybrid cache architecture replacing SRAM cache with future memory technology, in *2012 IEEE International Symposium on Circuits and Systems (ISCAS)*, IEEE, pp. 2481–2484.

22. G. Loh, Y. Xie, and B. Black, 2007, Processor design in 3D die-stacking technologies, *IEEE Micro*, vol. 27, no. 3, pp. 31–48.

23. J. Li, C. J. Xue, and Y. Xu, 2011, STT-RAM based energy-efficiency hybrid cache for CMPs, in *2011 IEEE/IFIP 19th International Conference on VLSI and System-on-Chip (VLSISoC)*, IEEE, pp. 31–36.

24. N. Magen, A. Kolodny, U. Weiser, and N. Shamir, 2004, Interconnect-power dissipation in a microprocessor, in *Proceedings of the 2004 International Workshop on System Level Interconnect Prediction*, ACM, pp. 7–13.

25. P. Chen, C. Wang, X. Li, and X.-H. Zhou, 2014, Accelerating the next generation long read mapping with the FPGA-based system, *IEEE/ACM Transactions on Computational Biology and Bioinformatics*, vol. 11, no. 5, pp. 840–852.

26. K. Nesbit, M. Moreto, F. Cazorla, A. Ramirez, M. Valero, and J. Smith, 2008, Multicore resource management, *IEEE Micro*, vol. 28, no. 3, pp. 6–16.

27. G. Sun, X. Dong, Y. Xie, J. Li, and Y. Chen, 2009, A novel architecture of the 3D stacked MRAM L2 cache for CMPs, in *IEEE 15th International Symposium on High Performance Computer Architecture, HPCA 2009*, IEEE, pp. 239–249.

28. S.-M. Syu, Y.-H. Shao, and I.-C. Lin, 2003, High-endurance hybrid cache design in CMP architecture with cache partitioning and access-aware policy, in *Proceedings of the 23rd ACM International Conference on Great Lakes Symposium on VLSI*, ACM, pp. 19–24.

29. G. Suo, X. Yang, G. Liu, J. Wu, K. Zeng, B. Zhang, and Y. Lin, 2008, IPC-based cache partitioning: An IPC-oriented dynamic shared cache partitioning mechanism, in *International Conference on Convergence and Hybrid Information Technology, 2008, ICHIT'08*, IEEE, pp. 399–406.

30. Y. -F. Tsai, F. Wang, Y. Xie, N. Vijaykrishnan, and M. -J. Irwin, 2008, Design space exploration for 3-D cache, *IEEE Transactions on Very Large Scale Integration (VLSI) Systems*, vol. 16, no. 4, pp. 444–455.

31. B. Verghese, A. Gupta, and M. Rosenblum, 1998, Performance isolation: Sharing and isolation in shared-memory multiprocessors, in *ACM SIGPLAN Notices*, ACM, pp. 181–192.

32. C. Wang, L. Gong, Q. Yu, X. Li, Y. Xie, and X.-H. Zhou, 2017, Dlau: A scalable deep learning accelerator unit on FPGA, *IEEE Transactions on Computer-Aided Design of Integrated Circuits and Systems*, vol. 36, no. 3, pp. 513–517.

33. X. Ma, C. Wang, Q. Yu, X. Li, and X.-H. Zhou, 2015, An FPGA-based accelerator for neighborhood-based collaborative filtering recommendation algorithms, in *2015 IEEE International Conference on in Cluster Computing (CLUSTER)*, IEEE, pp. 494–495.

34. S. Vangal, J. Howard, G. Ruhl, S. Dighe, H. Wilson, J. Tschanz, and D. Finan, et al., 2008, An 80-tile sub-100-w teraflops processor in 65-nm CMOS, *IEEE Journal of Solid-State Circuits*, vol. 43, no. 1, pp. 29–41.

35. B. Vaidyanathan, W. Hung, F. Wang, Y. Xie, V. Narayanan, and M. J. Irwin, 2007, Architecting microprocessor components in 3D design space, in *Proc. Int. Conf. VLSI Des.*, pp. 103–108.

36. M. Qureshi and Y. Patt, 2006, Utility-based cache partitioning: A low-overhead, high-performance, runtime mechanism to partition shared caches, in *39th Annual IEEE/ACM International Symposium on Microarchitecture, 2006, MICRO-39*, IEEE, pp. 423–432.

37. S. Wilton and N. Jouppi, 1994, *An integrated cache and memory access time, cycle time, area, leakage, and dynamic power model*, Technical report, Palo Alto, CA: Western Research Laboratory.

38. J. Wang, X. Dong, and Y. Xie, 2012, Point and discard: A hard-error-tolerant architecture for non-volatile last level caches, in *Proceedings of the 49th Annual Design Automation Conference*, ACM, pp. 253–258.

39. X. Wu, J. Li, E. Speight, and Y. Xie, 2009, Power and performance of read-write aware hybrid caches with non-volatile memories, in *Design, Automation & Test in Europe Conference & Exhibition, 2009, DATE'09*, IEEE, pp. 737–742.

40. S. Yazdanshenas, M. R. Pirbasti, M. Fazeli, and A. Patooghy, 2014, Coding last level STT-RAM cache for high endurance and low power, *IEEE Computer Architecture Letters*, vol. 13, no. 2, pp. 73–76.

CHAPTER 11

Accelerators for Classification Algorithms in Machine Learning

Shiming Lei, Chao Wang, Lei Gong, Xi Li,
Aili Wang, and Xuehai Zhou

University of Science and Technology of China

Hefei, China

CONTENTS

11.1 INTRODUCTION

With the rapid development of the Internet and the rapid expansion of electronic information, how to organize and manage this information effectively and how to find the information needed by users quickly, accurately, and comprehensively has become one of the hot topics of state-of-the-art information science and technology. Classification algorithms [1], as a key technology to process and classify large amounts of data, can solve the problem of information clutter phenomenon to a large extent, so that users can accurately locate information and diversion information. Also, as a technical basis for information filtering, information retrieval, search engines, text database, digital library, and other fields, classification technology has a wide range of applications.

In the current classification algorithm, integrated learning [2,3] is a hot topic for domestic and foreign scholars. Integrated learning is mainly based on a certain combination of rules to solve the problem; the algorithm has bagging [4] and boosting [5]. In the single classification algorithm, support vector machine (SVM) [6] has a high accuracy rate; it has a very good effect when there is no background information on the data set. A decision tree [7] can explain the established model very well. So with different data, background, and needs, different classification algorithms are needed to achieve good results.

In the era of Big Data, massive high latitude data greatly slow down the efficiency of classification algorithms, seriously restricting the development of all walks of life. With the rapid growth of data and the urgent need for key information, how to extract and classify the information quickly and efficiently has become particularly important. Therefore, the high performance of the classification algorithm has become an important topic for researchers to study. The traditional computer system has been unable to adapt to the typical needs of Big Data; a heterogeneous computing system based on graphics processing unit (GPU) and field programmable gate array (FPGA) has become an effective framework to deal with Big Data applications.

Compared with the difficulty of optimizing and improving the algorithm at the algorithm level, researchers have made effective progress at the hardware level. The main means of accelerating the current classification algorithm are the cloud computing platform [8,9] and the hardware acceleration platform [10]. The cloud computing platform consists of a large number of isomorphic CPU-based single node servers. Each node works in coordination. The computing model of cloud computing platform can be divided into two types: the MapReduce calculation model and graph-based computing model. The essence of the two calculation models is to divide the tasks using task-level parallelism and data set-level parallelism. The assigned tasks and data are distributed to each node computer distributed over the cloud, and these distributed computers return the results to the hosts on the cloud computing platform after completing the calculation tasks. Although the cloud computing platform can have good acceleration performance, the computing efficiency for each node on the cloud computing is low, and the performance of the acceleration is also limited by the network bandwidth. Its cost is relatively high and so is the energy consumption.

The hardware acceleration platform includes a general purpose graphics processing unit (GPGPU) [11], application specific integrated circuit (ASIC) [12,13], and field programmable gate array (FPGA) [14,15]. The GPU has a large number of hardware-level threads and a large number of parallel processing units; it is often used in data-level parallel mode to accelerate the implementation of various applications, such as the calculation of complex and parallel graphics processing. At present, programming standards such as CUDA [16], OpenCL [17], and OpenACC [18] have been proposed and implemented for the GPGPU platform, which greatly reduces the development threshold for GPGPU-based applications and makes GPGPU one of the most widely used parallel acceleration platforms. The GPU platform has a good acceleration effect but cannot avoid the high energy consumption overhead. In addition, in order to enhance the versatility, GPU chips integrate some functional components that many algorithms never use; this brings a larger chip area and extra overhead. If we need to design a dedicated hardware accelerator structure to accelerate the implementation of the classification algorithm from the bottom of the hardware level, the accelerator should have both high computational efficiency and lower operating power consumption. ASIC is used for specialized integrated circuits; the circuit structure cannot be modified after the completion of the circuit structure, so it is only suitable for specific applications. Compared with ASIC, FPGA has some characteristics such as reconfigurability, which means the user can dynamically reconstruct the FPGA on the functional modules, flexibility, low requirements of the developer, a short development cycle, and so on.

At present, researchers at home and abroad often focus on the study of the improvement of single algorithm based accelerator without much concerned about the versatility and flexibility of FPGA accelerators. So we aimed at designing a general classification algorithm accelerator based on FPGA.

In this chapter, we chose the FPGA platform as our accelerator design platform. The FPGA platform has characteristics such as programmability, high performance, and low power consumption. The design of the accelerator includes three kinds of classification algorithms, including the Rocchio algorithm [19], k-nearest neighbor algorithm [20], and naïve Bayesian algorithm [21], and supports five similarity measures between vectors. We extracted the key code after analyzing these three different algorithms and got the common logic between the key code. After that, we designed the common logic in the hardware and finally programmed the FPGA platform, which has an operating system. We also programmed the device drivers and the related user interface for the upper call to improve the applicability of the accelerator. This chapter will proceed from the following aspects:

1. We use the profiling tool [22] to analyze the Rocchio algorithm, k-nearest neighbor algorithm, and naïve Bayesian algorithm to generate the key code. Then the key code of these three algorithms is analyzed and modified to extract the common logic. At last, the common logic is programmed into the execute unit in our accelerator.

2. We design the overall framework of the hardware accelerator. We analyze the resource limits and features of the FPGA platform and decide to use the pipeline and parallel methods to optimize the execute unit of the accelerator to improve the efficiency of the hardware accelerator.

3. We use the data set to test our accelerator and compare its performance with the CPU platform. According to the performance, power, and energy consumption of the accelerator, we analyze the advantages and disadvantages of the accelerator and its performance influence factor.

11.2 RELATED WORK

In this section, we introduce the related works of a different kind of accelerator.

11.2.1 Cloud-Based Accelerations

The cloud computing platform is a typical example of distributed computing and also an important means of classification algorithm acceleration. In cloud computing, Chieh-Yen Lin and Cheng-Hao Tsai used MapReduce to accelerate the SVM algorithm on the Spark platform [23]. Likewise, in 2014, Hang Tao also accelerated the SVM algorithm on the Spark platform [24]. Although the cloud computing platform has greatly improved the performance of the classification algorithm SVM, the problem of increased power consumption with the increase in computer nodes still cannot be underestimated.

11.2.2 CPU-Based Accelerations

On the GPU side, Bryan Catanazaro used the CPU + GPU model to accelerate the SVM algorithm [25]. They used MapReduce technology to accelerate the kernel computing through the GPU parallel computing resources in Nvidia's Compute Unified Device Architecture (CUDA) model. The entire system can reach 20× speedup compared with the CPU. Marcos VT Romero and Adriana S. Iwashita implemented the optimum-path forest (OPF) algorithm in the CUDA model [26], which achieves a speedup of 50× overall. However, the GPU platform still cannot avoid the high energy consumption and high cost.

11.2.3 FPGA-Based Accelerations

There is much research at home and abroad related to FPGA and ASIC [27]. Srihari Cadambi used FPGA as a coprocessor to design the SVM algorithm accelerator [28]. The main idea was to use the CPU + FPGA model. The CPU was used to run the sequential minimal optimization (SMO) algorithm and the FPGA coprocessor was used to calculate the kernel dot product (key calculation). The point of their acceleration was to take a low-precision calculation, so that the vector processor cluster could be paralleled to deal with multiple multiplication accumulation operations. And finally it was able to achieve an average 20× speedup compared to a CPU. However, it did not fully use the heterogeneity of modern FPGA; it also did not address the specific needs of training and the resource utilization was not high. Fareena Saqib designed a decision tree algorithm accelerator based on FPGA [29]. They mainly use parallel and pipeline technology, which is to deal with data pipelined by establishing multiple parallel independent nodes. The final accelerator can reach an average of 110× speedup compare to the CPU. Ref. [30] introduced an SVM training process acceleration framework based on FPGA, which used a floating-point pipeline to accelerate the kernel function to improve the accelerator performance.

Ref. [31] proposed a new SVM accelerator based on logarithmic number systems (LNS). Similarly, Ref. [32] also used LNS to accelerate the SVM kernel and achieved good performance. However, their work is more inclined to use LNS to solve SVM problems rather than to accelerate the SVM algorithm.

In addition to the classification algorithm, there is some related work on acceleration for the current popular variety of Big Data algorithms on FPGA, mainly in deep learning, data mining, gene sequencing, and graph calculation. For example, Qi Yu designed an FPGA-based deep learning accelerator [33] that achieved a speedup of 30× in performance compared to a CPU by using methods such as optimized data transfer, approximation calculations, and accumulation tree. Xiang Ma [34] also used a similar acceleration method to achieve the acceleration of the recommended algorithm. The entire algorithm accelerator can achieve an average of 10× speedup. In gene sequencing, Peng Chen designed a gene sequencing accelerator system based on the Smith-Waterman algorithm on the FPGA platform [35], which achieves better acceleration compared to the current gene sequencing software. Chao Wang [36] proposed an acceleration method for the constrained shortest path finding (CSPF) algorithm, which was applied in a software-defined network. The method decomposed the CSPF problem and then processed it in parallel. He used the ARM + FPGA model, which means the CSPF steps are implemented on the FPGA, and other parts run on the ARM processor. The entire accelerator can achieve 43.75× speedup compared to the same ARM software operation.

11.3 ALGORITHM ANALYSIS

In this section, we select three representative classification algorithms to analyze, the naïve Bayesian algorithm, k-nearest neighbor algorithm, and Rocchio algorithm.

11.3.1 Naïve Bayesian Algorithm

The naïve Bayesian algorithm is simple, efficient, and easy to understand. It is one of the typical data-mining algorithms. The algorithm insists on the attribute independent assumption, that is, it is assumed that the attributes are independent of each other and ignore their interdependence. Although the hypothesis violates the fact that there is interdependence between the data, in reality, the naïve Bayesian algorithm is one of the most widely used algorithms in terms of its excellent classification accuracy and classification speed and is favored by many experts and scholars.

The basic idea of the naïve Bayesian algorithm is to compare the probability that data belong to a certain class and to divide the input data object into the most probable class.

Algorithm input: test data set D = $\{d_1, d_2, ..., d_n\}$; training data set T = $\{(x_1, y_1), (x_2, y_2), (x_3, y_3), ..., (x_n, y_n)\}$; where $x_i = (x_i^{(1)}, x_i^{(2)}, ..., x_i^{(n)})^T$; $x_i^{(j)}$ is the jth characteristic of the ith sample, $x_i^{(j)} \in \{a_{j1}, a_{j2}, ..., a_{jS_j}\}$, a_{jl} is the lth value that the jth characteristic may take, $j = 1, 2, ..., n, l = 1, 2, ..., S_j, y_i \in \{c_1, c_2, ..., c_K\}$, and c_i represents a certain class number.

Algorithm output: class number data set ID = $\{id_1, id_2, ..., id_n\}$, id_i is the class label of the instance data d_i, where $id_i \in \{c_1, c_2, ..., c_K\}$.

The steps of the algorithm:

1. Calculate prior probability

$$P(Y = c_k) = \frac{\sum_{i=1}^{N} I(y_i = c_k)}{N}, k = 1, 2, \ldots, K \tag{11.1}$$

2. Calculate the conditional probability

$$P\left(X^{(j)} = a_{jl} \mid Y = c_k\right) = \frac{\sum_{i=1}^{N} I\left(x_i^{(j)} = a_{jl}, y_i = c_k\right)}{\sum_{i=1}^{N} I\left(y_i = c_k\right)} \tag{11.2}$$

j = 1, 2, ... n, 1 = 1, 2, ... S_j, $y_i \in \{c_1, c_2, \ldots, c_K\}$

3. Given every instant $d_i = (x_i^{(1)}, x_i^{(2)}, \ldots, x_i^{(n)})^T$ in test data set D, calculate

$$P(Y = c_k) \prod_{j=1}^{n} P\left(X^{(j)} = x^{(j)} \mid Y = c_k\right), k = 1, 2, \ldots, K \tag{11.3}$$

4. Determine the class where instant d_i *belongs* to

$$id_i = arg \max_{c_k} P(Y = c_k) \prod_{j=1}^{n} P\left(X^{(j)} = x^{(j)} \mid Y = c_k\right) \tag{11.4}$$

The Bayesian algorithm assumes that the properties are independent of each other in practice, so in some cases, there is an error rate in the classification decision.

11.3.2 *k*-Nearest Neighbor Algorithm

The *k*-nearest neighbor (KNN) algorithm is a basic classification and regression algorithm. Initially proposed by Cover and Hart in 1968, it is a nonparametric classification algorithm, which is effective in statistics-based pattern recognition. For the unknown and not-normal distribution, the algorithm can achieve a high classification accuracy with a characteristic such as simple formula, good classification effect, easy to operate, and so on.

The basic idea of the KNN algorithm is very simple and intuitive. It calculates the similarity between a given data and each data in the training data set and finds the *k* most similar training data from the obtained similarity. Most of the *k* training data belong to class; then the instance is divided into this class.

Algorithm input: test data set D = {d_1, d_2, ..., d_n}; training data set T = {(x_1, y_1), (x_2, y_2), (x_3, y_3), ..., (x_n, y_n)}, $x_i \in R^n$ is the eigenvector of the training data, $y_i \in \{ c_1, c_2, ... , c_K \}$ is the class of the training data, c_i represents a class number, $i = 1, 2, ... , n$.

Algorithm output: class number data set ID = {id_1, id_2, ..., id_n}, id_n is the class label of the instance data, d_i where $id_i \in \{ c_1, c_2, ..., c_K \}$.

The algorithm contains the following steps:

1. According to the given metric, we calculate the similarity between each instance of the test data set and the training data set.

2. According to the similarity, the k data points that are most similar to the test cases are selected in the training data set, that is, k nearest neighbors.

3. In the k nearest neighbors of the test instance, calculate the weight of each class; the formula is as follows:

$$P(C|x) = \sum_{d_i \in k \text{ nearest neighbors of } x} sim(x, d_i) I(d_i, c_j) \tag{11.5}$$

where x is an instance, c_j is a known class label, d_i is the k nearest neighbor of x, sim $sim(x, d_i)$ is the similarity between x and d_i, and $I(d_i, c_j)$ is the instruction function, that is, when $d_i \in C_j$ when the function value is 1, otherwise 0.

4. Compare the weight; the instance will be assigned to the class with the largest weight.

The KNN algorithm is a lazy learning algorithm; the amount of calculation is large, and it will produce errors in the case of a small sample size.

11.3.3 Rocchio Algorithm

The Rocchio algorithm is an algorithm based on the vector space model and minimum distance. The algorithm has a good feedback function. It can modify the classification of the vector space according to its formula. The algorithm is widely used because the implementation is simple, the similarity calculation is reduced, and the training and classification speed is accelerated.

The basic idea of Rocchio algorithm is to calculate the central vector of the data of each class and then compare the size of the similarity between the test instance and each type of central vector. Finally, the test instance is classified into the class with the largest similarity.

Algorithm input: test data set D = {d_1, d_2, ..., d_n}; training data set T = {(x_1, y_1), (x_2, y_2), (x_3, y_3), ..., (x_n, y_n)}, xi $\in R^n$ is the eigenvector of the training data, $y_i \in \{c_1, c_2, ..., c_K\}$ is the class of the training data, c_i represents a class number, i = 1, 2, ... , n.

Algorithm output: class number data set ID = {id_1, id_2, ..., id_n}; id_i is the class label of the instance data d_i, where $id_i \in \{c_1, c_2, ..., c_K\}$.

The steps of the algorithm:

1. Calculate the central vector of each training data set, and the center vector is chosen using means such as sum center, average center, and normalized average.
   Sum center means the center is the sum of all the vectors of the same class:

$$C_i^S = \sum_{y \in c_i} x \tag{11.6}$$

The average center is the number of vectors in the class divided by the sum of centers in the same class:

$$C_i^A = \frac{C_i^S}{|c_i|} \tag{11.7}$$

The normalization center is normalized to the average center with two norms:

$$C_i^N = \frac{C_i^S}{\|C_i^S\|} \tag{11.8}$$

2. Calculate the similarity between the test instance and each of the central vectors.

3. Compare the size of the similarity; the test instance will be classified into the class with the largest similarity. The calculation formula is as follows:

$$P(D) = \max_{j=1,2,\dots,K} sim(C_j, D) \tag{11.9}$$

The disadvantage of the algorithm is the use of the central vector, which will depend on the distribution of the category. In the case of uniform distribution such as the case of spherical distribution, the performance is very good, and vice versa: in the case of irregular distribution, especially in the noise or isolated point, the performance is poor.

11.3.4 Similarity Measure

We find that the Rocchio algorithm and the *k*-nearest neighbor algorithm use the same similarity calculation of the vector [37,38]. The similarity metric is measured in the following ways.

To calculate Euclidean distance, which represents the distance between two points in the Euclidean space, the formula is

$$W_{uv} = \frac{1}{\sqrt{\sum_{i \in I}(r_{ui} - r_{vi})^2}} \tag{11.10}$$

To calculate Manhattan distance, which represents the absolute wheelbase sum between two points in the standard coordinate system, the formula is

$$w_{uv} = \sum_{i \in I} |r_{ui} - r_{vi}| \qquad (11.11)$$

The Jaccard coefficient, which represents the proportion of the intersection elements of the two sets in their cohesion, is calculated as follows:

$$w_{uv} = \frac{|N(u) \cap N(v)|}{|N(u) \cup N(v)|} \qquad (11.12)$$

Cosine similarity, which represents the cosine of the two vectors, is calculated as follows:

$$w_{uv} = \frac{\sum\limits_{i \in I} r_{ui} * r_{vi}}{\sqrt{\sum\limits_{i \in I} r_{ui}^2 \sum\limits_{i \in I} r_{vi}^2}} \qquad (11.13)$$

To calculate the Pearson correlation coefficient, used to reflect the linear correlation between the two variables of the statistics, the formula is

$$w_{uv} = \frac{\sum\limits_{i \in I} \left(r_{ui} - \hat{r}_u\right) * \left(r_{vi} - \hat{r}_v\right)}{\sqrt{\sum\limits_{i \in I} \left(r_{ui} - \hat{r}_u\right)^2 \sum\limits_{i \in I} \left(r_{vi} - \hat{r}_i\right)^2}} \qquad (11.14)$$

When we compare these five similarity measures, we find that the five similarities have some duplication. So we can use some intermediate variables to replace one of the formulas so that the five similarity operations can reuse some of the intermediate variables, to avoid duplication of operations. It ensures the efficiency of the hardware accelerator computing unit that used the five similarity measurements, improves the efficiency of calculation, and can save FPGA hardware logic resources. We reorganized to get the following formula.

The Euclidean distance metric formula contains $S_{(x-y)}^2$. $S_{(x-y)}^2$ represents the accumulation of squared difference of vector x and vector y:

$$w_{xy} = \frac{1}{\sqrt{\sum\limits_{i \in I} \left(r_{xi} - r_{yi}\right)^2}} = \frac{1}{\sqrt{S_{(x-y)^2}}} \qquad (11.15)$$

The formula for the Manhattan distance metric contains S_{x-y}. S_{x-y} represents the accumulation of the difference between vector x and vector y:

$$w_{uv} = \sum_{i \in I} |r_{ui} - r_{vi}| = S_{x-y} \qquad (11.16)$$

The Jaccard coefficient metric formula contains N_x, N_y, N_{xy}. N_x and N_y represent the number of nonempty eigenvalues of vector x and vector y; N_{xy} represents the number of common eigenvalues between vector x and vector y:

$$w_{xy} = \frac{|N(x) \cap N(y)|}{\sqrt{|N(x)||N(y)|}} = \frac{N_{xy}}{\sqrt{N_x * N_y}} \tag{11.17}$$

The cosine similarity metric formula contains S_x^2, S_y^2, S_{xy}. S_x^2 represents the accumulation of the squares of vector x; S_y^2 represents the accumulation of the squares of vector y; and S_{xy} represents the accumulation of the product of vector x and vector y:

$$w_{xy} = \frac{\sum_{i \in I} r_{xi} * r_{yi}}{\sqrt{\sum_{i \in I} r_{xi}^2 \sum_{i \in I} r_{yi}^2}} = \frac{S_{xy}}{\sqrt{S_{x^2} * S_{y^2}}} \tag{11.18}$$

The Pearson correlation coefficient metric formula contains S_x, S_y, S_x^2, S_y^2, S_{xy}, N_{xy}. S_x represents the accumulation of vector x; S_y represents the accumulation of vector y:

$$w_{xy} = \frac{\sum_{i \in I} r_{xi} * r_{yi} - \frac{\sum_{i \in I} r_{xi} * \sum_{i \in I} r_{yi}}{|I|}}{\sqrt{\left(\sum_{i \in I} (r_{xi})^2 - \frac{(\sum_{i \in I} r_{xi})^2}{|I|}\right) * \left(\sum_{i \in I} (r_{yi})^2 - \frac{(\sum_{i \in I} r_{yi})^2}{|I|}\right)}}$$

$$= \frac{S_{xy} - \frac{S_x * S_y}{N_{xy}}}{\sqrt{\left(S_{x^2} - \frac{(S_x)^2}{N_{xy}}\right) * \left(S_{y^2} - \frac{(S_y)^2}{N_{xy}}\right)}} \tag{11.19}$$

We found that all five similarity measures require the calculation of several intermediate variables such as S_x, S_y, S_{x-y}, S_x^2, S_y^2, $S_{(x-y)}^2$, S_{xy}, and N_{xy}.

11.4 ACCELERATOR SYSTEM DESIGN

In this section, we will elaborate the design of hardware acceleration system based on FPGA. We first profile the three kinds of classification algorithms (Rocchio, k-nearest neighbor, and naïve Bayesian) and analyze the hotspot of the three algorithms, which is the longest period. Then, the function logic of the key codes of three algorithms is analyzed, and the same logic function is extracted. We implement these logic functions in hardware on the FPGA platform. It can effectively improve the efficiency of the algorithm and save the FPGA hardware logic resources. At last, we introduced the overall design of the hardware acceleration system.

11.4.1 Algorithm Profiling

11.4.1.1 Rocchio Algorithm

According to the algorithm description in Section 11.3, the general calculation process of the Rocchio algorithm mainly includes the calculation of the center vector, the calculation of the similarity between the vectors, and the search of the minimum of the similarity. It first calculates the center vector of different classes; in this case, we choose sum center as the calculation metric of the center vector. It then calculates the similarity between the test data and all the class centers and finally finds the central vector, which has the minimum similarity. At last, the test data is attributed to the class to which the center vector belongs. However, the similarity measurement method is relatively mixed. In some similarity measures, the smaller value means that the two vectors are similar and in other cases, the larger value means the two vectors are very similar. So we will take the standard that when the similarity measure is small it means the two vectors are very similar, as is the case elsewhere in this article. Table 11.1 shows the results of the hot-spot analysis for the different similarity calculation methods of Rocchio algorithm. In the table, the column labeled "Center Vector Calculation" represents the calculation for finding the center vector. The "Similarity Calculation" column represents the calculation of the similarity between vectors. "Min" represents searching the minimum value of similarity.

From Table 11.1, we can see that the ratio of the calculation of similarity between vectors is the largest, which is 82.37%~96.74%. The ratio of the centroid vector calculation and the search minimum is 2.13%~11.41% and 1.13%~6.22%. Therefore, the calculation of similarity between vectors is a hot spot and a key code for hardware acceleration. At the same time, we can see that the similarity calculation time in the Manhattan distance metric occupancy ratio is lower than that of other similarity measurement methods, because it only involves operations such as subtraction of the vector, the absolute value, and the scalar summation, which means the computational complexity of this metering method is lower.

11.4.1.2 KNN Algorithm

The general calculation process of the k-nearest neighbor algorithm mainly includes the calculation of the similarity between vectors and the search of the minimum similarity. The k-nearest neighbor algorithm compares the similarity between the test data and all

TABLE 11.1 Profiling of the Rocchio Algorithm

Algorithm	Metric	Center Vector Calculation	Similarity Calculation	Min
Rocchio	Jaccard	2.13%	96.74%	1.13%
	Cosine	2.58%	96.06%	1.36%
	Euclidean	2.34%	96.52%	1.14%
	Pearson	2.45%	96.28%	1.27%
	Manhattan	11.41%	82.37%	6.22%

the data in the training set. Then it searches k training sets with the smallest similarity. Finally, the test data will be allocated to the class where most of the k training data belong to. Here the searching of k training sets with the smallest similarity is not through the sort. We maintain a two-dimensional k-length array that stores the similarity size and the class label. Each time when the similarity comparison between test data and training set data is over, we will find the maximum value from the two-dimensional array. If the maximum value is larger than the current similarity calculation value, the class number and the similarity value of the current training set data are stored in the array to replace the maximum value, and if it is smaller the array will remain unchanged. The reason for this is to reuse the logic of the search for the minimum. Table 11.2 shows the results of hot-spot analysis for different similarity calculation methods of the KNN algorithm. "Similarity Calculation" represents the calculation of the similarity between vectors, and "Min" represents searching for the minimum value of similarity. It can be seen that the proportion of the calculation of the similarity between vectors is the largest, which is 93.42%~98.91%, and the searching of the minimum value is 1.09%~6.58%. So, like the Rocchio algorithm, the calculation of similarity between vectors is a hot spot and a key code for hardware acceleration.

11.4.1.3 Naïve Bayesian Algorithm

The general calculation process of the naïve Bayesian algorithm mainly includes the probability calculation of vectors and the search of the minimum value. Naïve Bayesian calculates the prior probability and conditional probability to determine the class where the test data belongs to. The results of the hot-spot analysis for the naïve Bayesian algorithm are shown in Table 11.3. The "Probability Calculation" column in the table represents the probability calculation of vectors; "Min" represents the search for the minimum value of similarity.

From Table 11.3, we can see that the proportion of the probability calculation is the largest, 98.86%, and the minimum search is 1.14%. So the probability calculation is not only the hot spots of the algorithm calculation but also the key code for hardware acceleration.

TABLE 11.2   Profiling of the KNN Algorithm

Algorithm	Metric	Similarity Calculation	Min
KNN	Jaccard	98.91%	1.09%
	Cosine	98.63%	1.37%
	Euclidean	98.72%	1.28%
	Pearson	98.84%	1.16%
	Manhattan	93.42%	6.58%

Note: KNN, k-nearest neighbor.

TABLE 11.3   Profiling of Naïve Bayesian Algorithm

Algorithm	Probability Calculation	Min
Bayesian	98.86%	1.14%

Here, we need to modify the naïve Bayesian algorithm to make its algorithmic logic function more similar to the Rocchio and KNN algorithms, so that we can extract more of the same function code. The basic idea of the algorithm is that the training data set is not trained first to obtain the prior probabilities and conditional probabilities of all categories, but for each instance to be tested, compare it with each training instance in the training data set to get prior probabilities and conditional probabilities and then obtain the probability that the test instance belongs to each category. At last, we compare the probability and allocate the test instance to the class with the highest probability. The whole process of the algorithm is modified to be similar to the k-nearest lazy learning method by using the method of predicting while training instead of the method of predicting after training. The benefits of this modification are that the algorithm will have a similar logic function to the KNN algorithm, which can reduce the storage of intermediate data and greatly reduce hardware resource consumption in FPGA.

11.4.2 Hardware Accelerator Overall Design

After the hot-spot analysis, we can see that the calculation of the similarity between vectors is the key code of the three classification algorithms. So the accelerator design is mainly focused on this key code. In Section 11.2, we mentioned that there is some reusable logic in the measure of similarity between vectors. We find that in all five similarity measures, Euclidean distance, Manhattan distance, Jaccard coefficient, cosine similarity, and Pearson correlation coefficients, intermediate variables such as S_x, S_y, S_{x-y}, S_x^2, S_y^2, $S_{(x-y)}^2$, S_{xy}, and N_{xy} are needed for the calculation. The calculation of all these intermediate variables contains an accumulation of two vectors. So that we can implement an accumulator in the accelerator design to calculate the intermediate similarity variable, which simplifies the accelerator structure and makes it easier to hydrate and improves the performance of the accelerator. Since there is no dependency between the vectors when calculating the similarity, we can use multiple parallel IP cores to calculate the similarity between vectors. The overall structure of the accelerator is shown in Figure 11.1. The thick line of dark color represents the data bus. The fine line of light color represents the control bus. It can be seen that the overall structure of the acceleration platform is composed of Host PC, DDR RAM, and accelerator. The host PC controls the control unit within the accelerator by the control bus to manage the operation of multiple IP cores within the accelerator and the data transfer of DMA. DMA can replace the host CPU to manage the data transfer between the DDR RAM and the IP core so that the host PC can perform other tasks during DMA data transfer and greatly exploit the resources. Inside the accelerator, each IP core is equipped with a DMA, which ensures that the IP core runs in parallel while data transmits in parallel at the same time. In the design of the accelerator, we found that each IP core in the implementation of the same task calculation only differed in the input vector, and the difference between the data would not cause too much impact on the running time of the IP core. So we used the SIMD method to design the accelerator; each IP core completed the entire computing tasks in SMID mode. This simplified the hardware logic design and ensured the efficiency of each IP core.

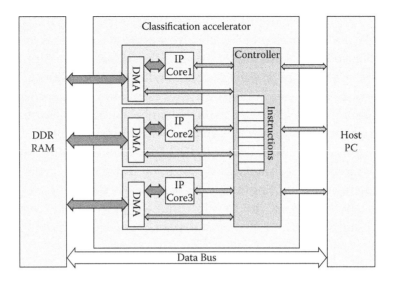

FIGURE 11.1 The overall structure of the accelerator.

The control unit inside the accelerator controls the operation of the IP core in the accelerator and the data transfer of DMA. The whole process is executed by instruction. And the instruction is written by the user to control the management of the accelerator. It is filled through the host PC to the instruction cache inside the control unit. In order to ensure the execution of the instructions one by one, the program counter and the storage of important information such as the length of vector and register group are also designed in the control unit. The IP core inside the accelerator runs the data that stored RAM and returns the result of the calculation to the DMA, which transfers the result and stores it back to RAM. It can be said that IP core contracted most of the calculation; its overall design is shown in Figure 11.2.

As can be seen from Figure 11.2, the IP core contains an input/output (I/O) module, central storage unit, arithmetic unit, and accumulation unit. The I/O module is responsible for the input and output of data in the IP core. The central storage unit is used to store the input vector, intermediate variables, training data, and final classification results. And the Ethernet controller controls the input and output of the I/O module, the calculation of the arithmetic unit, and the accumulation unit through the control bus. Both the accumulation unit and the arithmetic unit can read the data in the central memory cell to perform operations and return the result to the central storage unit. The final result is written back to the DMA through the output module. The overall design of the accumulation unit is shown in Figure 11.3. From the structure, we can see that the main task of the accumulation unit is to calculate the intermediate variables, including S_x, S_y, S_{x-y}, S_x^2, S_y^2, $S_{(x-y)}^2$, S_{xy}, and N_{xy} and save them in the cache. We note that S_{x+y} does not belong to any of the similarity calculations. However, it is used to calculate the center vector of the Rocchio algorithm so that the calculation of the similarity of vectors and the calculation of center vector are shared with the logic of the hardware. We do not need to waste hardware resources to design the calculation of the center vector and also to

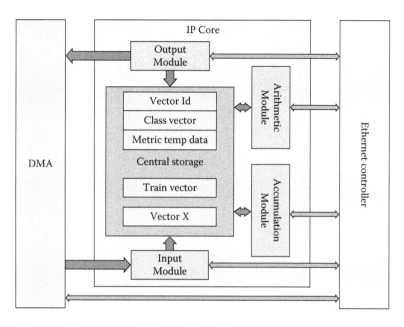

FIGURE 11.2 The overall structure of the intellectual property (IP) core.

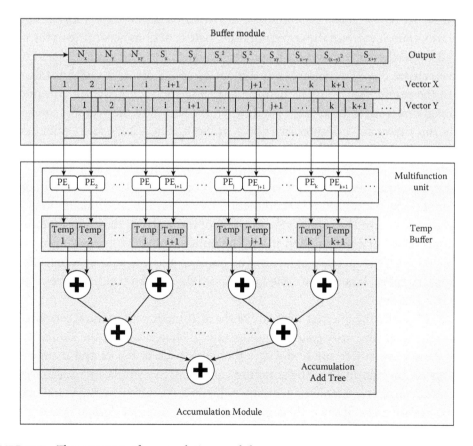

FIGURE 11.3 The structure of accumulation module.

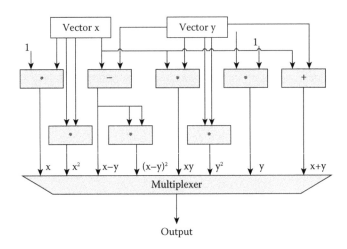

FIGURE 11.4   The structure of processing elements.

ensure the efficiency of the accelerator. The structure of the accumulation unit consists of three parts, a multifunction unit, a cache, and a cumulative tree.

The accumulation unit contains a number of processing elements (PE), which are responsible for the calculation of the two vectors in one certain dimension. The structure is shown in Figure 11.4; it can be seen that it is a function unit with two scalar inputs and one scalar output. It can run the corresponding logic functions according to the instructions and write the corresponding results to the cache via the multiplexer. From the figure, we can see one PE represents one dimension of the vector. As long as the number of PEs in the accelerator is larger than the length of the vector, we can run the vector operation at one time. On the other hand, when the length of the vector is too large, we can only run the vector operation part by part. So it is necessary to fragment the long vector. Each piece of vector length is less than the number of PE; we can complete the operation of the entire vector by multiple times. The temporary cache is used to store the temporary scalar generated by the PE, which corresponds to the PE one to one, and their numbers are the same. The accumulation tree is used to accumulate these temporary scalars and return the result to the position of the scalar in the cache module. There are multiple layers of accumulation trees. The number of add trees per layer gradually decreases 1/2 with the increase of layers. The number of the first layer is half the size of the temporary cache; it is also half the number of PE. You can see the entire calculation process is pipelined.

Figure 11.5 shows the internal structure of the arithmetic unit in the accelerator, which calculates the final similarity result using the intermediate scalar of the similarity calculated by the accumulation unit and writes the result back to the central memory in the accelerator via the multiplexer. The structure consists of five similarity measures, including Euclidean distance, Manhattan distance, Jaccard coefficient, cosine similarity, and Pearson correlation coefficients. The logic of Manhattan distance does not need to appear in the arithmetic unit, because it does not have to be calculated, but for structural integrity it will still be added to the structure.

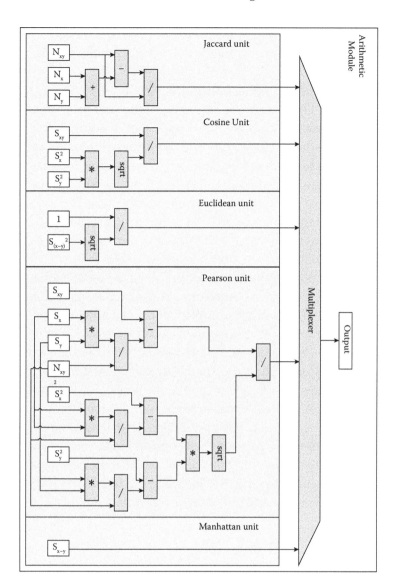

FIGURE 11.5 The structure of arithmetic module.

11.4.3 Accelerator System

We selected FPGA as the platform of our accelerator system. FPGA can work in both standalone mode and operating system mode. In standalone mode, the data must be written to the processor memory, which is RAM in advance, and the capacity of RAM is limited and valuable. We cannot store all data in RAM in standalone mode since our accelerator is used to process large amounts of data, which obviously does not meet our accelerator design. However, in operating system mode, the data can be transferred from external device to the RAM in FPGA. FPGA has a secure digital (SD) card interface and peripheral component interconnect (PCI) interface, so that the data can be read and written from the SD card to transfer to the RAM or through the PCI interface to the RAM, which can solve the problem of data storage. However, the data transfer from the SD card to the processor memory or transfer from the PCI interface to the processor memory will take more time.

We must first build the appropriate operating system on FPGA in order to run in operating system mode. FPGA platform can load a Linux operating system from the SD card. The operating system can be built in two ways, static loading and dynamic loading. *Static loading* refers to loading all the required drivers of the entire accelerator while migrating the operating system to the FPGA. Similarly, dynamic loading separates the migration of the operating system and the loading of all the required drivers of the entire accelerator, that is, you can complete the migration of the operating system and then manually load the relevant drive in operating system mode. It can be seen that static loading is simple and fixed, and the required work is done at one time. However, different designs bring about the preparation and generation of new device tree files. Moreover, dynamic loading is more flexible. We are free to choose any hardware driver to load as a module after the completion of the operating system. It will avoid generating the device tree file multiple times. So we choose dynamic loading to achieve the transplant of the operating system.

When the Linux operating system environment is completed, the next step is to write hardware logic into the FPGA platform. We use a set of IDE tools provided by Xilinx. The tool can transfer our logic implementation of the accelerator design into IP core, and then we will connect the accelerator IP core with other IP cores, such as DMA and Timer to generate a bitstream file. All the IP cores can be found in the toolkit provided by the IDE, except the accelerator IP core needs our own design. After we get the bit stream file, we must first create a reconfigurable character device file in Linux operating system; then the bit stream file will be written into the character device. We need to prepare the required drivers of the accelerator, including DMA, Timer, and accelerator IP Core so that the drivers can be called in the form of a file by an application to complete the operation of the entire accelerator.

11.5 EXPERIMENTAL SETUP AND RESULTS

11.5.1 Experimental Setup

Hardware platform: Xilinx Zedboard.

Comparison of the platform: Intel Core i7 CPU.

The experimental data set: Kyoto Encyclopedia of Genes and Genomes (KEGG) is one of the commonly used public data sets in the University of California Irvine (UCI) data set, which has 65,554 vectors and each vector has 29 data dimensions. In this chapter, the KEGG dataset is mainly used to test the performance and power consumption of the classification hardware accelerator.

Development tools: We used Xilinx's development tools chain, including Vivado HLS, Vivado, Vivado SDK, and Vivado ISE. The development tool can convert high-level language algorithms into the corresponding register transfer level (RTL) code [39] to encapsulate IP, speed up the hardware design development cycle, and reduce the difficulty of hardware development.

Energy consumption test tools: We used Intel's RAPL (Running Average Power Limit) [40] for the CPU power test. It only supports Sandybridge, Ivybridge, and Haswell architecture processors. We used Power report in the Vivado tool to access the power consumption of FPGA.

11.5.2 Speedup versus CPU

Figure 11.6 shows the speedup of the accelerator compared to the Intel Core i7 CPU. When the Rocchio algorithm uses the five similarities of Jaccard, cosine, Euclidean, Pearson, and Manhattan, the accelerators can achieve to about 1.5×, 1.6×, 1.9×, 2.1×, and 1.2× speedup compared to the Intel Core i7 CPU separately. For the KNN algorithm, it can achieve to about 2.2×, 2.3×, 2.6×, 3.2×, and 1.3× speedup. Overall, the Rocchio algorithm achieved a speedup around 1.6×, the KNN algorithm achieved a speedup around 2.3×, and Bayesian achieved a speedup around 1.3×. The average speedup of the accelerator was about 1.7×. Compared with the other four similarity metrics, Manhattan's speedup was relatively low. That is because our hardware accelerator is designed in the form of the pipeline so that the calculation time of the accelerator is independent of the different measurement of similarity. However, the CPU computes another similarity metric longer than Manhattan. So the speedup of Manhattan distance is relatively low.

11.5.3 Energy Comparison

Figure 11.7 shows a comparison of the energy consumption of the accelerator to that of the Intel Core i7 CPU. It can be seen that the Rocchio algorithm can achieve a 93×, 114×, 109×, 117×, and 87× power consumption ratio using the Jaccard, cosine, Euclidean,

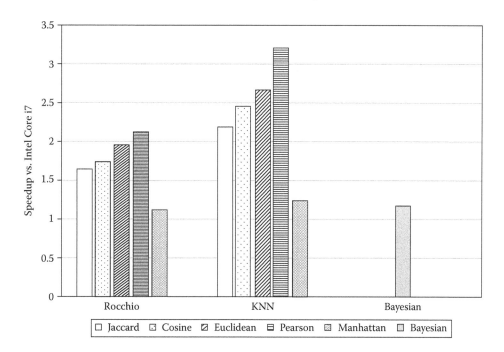

FIGURE 11.6 Speedup of the accelerator compared to the Intel Core i7 CPU.

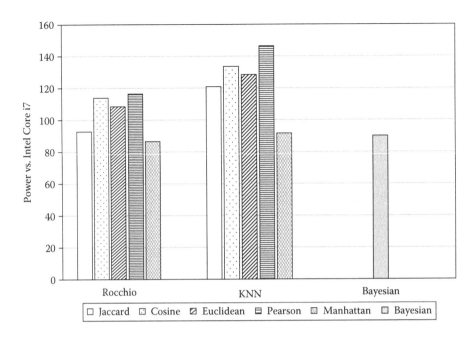

FIGURE 11.7 Energy consumption comparison between the accelerator and the Intel Core i7 CPU.

Pearson and Manhattan metrics, respectively. For the KNN algorithm, these figures are 121×, 134×, 129×, 147×, and 92× power consumption ratio. Overall, the Rocchio algorithm achieves a power consumption ratio of about 104×, the KNN algorithm achieves an energy consumption ratio of about 125×, and the Bayesian achieves an energy consumption ratio of about 90×. The average energy consumption ratio of the whole accelerator is about 106×. We can see that the energy consumption of the accelerator compared to the Intel Core i7 is very low, which is the advantage of the FPGA acceleration platform.

11.6 CONCLUSIONS

In this chapter, we proposed a general classification accelerator based on the FPGA platform that can support three different classification algorithms of five different similarities. The experimental results showed that our accelerator can achieve a 1.7× speedup compared to the Intel Core i7 CPU with low energy consumption.

11.7 ACKNOWLEDGMENTS

This work was supported by the National Science Foundation of China (No. 61379040), Anhui Provincial Natural Science Foundation (No. 1608085QF12), CCF-Venustech Hongyan Research Initiative (No. CCF-VenustechRP1026002), Suzhou Research Foundation (No. SYG201625), Youth Innovation Promotion Association CAS (No. 2017497), and Fundamental Research Funds for the Central Universities (WK2150110003).

REFERENCES

1. T. S. Lim and W. Y Loh, 2000, A comparison of prediction accuracy, complexity, and training time of thirty-three old and new classification algorithms, *Machine Learning*, vol. 40, pp. 203–228.
2. T. G. Dietterich, 2002, Ensemble learning, in *The handbook of brain theory and neural networks 2*, Cambridge: MIT Press, pp. 110–125.
3. A. C. Tan and D. Gilbert, 2003, Ensemble machine learning on gene expression data for cancer classification, *Applied Bioinformatics*, vol. 2, no. 3 Suppl., S75–S83.
4. A. Lipes, Packaging Automation Machinery Co., 1979, Automatic bagging machine, U.S. Patent 4, 172, 349.
5. Y. Freund and R. E. Schapire, 1996, July, Experiments with a new boosting algorithm, *ICML*, vol. 96, pp. 148–156.
6. S. V. M. Vishwanathan and M. N. Murty, 2002, SSVM: A simple SVM algorithm, in *Proceedings of the 2002 International Joint Conference on Neural Networks, 2002, IJCNN'02*, vol. 3, IEEE, Piscataway, NJ, pp. 2393–2398.
7. Y. Freund and L. Mason, 1999, June. The alternating decision tree learning algorithm, *ICML*, vol. 99, pp. 124–133.
8. D. Junbin, F. Pengcheng, and G. An, 2015, Design of test data management system architecture based on cloud computing platform, in *2015 AASRI International Conference on Circuits and Systems (CAS 2015)*, Atlantis Press, Amsterdam, The Netherlands, pp. 362–364.
9. P. Mell and T. Grance, 2011. *The NIST definition of cloud computing*.
10. M. Maruseac, G. Ghinita, M. Ouyang, and R. Rughinis, 2015, July, Hardware acceleration of Private Information Retrieval protocols using GPUs, in *2015 IEEE 26th International Conference on Application-Specific Systems, Architectures and Processors (ASAP)*, IEEE, Piscataway, NJ, pp. 120–127.
11. T. D. Han and T. S. Abdel Rahman, 2011. hiCUDA: High-level GPGPU programming, *IEEE Transactions on Parallel and Distributed Systems*, vol. 22, no. 1, pp. 78–90.
12. N. Tabrizi and N. Bagherzadeh, 2005, An ASIC design of a novel pipelined and parallel sorting accelerator for a multiprocessor-on-a-chip, in *Proceedings of the 6th International Conference on ASICON 2005*, vol. 1, pp. 46–49.
13. ASIC, https://en.wikipedia.org/wiki/Application-specific_integrated_circuit.
14. Y. J. Chen and W. P. Du Plessis, 2002, Neural network implementation on a FPGA, *Proceedings of IEEE Africon*, vol. 1, pp. 337–342.
15. FPGA, https://en.wikipedia.org/wiki/Field-programmable_gate_array.
16. C. Nvidia, 2007, *Compute unified device architecture programming guide*.
17. J. E. Stone, D. Gohara, and G. Shi, 2010, OpenCL: A parallel programming standard for heterogeneous computing systems, *Computing in Science & Engineering*, vol. 12, no. 1–3, pp. 66–73.
18. S. Wienke, P. Springer, and C. Terboven, 2012, OpenACC—First experiences with real-world applications, in Kaklamanis, C., Papatheodorou, T., Spirakis, P. G. (Eds.), in *Euro-Par 2012 parallel processing*, Berlin: Springer, pp. 859–870.
19. K. M. Leung, 2007, *Naive Bayesian classifier*, Polytechnic University Department of Computer Science/Finance and Risk Engineering.
20. T. Joachims, 1996, *A probabilistic analysis of the Rocchio algorithm with TFIDF for text categorization*, No. CMU-CS-96-118, Pittsburgh, PA: Department of Computer Science, Carnegie Mellon University.
21. P. A. N. Jeng-Shyang, Q. I. A. O. Yu-Long, and S. U. N. Sheng-He, 2004, A fast K nearest neighbors classification algorithm, *IEICE Transactions on Fundamentals of Electronics, Communications and Computer Sciences*, vol. 87, no. 4, pp. 961–963.
22. A. Matoga, 2013, Accelerating user space applications with FPGA cores: Profiling and evaluation of the PCIe interface, in *Proceedings of the 9th Portuguese Meeting on Reconfigurable Systems*, pp. 33–40.

23. C.-Y. Lin, C.-H. Tsai, C.-P. Lee, and C.-J. Lin, 2014, Large-scale logistic regression and linear support vector machines using spark, in *2014 IEEE International Conference on Big Data (Big Data)*, Piscataway, NJ, pp. 519–528.

24. H. Tao, B. Wu, and X. Lin, 2014, Budgeted mini-batch parallel gradient descent for support vector machines on Spark, in *2014 20th IEEE International Conference on Parallel and Distributed Systems (ICPADS)*, IEEE Computer Society, Piscataway, NJ, pp. 945–950.

25. B. Catanzaro, N. Sundaram, and K. Keutzer, 2008, Fast support vector machine training and classification on graphics processors, in *Proceedings of 25th International Conference on Machine Learning*, Association for Computing Machinery, New York, pp. 104–111.

26. M. V. T. Romero, A. S. Iwashita, L. P. Papa, A. N. Souza, and J. P. Papa, 2014, Fast optimum-path forest classification on graphics processors, in *2014 International Conference on Computer Vision Theory and Applications (VISAPP)*, vol. 2, pp. 627–631.

27. C. Wang, P. Chen, X. Li, and X. Zhou, 2013, A FPGA-based high performance acceleration platform for the next generation long read mapping, in *HPCC/EUC*, IEEE Computer Society, Piscataway, NJ, pp. 308–315.

28. S. Cadambi, I. Durdanovic, V. Jakkula, M. Sankaradass, E. Cosatto, S. Chakradhar, and H. Graf, 2009, A massively parallel FPGA-based coprocessor for support vector machines, in *Proceedings of 17th IEEE Symposium on Field Programmable Custom Computing Machines*, April 2009, IEEE Computer Society, Piscataway, NJ, pp. 115–122.

29. S. Lopez-Estrada and R. Cumplido, 2006, Decision tree based FPGA architecture for texture sea state classification, in *Proceedings of IEEE Int'l Conference on Reconfigurable Computing and FPGA's, ReConFig.*, Sept. 2006, IEEE Computer Society, Piscataway, NJ, pp. 1–7.

30. M. Papadonikolakis and C.-S. Bouganis, A scalable FPGA architecture for non-linear SVM training, in *Proceedings of International Conference on FPT Technology*, Dec. 2008, IEEE Computer Society, Piscataway, NJ, pp. 337–340.

31. F. Khan, M. Arnold, and W. Pottenger, 2005, Hardware-based support vector machine classification in logarithmic number systems, in *Proceedings of IEEE International Symposium on Circuits System*, May 2005, vol. 5, pp. 5154–5157.

32. K. Irick, M. DeBole, V. Narayanan, and A. Gayasen, 2008, A hardware efficient support vector machine architecture for FPGA, in *Proceedings of Annual IEEE Symposium on Field-Programmable Custom Computing Machines*, Apr. 2008, IEEE Computer Society, Piscataway, NJ, pp. 304–305.

33. Q. Yu, C. Wang, X. Ma, X. Li, and X. Zhou, 2015, A deep learning prediction process accelerator based FPGA, in *CCGRID*, pp. 1159–1162.

34. X. Ma, C. Wang, Q. Yu, X. Li, and X. Zhou, 2015, An FPGA-based accelerator for neighborhood-based collaborative filtering recommendation algorithms, in *CLUSTER*, pp. 494–495.

35. P. Chen, C. Wang, X. Li, and X. Zhou, 2014, Accelerating the next generation long read mapping with the FPGA-based system, *IEEE/ACM Transactions on Computational Biology and Bioinformatics*, vol. 11, no. 5, pp. 840–852.

36. C. Wang, X. Li, Q. Guo, and X. Zhou, 2015, RapidPath: Accelerating constrained shortest path finding in graphs on FPGA (Abstract Only), in *FPGA*, p. 273.

37. D. G. Perera and K. F. Li, 2008, Parallel computation of similarity measures using an FPGA-based processor array, in *22nd International Conference on Advanced Information Networking and Applications, 2008, AINA 2008*, AINA 2008, IEEE, Computer Society, Piscataway, NJ, pp. 955–962.

38. N. Sudha, 2015, A pipelined array architecture for Euclidean distance transformation and its FPGA implementation, *Microprocessors and Microsystems*, vol. 29, no. 8, pp. 405–410.

39. T. Davidson, 2015, Identification of dynamic circuit specialization opportunities in RTL code, *ACM Transactions on Reconfigurable Technology and Systems (TRETS)*, vol. 8, no. 1, p. 4.

40. V. Gil-Costa, C. Ochoa, and A. Marcela Printista, 2013, Suffix array performance analysis for multi-core platforms, *Computación y Sistemas*, vol. 17, no. 3, pp. 391–399.

CHAPTER 12

Accelerators for Big Data Genome Sequencing

Haijie Fang, Chao Wang, Shiming Lei, Lei Gong,
Xi Li, Aili Wang, and Xuehai Zhou
University of Science and Technology of China
Hefei, China

CONTENTS

12.1 INTRODUCTION

At present, the acceleration work for gene sequencing has a variety of development [3], there are a variety of acceleration algorithms for the Gene sequencing, and the acceleration platform is diverse. In this section, we will explain the different platforms used in gene sequencing.

12.1.1 Distributed System

The distributed system depends on the computer network [4]. A distributed system contains many computers. With the increase of the system scale, the number of computers can reach a high scale, which also makes the management and maintenance of a distributed system more difficult. The concept of the cloud is also derived from a distributed system [5].

Different from traditional work, an independent, distributed system is the cooperative work of many machines. To the user, a distributed system is not only a set of computers but also a separate object. After receiving a task, the distributed system partitions the whole task to different machines, then all the computers deal with the task in a parallel way. This point is different from the parallel work of a single machine. Usually these processes are similar tasks in parallel, but the distributed system needs to consider which machine resources can handle the task, not simple similar division. Compared with parallel computing, a distributed system has a higher degree of freedom and can handle larger tasks [6]. At the same time, the distributed system also has a higher tolerance. After all, a distributed system contains many machines; when a machine fault occurs, the distributed system loses only one of the local machine node tasks, and all processes will be affected in parallel [7].

We can find that the distributed system is suitable for the large-scale data processing of tasks scattered from the characteristics of the distributed system and the gene sequencing we want to study is such a problem.

Using the distributed system to process the acceleration of gene sequencing can start from the beginning of the task division. According to the task type of gene sequencing process, tasks can be divided into two categories: computing tasks and storage tasks. The acceleration of gene sequencing can start from these two aspects. In terms of computing, we can make full use of the resources of each computing node to improve the granularity and parallelism of computing. Storage is a large proportion in the distributed system; there are two kinds of storage for distributed systems, namely structured storage and unstructured storage. Through the analysis of data attributes, finding a reasonable storage mode based on the consistency of these data is also a direction to improve the system.

12.1.2 Graphics Processing Unit Platform

A graphics processing unit (GPU) is an integrated processor that handles images. Initially, the GPU helps the CPU improve image performance by rendering the screen to meet the needs of increasingly sophisticated quality. The image contains a large number of pixels; the higher the level of the image, the more points there are. To deal with these pixels, the GPU needs a very high capability for data processing. With the development of GPU [8], people are not only focused on the image processing; the powerful data processing ability gradually lets people attempt to accelerate the algorithm by making use of the GPU resources [9].

The simplest GPU acceleration is to turn part of the CPU calculation independently over to the GPU to complete, and this is also the initial GPU acceleration [10]. Then the GPU gradually developed into the GPGPU. GPGPU has many general-purpose computing units that can process data in a highly parallel ways to accelerate the execution of computing [11].

12.1.3 Field Programmable Gate Array Platform

Through the development of GPU, we can see that the custom hardware circuit [12] has a good effect on accelerating calculation [13]. The current mainstream hardware circuit design is divided into field programmable gate array (FPGA) and application specific integrated circuit (ASIC) design, and the advantages are briefly narrated in the following section.

The full name of FPGA is field-programmable gate array [14]. The programmable logic device can only complete some simple logic functions from PROM and EPROM to slightly complex PLD and then more complex CPLD. FPGA has experienced continuous progress, adapting to the design of large-scale circuit gradually. The computing resources of FPGA are more abundant, the programming is more flexible, the development cycle of FPGA is shorter, and the cost is lower.

There are many look-up-tables in the FPGA [15]. The look-up-table (LUT) is also a ram when we use the hardware description language to design the hardware circuit. The FPGA development tool will integrate all the possible results into a look-up table when we enter data; to find the output, FPGA just needs to search the table. All this makes full use of the hardware resources of FPGA and improves the efficiency [16].

12.1.4 Conclusion

Through the above description, the popular accelerated means mainly include the cloud computing platform, GPU platform and FPGA platform several aspects [17–19]. We compare all three platforms in Table 12.1.

At present, most of the research work on gene sequencing is carried out for a single gene sequencing algorithm, and its versatility and universality are very limited. There is

TABLE 12.1   Analysis of Three Different Platforms

Platform	Distributed	GPU	FPGA
Speedup rate	Overall it has a good acceleration effect, but it is the result of many nodes. A single node remains to be improved.	Integrated with high speedup, but the acceleration of a single computing unit—the effect of FPGAs.	Has a good acceleration effect.
Power cost	Essentially, CPU processing calculates the power consumption at normal power level.	Too many computing units in the GPU causes high power consumption.	Extremely low power.
Maintenance and design	Cluster maintenance produces a lot of costs, and the parallel of the task partitioning data set needs careful consideration.	The development is harder than for the other platforms.	Short development cycle, easy to modify, easy maintenance, easy to achieve large-scale design and implementation.

Notes: FPGA, field programmable gate array; GPU, graphics processing unit.

no general framework for a variety of gene sequencing algorithms. Moreover, the current hardware accelerator has to be improved in performance and power consumption optimization. Based on the above problem, this chapter implements a hardware accelerator framework for a gene sequencing algorithm based on FPGA.

In this chapter, two gene sequencing algorithms are accelerated on an FPGA platform and then the performance of FPGA acceleration is analyzed. Finally, we compare FPGA acceleration with other acceleration methods to evaluate its advantages. The main works are as follows:

1. *Design and analysis of gene sequencing algorithm.* Design two algorithms and put up each module in the algorithm, then do module design; the main modules of the algorithm are the displacement calculation module of KMP and the conversion module of BWA.

2. *Design of the accelerator.* Use the powerful calculation function of FPGA to accelerate the core module of the algorithm, in order to achieve the acceleration effect. Organize each module in a balanced way.

3. *Driver writing.* Drive design under Linux system.

4. *According to the results, analyze the performance of accelerator and evaluate the resource occupancy and power consumption.* Analyze and evaluate the advantages and disadvantages of the FPGA platform.

12.2 PRELIMINARIES

We will discuss the principle of KMP algorithm and BWA algorithm in this section.

12.2.1 Gene Sequencing

Gene sequencing is a combination of bioinformatics, computer science, statistics, and other disciplines. It is a hot direction of contemporary research and is important for research on human behavior mechanisms, to help humans understand themselves more deeply. The target of gene sequencing is a large number of gene fragments. Like most animals, humans use DNA as genetic material. DNA consists of four bases composed of A, T, C, G, respectively. The existence of DNA as a genetic material in the human body is as a pair of long chains of double spiral. The two chains are connected to each other, forming base pairs. Base pairs can be regular, A-T pairs, or C-G pairs, and different permutation sequences of base pairs exhibit different genetic information. According to the matching rule of base pairs, we can measure the base sequence of a single DNA chain and achieve the purpose of gene sequencing. Gene sequencing has gradually improved; it is generally believed that gene sequencing has three main stages. The first phase is basic chemical sequencing, the second phase is high-throughput sequencing, and the third stage is molecular sequencing.

The first-stage sequencing is mainly based on the degradation of DNA; the double DNA is degraded into a single nucleotide molecule by chemical means, and then the DNA base sequence is obtained by observing the permutation sequence of the denatured nucleotide molecules. The main methods of this stage are chemical degradation, terminal termination method, etc. According to the principle of sequencing, these methods have high accuracy point to a single base, but the sequencing speed is not ideal. The gradual degradation of DNA and the efficiency of subsequent electrophoresis separation need to be further improved.

The first stage of the limitations is the inability to deal with large-scale DNA sequencing, and the second phase of the sequencing approach is for large-scale sequencing of high-throughput sequencing [20]. Thanks to the development of PCR technology, we can copy multiple DNA from a given DNA at this stage and then sequence the DNA at the same time. Obviously, when thousands of sequences are parallel, it will greatly improve the efficiency of sequencing. The gene sequencing at this stage needs to consume a lot of DNA samples for synchronous analysis to improve the efficiency and then the cost is increased. The final result is synthesized through the analysis of all the DNA samples, so the accuracy is decreased.

In the face of the reduced accuracy of sequencing technology and the high cost, the third stage of gene sequencing method was gradually born. The previous sequencing method was to study the result after the end of the DNA reaction. The third stage of sequencing can be synchronized in the DNA replication process, which greatly enhances the efficiency while not losing accuracy, and there is great space for development. During this time, what decides the efficiency of sequencing are the rate of DNA replication, DNA sequencing is carried out *in vitro*, which poses a challenge to PCR technology. These three sequencing methods are collaborative work in gene sequencing; each method has its advantages.

12.2.2 KMP and BWA

The whole function of KMP is composed of two parts called *KMP-Match* and *Prefix*. The KMP-Match is the main part of the function. At first, we need two input strings, called *pattern string* and *source string*. Then we do a Prefix for the pattern string; the Prefix will generate a new array that contains some information of the pattern string. Last, we use the source string, pattern string, and the array to continue the KMP-Match function. The process of the whole function is shown in Figure 12.1.

We have explained that the difference between KMP and traditional pattern match is the KMP moves as far as it can when a matching mistake happens. How to know the right step is what the Prefix function does. The prefix function deals with the input string according to the attribute of the string. It will generate a prefix array that helps us to know how many steps we should move. As the algorithm shows, at the beginning of each time in the *for* loop, we set $k = F[q - 1]$. When the cycle runs for the first time, the condition in Lines 2 to 3 and Line 9 ensure the conditions that in each iteration. Lines 5 to 8 adjust the value of k, make it become the correct value for $F[q]$. Lines 5 to 6 search all eligible k, until we find a value that makes $P(k + 1) = P(q)$. At this point, we can think of that $F[q] = k + 1$. If we cannot find the k, in the Line 7 we set $k = 0$; if $P = P[q]$, we set $k = 1$ and $F[q]$ is set to 1. Otherwise we just make $F[q] = 0$. Lines 7 to 9 complement the set of the values of k and $F[q]$.

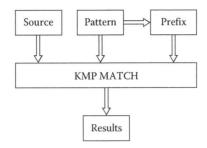

FIGURE 12.1   The process of KMP algorithm.

ALGORITHM 12.1   PREFIX ARRAY

1. m←Length[P]
2. F[1]←0
3. k←0
4. for q←2 to m
5.   do while k>0 and P[k+1]!=P[q]
6.   do k← F[k]
7.   if P[k+1]=P[q]
8.   k=k+1
9.   F[q] ←k
10.   return F

TABLE 12.2   An Example of Generating Table

i	1	2	3	4	5	6
P[i]	A	T	C	A	T	G
F[i]	0	0	0	1	2	0

The pattern string is ATCATG. Using the algorithm, we will generate a table like Table 12.2.

Since we have the prefix array, how does the array help us to find the most steps we can move? Here, the KMP-Match will give us the answer, according to the array. As the algorithm shows, we define the value of q as the number of characters that have the right match at first. Then we find the first matched character and judge the next character. If the next character is also matched, we set $q = q + 1$, which means we have another character matched. Otherwise, if the next character is not a match, we will use the generate array F[] to set q as F[q].

The essence of the KMP-Match is to find how many steps is the largest step for the next match. The algorithm just shows us that the right step is the value of q-F[q]. Take Table 12.2 as an example. At the first time of the cycle, we find that just three characters match. So we set q = 3; according to Table 12.2 we know F[3] = 0. Then we are sure that the next step should be three steps. As Figure 12.2 shows, if we move three steps we will have the second cycle. At the second cycle, all the characters match. In order to find a new match, we set q = 0 to repeat the algorithm.

ALGORITHM 12.2   KMP-MATCH

1. n←length[S]
2. m←length[P]
3. F←prefix(P)
4. q←0
5. for i←1 to n
6.   do while q>0 and P[q+1]!=S[i]
7.   do q←F[q]
8.   if P[q+1]=S[i]
9.   q=q+1
10.   if q=m
11.   print "match."
12.   q←F[q]

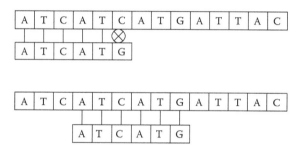

FIGURE 12.2   KMP search.

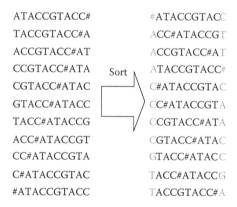

FIGURE 12.3   Burrows-Wheeler switch.

The process for BWA [21–23] is similar to KMP. The difference between the two algorithms is that the KMP does preprocess with pattern data but BWA does with the source data. After BW switch [24], we get an array that contains all the information of the source data [25]. The whole process of BW switch is like the Figure 12.3. The first row of the matrix is the array we need.

Once we have the array, how can we search for the pattern string [26]? As we see, the matrix is composed of all the suffixes of the source string [27]; we put all the suffixes in a tree and we will build a tree. The depth of the tree is the length of the source string. When we want to search a pattern, we just need to search the tree. If we put the suffix in alphabetical order, it will save lots of time.

ALGORITHM 12.3   BWA SEARCH

1. c←P[p], i←p;
2. top←C[c]+1, bot←C[c+1];
3. **while**((top<=bot) and i>=2) **do**
4. c← P[i−1];
5. top← C[c]+OCC(c, 1, top−1)+1;
6. bot← C[c]+OCC(c, 1, bot);
7. i=i−1;
8. **if**(top<bot) **then**
9.   **return** " cannot find";
10. **else**
11. Return "find(bot−top+1)";

12.2.3 The Principle of the Accelerate Base on Hardware

Hardware acceleration, as the name suggests, is using hardware to accelerate the process. The operation and calculations of the program are done in the processor, because the task of the processor is not a single task. The processor is designed more universally, and so the processing speed may not be satisfied. We can use specific hardware structure to deal with this data to achieve ideal efficiency. In essence, hardware acceleration is to transfer the relatively complex operations to the hardware during the processor processing program. The efficient processing of these data through specific hardware structure can reduce the burden of the processor and accelerate the efficiency of the whole system.

The typical representative of the processor is the CPU. The CPU as a general processor is designed to solve various tasks, so it has good versatility to deal with the various instructions of users and provide flexible and accurate processing, but its flexibility and universality causes its limitations. GPU is an image processor; its development was driven by the limitations of CPU universality. An image contains many pixels, and with the complexity of various image attributes, the amount of data contained in the image became larger and larger. It seems that the ability to deal with these data of CPU is weak. For this problem, GPU relies on its finer granularity and parallel processing performance compared to CPU. GPU is more targeted than the CPU but also has a relatively low applicability. However, it does not matter. A GPU stretched out by a CPU is good for image processing, which is also a hardware acceleration application. And with the development of science and technology, GPU is not limited to image processing. With its powerful floating-point data processing ability and high parallelism, it has gradually undergone long-term development in other areas. The development of GPU stimulates people to think about whether we can design more targeted processors to deal with other special tasks that reduce the efficiency of the system. FPGA is a programmable logic gate array, which has rich computing resources and powerful computing power. Because of its strong performance in data processing, people began to try using FPGA to customize the processor to adapt to a special direction and improve the efficiency of the system.

In summary, the application of FPGA in hardware acceleration is the result of technology development, is the need for professional.

From the above we know that hardware acceleration is essentially the transfer of data to dedicated hardware for processing. So how to select which part of the code will be transferred to the hardware? Our first idea is to transfer the most time-consuming and resource-intensive parts. We call this code *hot code*. At the initial stage of hardware acceleration, we need to find the hot code first. There are many ways to find the hot code; we select instrumentation as a method to find the hot code. Instrumentation has inserted a marker at a certain point of the program code as a wooden pile, through many running programs to analyze the code between two flags. The code cost most of the time is hot code; the hot code must be suitable for the hardware structure we select to accelerate.

After finding the hot code, we can take our second step and analyze the code structure to find the appropriate speedup. There are many hardware acceleration methods, and we need to choose the appropriate structure. The common methods are parallel computing, pipeline processing [28], and storage structure optimization; all these will be explained in the following section. Parallel computing is a common acceleration method; parallelism is running programs at the same time, which can save a lot of processing time through parallel computing for data processing, such as the correlation between the source string and pattern string in our string matching algorithm. Each processing module can be seen as an independent process; through parallel we can efficiently perform source string and pattern strings to save time expenses. Pipeline technology is a classical accelerating method and a method of high efficiency. The pipeline [29] is widely used in various fields. By dividing a complete production process into different flow segments, each segment runs the same segment independently to achieve high efficiency. Take a three-stage process as example. The processing time is assumed to be 1, and if we do not use any methods to improve these processes, we can significantly improve efficiency, and then start our second process after the first flow of the first process without waiting for the first process to complete, and then a process for each point in time. As the number of pipelines increases, as well as the pipeline refinement, we can increase efficiency. Of course, this will increase the occupation of resources; it is the strategy of space and time. Storage structure optimization is also a way to improve operational efficiency; data access has many methods. The classical one is the processor to select storage location and storage, call data through the processor to find and read; there is a great time spent on the interaction with the processor. At the same time, the storage of data can be reasonably planned; reducing the frequency of interaction with memory can also speed up the running efficiency of the program.

Finally, you can build the acceleration system to select the appropriate method of code acceleration for hot code, which will be described in detail later.

12.3 THE DESIGN OF ACCELERATOR

12.3.1 System Analysis

The system is designed as a system of hardware acceleration for the string-matching algorithm of gene sequencing. The overall framework of the system is as follows. First of our design is a user-oriented system design. The user operates an application to accelerate two algorithms directly. The system is the bottom hardware acceleration system. In order to complete the needs of users, we need to add a layer of intermediate stage support, which mainly contains some library function, API, and the driver corresponding to our bottom design [30].

The main contents of our design are as follows:

Design of String Matching Algorithm: The string algorithm adopts the KMP and BWA algorithms. First of all, we should complete the design of the two algorithms; the two algorithms are an excellent string algorithm and represent a considerable improvement compared to the traditional string algorithm.

Realization of Algorithm on the Board: This chapter uses a ZedBoard-based development board; it is based on the Xilinx Zynq FPGA development board and can run on the design of Linux, Windows, and other systems. In addition, the extensible interface enables users to easily access the processing system and programmable logic and implement the strong and powerful design. Our algorithm was tested on this development board.

IP Core: The package of the algorithm requires the tools of Xilinx. We are using the Vivado design suite. Vivado is an integrated design environment released by Xilinx in 2012, including a highly integrated design environment and a set of tools to generate IC from the system. The Vivado design suite can quickly synthesize and verify C language and generate IP cores for encapsulation.

The Implementation of Intermediate Stage Support: With the implementation of the IP Core, we need to write the appropriate driver to support its operation. This mainly includes our two IP cores, the driver of KMP BWA and the related DMA driver.

12.3.2 IP Core

The generation of the IP core requires the corresponding tool. The one mainly used is the High Level Synthesis (HLS) function of Vivado. HLS is a high-level synthesis, which refers to the process from the calculate description to the description of register transport level. The task goal of HLS is to find a hardware structure that satisfies the constraints and goals and costs the least. It has the advantages of increasing the design speed to shorten the design cycle, while easy to understand. HLS is generally composed of the following steps:

1. Compilation and conversion of calculating description

2. Scheduling (leaving the operation to control step)

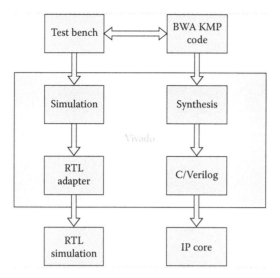

FIGURE 12.4   HLS and IP core.

3. Allocation of data paths (for each operation is assigned to the appropriate functional unit)

4. Controller synthesis (integrated controller of data-driven routing driver)

5. Generating (generating a low-level physical implementation)

After several steps, we can get an IP core (Figure 12.4).

12.3.3 The Implementation of the Accelerator

Our design framework is built on the above development board. The design framework of software and hardware co-design is adopted. According to the above description, we can see that the overall design of this system is divided into multiple modules: the software module design of the algorithm design level and the hardware design of the accelerator module. The traditional system design method often divides the whole module into software design and hardware design, gives priority to the bottom hardware design, and then develops the software for the hardware platform. On the basis of the design of software modules, the two processes are independent, although the relationship is not close. In many cases it will be difficult to meet the design of the software module, because independent design leads to a rough analysis of software requirements in the early stage of design, lack of understanding of the overall structure mechanism, and software operation analysis leading to problems. Figure 12.5 shows the traditional design process.

From the above design process, we can see that the whole system design cycle will be very long, because there will be a lot of time consumed in the solution of software and hardware system design contradictions, many changes will extend the overall design time, and there will be some unexpected problems; these things take a lot of time to solve. The hardware and software co-design is an improvement of system design for this problem.

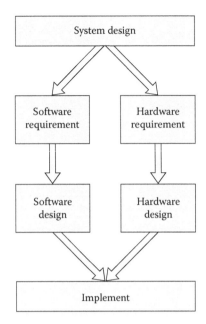

FIGURE 12.5   The traditional design process.

The hardware and software co-design takes system design as a whole, carries on concurrent software and hardware design, and finds the best contact point between the two aspects, so as to achieve the high efficiency of the design. Its design cycle is different from traditional design; Figure 12.6 shows the process of co-design.

We can see that the main advantage of hardware and software co-design is to link software with hardware at the beginning of development. Paying attention to software and hardware resources early can let us reduce later time investment greatly; we can find problems and solve them during the design phase. We will next describe the design process in detail according to the process of hardware and software co-design.

First is the overall system design. This process mainly uses the system-level description language to transform the system design into the system function performance and aspects of the digital circuit. Then according to the description, we organize function modules and establish the system model. After the completion of the system modeling, we begin to design the hardware and software modules, at the beginning of which we want to know the hardware module and software module clearly. The hardware part is highly efficient, programmable, and its programmability is strong. The hardware parts are mainly used to cure some of the more fixed general calculation parts; the software module is mainly responsible for the calculation of other parts. The whole design has the advantage of flexibility and ease of modification and maintenance. In the design, the hardware implementation can also be a software implementation, so we need to analyze further and find the most suitable way. We can see that this part of the design will occupy the main time period of our design cycle. In this stage, we have completed partition functions of hardware and software, and the function module design

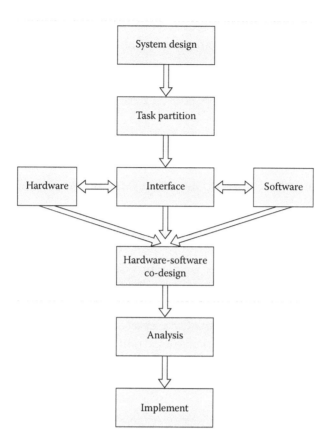

FIGURE 12.6   The process of co-design.

after the foundation is based on this. So at this stage, we need to be extremely careful. After the completion of the system module division, we have to do the interface design to complete the mapping of the whole system. This is mainly the process of layout; we combine the software and hardware modules involved in our design during the process, specifically the selection of each hardware module and the data transmission path communication mode, etc. Finally, we can complete the software and hardware co-design. After the completion of the system function design, we need to analyze and verify to modify the performance of the system to improve the system. This is not just validation of the accuracy of the system but also a holistic improvement of our design system. In this process, we found the combination of hardware and software problems and made modifications to avoid having various problems in the final system. When we complete the above process, we can get a designed model. For the system design of this chapter, we organize the whole design process according to the hardware and software co-design, as follows:

1. Build the basic model of the system and analyze the system.

2. Select the accelerated algorithm and analyze the hot code.

3. Design the hardware code that needs acceleration into the design of hardware circuit, including the selection of hardware resources and the data transmission path between hardware resources.

4. Synthesize hardware code, judge whether its function is correct, and analyze its performance.

5. Generate the IP core according to the designed hardware module; simulate and verify the layout routing of this accelerator.

6. Generate the hardware bitstream file and move the file to our board.

7. Finish all the above, begin to package the whole system, and do the support between the system and our hardware accelerator.

The whole software and hardware co-design system framework is divided into two parts: program system (PS) and program logic (PL). As shown in Figure 12.7, PS as the control terminal of the whole system is located in the host, including the processor and storage unit to complete the operation of the server-side software code and the control of the hardware part. PL is the programmable logic unit of FPGA part, and it is the hardware acceleration part of the whole system. We can load different IP core to achieve our task. The IP core in PL can work highly efficiently in a parallel way.

12.4 CONCLUSION

In this chapter, we proposed an accelerator based on the FPGA platform to accelerate a gene sequencing algorithm. We put up two gene sequencing algorithms, namely KMP and BWA. During the process, we designed the two algorithms and implement them in a digital circuit.

The experimental results showed that our accelerator achieves a high speedup rate. For KMP, the speedup rate can reach 5.1×, and it will increase with the data. As to BWA, it also can reach a speedup rate at 3.2× and if the pattern string is the large amount the speedup

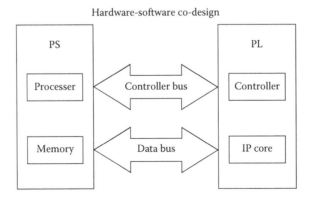

FIGURE 12.7 Outline of the co-design process.

rate will reach a higher speedup rate. What is more, the accelerator costs less power: it only needs 0.10 w to support the accelerator.

REFERENCES

1. M.H.J.D. Owens, D. Luebke, S. Green, J.E. Stone, and J.C. Phillips, 2008, GPU computing, *Proceedings of the IEEE*, pp. 879–899.
2. A.F.M. Armbrust, R. Griffith, A.D. Joseph, R. Katz, and A. Konwinski, 2010, A view of cloud computing, *Communications of the ACM*, pp. 50–58.
3. B.S.A. Mahajan, S.K. Parsi, N. Weng, and H. Wang, 2008, Implementing high-speed string matching hardware for network intrusion detection systems. *Parallel and Distributed Processing Techniques and Applications*, pp. 157–163.
4. M.C. Schatz, 2009, CloudBurst: Highly sensitive read mapping with MapReduce, *Bioinformatics*, vol. 25, no. 11, pp. 1363–1369.
5. X.L. Chao Wang, P. Chen, A. Wang, X. Zhou, and H. Yu, 2015, Heterogeneous cloud framework for big data genome sequencing, *IEEE/ACM Transactions on Computational Biology and Bioinformatics*, pp. 166–178.
6. T. S, S. Dharmapurikar, P. K, and J. Lockwood, 2003, Deep packet inspection using parallel bloom filters, *High Performance Interconnects, IEEE Micro*, vol. 24, no. 1.
7. H. W. a. V.D.X. Guo, 2012, A systolic array-based FPGA parallel architecture for the BLAST algorithm, *ISRN Bioinformatics*.
8. S.A. M. a. G. Valle, 2008, A compatible GPU cards as efficient hardware accelerators for Smith-Waterman sequence alignment, *BMC Bioinformatics*, vol. 9, no. Suppl. 2, p. S10.
9. a. D.E.D. Thambawita RR, 2014, To use or not to use: Graphics processing units (GPUs) for pattern matching algorithms, *Information and Automation for Sustainability (ICIAfS) 2016 IEEE International Conference*, pp. 1–6.
10. S.-H.L. N.-F. Huang H-WH, Y.-M. Chu, and W.-Y. Tsai, 2008, A GPU-based multiple-pattern matching algorithm for network intrusion detection systems, *Advanced Information Networking and Applications-Workshops*.
11. C.-H.L. C.-H. Lin, L.-S. Chien, and S.-C. Chang, 2013, Accelerating pattern matching using a novel parallel algorithm on GPUs, *Computers, IEEE Transactions*, pp. 1906–1916.
12. S.N.Y.H. Cho, and W.H. Mangione-Smith, 2002, Specialized hardware for deep network packet filtering, *Field-Programmable Logic and Applications, Proceedings*, pp. 452–461.
13. G.F. A. a. N. Khare, 2014, Hardware-based string matching algorithms: A survey, *International Journal of Computer Applications*, pp. 435–462.
14. S. Brown, 1996, FPGA architectural research: A survey, *Design & Test of Computers, IEEE*, vol. 13, no. 4, pp. 9–15.
15. R.T.I. Kuon, and J. Rose, 2008, FPGA architecture: Survey and challenges, *Foundations and Trends in Electronic Design Automation*, pp. 135–253.
16. C.W. Peng Chen, X. Li, and X. Zhou, 2013, A FPGA-based high performance acceleration platform for the next generation long read mapping, *HPCC/EUC*, pp. 308–315.
17. C.W. Peng Chen, X. Li, and X. Zhou, 2014, Accelerating the next generation long read mapping with the FPGA-based system, *IEEE/ACM Transactions on Computational Biology Bioinformatics*, pp. 840–852.
18. C.W. Peng Chen, X. Li, and X. Zhou, 2013, Acceleration of the long read mapping on a PC-FPGA architecture (abstract only), *FPGA*, p. 271.
19. X.L. Chao Wang, X. Zhou, Y. Chen, and R.C.C. Cheung, 2014, Big data genome sequencing on Zynq based clusters (abstract only), *FPGA*, p. 247.
20. C.T.M.C Schatz, A. L Delcher, and A. Varshney, 2007, High-throughput sequence alignment using graphics processing units, *BMC Bioinformatics*, vol. 8, p. 474.

21. B.M. a. S.F.N.N. Homer, 2009, BFAST: An alignment tool for large scale genome resequencing, *PLoS One*, vol. 4, no. 11, p. 7767.
22. C.T.B. Langmead, M. Pop, and S.L. Salzberg, 2009, Ultrafast and memory-efficient alignment of short DNA sequences to the human genome, *Genome Biology*, vol. 10, no. 3, p. 25.
23. W.W.W. Tang, B. Duan, C. Zhang, G. Tan, P. Zhang, and N. Sun, 2012, Accelerating millions of short reads mapping on a heterogeneous architecture with FPGA accelerator, *Proceeding of IEEE 20th International Symposium on Field-Programmable Custom Computing Machines*, pp. 184–187.
24. L.R.A, 2015, Space-efficient whole genome comparisons with Burrows-Wheeler transforms, *Journal of Computational Biology*, vol. 12, no. 4, pp. 407–415.
25. H. L. a. R. Durbin, 2009, Fast and accurate short read alignment with Burrows-Wheeler transform, *Bioinformatics*, vol. 25, no. 14, pp. 1754–1760.
26. H. W-K, 2007, A space and time efficient algorithm for constructing compressed suffix arrays, *Algorithmica*, p. 48.
27. J.S. Grossi RaV, 2000, Compressed suffix arrays and suffix trees with applications to text indexing and string matching, in *Proceedings on 32nd Annual ACM Symposium on Theory of Computing (STOC 2000)*.
28. W.L.D. Pao, and B. Liu, 2010, A memory-efficient pipelined implementation of the aho-corasick string-matching algorithm, *ACM Transactions on Architecture and Code Optimization (TACO)*, p. 10.
29. A. M. a. M.C. Herbordt, 2012, FMSA: FPGA-accelerated ClustalW-based multiple sequence alignment through pipelined prefiltering, *Proceeding of IEEE 20th International Symposium on Field-Programmable Custom Computing Machines*, pp. 177–183.
30. C.W. Shiming Lei, H. Fang, X. Li, and X. Zhou, 2016, SCADIS: A scalable accelerator for data-intensive string set matching on FPGAs, *Trustcom/BigDataSE/ISPA*, pp. 1190–1197.

Index

For Product Safety Concerns and Information please contact our EU representative GPSR@taylorandfrancis.com
Taylor & Francis Verlag GmbH, Kaufingerstraße 24, 80331 München, Germany